The Complete
Book of
GARDENING

The Complete Book of GARDENING

MARSHALL CAVENDISH

This edition specially printed for Dealerfield Ltd, Glaisdale Parkway, Glaisdale Drive, Nottingham, NG8 4GA,
by Marshall Cavendish Books, London (a division of Marshall Cavendish Partworks Ltd).

Copyright © Marshall Cavendish Limited 1996

This edition printed 1996

ISBN 1-85435-866-9

British Library Cataloguing in Publication Data:
A catalogue record for this book is available from the British Library

Printed and bound in Italy

Some of this material has previously appeared in the
Marshall Cavendish partwork *My Garden*.

CONTENTS

Foreword

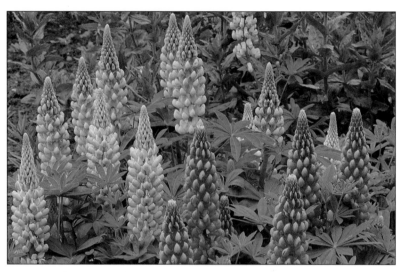

Whether your garden covers acres, or is just a tiny patch,
you can make it a pleasing refuge from the workaday world.

Not another gardening book, you may say! There are dozens of gardening books on the shelves, with new ones being published every day. Some claim to be complete guides but few live up to their aspirations. This new edition has been a pleasure for me to work on: its simplicity in layout and style is refreshing. Although I've been a keen gardener for over twenty years (as well as editing and indexing at least a hundred books on the subject), it demonstrates there is still plenty to learn.

Pluses and minuses in the garden

I was brought up by parents who loved gardening – they had a reasonably sized plot in Essex and it was my mother who instilled in me my love of plants, plant names (especially Latin) and the sight of a well-weeded bed. That garden had its share of horrors, and a large area of mare's tail, a dreadful deep-rooted weed which sat in a boggy patch near the stream which

ran at the end of the garden. But there were pluses too: a soil verging on acid which made rhododendrons and pieris easy to grow, a slope which lent an interesting aspect, and a huge fence which was covered with climbers such as *Clematis montana*. Other highlights were a *Magnolia stellata*, a *Hamamelis mollis* (with a beautiful set of syllables to go with those spidery, yellow flowers appearing in the depth of winter), a rose named 'Michèle Meilland' which my parents bought for me, and a huge patch of bronze chrysanthemums, carefully tended one year to be at their best on one specific day in mid autumn, for my sister's wedding.

The learning curve

After that, there was a hiatus of some years when I was at college: I really missed having a garden. When I started gardening on my own, it was on a long thin strip of Hertfordshire behind a terraced cottage, a plot whose soil was in good heart from 100 years of tending, but whose design was unimaginative. There I cut my teeth on the use of a cold frame, creating a lawn from seed, growing chrysanthemums, coping with clematis wilt and growing my own strawberries. My next garden was a handkerchief-sized back garden and a larger front garden. There I experimented with 'different' plants (at least to me) such as *Leycesteria formosa*, hebes and a tiny *Cedrus libani atlantica* 'Glauca', which I now note is higher than the house. No one has had the heart to take it out.

There is no substitute for experience
The best bonus of all is to marry a gardener – one who has all the qualities that you may lack yourself. My partner has an eye for design and practices what the gardening text books tell you so often: prepare the site properly for any planting, be it a tree or an annual bedder, and the plants will repay your effort. The two of us have transformed, over fourteen years, our half-acre plot from a lawn with one bed and many nettles (often thought to be a sign of good soil), plus dock and bramble, to a garden which now includes: patio, rockery, conifer bed, herb bed, fruit frame and vegetable plot, rose bed, and beds of shrubs and herbaceous perennials.

Get to grips with mulch
If I had to pass on one tip to new gardeners, it is to really till the soil. When I started gardening, it did not occur to me to put anything into the soil apart from the plant itself. I obviously had not picked up the idea of adding humus, which my parents were doing all the time. Now we have two compost heaps and buy large loads of manure, plus wood chips when we feel rich. Mulching plants, especially after rain, is important – we really notice the difference in those unmulched areas, particularly when we come to dig them.

The Complete Book of Gardening
All this has been a lot of work – we still spend twenty or more hours a week in the garden in spring and summer, despite two full-time jobs. Not everyone likes gardening as much as we do, but a book like the *Complete Book of Gardening* has much to commend it to both beginner and experienced gardener alike, and to those who have much or only a little time to spend in the garden. You will not have to 'hunt' in various places for bites of information on the same plant or job, as each chapter is devoted to specifics, be it on how to propagate a coveted shrub, or all there is to know about irises.

The book has been divided into four parts. First come the basics of gardening: the 'how to' aspects of sowing seeds, or the 'what' aspects of plant diseases. Next, a section on container gardening, so there is no excuse for a bare patio or window ledge. A section on 'types' of gardens follows – with chapters describing how to create a wildlife haven, a water garden or an italianate formal hedging area. Finally the stars of the show are presented, those flowers that always catch the eye in their season, from flashy fuchsias to heady hyacinths. This invaluable book should fill a large gap on every gardener's bookshelf.

Michèle Clarke

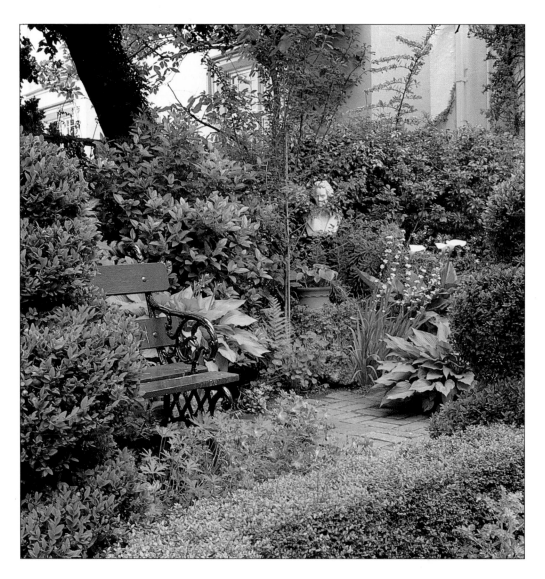

With some basic gardening knowledge you can create whatever gives you pleasure in your garden, whether it is a beautiful border of herbaceous perennials or a leafy refuge planted with evergreens.

CHAPTER ONE
Gardening Know-How

SOIL TYPES

For successful, satisfying gardening, you need to know what kind of soil you have and how to make the most of it.

It does not matter whether you are a complete beginner or consider yourself a bit of an expert; unless you know your soil you will never obtain the best results from your garden. Every plant has different preferences – for instance, some thrive on an acid soil while others do not.

Soil is made up of four basic components which are present in varying amounts.

Organic matter is essential to any fertile soil. It is composed of decaying plants and animals and puts back into the soil what the plants have taken out (worms help by pulling leaf litter underground as they tunnel). It is also referred to as humus.

Air is necessary to ensure that the organic matter is broken down and to prevent waterlogging, while **water** carries the nutrients to the plant and clings to the soil particles. Some soils are less able to hold water than others: sand for

The glorious hydrangea (above) is a mixture of colours because the soil is limy and alkaline and is turning the blue hydrangea pink. The hydrangea would be purely blue on an acid soil.

example drains very quickly giving the plant less time to take it up.

Minerals are the rock particles in the soil and they are chiefly responsible for the texture. When these vital components are well balanced good humus results and the soil is healthy and fertile.

Soil texture

The soil is made up of pieces of material of different sizes. A soil which is made from large,

FROM TOP TO BOTTOM

There is usually a distinct difference between the top layer of your soil, the topsoil, and what lies below it, the subsoil. Depending on how well established your garden is and what are the geological qualities of the area, the topsoil may vary from a couple of inches to several feet deep. There may even be a range of different soil types and this can work to your advantage as well as against you. Gravel under clay provides good drainage and chalk under acid neutralises acidity. Take care not to bury the topsoil under the subsoil when digging.

TOPSOIL

Topsoil (the dark, shaded part of the diagram, left) can vary in depth from a couple of inches to several feet. More open in structure and darker in colour, it is organic material and rich in nutrients. Plants, especially small ones, feed mostly from this layer. Worms are vital because they mix up the material.

SUBSOIL

Lying below the topsoil, subsoil is a less rich layer, providing water and a firm anchorage for larger plants, trees and shrubs.

This magnificent scented lilac border flourishes where most plants would flounder. Lilac grows well on thin, starved chalky soils.

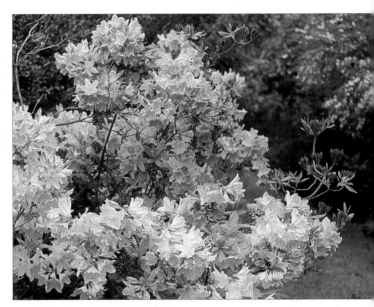

This aptly named 'Fireglow' azalea is a member of the rhododendron group of plants and, like its relatives, it grows well on acid, peaty soils.

coarse particles is known as 'light' while a 'heavy' soil is made up of tiny grains. Ideally the composition should be somewhere between the two: a mid-textured soil is known as a loam.

The way soil particles are held together is known as the structure. A clay soil has minute particles which cling together in clumps. Other soils form flat layers or plates, but the best structure is one which is crumbly. This is known as a 'good tilth'. A crumbly loam has the perfect structure and texture but you must also find out how acid or alkaline your soil is in order to decide which plants you will be able to grow. This can be done very cheaply and easily with a soil testing kit. It will only take a few minutes and may save you years of unsuccessful attempts.

Whatever your soil, you will not be able to change either the structure or the acid/alkaline balance completely. But do not despair. Even if you have a heavy clay or a highly

alkaline soil you can still improve it enormously. Finding out all you can is the first step.

Basic soil-types

Peat It is rare to find a garden soil that is very peaty, but it does occasionally happen. The area has at some time in the past been wet and boggy, like the fen lands of East Anglia.

Dark in colour, with a light and spongy texture, peaty soils have a high fibrous content – if you squeeze a handful it will fall apart easily.

Peat soils are capable of absorbing and retaining large amounts of water, which they can hold right up to the surface. Drainage can sometimes be a problem but generally it is a soil which is easy to work and very fertile.

This open texture and high moisture content is ideal for growing hydrangeas, rhododendrons, pieris and the many kinds of heathers. Primulas and lilies do well, and so does blue poppy (meconopsis).

All these plants appreciate

Roses, like this delightful hybrid tea 'Le Havre', grow particularly well on clay soils; although some roses will grow quite happily on sandy soils too.

CLAY

SAND

	How to recognise	Advantages
CLAY	A heavy, sticky soil. A squeezed handful will stick together and retain its compressed shape.	Usually rich in nutrients. A clay subsoil is ideal for making ponds.
SAND	Light, crumbly and free-draining. A squeezed handful will fall apart easily.	Fast to warm up in spring. Lawns will drain freely, and borders can be worked on all winter if the weather permits. Does not stick to tools.
CHALK	Limy soils vary a great deal, from thin, stony loam over chalk bed to a deep clay soil. But they all have a high pH value (= alkaline).	A moderately limy soil will grow a wide range of plants.
PEAT	A dark, fibrous and spongy soil. A squeezed handful will not hold together. Water may sometimes be squeezed out.	Ideal for acid-loving plants and those which need a high moisture level at all times.
LOAM	Brown or red, medium-weight soil, with plenty of organic matter. A squeezed handful will hold together but can be made to crumble easily.	A loam soil of neutral pH (7) is the ideal soil for growing a wide range of plants, especially vegetables.

PEAT

CHALK

LOAM

Disadvantages	Will grow/won't grow
Slow to warm up in spring. Lack of free drainage is hostile to many kinds of plants. Difficult to weed, and compacts easily in borders and under lawns.	Good for roses, irises and many water-side plants. Unsuitable for rhododendrons, heathers, tenders shrubs, bulbs and alpines.
Can be very lacking in nutrients, requiring the addition of much organic matter and fertilizer. Dries out quickly, even when mulched.	Grows most things, but poor for moisture-loving plants such as many primulas, hostas and bergenias.
Often dry, thin and starved, over rock. Will not support acid-loving plants at all. Some plants become 'chlorotic' (yellow leaves).	Good for lilac, cistus and hebes. Bad for most heathers, rhododendrons and hydrangeas.
Constant high moisture level is bad for tender/drought-loving plants which need sharp drainage. Lawns can be poor.	Good for rhododendrons, azaleas, heathers, lilies and primulas. Bad for cistus and dianthus. Extra lime needed for good vegetables.
Loam can be acid or alkaline, and therefore plant choice is limited accordingly.	Alkaline loams will NOT support acid-loving plants.

moisture, but some of them, especially those in the heather family, must have another of the qualities of peaty soil: acidity. If a soil is acid, it means it is lacking in lime, a substance which some plants will not tolerate. Soil acidity is measured on the pH scale. Rhododendrons and heathers prefer a pH of about 5-6.5.

Lime Soils containing lime can be very varied. At worst they can be dry, thin and stony, over solid chalk or limestone. But at best they are excellent, rich, loamy soils, which happen to be alkaline.

The only way to be sure whether a soil is alkaline is to test its pH value, and see if it is above pH7.

There are very few limitations of a rich but alkaline soil. It will not grow plants such as rhododendrons, pieris and summer-flowering heathers, because they must have acid soil. But it will grow good roses, vegetables, lawns and an enormous range of flowers and shrubs.

Extreme alkalinity may, however, cause yellowing of the leaves (chlorosis) in some plants such as camellias. Blue-flowered hydrangeas also turn pink on limy soils.

Thin, dry alkaline soils over

chalk are more of a problem, and can be very limiting. They tend to be lacking in nutrients and are often stony and difficult to work and are sticky and soft in wet weather. Not all plants flounder on limy soils, some prefer it: cistus, rosemary and carnations (the dianthus family), will be perfectly happy there.

Sand Crumbly and free-draining, sandy soils are without doubt the easiest to work with. Tools keep themselves clean with almost no effort, and the soil warms up quickly in spring which means it is suitable for early crops.

Although this type of soil is good for growing alpines, and shrubs and perennials of doubtful hardiness, the real problem with sand is likely to

In hot and dry weather, clay will shrink and crack, because of its poor drainage. Plants with shallow root systems such as these dwarf herbaceous plants (top) cannot cope with the extreme conditions that clay produces. Roses or hardy shrubs make a better choice for clay beds.

Rhododendrons are unable to extract vital nutrients from chalky soils, such as this shrub (above), which is showing its suffering with yellowing, or chlorotic, leaves.

GARDEN NOTES

ACIDITY AND ALKALINITY

The term pH (potential of Hydrogen) is a scale for measurement of the chemical alkaline/acidity level of soil. The full scale runs from 1 to 14, but most garden soils are within the range of 4 to 8. When a soil contains enough lime or chalk to give a pH value of over 7, it is said to be alkaline. A pH balance of 6.5 or less is acid. A pH reading of 7 is neutral.

TESTING YOUR SOIL

Soil testing kits can be bought from garden centres and other gardening outlets. They take only minutes to do and can save you years of trial and error in trying to grow the wrong plants on the wrong soil. These kits test the pH value of your soil; pH is simply a scale, ranging from 4–8, which measures the acidity or alkalinity of your soil. The range of 3–6.5 indicates acidity, 7.5–8 alkalinity, 7.0 is neutral.

Remember to test several parts of your garden to get an overall view and if you are treating the soil, test after treatment and compare the results.

A rich, neutral loam is the ideal soil and if you are lucky enough to have it in your garden you will be able to grow practically anything. It has an excellent moisture content and a good crumbly texture. Plenty of organic material ensures that your plants get maximum nutrition, so there is less need to feed. Here it has been used to create a beautiful flower-filled garden.

be dryness. The topsoil, and even the subsoil, can be so free-draining because of its open texture that, in times of drought, thirsty plants will soon wilt for want of a good drink of water and even trees, with their extensive roots may show signs of suffering.

The topsoil, of course, can be made to hold more water by adding some humus to it. Nutritional enrichments – fertilizer – is often necessary, too, in large quantities.

Most plants will grow well on sandy soil but be careful with shallow-rooted varieties.

So long as it is on the acidic side (with a pH value below 7), even summer heathers and rhododendrons thrive. They enjoy the open texture of sandy soils; for your part, give them sufficient water and they will do very well.

Clay Probably the hardest type of soil to deal with. In winter, clay is cold, wet and sticky, so that you cannot work on the garden for fear of compacting the soil into a solid mass. Plants can literally drown when clay soils become waterlogged. In summer, clay can dry out and crack. Because

of poor drainage, the moisture will simply evaporate. It is never easy to weed. Seedling weeds seem to be stuck to the soil in winter and baked on during a dry summer.

Good for roses

Clay soil is not all bad news, however. It can be very fertile, it is well supplied with plant foods, and they are not drained away by a heavy rainfall. Roses grow best of all, along with a good range of shrubs and perennials. And the texture can be improved with effort over the years. It will never make a light, open soil, so it is better to stick to plants which will tolerate clay successfully, rather than try those which will just survive and never look at their best.

Clay soils can be either on the acidic or alkaline side, but generally the lime-loving plants like lilac and cistus do best on it. Often a heavy loam topsoil will be found overlying a clay subsoil, and this is a satisfactory combination.

Loam The ideal soil for gardening, loam will grow much the widest range of plants. It possesses all of the good points of sandy and clay soils but few of their disadvantages. It can be acidic or alkaline, which will limit the choice of plants a little, but, broadly speaking, you can grow anything on loam. Certainly a medium acidic loam will grow rhododendrons perfectly well.

Best of all

The advantage of loam is that it has a high content of organic matter, which is full of nutrients and holds water well. A handful of an average loam, when squeezed, will have enough fibre and moisture to stick together afterwards, but will not be so sticky that you cannot easily make it crumble again.

This is just what growing plants need for healthy foliage and root systems. For vegetables you could not do better.

BOTANICAL NAMES EXPLAINED

Boggled by botanical terms and at a loss with Latin? Help is at hand! Here is a simple explanation of what's in a name . . .

Many new gardeners are puzzled and put off by Latin as the language of flowers. Difficult to pronounce and even harder to remember, Latin seems to make things even more complicated. What is wrong with using simple names in the language we all understand – like 'black-eyed Susan' or 'forget-me-not'?

Being choosy

There are good reasons for cracking the Latin problem. Nowadays, whether shopping for food or shopping for the garden, there is the chance to

be more selective. Not so long ago, gardeners would have been perfectly happy to buy something labelled 'carnation' and not mind too much how it eventually turned out.

Pretty, but unreliable

With so many wonderful new varieties on offer – that are often startlingly different in size and bloom – customers want to be more sure of what they are buying.

Common names are simply not reliable – and this is where the proper botanical names are helpful. Often, one common name serves two owners. Love-lies-bleeding is the name

As they are both bright, sunny flowers with a sharply contrasting black central 'eye', it is easy to see why these two plants have acquired the common name black-eyed Susan. It is easy to distinguish the plants when looking at them, but if you want to buy one in particular, it is crucial to know its Latin name. Thunbergia alata (left) is a climber, while the daisy-like Rudbeckia hirta (above) is not.

15

Beware of imposter poppies. Common names are often very inaccurate and can lead to confusion. Although both these plants share some of the features of the poppy family, they have no botanical links and come from separate families. The delicate little perennial, Meconopsis cambrica (right) is commonly known as the Welsh poppy.

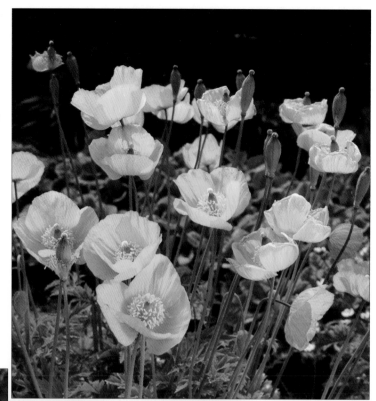

The rich orange eschscholtzia (below) is an annual, but can be confused with the poppy family (papaver) too, as it bears the common name of Californian poppy.

Although common names are usually misleading, the common name of this Limnanthes douglasii (right) is perfect. Known as the poached-egg flower, it is instantly recognisable. It looks exactly as its name suggests; its rich yellow centre forming a perfect 'yolk' with clearly defined white petal tips. The flowers are delicately scented and are very appealing to bees. An annual, it flowers from early midsummer and can be used as an edging plant for borders.

thereby transcends language barriers and avoids confusion.

The 'scientific' system of plant naming is simpler than it looks. With about half a million plant species that are known of in the world, it is important to categorize them. Once you understand the structure of botanical names, you will discover just how informative they can be.

Getting to know you

For a start, many plants are known commonly by the first part of their scientific name anyway. Dahlia, zinnia, begonia, aubrieta and magnolia are some well-known examples. So when you want to know exactly which magnolia or dahlia to grow in your garden, you should refer to the system of full Latin names.

used by some gardeners to describe the long-tasselled amaranthus and by others when talking about a viola. It's not unusual that a plant, especially a well-loved one, will, over the years, have gathered a bouquet of different names. For instance, heartsease, Jack-jump-up-and-kiss-me, love-lies-bleeding and love-in-idleness are just four of at least 25 common names given to *Viola tricolor*, the parent of the garden pansy.

Common names, cheerful though they are, often convey incorrect information about the plants attached to them. The Guernsey lily in fact originally comes from as far away as South Africa.

Alas, common names do not cross the language barrier. What we call lily-of-the-valley is known as muguet in France and as Maiglöckchen in Germany. Yet the Latin name, *Convallaria majalis*, is understood in all countries and

The Latin system gives every species of plant a two-word name. Think of it like a telephone number, where one part of the number is your area code and the other is your personal number.

Take the scientific name for the species commonly called primrose – *Primula vulgaris*. *Primula* is the name of the genus or related group to which the primrose belongs. There are about 500 species in the Primula genus – many very different in colour, but all with a family resemblance. *Primula veris*, the cowslip, is a first cousin. The offspring of these two species can also be grown in your garden. The result of long breeding, these hybrids are the bright and cheery colourful plants that fill window boxes in the spring –

WHAT WENT WRONG?

PLANT POSERS

Q My mother's favourite plant is a climber called black-eyed Susan. I went to the garden centre to buy one but the one I bought never climbed, it just spread with a daisy-like flower in my border. What do you think it was?

A The plant you were trying to buy is *Thunbergia alata*, sometimes sold in pots with a small trellis. In warm climates it grows outdoors, but usually it is treated as a house plant. The plant you brought home is *Rudbeckia hirta*, a perennial plant with yellow daisy-like flowers. Confusingly both plants share the common name black-eyed Susan.

Q I recently tried to buy a geranium for a hanging basket. The assistant told me that I should in fact, be looking for a pelargonium. What should I have asked for in the first place?

A *Geranium* is a group of hardy perennials commonly called cranesbill. Pelargoniums are not hardy, but are invaluable in summer bedding schemes, hanging baskets and window boxes. They are commonly known as geraniums.

The second part of a plant's Latin name distinguishes it from the rest of its family. Plants from different families may share an attribute but it does not mean they are related. Anemone japonica 'Alba' (above) and Primula japonica (right) may both share the characteristic of having originated from Japan, but this is as far as the similarity goes.

Likewise the shrub Rosa primula (below) is so called because its primrose-yellow flowers closely resemble the familiar herbaceous primulas.

Primula polyantha. It is a similar story for roses. You can tell when a flower is a rose of some kind, they all belong to the family genus of *Rosa*.

First name terms

So, the first word in a plant's name is the genus name. It is always written with a capital letter. The second word (like your personal telephone number), tells the rest of the story. The two names together describe just one particular species of plant and this name

Often the second part of the Latin name gives a clue to what the plant looks like. There's no need to be a Latin expert-you can guess the meaning of many of them. Cotoneaster horizontalis (above), spreads horizontally as its name suggests.

To the delight of gardeners there are often differences within a species which occur naturally. These have three latin names; Heliopsis scabra incomparabilis (right) is an example of this.

A hybrid is the result of the interbreeding of two separate species, often from different families. This can occur naturally or may be the product of careful breeding in specialist nurseries, such as this Lilium × 'Yellow Blaze' (right).

is the same the world over. It is also generally written in gardening books in italics.

A family likeness

The second part of the name usually describes a basic characteristic of the species. In the case of *Primula vulgaris* the second word tells us that it is the 'vulgar' or 'common' species of *Primula*.

The word *japonica* means Japanese and many flowers and shrubs bear that description. For example there is a *Primula japonica* and an *Anemone japonica*. They may both have originally come from Japan but they are completely different flowering plants belonging to two separate families.

The second name is not given a capital letter. When you see plant names in books and on labels at the garden centre, you will notice that the two words are written in italics, to show that they are in a different language. Using the two words together, you can be certain the plant you bring

home will grow to be exactly like the one you saw in the book or on television, or heard about on the radio.

Many Latin words have similar English equivalents so it is often easy to guess their meaning. A plant whose second name is *stellata* has star-like blooms and you can be sure that *spinosa* will be spiny. Anything called *horizontalis* will be low-growing, as it grows horizontally rather than vertically.

Some cannot be worked out at all, however, because they have been named after the person who discovered them. Zinnias were named in honour of botanist Johann Zinn and fuchsias after Dr Fuchs.

Word games

The word 'species' means a group of individuals that have a lot of features in common, can breed together and have fertile offspring. Plant nurseries, however, not content with the results of natural breeding, have been creating new varieties of plants for centuries. These are known as cultivated varieties. Nature produces lots of varieties on her own account, but to sort out which are natural and which are cultivated, another name must be added to the two-word species name.

Natural varieties have a Latin name. The low-growing form of horse chestnut is called *Aesculus pavia humilis*.

Nursery-bred varieties can use Latin or the local language – be it English, French or whatever – but the variety name must be written in single quotation marks. That is why you will see daffodils named as 'Arctic Gold' or an iris called 'Blue Rhythm'. These specially cultivated varieties are called *cultivars*.

Buying power

Armed with these basic botanical rules – the naming of species and varieties – you can purchase your plants from the

CHARACTERISTICS

Some Latin words which describe plants' colour and appearance:

alba	white
aurea	gold
nivea	white and snowy
caerulea	blue
rosea	pink
lutea	yellow
purpurea	purple
rubra	red
sanguinea	red
viridis	green
flore pleno	double flowered
ferox	prickly
horizontalis	low-growing
nana	dwarf
pubescens	downy
pumila	dwarf
repens	creeping
sempervirens	evergreen
stricta	rigid
variegata	mixed colours

WHERE AND WHEN

These give the origins, desirable conditions and the growing or flowering season:

alpinus	alpine
campestris	field
maritima	sea
montana	mountain
saxatile	rock
aestivalis	summer
autumnalis	autumn
vernalis	spring

Hybrids which have occurred from the interbreeding of two separate species from within the same family group are classified with an × between the names of the two species. The sunny, orange Geum × borisii (right) is such a hybrid.

If species from different families mix, the resulting plant is called a hybrid genus. The Leyland cypress (below) is a cross between Cupressus macrocarpa and Chamaecyparis nootkatensis. Its proper Latin name is × Cupressocyparis leylandii.

GLOSSARY

genus – a family group of plants or the plant's 'surname'

species – the family members: the parents, aunts, uncles and the cousins

varieties – the offspring, whether they occur in nature or are cultivated

hybrids – the result of interbreeding between two species or varieties, usually from the same genus

garden centre with confidence. You need not be nervous about pronouncing these unfamiliar words, either. Remember, no-one actually talks in Latin!

The last section to make up the picture is the hybrid. This is a plant that results from the interbreeding of separate species. In the animal world, a donkey is a species and so is a horse. If you breed the two you get a mule. The mule will not be able to breed. If you want another mule, you have to start from the beginning with a horse and a donkey.

Unlike mules, some of the new hybrid plants are fertile. You might have a new kind of orchid, created by breeding two species of orchid. That new orchid could then breed with either of its parents, creating more new plants. But not all hybrids are fertile.

For now, all you need to know to guide you through the garden centre or seed catalogue, is when you see a plant with an × it is a hybrid.

Once you have become used to using the proper Latin botanical names you will find it is one of the best tools a gardener can have.

GARDEN COMPOST

Improve your soil while reducing waste by making your own garden compost. It is easy to do and very satisfying.

Making your own compost is perhaps the ultimate in recycling. There is nothing magical about composting: all plant and animal material will rot down eventually. By making a compost heap, you are just speeding up the process, concentrating it in one place.

In the past, garden compost was used both to enrich the soil and for growing seedlings and pot plants. There is now no point in using it as a growing medium as the widely available specialist composts produce much better results.

The nutrient value of your compost will depend on what has gone into it, but the main function of all garden compost is to contribute to the creation and maintenance of a healthy soil by nourishing the micro-organisms that live within it. These micro-organisms in turn release nutrients that will benefit your growing plants.

Better texture

Like all bulky organic material, including farmyard manure, compost helps free-draining sandy soils to retain moisture and conversely opens up sticky clay soils and helps them drain. Used regularly and fairly generously, this or-

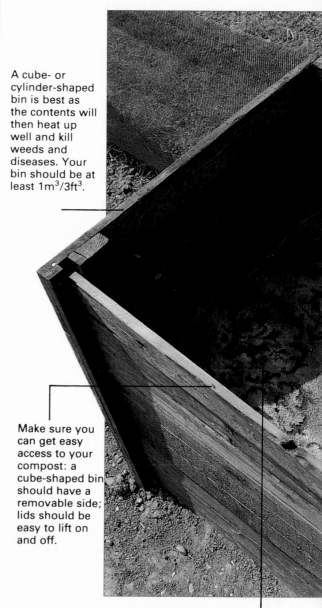

A cube- or cylinder-shaped bin is best as the contents will then heat up well and kill weeds and diseases. Your bin should be at least 1m³/3ft³.

Make sure you can get easy access to your compost: a cube-shaped bin should have a removable side; lids should be easy to lift on and off.

Cover your heap to keep heat in and rain out.

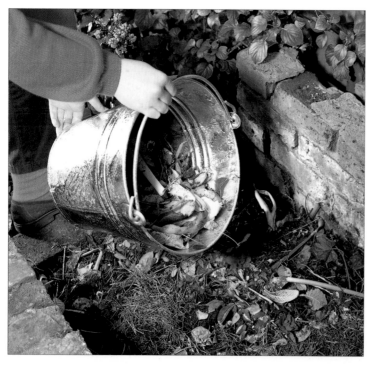

Keep a bucket in the kitchen and empty your vegetable waste into it instead of just throwing it out. You can use anything from egg shells to cabbage leaves, apple cores to leftover carrots – it will all make excellent compost. Once you have filled the bucket (left) tip the contents onto the compost heap where it will soon decompose. Do not mix it. Remove compost from the bottom of the heap at regular intervals.

ganic material helps to make the soil more workable and more able to support a wide range of plants.

Do not, however, expect instant results: feeding the soil is a slow, steady process and it takes time to see the benefits of continually adding compost.

Some experts manage to make compost-making sound very complicated. It need not be so. Garden compost is simply free organic matter and need not take hours of your

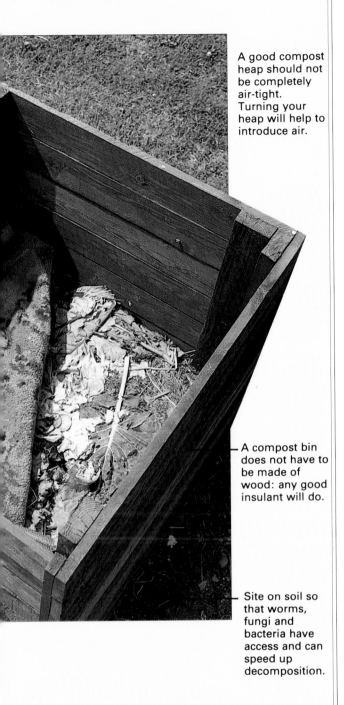

A good compost heap should not be completely air-tight. Turning your heap will help to introduce air.

— A compost bin does not have to be made of wood: any good insulant will do.

— Site on soil so that worms, fungi and bacteria have access and can speed up decomposition.

produce your own food, especially organically, you will need to feed your garden a lot and will probably want to make as much compost as possible. Use everything you can, from the garden, the house and even what you can beg from the neighbours.

You can almost never overdo the amount of compost you add to the vegetable patch, especially where you intend to grow potatoes, peas, beans and other vegetables which need a lot of moisture in order to crop satisfactorily. Aim to dig in a full barrow-load for every square metre.

Using grass cuttings

If your garden is mainly ornamental, on the other hand, and you have a large lawn, the compost heap is a convenient way of dealing with all those mowings. Mowings on their own do not make a satisfactory compost – much more than 30 per cent of mowings will result in a slimy although still usable mess, and you will need other ingredients.

All the waste products from flower beds and borders will help, together with the various types of kitchen waste.

The compost you make can

be used as a mulch on the borders, around individual plants, or dug into the soil when you are preparing the ground for planting or are lifting, dividing or moving plants.

A mulch of compost

If you decide to use your compost as a mulch – a layer of material laid on bare soil to suppress weeds and retain moisture – you will need a 5-8cm/2-3in deep layer for it to be effective. When you apply the mulch, first place it around precious plants which could suffer during droughts and hosepipe bans. If you have any left over, spread it around other plants next, and finally on any bare ground. Be careful not to let the mulch touch the stems or trunks of any plants, as it could kill them – these parts are meant to be above

SHORT CUTS

SPEED UP DECAY

Bag up weeds and accumulate kitchen waste until you next mow the lawn. Then add all these materials at the same time, so that the heat from the grass mowings can start work on the rest straight away.

time to produce. Likewise, choosing what to add to your heap is not difficult. Suitable composting materials are anything that once lived, so do not restrict yourself to garden waste. Think about what you throw in the dustbin now: tea leaves, egg shells, vegetable peelings, for example.

How much to make

You do not need to make vast amounts of compost for it to be worthwhile. If you are keen to

Compost is a wonderful substance that can be used in a number of ways. In autumn it can be used as a feed. It will not only add valuable nutrients but it will also greatly improve the soil texture. It should be dug into the soil with a spade. This is especially useful for any vegetables you may be growing. Alternatively it can be used at any other time of the year as a mulch (right) or be forked into the soil around shrubs.

Compost bins can be bought in a wide variety of forms and work in slightly different ways, but the end product is invariably very similar. This wire mesh bin (left) is fairly inconspicuous and allows lots of air to circulate, ensuring rapid breakdown of the compostable material. For something that looks a bit more professional this twin bin (below) is made from strong steel tubes and rot proof material which allows the air to circulate. Fill the first bin and allow the compost to make while you fill up the second. The compost which is ready is easily removed from the base.

WHAT TO ADD TO A COMPOST HEAP

- plant material
- lawn mowings
- wood ash
- kitchen waste, including vegetable parings and tea bags
- newspaper and other waste paper
- sawdust and straw
- finger-thick woody prunings
- thorny prunings (wear gloves when handling compost – thorns stay intact)
- manure mixed with 'bedding' (for example, straw, shredded paper or sawdust)
- droppings from poultry, pigeons and farm animals

MAKING A COMPOST HEAP

You can use wood, mesh panels, a plastic dustbin or barrel or even straw bales. Make sure you incorporate enough ventilation when you are building, or drill holes in solid sides. If you use mesh, line your bin with cardboard or plastic sheeting to reduce some of the airflow. Make sure you can get easy access to the heap, for adding and removing material.

The first layer of the heap should be brushwood, thick woody prunings or tough stems (e.g. cabbage). Lay this directly on the soil to help ventilation.

Add your compostable material in 15-30cm/6-12in layers. Each layer should be a well-mixed combination of soft, sappy greenery (like mowings) and drier, coarser material (like dead flower stalks or woody prunings). Water this layer if necessary to make it moist but not sodden and fit the lid.

Start collecting material again until you have enough to add another layer and repeat the process. Once the container is full, leave it with the lid on until the contents have rotted and you need to use it. Keep the outer edges for adding to the new heap as they will not have rotted down completely.

ground, not buried!

There are three main options when choosing where to make compost: burying compostable material in a trench; placing it in a bought or home-made container; or simply building a heap.

Making a trench

Burying compostable material in a trench is an ideal method for use with bare ground where you intend to grow vegetables. It gets rid of the need for a heap or bin and once you have dug your trench, all you have to do is place mowings

WHAT WENT WRONG?

Q Last year I decided to make my own compost from lawn-mowings, but after 12 months all I have got is a slimy mess that smells frankly offensive.

A This happens when too many grass mowings are added, all at once. Your 'compost' can still be used – dig it into the ground or spread it as a mulch – but in future, mix dry and bulky material with the mowings and you will get better results.

This compost is unsuitable for use, in parts it has not decayed and in others it is too slimy.

Q The ingredients of my compost look just the same now as they did six months ago. Why should this be and what can I do?

A Your heap has not become hot enough to start decomposition. Re-build it, including a source of nitrogen – mowings, nettles, comfrey or urine – to help the bacteria to digest the heap. Prevent drying out by lining a bin with cardboard or cover a heap with polythene.

WHAT NOT TO ADD TO A COMPOST HEAP

- diseased plant material
- coal ash
- bones
- meat scraps (as these attract vermin)
- cardboard
- lumps of soil
- very thick prunings (unless shredded first)
- seeding weeds and roots of perennial weeds (unless the heap is very hot)
- dog and cat manure (unless the heap is very hot and compost is not to be used on food crops)
- tree leaves (make a separate leaf heap)

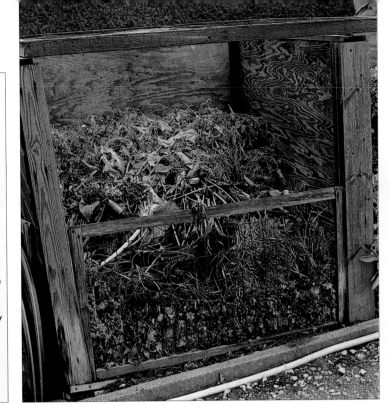

and other material into the base. When you have a fairly thick layer, cover it with soil and tread it down.

Waste composted in this way will not heat up much, so you will not be able to put perennial weeds and seedheads in the trench and you will also have to avoid adding anything which animals may want to dig up. Leave it to rot until the following spring, then plant your vegetables – especially moisture-loving runner beans – or potato tubers.

If you do not have enough bare ground to bury your

If you don't want to go out and buy a compost bin why not build your own? It doesn't have to be anything too complicated but a cube or cylindrical shape is best. This bin (above right) has been made from wood and the mesh front ensures there is plenty of ventilation. Easy access to the heap is important. This bin allows you to add material to the top and to slide the mesh panel up to enable you to remove compost from the bottom.

waste, you will need a compost heap or bin. Your bin need not be large as mowings and other material sink down surprisingly quickly. Start with a small container and buy or make a second one if the first begins to overflow.

Natural allies

Whichever type you choose, place it directly on to the soil so that the fungi, bacteria and worms, which all contribute to the decomposition process, have access to it.

The commonest bins on sale are either plastic cylinder shapes or cubes made of wood slats or mesh panels. Slats and mesh can let in too much air, so you may have to line the sides with plastic to cut down on draughts. Neither type is very expensive, but you could easily make your own.

The right mixture

Provided you put in a good mixture of materials, ensure the right amount of air and keep the heap damp, you should be able to make good compost in any container.

If you think of a compost heap as similar in principle to a fire, you will appreciate what is needed. Fuel, in the form of compostable material; air, to

BRIGHT IDEAS

SPECIAL TREATMENT

- Chop or shred dry materials such as straw and paper, then soak in water
- Shred or chop woody prunings of more than finger thickness to help them rot more quickly
- Use mowings from a lawn recently treated with weedkiller only if the compost is not used for 12 months (check weedkiller instructions for details)
- Compost leaves separately

fan the flames but not put them out; and heat, which in turn helps more heat be generated, are all essential.

With a small compost heap, after the initial heat has diminished, mix up or 'turn' the contents, so that the material that was formerly on the outside is on the inside. This process adds more air to the remaining uncomposted material and re-kindles the 'fire'. To avoid doing this manually, you can buy tumbler bins which you regularly turn on their axis to re-mix the contents, but this can be hard work as the bin gets fuller.

GREEN FEED

Comfrey leaves or stinging nettles on a compost heap will add nutrients and speed up decay.

A compost heap is the basis of good organic gardening and is also a productive way of re-cycling various materials. Do not limit yourself to re-cycling your garden waste; save your kitchen waste too (in a covered bucket). Use natural or recycled materials to construct your bin and mowings, nettles, comfrey or urine as a nitrogen source to speed decay. For true organic gardening use ingredients from organic gardens and farms only.

FERTILIZERS

Keeping your soil nourished with the right feed is vital for healthy, attractive plants. Find out what kind of soil you have, and what fertilizer it needs most.

A dressing of organic bone meal on a freshly dug vegetable plot in autumn. It needs to be forked in to the soil.

Fertilizers will help to make your garden soil more fertile and productive. They improve sandy and peaty soils which are not very fertile. They also replace nutrients where constant cropping has robbed the soil of the plant waste that would otherwise have been returned to the ground to rot down (thus recycling the nutrients).

Using fertilizers is just as important in your fruit and vegetable garden, where you remove all or part of a plant, as it is on farmland.

Modern methods

When you prune or harvest a plant, you are removing some of its food reserves, and these have to be replaced. Fertilizers are also useful on your lawn, if you always remove the dead grass clippings.

Fertilizers were originally applied in the form of animal dung, garden compost, seaweed or crushed, quarried minerals that were rich in certain nutrients.

WHICH FERTILIZER?

Fertilizer	Uses	Source	Features
Nitrogen (N)	When the whole plant appears weak and the lower, older leaves are yellow, small and curling, and the plant flowers and fruits poorly.	Urea Blood Hoof and horn Soot (old) Seaweed Ammonium sulphate Nitrates (various)	Organic, fast, acidic Organic, fast, acidic Organic, fast, acidic Organic, fast, neutral Organic, steady, neutral Inorganic, fast, acidic Inorganic, fast, most neutral
Phosphorus (P)	If older leaves have red or purple margins, and are small, drop prematurely and the plant is dark green and stunted.	Bone meal Seaweed Basic slag Mineral phosphate Super-phosphate	Organic, slow, alkaline Organic, steady, neutral Inorganic, slow, alkaline Inorganic, steady, alkaline Inorganic, steady, neutral
Potassium (K)	When older leaf margins are scorched and there are small spots of dead tissue at the leaf tip and between the veins	Wood ashes *Potassium sulphate *Potassium nitrate	Organic, fast, alkaline Inorganic, steady, acidic Inorganic, fast, alkaline

*Potassium sulphate is also known as sulphate of potash
*Potassium nitrate is also known as nitrate of potash

Dried Blood — Organic nitrogen fertiliser for rapid plant growth

Hoof and horn

Bone meal

Wood ashes

Seaweed extract

Blood

Ammonium sulphate

Nitrogen (N)

Phosphorus (P)

Potassium (K

Nowadays most fertilizers used in agriculture and horticulture are manufactured synthetically. These are known as inorganic fertilizers, because they are not produced from once-living matter.

Restoring soil

Plants and flowers require many chemicals in small amounts for healthy growth. Some, especially nitrogen, which is required for leaf growth, are absorbed from the soil in greater quantities than others, quickly exhausting the supply.

Those elements required in the greatest quantity – nitrogen, potassium and phosphorus – are known as major nutrients. Other chemicals in the soil, known as minor nutrients, are also necessary to plants but are used in such

After aerating the lawn in autumn apply a sedge peat dressing and brush it into the holes to improve the soil (right). Then apply an autumn lawn fertilizer that is low in nitrogen and high in phosphorus to encourage root growth.

small quantities that there is rarely a deficiency of them.

Plants in containers can also exhaust the soil's nutrients, major and minor, and need to be fed with fertilizers for good growth.

If you do not use fertilizer the plants will grow less well and be far more likely to succumb to pests and diseases. The exceptions are some culinary herbs, which thrive on poor soils, and should not be fed with fertilizers.

Choice of food

Whatever soil and type of garden you have, you need to supply a balanced diet to your plants. Bulky fertilizers such as stable or farmyard manure mixed with straw should contain a little of everything, and will improve the drainage of sticky soils, while helping dry soils to retain moisture for longer than usual. Manures should be stacked for a few months before they are used.

Many people, especially those living in towns, have no access to manure and use peat instead. But peat does not contain any nutrients.

For town dwellers, the main alternative to manure is garden compost. This can provide the whole range of nutrients in the same way that manure and straw do.

Lawn mowings make a good base for composting and, when mixed with shredded paper and kitchen waste, should allow you to produce enough compost for the vegetable garden and also some to place in

Fertilizer	Uses	Source	Features
Calcium (Ca)	If newer leaves and tips of shoots are turned inward, ragged, scorched or even dead. But first look for caterpillars and aphids, which cause curling on leaves	Calcium compounds Lime/chalk Gypsum	Inorganic, fast, alkaline Organic, slow, alkaline Inorganic, slow, acidic
Magnesium (Mg)	When older leaves are mottled with spots of dead tissue and the leaf margins curl upwards and have slender stalks. But these symptoms may also be the result of excessive potassium fertilizer.	Kieserite/ dolomitic limestone Epsom salts/ magnesium sulphate	Organic, slow, alkaline Inorganic, steady, alkaline
Iron (Fe)	If newer leaves are yellow or bleached, with the veins remaining green, and the plant is growing poorly.	Iron sulphate Sequestrene	Inorganic, steady, acidic Inorganic, steady, neutral Cures iron deficiency.

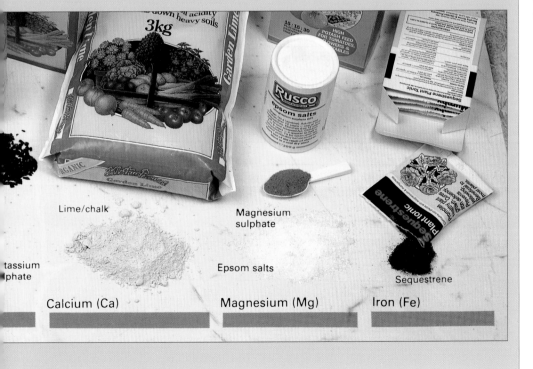

Lime/chalk

Magnesium sulphate

tassium phate

Epsom salts

Sequestrene

Calcium (Ca)

Magnesium (Mg)

Iron (Fe)

planting holes for ornamental plants. If you have no space for a compost heap you can buy bagged up manure-based composts.

Bulky manures supply the complete range of nutrients, albeit in very small amounts. But some plants need more of some elements than manure or garden compost can provide. You will have to add these extra elements in the form of concentrates.

Strike a balance between your use of fertilizers and farmyard manure or garden compost. Use manure or compost for the value of their physical bulk and use fertilizers to feed your plants.

Organic gardens

It is important to give plants the exact nutrients they need. So consider whether or not you want to use organic methods.

Organic growing is based on the long-term health of the soil. It uses bulky manures and nutrients that feed the soil organisms as well as the plants. These nutrients are supplied by organic fertilizers, which means that they have

been produced from once-living matter, such as bone meal or compost.

Limestone, formed from the shells of ancient sea creatures, is an organic fertilizer, and quarried rock phosphate and potash (potassium) are also used by organic growers.

Organic fertilizers usually have to be broken down by organisms in the soil before their chemicals take a form which can be used by the plant. So, usually, they have a steady or slow effect on the plants, though this is not always the case. The exceptions are blood, urea and wood ashes.

Fast action

Inorganic fertilizers provide the same chemicals to the plants but in a soluble form with a fast effect. Their solubility means that some of these manufactured fertilizers can be quickly washed away from the root zone.

To counter this, firms have developed controlled, or slow-release, fertilizers for lawns, flower beds and pot plants. The particles of fertilizer are bound with a substance which either allows the nutrients to pass through gradually when wetted, or needs bacterial action to break down the coating. These coated particles are those often mistaken for slugs' eggs in the potting compost of purchased plants.

Choosing with care

Fertilizers are sold as straights, compounds and soil improvers. Straights are those which contain one nutrient, such as superphosphate, which provides phosphorus, or ammonium sulphate (sulphate of ammonia), which provides nitrogen.

Compounds are a mixture of materials which give a variety of nutrients in a certain ratio. You will find this ratio printed on the package.

The items are always listed in the order of nitrogen, phosphorus and potassium (often re-

ferred to as N:P:K, the abbrevations used by chemists), followed by other components.

For example, when you see a ratio described as 7:7:7, this shows an equal amount of nitrogen, phosphorus and potassium. The figures 10:0:6 would indicate that no phosphorus is contained in this particular compound.

The actual figures used refer to the percentage of each nutrient. So 7:7:7 shows that each component forms seven per cent of the compound.

You also find that the package shows the proportions of other nutrients in the overall weight of the compound. So 10g/kg means that 10 grammes of the nutrient is present in every kilogramme, or 1000 grammes, of the fertilizer, which works out at one per cent. This is handy to know when comparing brands.

Special treatment

Fertilizers are often sold for specialist uses. These include tomato fertilizer, chrysanthemum feed and spring or summer lawn dressing. If you look at the ratio given on the package, you will see that many are similar.

Tomato fertilizer, for example, which is only used once the fruit sets, contains a high proportion of potash which is required by the developing

Those without access to farmyard manure and without space for a compost heap can buy bags of concentrated organic manure (top). Though not cheap, it is convenient. Fertilizers are best applied to seed beds before planting (above).

Foliar feeds (above) are sprayed onto a plant's leaves. Here one is being applied to perk up a weak rhododendron. Add lime (below) to a lawn if a soil test shows the soil to be very acid. This is a rare problem as most grasses tolerate acidity.

fruits. It can be used for most flowering plants if necessary. Foliage plants, however, prefer fertilizers high in nitrogen.

Liquid or dry

Fertilizers can be applied as liquids or as dry granules or powders. Dry fertilizer is scat-

---

FEEDING PLANTS

● The way your plants grow tells you what nutrients are lacking and need replacement.
● Some plants take up a nutrient early in the growing season and quickly exhaust the supply.
● Look out for signs of deficiency in the growing season, not in autumn when the leaves change colour and die.
● General purpose fertilizers supply a balance of the major nutrients. For specific nutrients, choose one that is readily available to you.

---

tered over the surface of the soil and raked in before sowing or planting. This process is called base dressing. When applied to growing plants, it is known as top dressing.

Handling and storage

Dry fertilizer has to be weighed out for accurate dosing and can blow into your eyes during use on all but the stillest day. Lawn fertilizer spreaders are sold which help you to apply the material evenly. Take care not to overlap or miss strips as you apply it, or you will have stripes of different greens on the lawn.

These dry fertilizers must be stored in a dry place. If they get wet they will set rock hard in their packs and be extremely difficult to use. The packs are easily damaged and can leak the material everywhere. Fertilizer is also very corrosive to metals so keep it well away from your car.

Special dry mix fertilizers can be bought to add to other ingredients, such as loam, peat, perlite and sand, to make your own potting compost.

Keeping stocks

Some dry fertilizers can be diluted with water and kept as concentrated stock solution, to be diluted further when required. You can also buy liquid fertilizers that are ready to dilute; these can be kept in a damp place.

Liquid feeds can often be applied to leaves, and not just the soil, and can be used in a hose-end dilutor to spray the material to the far corners of flower borders and beds.

Hose-end dilutors also make feeding the lawn easy, with no danger of leaving stripes, and save you carrying watering cans across the garden. Some hose-end dilutors are designed to take tablet fertilizers.

Correct timing

It is important to apply fertilizer at the correct time. The fast-acting types will soon be

---

SOILS THAT 'LOCK UP' FERTILIZERS

Some plants find it difficult to absorb certain nutrients – particularly iron – from neutral or acid soils. Acid-loving plants, in particular, such as rhododendrons, camellias, skimmias and most heathers, find that the nutrients are 'locked up' chemically.

Using fertilizers that make the soil more acid (sulphate of ammonia instead of Nitro-chalk if you want a nitrogenous fertilizer, for example) may help over time, but can never be an adequate solution on a very chalky soil.

For more immediate results you can use a product called Sequestrene, which provides the necessary nutrients in a form that acid-loving plants can absorb even on ordinary soils.

Sequestrene is available as a powder or granules, so it can be diluted and watered on the soil or added dry and left for the rain to wash in.

---

washed from the soil, beyond the reach of the plants, so apply them at the appropriate stage of growth, which is usually the spring.

Slow-acting types can be effective for a year or more, so the timing is less critical, especially if you apply them annually or more often to ensure a continual supply to your valuable plants.

It is better to apply dry material to growing plants with dry leaves. If the leaves are wet from dew or rain, the material can stick to the leaves and scorch them.

If you are foliar feeding, do so on a dry day so that the nutrients stay on the leaves where the plants can quickly take them up. If washed off onto the soil, the effect may be slower.

Nitrogen encourages soft, leafy growth, so avoid applying it after mid-summer, or new growths could be damaged by the first frosts and cold winds.

COMMON PESTS

Gardeners often worry about pests and the damage that they may cause. However, prompt action of the right sort will usually prevent them becoming a problem.

Not all creatures are pests and many of those labelled as pests are unlikely to be a major problem in your garden. But it pays to be familiar with the common pests and the problems they cause.

Gardeners have come to rely on remedies out of a pesticide bottle, but often there is a cheaper and simpler way of dealing with the problem. A combination of good gardening practice, eagle eyes and resorting to chemicals only when necessary, should keep pest numbers below problem levels.

Organic controls avoid the use of any chemical except those derived from plants (crushed rhubarb leaves in water for example). But unfortunately these pesticides are often non-selective, killing all in their path, including pest predators. Modern specific pesticides are more useful.

Problem areas

Pests can build up in gardens because there are many similar plants growing together. These provide a good meal and breeding sites for creatures that then become pests, damaging the appearance and yield of your plants.

If you have little time free for gardening, it makes sense to choose plants that are not troubled by pests. Avoid, for instance, roses, which can become smothered in greenfly and sooty mould to the extent that their blooms are spoiled.

In a greenhouse or conservatory, the sheltered environment and abundance of food enable pest numbers to build

Weevils (above) cut scalloped holes from the edges of leaves.

Sawfly larvae (left) can cause extensive damage to leaves.

When spraying (opposite page), wear protective gloves and make sure to spray the underside of leaves where pests often hide.

up. If you are loathe to fill the air with pesticide sprays, try using a cardboard spike that has been impregnated with pesticide. The spike is pushed into the plant container and the pesticide moves into the soil and is taken up by the plant. When pests feed on the plant they are poisoned.

Types of pesticide

There are two types of pesticide. Systemic ones are taken up by the plant, while contact (non-systemic) pesticides are sprayed or dusted on to the plant and have to touch the pest to work.

Check the label to see which type you are buying. The label will also list the chemicals the pesticide contains, the pests it will kill and common plants it should not be used on.

Some plants are damaged by certain pesticides. Follow the maker's instructions carefully, especially when using pesticides on food crops.

Bees are very susceptible to pesticides, so if you must spray a plant in flower (which will be visited by bees and other pollinators), wait until evening when they have stopped flying. There is then plenty of time for the spray to settle before the morning.

How do you know what is attacking the plant? If you cannot find the creature, look

A CHOICE OF CHEMICALS

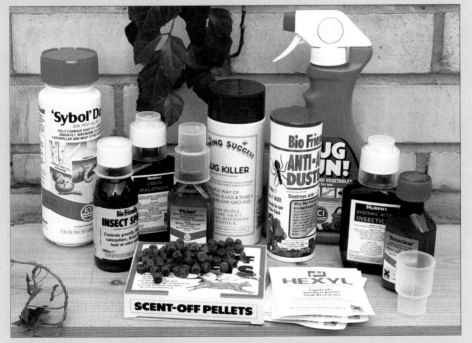

There is a wide variety of pesticides on the market and good stockists will have several alternative brands for whatever pest problem you may need to counter. Read the labels carefully before you buy and when using any insecticide.

SOME COMMON PESTS

Ants
Symptoms: Mounding of plants, especially in rockeries.
Control: Spread ant-killer near nests and over ants.

Aphids
(greenfly, blackfly)
Symptoms: Stunted or curled up leaves; lower leaves sticky.
Control: Derris, malathion or pirimicarb. Systemic dimethoate.

Capsid bugs
Symptoms: Tattered leaves and distorted flower buds.
Control: Remove leaf litter from base of plants.
Dimethoate or malathion in spring, summer.

Caterpillars
Symptoms: Holes eaten in leaves. Can be found on underside of leaves or pupating on soil below.
Control: Pick off by hand. Hoe to expose pupating stages to birds. Malathion / permethrin.

Eel worms
Symptoms: Distorted growth of stems and leaves of bulbous plants.
Control: Burn affected plants.

Fly larvae
Symptoms: Root and stem base damage.
Control: Diazinon and bromophos.

Leafhoppers
Symptoms: Cuckoo spit on plants. Not harmful.
Control: Hose off if necessary.

Leaf miners
Symptoms: Found between upper and lower surface of leaves, particularly chrysanthemums.
Control: Dimethoate. Pick off severely affected leaves.

Leather jackets
(larvae of crane flies)
Symptoms: Damage to roots in lawns, and in ground once used as lawn.
Control: Good care of lawn and soil, so birds eat larvae.

Mammals (rabbits,
dogs, cats, squirrels)
Symptoms: Damage to bulbs, fruit, tree bark etc. Fouling.
Control: Barriers. Bulbs in wire cages. Repellants discourage fouling.

Scale insects
Symptoms: Leaves sticky with honeydew. Slow growth. White waxy deposits on stems.
Control: Winter tar wash for trees. Malathion or pirimiphos-methyl. Wipe with cotton-wool buds soaked in white spirit.

Slugs or snails
Symptoms: Irregular holes in leaves. Slime trail usually evident.
Control: Slug pellets. Surround plant with ashes, egg shells etc.

Spider mite
Symptoms: Pale and speckled leaves. Very fine strands of web visible on leaf and stem.
Control: Good greenhouse hygiene. Spray to keep up humidity level. For pot plants, plant spikes containing butoxy-carboxim. Biological control with Phytoseiulus persimilis.

Weevils
Symptoms: Leaves bitten in scallop shape. Vine weevil attacks roots / stems, especially of pot plants.
Control: Malathion. Larvae can be controlled with careful hygiene and HCH.

Whitefly
Symptoms: Clouds of small flies when plants are tapped.
Control: Many now resistant. Spray at 5-day intervals. Biological control / Encarsia formosa.

at the damage for a clue.

Types of Pest

If the whole plant keels over and dies, suspect a root or stem eater or fungus disease. Have a look in the soil for grubs and go out at night with a torch to see if slugs are about. If you cannot find the culprit, it will probably have moved on, so there is no point in spraying.

Most damage can be easily identified if the plant is studied closely enough. It is always better to catch infestations at an early stage, so regular inspections are important.

If rabbits, dogs and cats are a problem in your garden, the base of young trees will need to be protected with a guard. The best solution, though an expensive one, is to fence your garden with rabbit proof fencing.

DON'T FORGET!

PESTICIDE SAFETY

• Read the label before you buy the pesticide to ensure that it is the correct one for the pest and the plant.
• Read the instructions for protective clothing (usually gloves and perhaps goggles) and dose rate.
• Keep a sprayer or watering can for pesticide use only and mark it accordingly. Keep a measuring jug and mixing stick solely for this job too.
• Take water out to the sprayer in a bucket, don't bring the sprayer into the kitchen.
• Don't spray on a windy day and if the plant is in flower, wait until evening when the bees will have left.
• Observe harvest intervals on maker's instructions if spraying fruit or vegetables.

Leaf miners (left) leave tell-tale pale tunnels in the leaves they attack. This is chrysanthemum leaf miner. Outdoors, the problem occurs in late spring and summer, but under glass it can be continuous. Spray at the first sign of infestation, and pick off severely affected leaves.

Red spider mites (below left) attack plants indoors and in the greenhouse, and may attack herbaceous plants and shrubs in the garden. Try biological control by introducing the predatory mite Phytoseiulus persimilis (below), and by good greenhouse hygiene.

PLANT DISEASES

Diseases are hidden dangers to plants, often remaining undetected until infection is severe, but there are ways to prevent and control them.

There are three main types of diseases that attack plants – fungal, bacterial and viral. Some other problems are disease-like, but are caused by unsuitable environments and errors in cultivation. These types of setback are known as physiological disorders.

All of these problems have distinctive characteristics, and each requires separate treatments to control them.

Fungal diseases

There are numerous fungal diseases and some are widespread, including mildews and rusts. Once a fungus enters a plant, minute and thread-like growths, known as hyphae, spread throughout the stems, leaves and shoots.

The disease spreads from one plant to another by microscopic spores that develop on the plant's surface, sometimes entering through cuts and other damage. Once the spores germinate, the hyphae rapidly take over the plant.

Some fungal diseases attack a wide range of plants, while others restrict their attention to just one or a few hosts.

Bacterial diseases

The bacteria that cause disease are microscopic, single-celled organisms that develop within a plant and cause damage. They are not so easy to control as fungal diseases.

Bacterial infections enter plants through wounds, prun-

Fireblight (above) is a bacterial disease which affects trees and shrubs in the Rosaceae family. Here it has attacked the leaves of Sorbus sargentiana.

There are many different types of rust, some of which affect only certain species. All are caused by a fungal infection. Here (left) rust spots have affected the leaves of a hypericum.

Most virus diseases are spread by tiny creatures such as greenfly (right).

Grey mould (below) is a fungal disease that can affect all plants. Spores spread easily.

sects previously in contact with contaminated plants. Activities such as removing side-shoots on tomato plants can increase the chance of infection because they open up a sappy wound to insects.

Once a plant is infected, nothing can be done to remove the virus. Avoid propagating from infected plants.

Greenfly (aphids) are the main cause of a virus spreading and it is, therefore, vital that insect pests are controlled by regularly spraying plants.

Viruses seldom kill plants. Indeed, if they did, the virus would not have a host. Rather, they cause loss of vigour and a general lack of well being.

In a commercial situation, with the aid of science, the shoot tips of infected plants can be encouraged to grow rapidly and produce virus-free cuttings. A home gardener,

ing cuts, natural cracks in stems and damage to leaves. Moisture is vital to bacteria and therefore infection is worse during wet weather, especially when it is warm.

Examples of bacterial diseases include gladiolus scab and crown gall, a disease that attacks a wide range of plants, from gladioli to brambles, creating wart-like growths.

Virulent viruses

A virus is a living organism, so small that it can only be seen with the aid of an electron microscope. Therefore, it is only the effect of a virus that is seen, not the cause.

Viruses are often introduced into the sap of plants by in-

PLANTS AT RISK

Warmth and high humidity, coupled with soft stems, leaves and fruits, are a dangerous combination when disease spores are about.
Do not . . .
● excessively feed plants with nitrogen, or they will produce soft, floppy stems and leaves.
● set plants too close together, as this will prevent the circulation of air around them. Moist, stagnant air in confined places encourages diseases.
● create a stuffy, warm atmosphere in greenhouses and conservatories. And avoid cold winds blowing on plants in winter. Always open the ventilator on the lee side.
● damage plants and fruits, as this quickly allows disease spores to enter. Apples and pears soon become infected if roughly handled.
● leave infected fruits on plants – destroy them immediately.
● neglect treating diseases. The earlier plants are dusted or sprayed, the better the chance of recovery – it also prevents the disease from spreading further.

SYSTEMIC FUNGICIDES

The best way to control diseases is to spray before an attack and then to give further treatments at regular intervals. As with insecticides, there are also systemic fungicides. They enter a plant's tissue and remain active against diseases for several weeks.

The chemical **carbendazim**, for instance, is a systemic fungicide for the control of a wide range of diseases of flowering plants, bulbs, shrubs, vegetables and fruit. The chemicals **bupirimate** and **triforine** can also be used to control diseases on flowering plants, shrubs, roses and fruit, controlling black spot on roses, powdery mildew and apple scab.

however, has no choice but to remove and burn infected plants. Try also to ensure that infection is not taken into your garden on infected plants.

Occasionally, plants with viruses are specially selected because of the attractive mottling and coloration that viruses can produce.

The multi-colouring and streaking in some tulips is sometimes caused by viruses. So, too, is the attractive mottling on spotted flowering maple, *Abutilon pictum* 'Thompsonii'. This widely grown houseplant is also often used in summer-bedding displays.

Physiological disorders

Plant disorders brought about by environmental factors and incorrect cultivation are not contagious. One such example is the practice of spraying soft leaves with water when they are in strong sunlight; the water droplets act as lenses, causing the tissue to burn.

Fruits that are roughly

Tulips with broken colours, such as the two burgundy and white ones (above left), are popular. The colours are often caused by a virus. Rembrandt tulips are old varieties of this type.

A good chemical sprayer (top) will focus your fungicide where it is needed.

Immersing cuttings in a fungicide (above) before planting them will protect them at a vulnerable time.

Apple scab (left) damages fruit, leaves and the young shoots of apple trees. It is a fungal disease which can be particularly bad after a wet spring.

handled when being picked will, when stored, develop bruises that encourage the entry of storage rots.

Plants can also be damaged through being given too little or too much nutrient. Lack of water will also cause damage.

Badly drained soil prevents plants growing properly, as they require a healthy balance between moisture and air around their roots.

Garden husbandry

Whenever a plant disease – or pest – is mentioned, the first reaction is to ask, 'What can I spray it with?' But usually this is not the only solution. Good garden husbandry is actually just as important.

SOME COMMON DISEASES

Name	Description	Control
American gooseberry mildew	Attacks leaves, shoots and fruits of gooseberries, creating a white powdery coating that changes to pale brown. If not controlled, bushes eventually die. Blackcurrants are also infected, but late in the season.	Spray with benomyl or thiophanate-methyl in spring and repeat at two-week intervals. A good air circulation around plants reduces infection. Do not over-feed plants with nitrogen, as this encourages lush shoots that are liable to infection.
Apple canker	Attacks both apples and pears, entering through damage caused by pests. Sunken patches that resemble small oyster shells form around damaged areas, spreading and girdling limbs. Young shoots die.	Cut out and burn infected shoots and branches. Cover large pruning cuts with a fungicidal paint. Regular spraying against insects prevents them causing damage through which the disease gains access.
Apple mildew	Creates a white, powdery coating on leaves and shoots of apples, pears, crab apples, medlars and quinces. 'Cox's Orange Pippin' is an apple variety that is especially susceptible.	Remove and burn seriously infected shoots and spray with benomyl or thiophanate-methyl at the pink bud stage in late spring, repeating the spray every 10-14 days until midsummer.
Apple scab	Attacks apples and other members of the *Malus* family. Creates matt, green-black spots on leaves and fruits, often causing them to split.	Fungus overwinters on fallen leaves, so collect and burn them. Spray trees with benomyl or thiophanate-methyl.
Bacterial canker	Attacks plums, peaches, cherries and ornamental *Prunus* trees, especially young ones. Cankers form and shoots slowly die.	Disease enters branches through cuts. Therefore, only prune these trees in summer, when the sap is rising. Coat all pruning cuts with a bacterial wound paint.
Black leg	Mainly attacks cuttings, especially pelargoniums, causing the bases of stems to become soft and black.	Infection is encouraged by wet, cold, air-less and compacted potting compost. Remove and destroy seriously infected cuttings, but those slightly damaged can be saved by cutting away black areas and re-potting in clean compost.
Black spot	Common on roses and first seen on young leaves in spring, developing from overwintering spores. Slowly, the black spots spread and merge. Infected leaves fall off prematurely.	Remove and burn infected leaves, as well as all shoots removed during pruning. Immediately after pruning, spray with or thiophanate-methyl every two or three weeks until late summer.
Brown rot	Infects insect-damaged fruits, creating concentric rings of raised spores. Fruits that have been roughly picked often begin to rot later.	Spray trees regularly and avoid damaging fruits when they are picked. Check stored fruits and remove infected ones.
Clematis wilt	Results in wilting and die-back in clematis, especially with large-flowered varieties of *Clematis* × *jackmanii*. Plants suddenly wilt, but are rarely killed. Fresh shoots develop below infected areas or grow up from the ground.	Cut out infected shoots. In spring, spray with Bordeaux mixture.

See the next page for details of more diseases.

Powdery mildew can affect the leaves and stems of a rose (left), and also the buds. Many different mildews attack a wide variety of plants, though some are specific to certain hosts. Remove and burn all diseased growth, especially in autumn to prevent the fungus overwintering. If need be, spray in spring and summer.

Name	Description	Control
Damping off	Widely damaging to seedlings in seed boxes in greenhouses. Overcrowded seedlings in very wet, unsterilized and compacted potting compost collapse and die. High temperatures encourage this disease.	Ensure compost is sterilized. Also, wash seed trays and boxes. Attacks can be checked by watering the compost with Cheshunt compound.
Fireblight	Affects pears and apples, as well as ornamental trees and shrubs such as *Cotoneaster* and *Crataegus*. Fruit spurs are attacked, leaves shrivel and turn brown, then black.	All infections in England and Wales must be notified to the Ministry of Agriculture. Cut out and burn infected shoots, 90cm/3ft below the infection.
Grey mould (also known as botrytis)	Infection enters plants through wounds and cuts. Grey, fluffy spores appear in clusters. They spread rapidly in wet weather, covering soft leaves, petals and fruits.	Remove and burn infected parts. Avoid excessive watering and ensure plants in greenhouses are well ventilated. Sterilize the potting compost and containers, and spray with benomyl or thiophanate-methyl.
Peach leaf curl	Mainly attacks peach trees, but also seen on apricots, almonds, nectarines and ornamental cherries. In early spring, young leaves assume a crimson flush, then thicken, curl and crumple. They become covered in a white bloom and soon fall off the tree.	Pick up and burn all fallen leaves. Spray trees in spring with Bordeaux mixture, repeating two weeks later. Additionally, spray trees when the leaves start to fall.
Rose mildew	Infects roses, especially in wet weather and when days are warm and nights cold. Small grey or white spots appear, spreading to form a felt-like grey down. Also, shoot tips are killed and buds fail to open.	Do not plant rose bushes close together – they need good air circulation around them. Spray infected leaves thoroughly with a copper-based fungicide or with bupirimate with triforine.
Rusts	Complex diseases. Many types, with varied life styles and range of hosts. Brown or black spots develop into irregular, raised blotches. Makes plants unsightly and impairs growth.	Difficult to control. Burn seriously infected plants, reduce humidity and ventilate freely. Soft stems and leaves encourage rusts. Spray with mancozeb or propiconazole, or with myclobutanil for rose rust.
Tulip fire	Encouraged by wet, cold weather in early spring. Infection first appears as deformed shoots and leaves, revealing small, sunken, grey spots that spread to form patches. Fungal spores live in the soil for several years.	Carefully remove infected plants and immediately burn. In spring, spray with benomyl when shoots are 5cm/2in high. Repeat the spraying at 10-day intervals until plants start flowering.

Removing and burning infected plants is vital. For instance, rose leaves infected with black spot – as well as shoots that have been cut off during pruning – should be burned immediately. The spores of apple scab overwinter on leaves and shoots, and these should be burned to stop it spreading.

Rotate plants throughout the garden from year to year. This particularly helps to prevent the build up of plant problems in vegetable plots.

Good stock

Only buy plants from reliable sources that claim to sell disease-free plants. Virus-free strawberry plants, for instance, can be bought from specialist nurseries. And remember that insects transmit diseases, so ensure that plants are free of these.

It is more likely that infected plants will be given to you by friends, rather than bought from nurseries.

A CLEAN START

Preventing infection is essential. Once a disease is established, eradication is difficult.

For instance, the notorious club root disease in cabbages and other plants in the brassica family (including wallflowers and stocks) can be controlled by dipping the roots of young plants – when they are being planted – in a fungicidal paste.

Alternatively, plants newly transplanted can be watered with a fungicide.

Additionally, dusting the seed drills of many vegetables with a combined disease and pest dressing helps to prevent the onset of diseases and pests. Importantly, it reduces the chance of diseases entering seedlings through damage caused by insects.

GARDEN NOTES

SOWING SEEDS INDOORS

Growing from seed is immensely rewarding. Not only is it the cheapest way to fill your garden with masses of blooms, but it is also easy to do.

Fill your garden with masses of summer flowers for a fraction of the cost of ready-grown bedding plants.

Growing plants from seed is not a difficult business and it is enormously satisfying to bring on a plant from seed right through to flowering.

Buying seed is, of course, cheaper than buying plants, even allowing for a certain outlay on pots and compost. Perennials, trees and shrubs are slow to grow from seed, and it is usually better to buy an established plant. Annual bedding plants and vegetables, on the other hand, are best raised from seed and this can be done with the minimum of space and equipment.

There is no need for a greenhouse or cold frames. A warm, light windowsill will do perfectly well. By following a few simple guidelines you can produce an excellent stock of bedding plants.

Tools of the trade

You will need compost, a few pots and trays and the seed. Apart from compost and seeds, every piece of equipment can be improvised.

Begin by clearing a table or draining board and set out the containers (seed trays or pots) needed for each batch of seed. Shallow (half) pots or plastic seed trays are best for sowing seed. The seedlings are 'pricked out' soon after their first leaves appear so a greater depth of compost would be wasted. The plastic punnets or trays in which you buy your fruit and vegetables from the supermarket are ideal. Yoghurt pots or old plastic cups will do the job too. With a screwdriver, punch holes in the bottom for drainage. Cut cups down to 6cm/2½in high if you want to be economical with your compost.

Most seed packets contain a generous amount and you will

Show lupins off to best effect in the middle of a border.

Easy-to-grow sweet peas make wonderful cut flowers.

Begonias, in beds or containers, will flower all summer long.

EASY STEPS TO SOWING SEEDS

1 Fill the seed tray with compost almost to the top. Compress the compost with another tray.

2 Water thoroughly by setting bas of tray in a bowl of water. Leave for a few moments.

6 Lupin seeds are quite large. Sow two then discard the weaker seedling later.

7 Cover seeds with 1.5cm/¹⁄₂in of compost. Water lightly so the seeds are undisturbed.

not need the entire contents. Sow some of the seed into a small tray or 'half tray' (15 x 20cm/6 x 8in) and save or give away the rest.

Some seeds, such as sweet peas, lupins and pot marigolds are best sown in individual pots, which allows them to grow on with their roots undisturbed right from the start. (Small yoghurt pots are quite big enough to start with.)

There are many brands of seed compost available, and one will work just as well as another. The advantage of these composts is that they are fine-textured and contain no strong nutrients which might upset tiny seedlings. So do not be tempted to make do with stronger potting composts. Invest in a little of the right compost and it will help you to avoid set-backs with your seedlings' growth.

See the light

The seed containers should be filled evenly with compost, including the four corners of trays. Fill them loosely to the top, then take a second container of the same shape and use its base to press down the compost, firming it to a level within 6mm/¹⁄₄in of the top. If

3 Alternatively, gently pour water over the seed tray (without disturbing the surface too much).

4 Begonia seeds are like specks of dust. A capsule that may come with the seeds helps sow them evenly.

5 Do not cover begonia seeds with compost. Cover with cling film to create humidity for germination.

8 A plastic bottle 'cloche' provides moist conditions for germination. For ventilation, open the bottle top.

9 Sow sweet pea seeds in moistened peat pots. These can be put straight into the ground at planting time.

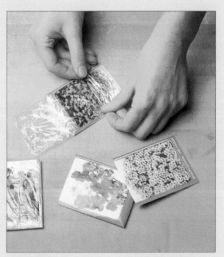

10 Seal opened seed packets with cling film and store in a cool, dry place until next year.

you leave the compost level much below that, the sides of the pot will reduce the light which reaches the seedlings. Maximum light and air are vital for healthy seedlings.

It is more practical to water the compost thoroughly at this stage. This avoids the need to water heavily after sowing, which can wash the seeds around on the surface of the compost and undo all your careful, even sowing.

The best method of watering is with a watering can with a good quality, fine metal rose on the end. Plastic roses are often very crude and spluttery,

suitable only for garden use; it is worth buying a good rose that will fit your can. Alternatively, lower the pot's base gently into a bowl of water to soak the compost for a few seconds – *before* you sow your seeds. Allow the compost to drain a little before sowing.

Indoors or out?

Before rushing to sow, first check the seed packet for the precise instructions and requirements. For example, some annual flowers can be sown outdoors in situ. Others need to be sown indoors, but not covered with soil, since

they require light for germination, for example, begonia.

To sow seed from a packet into the prepared container, shake the seed down to the bottom of the packet before tearing off the tip. This prevents spillage; generally seeds come in a sealed pack within the packet. Then, holding the packet on its side over the container, between thumb and middle finger, gently tap the packet with your index finger to produce a gradual trickle of seed. Move the packet around until the surface of the compost is thinly and evenly covered. Too thickly sown

WATERING

Small seedlings require very little water (except sweet peas), and there is no need to water often. As you grow them on and the plant develops, they will require more water. In the early stages, moistness is all that is necessary.

A cling film covering or home-made cloche helps provide a moist environment.

39

SUMMER BEDDING PLANTS FROM SEED

Raise your own colourful bedding plants on your windowsill. Most of the plants will start to flower later than the plants from shops and garden centres, but they will reward you by flowering later into the season. These quick and easy seeds can be sown indoors and germinated on a windowsill.

Flowering plants:
African marigold
alyssum
aster
French marigold
busy Lizzie
mallow
lobelia
Livingstone
 daisy
nemesia
nicotiana
pansy
petunia
rudbeckia
salvia
tagetes
verbena
zinnia

For foliage:
*Cineraria
 maritima
Kochia childsii
 and K. tricophylla
Ricinus
 communis*

seed will produce crammed, crowded seedlings that are difficult to separate and pot on. They are also much more likely to go mouldy.

Do not feel you have to use the whole packet of seed. Save some for a later sowing, perhaps, or even for next year. Most seed will keep for 12 months in a cool place in an airtight container, even if it gives a slightly lower percentage of germination. Seal the packet in foil or cling film to help prevent deterioration.

Once the seed is sown it needs to be covered with the required depth of compost. (Check the seed packet details.) You can do this by using a loosely cupped hand as a sieve, shaking it over the pot to allow a thin trickle of compost to escape between your fingers. A very coarse kitchen sieve will do the job nicely too, but fine meshes hold back too much of the compost fibre.

Settling in

Give the containers a final watering to bed in the seed. Using a fine rose, pass the watering can once or twice quickly over the top; just enough to settle the surface. Try to make sure the can is already flowing before you spray it over the compost, to avoid the first, sudden spurts of water. This

can splash in the earth and disturb the surface.

Find a warm and (in most cases) dark place to keep the containers until the seeds germinate. Once again, the seed packet will say whether a particular variety needs light and, sometimes, how long the seed will take to germinate. Some can sprout in just a few days, others take up to three weeks. (Some can take months, but these are usually hardy perennials rather than annuals).

Some seeds demand higher temperatures to germinate. In these cases, an airing cupboard provides an even, warm environment for germination, both day and night.

Covering up

To stop the compost drying out and save you the daily task of methodical watering, cover the containers. There are various methods. Glass used to be the traditional way, but, with small pots of seed, a little 'mob cap' made from polythene with an elastic band to hold it in

For a modest outlay, this propagation kit (right), available from garden centres and shops, contains seed trays with lids and separate modules for pricking out. This kit allows you to grow 24-96 plants.

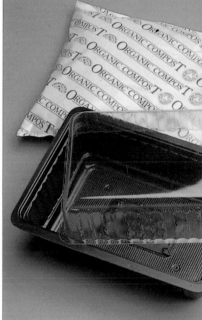

P ROJECT   PROPAGATING SEEDS ON A WINDOWSILL

The most ideal conditions for raising seeds are in a greenhouse or conservatory. This propagator box will give you excellent results from your windowsill. The foil acts as a reflector, so the seedlings receive all round light. This prevents 'legginess' – a common problem.

All you need is a cardboard box, kitchen foil, glue, sticky tape or stapler.

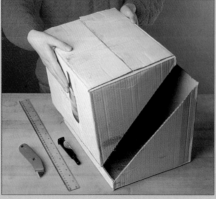

Choose a box which has a base area large enough for one or more seed trays but which can also fit near a light window. Cut the box as shown above.

Cover the inside with kitchen foil, shiny side outwards. Fix into position. Place seed trays in as shown. Remove from windowsill in frosty weather.

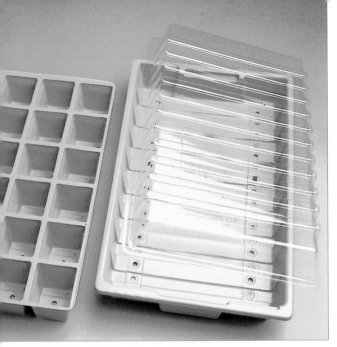

There are several variations of a more complete sowing kit on a smaller scale. This kit (left) contains seed tray, with drip tray and lid, seeds and compost. All you need to add is water and warmth.

Put together your own seed-raising kit for free. Recycle plastic vegetable and fruit packaging trays (below), yoghurt pots and margarine cartons. Don't forget to make some holes for drainage.

place will do just as well. Pierce a couple of holes to stop the air getting stale.

The condensation that builds up on the underside of the polythene drops onto the compost and keeps it moist. It will, however, need to be wiped off or turned over every other day or so. While you are doing this, keep a sharp eye open for the first emerging green shoots.

As an alternative to polythene covers, use very large clear plastic lemonade bottles with their bottoms cut off. These make splendid little 'greenhouses' and the screw-top serves as an excellent ventilator. For seed trays, use sheets of cling film or polythene pierced with a few fine holes for ventilation.

Timing counts

If you are growing annuals from seed without a cold frame, do not be tempted to sow too early. Without a cold frame in which to harden off young plants and accustom them to life outdoors, it is always best to sow at the end of the advised period on the packet. If you sow too soon your plants will be ready to go outside before the weather is warm enough and danger of frost is past.

Windowsills often have inadequate light which makes seedlings 'leggy'. To overcome this, make a propagator (far left) which maximizes the amount of light available. Plants which are grown late, but well, often overtake plants which were sown too early and have suffered setbacks.

The first shoots

Once the seedlings germinate and the shoots appear, uncover the containers and move them to a light windowsill which is also warm. A cold, draughty sill may kill off your seedlings. If this is the case, move them off the window-sill to a warmer position overnight when the temperature drops.

DON'T FORGET!

SHOW A LEG

Q Why do my seedlings often grow long stems in a lop-sided way?

A Seedlings grow towards the light. As soon as seedlings appear, turn the tray regularly so they receive even sunlight.

Modern, draught-proof and double-glazed windows are perfect. Here, the seedlings can continue to develop steadily until the first pair of 'seed leaves' are fully formed.

This is the time to separate the seedlings and prick them out into trays or pots. Whether you use one or the other at this stage is largely a matter of space. Trays allow you to put more plants into a smaller space, but when you come to plant them out there is more chance of disturbing the plants' roots.

One for the pot

Individual pots, however, allow the plants to develop a root system which can be lifted out without any disturbance or setback at planting time. For instance, sweet peas can be planted singly in peat pots. These can be planted straight into the ground, where they break up into the soil. Seedlings in individual pots can also be moved and spaced out individually as they grow on, to give them maximum light for bushier growth.

If you are limited to growing plants on your windowsills, then you might try modular trays. There are many brands available, but the basic idea is the same. A rectangular tray is divided into smaller units. Each plant has its own container, but the plants are held conveniently together. When you want to remove the young plants from the modules, simply press the bottom of the individual pocket to release the rootball.

SOWING SEEDS OUTDOORS

Raising plants from seeds sown outdoors is easy if you know how. Make the most of a variety of seeds with these handy hints.

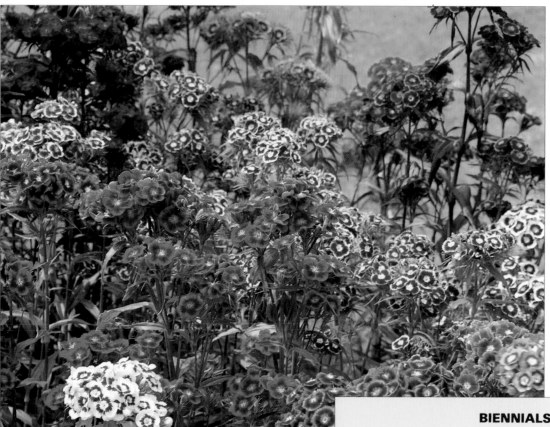

A vibrant display of sweet Williams (Dianthus barbatus) can be grown from seed (left) at a fraction of the price of bedding plants. As this is a biennial, sow the seeds first in a nursery bed and allow the seedlings to develop into strong plants before moving them to their final flowering position. Sweet Williams thrive best in an open position and well-drained soil.

BIENNIALS

Name	Flowering	Planting spacings
Common daisy (*Bellis perennis*)	Mid spring to mid autumn	13-15cm/5-6in
Canterbury bell (*Campanula medium*)	Early to mid summer	25-30cm/10-12in
Siberian wallflower (*Cheiranthus [now Erysimum] × allionii*)	Late spring to mid summer	25-30cm/10-12in
	Early to mid summer	20-25cm/8-10in
Sweet William (*Dianthus barbatus*)	Early to late summer	30-45cm/12-18in
Foxglove (*Digitalis purpurea*)		
Honesty (*Lunaria annua*)	Mid spring to early summer	25-30cm/10-12in
Forget-me-not (*Myosotis*)	Late spring to early summer	15-20cm/6-8in

Whatever their size and shape, seeds need moisture, warmth and air to encourage germination. The majority germinate in darkness, while a few require light. They are therefore scattered on top of the soil or compost rather than being slightly buried.

Moisture is needed to soften the seed's coat and chemically activate the process of growth, while air is required to enable respiration in the roots and developing shoots.

Warmth controls when, and at what rate, the process of germination takes place. As long as the soil or compost is moist, but not waterlogged, and has an open texture to enable air to circulate, the only variable in the process of germination is the temperature.

Germination

The warmth needed to encourage seeds to germinate differs from one type of plant to another. Seeds sown in greenhouses can, of course, be given optimum temperatures to

HARDY ANNUALS

Name	Flowering	Sowing depth	Thin to
Love-lies-bleeding (Amaranthus caudatus)	Mid summer to mid autumn	3mm/½in	30-38cm/12-15in
Pot marigold (Calendula officinalis)	Early summer onwards	12mm/½in	25-30cm/10-12in
Cornflower (Centaurea cyanus)	Early summer to early autumn	12mm/½in	23-38cm/9-15in
Chrysanthemum carinatum (syn. C. tricolor)	Early summer to early autumn	6mm/¼in	15-23cm/6-9in
Clarkia elegans	Mid summer to early autumn	6mm/¼in	25-30cm/10-12in
Clarkia pulchella	Mid summer to early autumn	6mm/¼in	25-30cm/10-12in
Convolvulus tricolor (syn. C. minor)	Mid summer to early autumn	12mm/½in	23-30cm/9-12in
Larkspur Consolida ajacis (syn. Delphinium consolida)	Early to late summer	6mm/¼in	15cm-23cm/6-9in
Californian poppy (Eschscholzia californica)	Early summer onwards	6mm/¼in	23-30cm/9-12in
Gypsophila elegans	Early summer to early autumn	6mm/¼in	23-30cm/9-12in
Sunflower (Helianthus annuus)	Mid summer to early autumn	12mm/½in	30-45cm/12-18in
Candytuft (Iberis umbellata)	Early summer to early autumn	6mm/¼in	23cm/9in
Sweet pea (Lathyrus odoratus)	Early summer to early autumn	12mm/½in	23-30cm/9-12in
Poached egg plant (Limnanthus douglasii)	Early to late summer	3mm/⅛in	10cm/4in
Scarlet flax (Linum grandiflorum)	Early to late summer	6mm/¼in	30-38cm/12-15in
Virginian stock (Malcolmia maritima)	Summer (repeat sowings necessary)	6mm/¼in	15cm/6in
Night-scented stock (Matthiola bicornis)	Mid to late summer	6mm/¼in	23cm/9in
Love-in-a-mist (Nigella damascena)	Early to late summer	6mm/¼in	15-23cm/6-9in
Field poppy (Papaver rhoeas)	Early to late summer	6mm/¼in	25-30cm/10-12in
Mignonette (Reseda odorata)	Early summer to mid autumn	3mm/⅛in	23-30cm/9-12in
Black-eyed Susan (Rudbeckia hirta)	Late summer onwards	6mm/¼in	30-38cm/12-15in

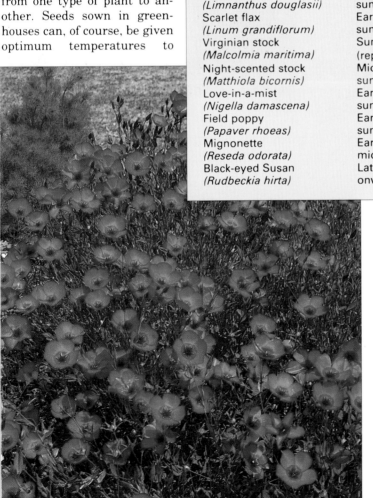

Hardy annuals such as scarlet flax (Linum grandiflorum 'Rubrum', left) are resilient plants which can simply be sown outdoors where you want them to flower. If they are to form part of a larger bed, make sure you take varying colour combinations into account before sowing.

Encourage sweet pea seeds (right) to germinate rapidly by nicking them lightly with a knife before planting. This helps the hard seed coat to break down.

HARDY HERBACEOUS PERENNIALS

Name	Flowering	Sowing depth	Transplant to
Yarrow (*Achillea filipendula*)	Mid summer to early autumn	6mm/¼in	38-45cm/15-18in
Yarrow (*Achillea millefolium*)	Early summer to early autumn	6mm/¼in	30-38cm/12-15in
Anchusa azurea (syn. *A. italica*)	Early to late summer	12mm/½in	30-38cm/12-15in
Cupid's dart (*Catananche caerulea*)	Early to mid summer	6mm/¼in	30-38cm/12-15in
Shasta daisy (*Chrysanthemum maximum*)	Early to late summer	6mm/¼in	30-45cm/12-18in
Coreopsis grandiflora	Early to late summer	6mm/¼in	30cm/12in
Delphinium	Early to mid summer	6mm/¼in	45-60cm/1½-2ft
Globe thistle (*Echinops ritro*)	Mid to late summer	12mm/½in	45-60cm/18-24in
Blanket flower *Gaillardia aristata* (syn. *G. grandiflora*)	Early summer to mid autumn	6mm/¼in	38-45cm/15-18in
Avens (*Geum chiloense*)	Early summer to early autumn	3mm/⅛in	30-38cm/12-15in
Baby's breath (*Gypsophila paniculata*)	Early to late summer	6mm/¼in	45-75cm/1½-2½ft
Sweet rocket (*Hesperis matronalis*)	Early summer	6mm/¼in	38cm/15in
Oriental poppy (*Papaver orientale*)	Late spring to early summer	6mm/¼in	45-60cm/1½-2ft

The hardy herbaceous perennial blanket flower (Gaillardia aristata) will provide a profusion of brilliant yellow blooms (above) for several years, if grown initially from seed in a nursery bed.

encourage germination. Outdoors, this is dictated by the weather and especially by the area in which you live.

Spring is the traditional time of year for sowing seeds because the rising temperatures make germination possible. The range of ornamental plants for sowing outdoors is extremely wide and includes annuals, biennials, herbaceous perennials, trees and, of course, shrubs.

Annuals

Some annuals are half-hardy and must be raised under glass early in the year, ready for planting outdoors as soon as the risk of frost has passed. Hardy annuals have a tougher image and can be sown outdoors in the positions where they are to flower. Most are sown in spring.

Preparation for sowing hardy annuals should begin in the autumn of the previous year, when the soil is dug to a depth of about 25cm/10in (a spade's blade). Well-rotted manure and decayed garden compost can be dug into the soil at this stage, but remember annuals flower best in soil that is not too rich.

Winter weather breaks down large lumps of soil and by spring creates a fine tilth. In early spring, rake the ground level, further breaking down the soil. Firm light soils by systematically treading over them, but take care not to compact them too much.

Small and narrow flower beds at the side of paths can be sown without too much preparation. But large borders need to be carefully planned on paper first, taking into account the differing heights and colour combinations.

After raking and treading the surface, use a thin line of sand to mark out the areas for each type. Alternatively, mark the areas by using a stick to draw shallow lines.

A garden-line and the corner of a hoe or rake can be used to create drills in which seeds can be sown. Sow seeds thinly and evenly and use the back of a rake to cover them. Alternatively, shuffle along the

When preparing the soil in spring for sowing, first mark out the positions of the different plants you intend to sow with a thin line of sand (right). Then form drills with the side of a hoe. When the seeds are sown, use the back of a rake (inset) to cover them with soil to the required depth.

drill, with your feet on either side of it, gently pushing soil over the seeds.

If you need to lightly rake the surface at this stage, do this in the same direction as the drills. Raking across them may disturb and scatter seeds in the wrong places.

Place brushwood-type sticks over the area to prevent birds and cats scratching the seed. Alternatively, use black cotton stretched between canes inserted at the edges of the border. Extra protection can be given by threading pieces of tin-foil along the cotton.

During dry spells, keep the border moist. After germination, remove the sticks and, when large enough to handle, thin out the seedlings to the distances in the Hardy Annual table on page 43.

Most of the plants in this table are true hardy annuals

but some, such as black-eyed Susan (*rudbeckia hirta*), are short-lived perennials which are normally cultivated as hardy annuals.

Biennials

These are plants that are usually sown in shallow drills, about 30-38cm/12-15in apart, in a nursery bed in early summer for flowering during the following year.

During the first few months they germinate and develop into strong plants. Transfer them to their flowering positions in late summer or early autumn.

Many plants naturally have a biennial nature, but others although normally perennial are treated as biennials.

Herbaceous perennials

These are plants that live for several years, dying down to soil level in autumn and sending up fresh shoots the following spring.

They are raised by sowing seeds thinly in shallow drills in a nursery bed in late spring and early summer. The sowing depths are indicated in the

Hardy Herbaceous Perennial table on page 44.

After germination, thin the seedlings slightly so that they are not congested, and in late summer or autumn plant them into their flowering position. The spacings are also indicated in the table. These distances may need to be adjusted according to the height and vigour of a particular variety.

Trees and shrubs

Seeds of trees and shrubs are increasingly offered in seed catalogues and, although it takes many years for a reasonably-sized tree to be raised in this way, to do so always creates a lasting sense of personal achievement.

Seeds of some trees and shrubs are large, with thick coats that reduce the speed of germination. Therefore, it is often necessary to soften or remove part of the seed coat, or to submit them to alternating periods of cold and warmth before they are sown.

Some ways of encouraging the rapid germination of seeds are suggested below.

ENCOURAGING SEEDS

Soaking seeds in water helps to leach out chemicals that inhibit germination. Soak for up to three hours in hand-hot water. If the packet advises soaking for longer, change the water periodically. Some seed, such as clianthus, caragana and broom swell when soaked. If this happens, sow immediately – before they have time to dry out.

Seeds such as sweet peas and morning glory have hard seed coats that benefit from being chipped. Scratch the outer surface with a sharp knife, rub the seeds on fine sand-paper or, with small seeds, prick with a sharp needle.

Some perennials, such as a number of trees, shrubs and many alpines, need a cold period to break their dormancy. This used to be done by putting the seeds between layers of sand and leaving them outside for the winter. Today it is easier to use a refrigerator.

Sow the seeds on several layers of moist kitchen paper placed in a small plastic container with a close-fitting lid. Keep them at room temperature for about three days then place in the refrigerator for several weeks. Check periodically to make sure the kitchen paper has not dried out. Then remove the seeds and sow them in compost.

BRIGHT IDEAS

SEEDLINGS

Once your seeds have germinated, the fiddly job of 'pricking them out' is the next stage.

As soon as your seedlings have produced their first pair of tiny green leaves it is time to give them a bit of space, or 'prick them out'.

Densely sown crops of seedlings are prone to damping off at this stage, so pricking them out while they are still small is very important. With tiny seed-lings, it can be a rather fiddly job, but it is perfectly possible with a little practice.

As a general rule, prick out only the strongest seedlings and discard any that are weak or spindly. However, with mix-tures prick out both strong and weak to ensure a good col-our balance. Lobelia seedlings are tiny and are pricked out in small clusters, so some will in-evitably be at a later stage of development than others.

Seedlings can be pricked out into pots, trays or modules (trays with their own internal divisions). Modules are econ-omical on compost and space and are easy to handle. There

Growing plants from seed is not only immensely satisfying it is also very economical. Once your seeds have germinated you will be rewarded with trays full of densely packed seedlings (above). This is the stage at which you prick them out, to prevent overcrowding.

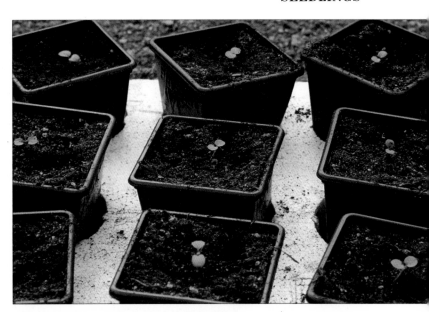

When the first two leaves appear the seedlings should be transplanted in order to give their root system adequate space to develop. The seedlings (left) have outgrown their tray and are being transplanted into another container where they will have adequate breathing space. The pansy seedlings (right) have been planted in individual containers until they are ready for planting out. Seedlings, like babies, cannot digest strong foods so plant in specially balanced seedling compost.

is also no disturbance to roots when the time comes to plant out, so the plants suffer no disruption to their growth.

Traditional seed trays (containing five rows of eight plants) are fine, but there will be a period, after the roots have been disturbed at planting out time, when growth is temporarily slowed down.

Which pot?

Pots can be used for seedlings, but they must be small (6-7.5cm/2½-3in across). A smaller pot is more economical on both space and compost and seedlings can later be moved to a larger one, if necessary.

To prick out seedlings, first fill your trays, pots or modules with compost, right up to the top. Press the compost down gently to leave space for watering. Make a hole with a pencil or a piece of fine cane. Then, using finger and thumb, take hold of the first seedling by one of its leaves. Use the pencil to gently tease up the root from the compost, then lower it into the prepared hole. Use the pencil again to bring the soil up to the root. When the tray is full, give it a thorough watering with tepid water through a fine rose. Seedlings hate an icy shower! Once the tray has drained, it is ready to go on the window sill.

The temperature needed

Not all seedlings look the same. Some, like these cyclamen (left) are quite developed and already share a family resemblance. They produce 'true' leaves unlike most seedlings whose first pair of leaves bears no resemblance to their final form.

The cyclamen produces a root ball which can easily be replanted while the sweet peas (below) set out a long tap root which must be handled carefully. Make a deep hole and insert the seedling, taking care not to break the root.

DON'T FORGET!

VITAL NEEDS

To ensure that seedlings grow into compact, healthy plants remember to give them:
- maximum light
- maximum ventilation
- an even temperature
- soil that is moist but not saturated

now is not quite so high as it was for germination. Over the next few weeks it needs to be gradually lowered to steady the growth of your little plants. Remember, though, that the temperature should not vary too much. If you are growing your plants on the window sill, lift them away

PRICKING OUT SEEDLINGS

When your seed tray begins to look overcrowded, the time has come to give the seedlings a bit of room. The next stage in the process of raising seedlings is known as pricking out. It is a fiddly job because the seedlings are so small but it will pay dividends in the long run. The size of the seedlings depends on the plant. Some, like the begonias pictured below, have tiny seeds and very small seedlings. Cyclamen and sweet pea seedlings are larger and easier to handle. They can be transplanted into modular trays which have individual compartments for each seedling or into individual small pots.

1 *Fill a modular tray with special compost suitable for seedlings and water well.*

2 *Using a pencil, ease out the roots and lift by the leaves using thumb and forefinger.*

3 *Make a hole in the compost with the pencil, insert the seedling and firm in.*

4 *Using the blunt end of the pencil gently firm in the soil around the seedlings.*

5 *Put a lid on the tray or cover pots with cling film to preserve moisture.*

OUTDOOR SOWING

Of course, the information on these pages applies only to seed sown indoors, and if the notes on your seed packet tell you to sow directly into the ground where the plants are to flower, you should follow this advice instead. Not all plants are automatically better suited to being nurtured indoors. Poppies, larkspur and pot marigolds will all produce far better plants when sown straight into the soil outdoors.

from the window into the room at night, so they do not get chilled. This is especially important at first, while the seedlings are getting established. Later, they will need to become accustomed to a colder night-time temperature before they go outside. A temperature of about 15-18°C/60-65°F is suitable for most new seedlings, reducing to 10–13°C/50-55°F later on.

While your seedlings are growing on, it is important to maintain as high a level of light as you possibly can. This will prevent the plants from becoming drawn and leggy.

Hardening off

As the days grow warmer it will be necessary to acclimatize your young plants to conditions out of doors. Hardening off is

WHAT DOES IT MEAN?

- **Pricking out** – spacing out seedlings in seed trays or pots.
- **Hardening off** – the process of acclimatizing tender and half-hardy seedlings raised indoors or under glass to the harsher conditions which exist out of doors.
- **Growing on** – the stage during which transplanted seedlings establish themselves and grow larger, before they are finally planted out of doors.
- **Damping off** – not a technique, but a fungus that can infect seedlings soon after they have germinated. For this reason, you should use only sterilized compost. Poor drainage and over-watering can also encourage the problem. Remove plastic coverings for a short period each day so that the atmosphere is not too humid. Always wash old pots and trays thoroughly before use, and water seedlings with fresh tap water.

Prevention is better than cure for controlling damping off. Keep tools clean and never use garden soil.

just a matter of easing the transition from a warm inside window sill to life in the real world of the flower bed.

Choose a mild, dull day to lift your pots and trays outside for a few hours. The temperature will not be too much of a shock, but they will not be used to the movement of air and it will take time for them to get used to transpiring, or breathing, at a faster rate. Eventually, after a few spells outdoors, they will be ready to take direct sun and wind. At this stage they will need more water than before. Alternatively, the easiest place to harden off seedlings gently is in a cold frame.

A permanent cold frame is often a wooden construction with a glass top. This very professional looking example (right) is located in a sheltered spot by the side of a large greenhouse. The chains attached to the glass top allow the amount of ventilation to be controlled according to the specific requirements of individual plants. Because it is in sections there can be a degree of flexibility – so that some plants can have full ventilation while others are only exposed a little.

PROJECT

BUILDING A SIMPLE COLD FRAME

A cold frame need not be large or permanent. It can be made from readily available materials and requires no special skill to assemble.

Site your frame in a warm, sheltered position that receives maximum light. For a frame measuring 1m/3ft 4in square, build up 48 bricks, layer by layer, following the photographs. There is no need to use mortar between the bricks so the frame can be dismantled easily and moved or stored for the winter.

Once you have built the walls of the frame, place a sheet of rigid clear pvc on top and secure around the edge using more bricks. For a cheaper alternative to rigid pvc you could try using polythene, or a sheet of glass in a wooden frame, though this can be risky with children around. Corrugated plastic is strong, but will leave a gap around the sides, even when closed.

Ventilate the frame on warm sunny days by lifting the pvc away from the bricks, but close it at night until the plants are acclimatised. If frost is forecast, lay a sheet of newspaper over the plants before closing the frame. A blanket over the whole frame will provide further protection. Once the risk of frost is over, put the plants in their final flowering positions.

1 *Using 48 ordinary household bricks, make a base for your cold frame.*

2 *Place a sheet of rigid clear pvc on top of the wall of bricks.*

3 *You will need another 8 bricks to secure the corners of the pvc.*

4 *To ventilate, simply raise the pvc up one level of the securing bricks.*

LAWN CARE

Whatever the present state of your lawn, the right treatment will quickly restore its condition and keep it looking its best throughout the year.

MOWING TIPS

● Reduce the height of long grass in several stages, rather than all at once, or the lawn will go brown.

● Let long grass dry before cutting, or it will look ragged.

● Always use a grass box when mowing fine lawns; this is not essential on hard-wearing lawns, provided you cut before the grass gets too long – short clippings soon vanish.

● Use grass clippings as a mulch under mature trees and shrubs or add them to the compost heap. For best compost results, use alternate 15cm/6in layers of grass clippings and kitchen waste or similar.

A lawn is like a large outdoor carpet. The big difference is that lawns are alive. Each square metre contains hundreds of tiny plants, each of which needs food and water. The lawn is regularly mowed and trampled on and, though few plants would put up with such punishment, grass thrives on it. Even so, lawns require regular attention if they are to look their best.

Types of grass

There are two basic types of lawn. Fine lawns are made up of narrow-leaved grasses which give a soft velvety texture, but need a lot of care and attention. They do not stand up to much wear, and have been traditionally used for front gardens.

Hard-wearing utility lawns are made of coarser grasses which grow fast and so stand up well to family use.

Families with small gardens are just as likely to have hard-wearing lawns everywhere, for ease of maintenance and low cost. Garden enthusiasts, particularly older people whose families have left home, often prefer fine lawns front and back for their better finish.

Mowing

Grass needs cutting regularly all the time it is growing – even in winter if the weather is mild. Rather than mowing once a week regardless, cut the grass when it actually needs it. Mow hard-wearing lawns when the grass reaches 5-6cm/2-2½in, and fine lawns when the grass is 2.5-3cm/1-1¼in high.

In late spring, when growing conditions are good, this

CHOOSING MOWERS

Electric Cylinder and rotary types available. Cheapest to buy and no regular servicing needed; sharpen or replace blades each year.
Motor Cylinder and rotary types available. Expensive to buy and need regular servicing each winter; costly unless you do it yourself.
Hand Small 'push' cylinder mowers are still available new. Cheap to buy and produce a good finish; ideal for a small fine lawn.
Rotary mowers (including hover types). Can cut wet grass but, for safety reasons electric models should not be used in the wet. Hover types are useful for awkward areas like banks. Rotary mowers with a roller will produce a striped effect.
Cylinder mowers Best for fine lawns. Give a closer cut and will produce zebra stripes if you mow up and down the lawn in alternate directions in neat parallel lines. (The stripes are caused by grass in alternate rows lying in opposite directions after the mower's roller has passed over it).
Width of cut Wider mowers make less work of cutting big lawns; narrower mowers are easier to manoeuvre round fiddly beds.

There is something satisfying about trimming lawn edges in a straight line. If doing it manually you will need a pair of long-handled edging shears (above).

For an even effect all over, apply lawn feed and weedkiller with a fertilizer spreader (below).

A fine lawn (left) is the perfect complement to bright borders of flowers. Neat edges complete the effect. A good petrol mower with a roller (below) will produce alternate stripes. A grass box saves you the unnecessary chore of having to rake up the lawn clippings.

may mean cutting twice a week. In late autumn, once every three to four weeks may be enough. Hard-wearing lawns should not be cut too closely – leave the grass at least 2.5cm/1in high. Fine lawns can be mown more closely, but not shorter than 1.25cm/½in.

Leave grass slightly longer in spring and autumn and whenever growing conditions are poor (during a summer drought, for instance) to avoid over-stressing it. Set the mower blades 6-13mm/¼-½in higher. Longer grass can look greener during a drought.

Edging lawns

After mowing, use a pair of long-handled shears to neaten the edges of the lawn. Nylon-line trimmers are handy for tidying up grass along walls and around trees. An electric lawn-edger is a labour-saving device for trimming the grass along the edges of beds. It only works properly if your lawn has well-made edges.

To make a neat lawn edge, use a half-moon edger (also called an edging iron or edging knife) to cut along a garden line marking the correct posi-

tion of the edge of a flower bed. Make the cut vertically, about 5cm/2in deep, turning the turf forward into the bed as if digging. Lawn edges may need re-making every few years. To avoid beds getting bigger and the lawn smaller, use hard edging strips.

Feeding

Lawns need feeding regularly, especially if you use a mower with a grass box. (By removing clippings you are also removing nutrients that would otherwise find their way back into the soil to improve it).

LAWN CARE PROGRAMME

Early spring
Start cutting when grass starts growing; set the blades high.
Mid spring
Apply lawn feed; if moss or weeds are a problem use a treatment combined with a feed. Continue to feed at 6-8 week intervals during the summer, unless you used a slow release feed (one application only will be needed). Reduce height of cut to 1.25cm/½in for fine lawns and 2.5cm/1in for utility lawns.
Summer
Avoid feeding lawns during drought, as grass may be scorched. Mow twice weekly when the grass is growing fast.
Early autumn
Rake lawn hard to remove moss and organic debris. Spike lawns on heavy soil or those which get a lot of wear. Apply sieved topsoil, peat and sharp sand at one bucketful per square metre as a top dressing on fine lawns. Apply an autumn lawn feed. Raise mower blades.
Autumn/Winter
Continue cutting until grass stops growing. Rake up fallen leaves. Avoid walking on the lawn when it is either wet or muddy as this can damage it.

Utility lawns will survive on one feed a year; this should be given at the start of the growing season, in mid spring. Instead of expensive lawn feed, you could use a product such as Growmore which thickens the grass without making it greener or grow too fast (but all fertilizers will speed up growth). Fine lawns must be regularly fed to keep them looking their best.

LAWN PROBLEMS

Weeds
Cause: thin, patchy grass, lack of feeding. Remedy: feed regularly, treat with liquid weedkiller or with weedkiller plus feed in spring.

Moss
Cause: thin, patchy, underfed grass; poor surface drainage; shade.
Remedy: apply mosskiller in spring and rake out dead moss; feed regularly; rake and spike in autumn and top dress with sharp sand (one bucket per square metre). In shade where moss is a regular problem, use a shade tolerant grass mixture.

Green slime
(algae and liverworts) Cause: as for moss. Remedy: apply lawn sand or liquid mosskiller, follow lawn care programme as for moss.

Fungi
Cause: occasional fungi in autumn are due to organic matter in the soil plus the damp weather. Persistent fairy rings are permanent unless treated – grass inside the ring is yellow and stunted due to removal of nitrogen by the fungi.
Remedy: autumn fungi soon go, or can be removed by hand. Fairy rings should be excavated to a foot deep and a foot beyond the ring, and the soil disposed of away from the garden. Refill with new topsoil and reseed.

Bumps and hollows
Cause: poor preparation before sowing or turfing. Remedy: lift turf from affected area and either remove or add soil until the ground is level. Firm the soil and relay the turf. Slight hollows can be levelled by top dressing.

Any lawn which is poor, starved or patchy, can be quickly restored by regular feeding. Choose a spring and summer lawn feed (high in nitrogen to promote leafy growth) for use from mid spring to late summer, or a slow release lawn feed (one application in spring will last all summer too).

In early autumn, use an autumn formulation that is high in phosphates to promote strong healthy roots; one application is enough.

Lawn feeds come as granules or liquids. Granules can be broadcast by hand, though irregular spreading can give patchy results. Liquid lawn feeds should be watered on with a watering can and some

can be applied using a hose-end diluter.

Weeds and moss

If the lawn contains weeds or moss, use a weedkiller or a mosskiller that is combined with a lawn feed. Apply this in mid spring in place of a plain feed. If you prefer to use a liquid mosskiller or weedkiller, apply it about three weeks after using a feed. Several applications may be needed for persistent, established weeds.

If you dislike using chemicals, you can remove moss with a spring-tined rake (one with long springy tines) or a powered lawn raker. Weeds can be dug out manually using a daisy grubber.

Utility lawns are relatively

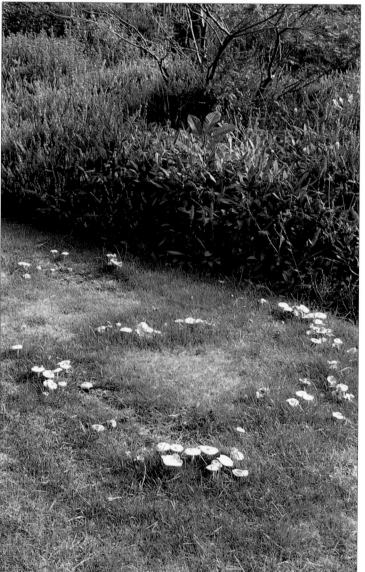

A twiggy birch besom is the perfect tool for brushing in a good top dressing (above). On fine lawns this only needs to be done once a year in autumn. Top dressing is also a good way to level out any shallow hollows and can be done every few months on all types of lawn.

A fairy ring (left) will kill the grass and spoil the look of your lawn. Removing the visible fungi is not enough, as the underground thread-like hyphae – a type of root – spread out year by year to find fresh nutrients, having exhausted those within the ring. You will need to dig up the soil, replace it and reseed the area.

Lawns need watering during hot, dry spells (left). If there is no ban on hoses and sprinklers, give the grass a good soaking.

This picture (below) shows how effective a selective weedkiller can be if you have a problem with daisies and white clover. The central strip was sprayed ten days before the photograph was taken and is virtually clear of all weeds.

tined rake. But now there are relatively cheap electric lawn raking machines which make light work of it. Larger petrol-driven machines can be hired.

Top dressing
Top dressing is used regularly for maintaining fine lawns, and is also useful for filling small depressions in a utility lawn. Make up a mixture of equal parts good topsoil, with peat, cocopeat or garden compost and sharp sand. Sieve it to remove any lumps.

Spread it in a layer 1.25cm/ ½in deep over the whole lawn (if treating a fine lawn), or in any shallow depression in a utility lawn. Work the mixture into the grass with the back of a rake. The grass should show through the dressing and not be smothered by it.

One top dressing a year, in autumn, is enough for fine lawns. If you are filling hollows in utility lawns, you can top dress every few months until the hollow is level with the rest of the lawn. This works fine so long as the grass is allowed to grow through the dressing and never smothered by it (which would kill it).

drought tolerant, and usually survive dry summers with little or no watering. Even if they go brown, they quickly green up again when the rain comes in autumn. Fine lawns are quicker to show signs of stress, and really need watering regularly in dry spells. If you cannot water, bare patches may need reseeding in autumn.

Avoiding drought
You can 'drought-proof' a lawn to a considerable degree by adding lots of organic matter before sowing or turfing, and then following a good lawn care programme (see box) which encourages deep rooting and builds up organic matter.

If you have to water a lawn, the golden rule is 'do it thoroughly'. Stand a dish under the sprinkler. When the dish

holds 4cm/1½in of water, the lawn is well watered.

Scarifying
Over a period of time, a lot of decomposed lawn clippings, dead moss and creeping grass stems build up in a lawn. This occasionally needs clearing out, to make way for fresh new growth. Scarifying, as it is called, is done in autumn.

Mow the lawn as usual, then run over it with the lawn raker in the opposite direction to that of the mower. Repeat both mowing and raking at 90 degrees to the original angle, then apply autumn lawn feed.

Fine lawns need scarifying every year, and utility lawns benefit from it every two years or so.

In the past, scarifying had to be done by hand with a spring-

LAWN FROM SEED

Sowing your own lawn is cheap, easy and not too back-breaking. The key to a good-looking lawn is to prepare the ground thoroughly first.

New lawns can be created from seed or by laying turf. There are pros and cons to each method, but there is no doubt that seeding is cheaper.

A lawn is usually one of the major features of a garden, and perhaps the one we take most for granted. Most of us hope to get away with weekly cutting and edging, and occasionally dealing with broad-leaved weeds. To make this possible, the secret is proper preparation of the ground. Time spent on initial preparation will pay off later.

Shape and position

The first things to consider when creating a lawn are its shape, size, level and position.

Rectangular lawns with sharp corners and straight edges look right in a formal context but are harder to maintain well. A curving outline will allow you to mow with much less stopping and turning. This means cutting will be faster and you are less likely, especially when the ground is wet, to damage the lawn when turning the mower.

Lawns look better without too many beds or trees. It may be worth extending a bed to include a tree, in order to leave a long clean edge to the lawn.

Choosing the area

There is no point in trying to put down to lawn land which is unsuitable for grass. For instance, grass will never grow well in deep shade under trees, even when using one of the grass seed mixtures in-

tended for shade. And boggy, ill-drained parts of the garden will always be a problem as lawn, unless you undertake some serious land drainage first. Try to site your lawn in the open, on soil which is naturally adequately drained.

Having decided on the extent of your lawn-to-be, you

can begin to prepare the ground. Ideally this should be done in the autumn, ready for spring sowing, but it can be prepared in the summer for sowing in late summer or early autumn. The procedure for autumn sowing is exactly the same but instead of leaving the ground roughly dug for the

Existing paths and beds of shrubs (above) in an established garden may dictate the shape of your lawn. For ease of maintenance keep the number of beds within a lawn to a minimum. In the garden of a new house you will have more flexibility.

SEED MIXTURES

Seed mixtures are designed to produce different types of lawn. They contain different species of grass according to how short they are to be cut, how hard-wearing they are, and how much light they need. The tougher mixtures usually contain ryegrass, which gives them strength but also a coarse texture. For a finer lawn, not intended for heavy use, choose a mixture without ryegrass.

You will usually find a slightly higher application rate recommended for the finer mixtures, as they are slower to establish and more likely to suffer from the competition of weeds in the early stages.

The way your lawn is to be used will determine your choice of a suitable seed mixture.

On the left (above) a ryegrass mix with some coarser grasses, contrasted with, right, a fine grass mix.

frost to break down over the winter, you must cultivate it manually there and then.

If the land you wish to make lawn is already under grass, or has perennial, deep-rooted weeds in it, like dandelion and dock, it is best to use a weed-killer on the ground in the autumn. Use, for example, a herbicide such as Tumbleweed that contains glyphosate.

Many lawns begin life from the bare soil of a building site around new houses. This often means that there are chunks of rubble to be removed before work can begin. It also means, all too often, that subsoil from the house's foundation will have been spread over the topsoil. This needs to be dug off, especially if it is clay subsoil, to get back to the proper topsoil. This will restore the natural drainage and means your lawn will be rooting into fertile topsoil instead of leaner subsoil. Do not be tempted to dig the subsoil into the topsoil and hope for the best. It will only lead to problems later.

A town garden (below) with a semi-circle of grass that has a wavy edge to accommodate flower beds and tubs.

Digging

Having got back to the topsoil and killed the existing vegetation, the ground can be rough dug, just as you would a vegetable patch, and left in large clods for the winter frosts to break down. If the land has had heavy machinery on it, then it is worth digging to two spade-depths. Otherwise one good spade-depth is sufficient.

On poor, thin soils this is also the time to incorporate any compost or well-rotted manure you have available, to increase the soil's fertility and

GROWING TIPS

RESEEDING

If any bare patches appear after germination, lightly reseed them using the same mixture. Remember to save some seed for the purpose, rather than sowing it all at the outset.

IMPROVING SOIL

During the winter, test the soil's pH, to see how acidic or alkaline it is. Do not over-lime, but if the soil is very acidic, then 85g/3oz of ground limestone to the square metre/yard will probably put matters right.

Heavy clay soils will benefit from the addition of 4.5kg/10lb of coarse, gritty sand to each square metre, incorporated into the soil, like the lime, with the spring digging.

moisture retentiveness.

In late winter or early spring the rough-dug land should be dug over again, breaking down the lumps to leave a smoother surface. Work in well any grit, lime or compost that has been added. A rotovator is excellent for this purpose if you have the muscles to handle one, or can make use of someone else's muscles! Afterwards the surface can be raked roughly level and any stones picked off.

Between now and the time to sow the grass seed, unsuitable grasses and weed seedlings, such as chickweed and shepherd's purse, will spring up in mild spells. The more that germinate now the better.

Once the soil has been dug over, tread it (above) to firm the ground. Work up and down, breaking up any clods. Rake it and then tread it again in the other direction. Seed can be broadcast by hand (below left). Working from a string line will ensure even coverage.

You can easily hoe off the seedlings or spray them with a contact weedkiller such as Weedol, based on paraquat with diquat. The more weeds you can eliminate, the better the seedling grasses will grow.

A week or two before you are ready to sow, scatter a handful of Growmore or a similar balanced fertilizer over each

square metre/yard and rake it in thoroughly. This will give the seedling grasses a little boost to get them going.

Firming the surface

Now the ground has been dug and broken down, it needs to be consolidated to give an even, level surface.

On a dry day, tread the soil down firmly all over with your heels, working in lines up and down the soil. Then rake it over to fill any depressions that have appeared. Repeat the process in the opposite direction and rake again. Work the soil surface with the rake, removing small stones and bits of root, until you have a smooth, fine surface, with no bumps, hollows or soft spots. You can now sow the seed.

Seed sowing

Most garden centres stock well-known, reliable brands of grass seed, supplied in various mixtures of species, which will

GARDEN NOTES

WEEDING AND FEEDING

Until the new turf is established, weed seedlings should be removed by hand when they are large enough to handle. Selective weed killers should not be used for the first six months as they can harm the young grasses.

A new lawn on well-prepared soil will require no further feeding for several months at least. Autumn-sown lawns should not be fed until the following spring, as late feeding can lead to fungal diseases attacking the young growth.

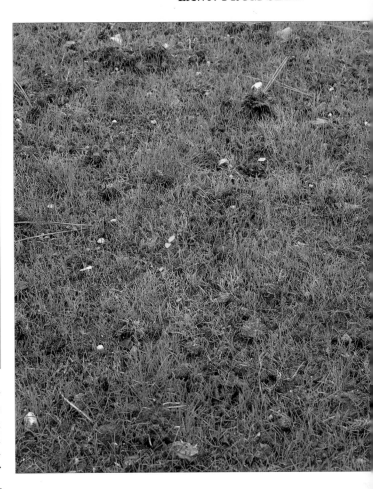

give you the turf suitable for different kinds of lawn. Before you buy, decide whether you want a very fine, ornamental lawn which will not be hard-wearing, or something tougher

Grass seedlings coming through (above) on a newly sown lawn. Unfortunately the surface has been poorly prepared, leaving too many clods and stones which will prevent seedlings growing. The clods will be broken up when the lawn is rolled but the stones will have to be raked off to prevent damage to the mower blades.

A pot standing in the middle of a lawn (left) can be as effective as a flower bed. It can be moved when it comes to mowing.

for children to play on, or perhaps something to tolerate shade. Check the recommendations for use on the packet, and also check the advised rate of application.

A rough rule of thumb for seeding lawns is 30-45/1-1½oz per square metre/yard. Increasing the rate does not necessarily lead to a better, faster lawn, as densely sown seedlings can easily damp off and die. Stick to the manufacturer's recommendations, and select seed treated with fungicide and bird-repellent.

Choose a dry day to sow the

MOWING

When the seedling grasses are 2.5cm/1in high they can be rolled to firm them in. At about 4cm/1½in the grass can have its first cut with a mower, down to about 2.5cm/1in. Continue to top off the grass at that height until it becomes established. Then you can begin to lower the blades to 1.5cm/½in. Autumn-sown lawns will probably only need two or three cuts before winter. Take care not to let autumn leaves lie on the new grass or it will die out beneath them.

seed, when the soil surface is dry but there is plenty of moisture underneath. First rake the soil surface lightly, then scatter the seed over the soil, covering the whole lawn twice, first in one direction, then in the other, using half the mixture in each direction. This should help to rule out any bare patches. Alternatively, you can borrow seed spreaders from some garden centres when you buy the seed. These can be useful for larger lawns.

Final touches

Now rake again very lightly, just to turn in the seed and cover it. Inevitably some seed will remain on the surface, but sowing rates allow for losses to wind and birds.

There is no need to roll or water-in the seed. Simply let it germinate. Sprinklers can do harm by puddling the surface, so only water if the soil really begins to dry out. If the ground is very dry, water two or three days before you sow. Germination times vary according to temperature and humidity levels, but the finer grasses are generally the slowest. Patience is almost always rewarded!

SEED VERSUS TURF		
There are advantages and disadvantages to the use of seed instead of turf when making a lawn.		
	SEED	**TURF**
ADVANTAGES	Seed is cheaper. It is easier to put down. A greater choice of seed mixture and type of grass is available. Sowing can be delayed.	The lawn is usable much sooner, in eight to ten weeks.
DISADVANTAGES	The ground needs finer preparation. The lawn is slower to become usable: autumn-sown lawns will be ready next summer, spring-sown lawns will be ready that autumn.	Cheaper meadow turf contains weeds and poorer grasses, and costs much more than sowing seed. Fine turf, grown from seed, is even more expensive, but very good. Turf is hard work to lay. Turf must be laid without delay once it has been delivered.

A lawn sown with 'Hunter' grass seed mixture in mid-autumn has made good progress by late winter (right). By early summer, when it will have been rolled and then mown several times, it will be ready for use.

A circular lawn (below) is easy to mow in ever decreasing circles. If a small lawn like this, surrounded by a brick wall, were square it would be much more difficult to mow.

PAVING OPTIONS

Paths and paved areas provide the framework for a garden. Choosing the right materials provides the finishing touch to a garden design.

Paths and paved areas are as important to the success of a garden as lawns, beds and borders. Providing the links between the different elements of the garden, they determine the way we use it – how we move around it, where we gather to sit, talk, or eat, and whether we do so in a formal or informal setting. They establish the frame within which the garden is viewed and enjoyed.

Paths and patios

The key to success in laying out paths and patios is to balance aesthetic and practical needs. If there is sufficient space, wider paths can invite more than one person to wander together, while smaller paths winding between tall shrubs will generate a welcome sense of privacy.

Small paths are all you need for access to dustbins or the garage, whilst the movement of prams, lawnmowers, or wheelchairs may require wider routes, as well as corners that are not too awkward to be negotiated.

Straight lines lead the eye, and the feet, directly to their destination, whether it be a decorative seat in an arbour or the front door.

In more rural, informal settings, a meandering path echoes the natural landscape and encourages the leisurely enjoyment of plants. This apparent naturalness must be well contrived, for the urge to take the shortest route is strong. Bends must have a reason – curving round a shrub, for example – or the

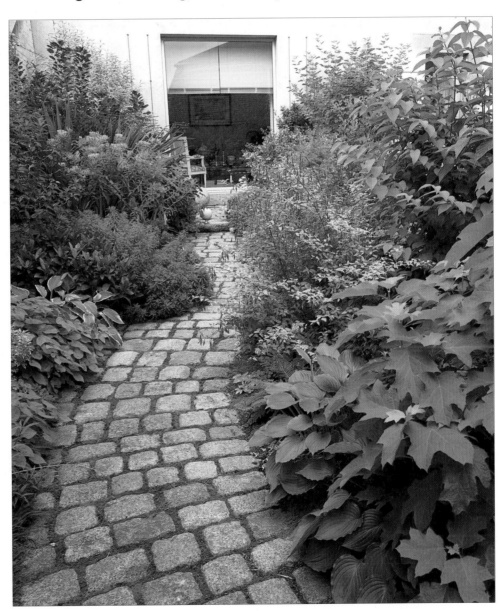

temptation to cut across may prove too great.

Patios should be generous in size, allowing chairs to be pushed back after a satisfying meal without toppling backward onto the adjoining lawn! It is a good idea to set out the furniture before defining the patio area.

A patio does not have to be against the house. Look for the best position for sun, shelter from winds, a good view and privacy when choosing the main paved area. The site should be well-drained and not heavily overhung by deciduous trees which will shed their leaves in autumn. If you have

A stone path brings a sense of structure and permanence to a garden. Natural stone setts (above) combine practicality with informality. The growth of moss between the individual stones and the use of overhanging edging plants helps to tie the path in with the borders.

BRIGHT IDEAS

CRAZY PAVING

Crazy paving can be a relatively cheap surface for paths or patios. Broken pieces of natural stone or paving slabs are less costly than whole paving. Pieces of concrete slabs may be available from your local authority.

Do not be deceived; laying the irregular shapes into a tight-fitting jigsaw is difficult and time-consuming, and best worked out *in situ* before being mortared into place. Use larger pieces at the edges, since smaller fragments can break away.

The random pattern is ideal for informal settings. Leave a few joints at the edges free of mortar, so that creeping plants can be inserted to enhance the natural effect.

Crazy paving (right) provides a bright and breezy alternative to formal pavers, but fitting the pieces together can be a difficult task. You can either leave a ragged edge and mask it with plants, or line it with bricks, as here. A more formal material, such as rectangular concrete setts (below), allows you to edge beds neatly and harmoniously.

the space, you may be able to establish more than one sitting-area for different times of the day or year.

A question of balance

When choosing from the enormous variety of paving materials available, the balance should, again, be between what looks good and what is practical. The material should suit the purpose to which it will be put and be within the limits of your budget. Gravel, for example, is relatively cheap, and excellent for scrunching around borders, but is a hazard for tumbling young children and can be difficult to wheel things across.

A mix of materials has several invaluable advantages. Large areas of a cheaper material such as concrete or gravel can be enlivened with insets or a decorative edging of more expensive elements like brick, natural stone or slate.

Combining materials in this way can spread costs, create imaginative patterns of contrasting colours and textures, and establish continuity between house and garden, picking up materials used in the construction of the house and carrying them through as features in paving or paths. This requires careful planning and a degree of restraint, or the results could be messy and confusing to the eye.

If you are planning to carry out the work yourself, think of

the skills needed and the time it will take when choosing materials. Enlist the help of family and friends to lighten the work – with good planning and thorough preparation, doing it yourself can be great fun and the results very satisfying.

There are few of us who do not covet the idea of natural stone paving for our gardens. The mellow colours and rich textures, enriched by long weathering, are as much a part of nature as the plants, and are sympathetic companions. However, stone is very expensive – even if you can get hold of second-hand slabs – and its weight and varying thickness makes it difficult to lay.

Fortunately, there are many good artificial alternatives

Though good to look at, gravel does require maintenance; pavers set as stepping stones (above) cut down the work.

An advantage of natural or reconstituted stone pavers (right) is that they look just as good – sometimes better – in the rain as in the sunshine.

Cobbles can be hard on the feet, and are perhaps best used as decorative inserts (below).

now available, some fashioned from reconstituted stone chippings or dust, or moulded from natural stone masters. These come in a range of sizes, are thinner, and of a uniform shape, making them easier to work with.

Concrete

Concrete is one of the cheapest and most versatile means of paving. Durable and virtually maintenance-free, pre-cast concrete paving slabs come in a vast array of finishes, colours, shapes and sizes. Textures vary from decorative stippling and brushing to irregular surfaces which attempt to simulate the look of natural weathered stone.

Because they are moulded, rather than cut, concrete pavers come in many more shapes than simple rectangles. They may be neatly hexagonal (with half-hexagons ready-made for edges), or tapered for edging curves. Circular slabs, though impractical for large areas, make unusual informal paving, with gravel and low-growing plants between. There are even concrete slabs that resemble sections of cobble or granite setts.

Look at catalogues for ideas, but remember to keep it simple. Use graph paper to work out the quantities you will need, and add about five percent for breakages.

Even concrete laid *in situ* can be enriched with textured finishes before it dries. Try drawing a stiff broom across damp concrete, or dropping a scaffolding pole onto the surface to form parallel ridges. For an exposed aggregate finish, damp gravel is pressed into the wet concrete, then cleaned up by a light brushing and hosing down.

Be warned: laying concrete is a messy job and needs precise planning and preparation, since it becomes unworkable after about two hours.

Beautiful bricks

Bricks make handsome paving. Their warm, mellow colouring and small scale make them ideal for the smaller garden. They are light to use and easily laid in attractive geometric patterns. They make excellent edging, and sit happily in combination with many other materials.

Ordinary house bricks are not necessarily suitable for paving, and you need to be sure that those you choose are frost proof and hard-wearing enough for the purpose. Buying second hand means you cannot reliably check the suitability of the bricks, while buying new can be expensive.

Engineering bricks are ideal, but can give a very smooth and rather clinical finish, and are perhaps best suited to modern settings.

If you prefer the effect of house bricks, clay pavers make good alternatives. These come in a variety of colours and textures and, being both thinner and more uniform in shape, are even easier to work with than brick.

Concrete also has a role to

SINKING STONES

Stepping stones in lawns should be set about 2cm/¾in below the level of the turf, so they don't catch your feet or the blades of lawnmowers.

SAFETY FIRST

ON THE EDGE

Loose paving materials such as gravel and bark often need a containing edge to help prevent the particles spilling onto adjoining lawns and other paved areas.

A decorative edging will give the final flourish to any paving, whether it's of the same material or something to provide interesting contrasts. All manner of materials can be used, from bricks laid on edge to granite setts and railway sleepers. A sympathetic idea for bark paths is the half-round timber generally sold for farm fencing.

Try using bricks or pavers as a mowing edge between the lawn and borders. The lawnmower will not tip into beds, and edging plants will keep their heads.

Wood never looks out of place in a garden (above). Here, a path of decking lined with gravel leads between raised beds edged with half-round timbering and logs.

Creative combination of paving materials can give a richly textured effect (left). Here, bricks, wood and paving slabs are combined on different levels.

play on this smaller scale. Concrete pavers have less colour variety to offer, but plenty of shapes, including interlocking geometric patterns. These often have bevelled top edges, which form a groove between pavers once they are laid, effectively highlighting and enhancing the pattern.

For many people, wood is the most appealing material for the garden. Its very naturalness, its colour and graining, make it eminently qualified for the job. However, this country's climate is not kind to wood, rendering it both expensive and impractical in the long term. If you are determined to incorporate wood into your design, then railway sleepers are probably the most durable, weatherproof option, and they are well-suited to mixed paving schemes.

The material which is easiest on the pocket and on labour is probably gravel, which will fill almost any shape with lovely, sparkling variations of texture and hue, and is well-suited to formal and informal settings alike. Colours vary according to the rock or stone from which the gravel comes,

SPRUCING UP

There are a number of cleaning agents available at garden centres, DIY and hardware stores for removing moss and stains such as rust, oil and grease from paving. For tougher problems, look through local papers for firms that will do the job for you, or hire a high pressure cleaner.

Bricks lend themselves to rectangular layouts but also look good in herringbone patterns (above).

Synthetic stone slabs are usually supplied in a 'weathered' finish (right).

The precise shapes and varied colour finishes of moulded concrete pavers allows you to create complex geometric patterns (below).

and it is available in several different grades or sizes.

There are, however, a few problems. Gravel is easily picked up on muddy boots, though where this is most likely to be a problem – near the vegetable patch, for example – 'stepping stones' of small paving slabs set into the gravel at intervals will help.

Containing edges are needed to prevent particles straying onto adjoining lawns, where they are a hazard to mowers, and you will need to rake the surface regularly to keep it tidy. You will also have to top up the gravel occasionally, and spray to deter weeds.

Gravel is particularly adaptable in more natural settings, where planting holes are easily scooped out and planted up for a softly informal edging.

Pebbles

Larger stones, such as cobbles and pebbles, are also now available at many garden centres. Unless set deep in concrete or mortar, they are uncomfortable to walk on, but make splendid decorative insets when laid in patterns in relief. Or, pile them around a water or plant feature.

In the same way, the blue-grey colouring and rich texture of granite setts add decorative contrasts to other paving materials. They are sometimes available second-hand from local authorities, but are generally too expensive for garden use on a large scale.

63

FIRST STEPS TO PRUNING

Knowing why and when to prune is the essence of good gardening. Learn the basic needs of plants and you will soon cut with confidence.

Are your roses rambling when they are not really meant to and your small shrubs beginning to form an untidy thicket? Then it is time to master the art of pruning.

Don't panic – pruning is not always the difficult and technical business it is sometimes made out to be. No plant is going to die simply because it has not been pruned, but without a bit of careful cutting the plant may not flower as well as it might or can become overgrown and shapeless.

Best results

Pruning really is just a matter of encouraging the best from your plants. It can help them to grow more efficiently and bear as much fruit and as many flowers as they can – for as many years as possible.

Pruning is easy to carry out at the right time once you have a grasp of the special needs of different groups of plants.

Keep them blooming

One important use of pruning is to induce plants to make flowers rather than leaves. Fruit trees require this kind of pruning so that a sensible balance is achieved between fruit production and the foliage which feeds the tree.

Often, however, pruning serves two purposes at once: while encouraging flowering shoots, at the same time it allows light to reach the fruit or flowers. Rambler roses and mock orange (philadelphus) have the older flowered shoots

Pruned to perfection, the splendid yellow rose bush (above) shows how a little work pays dividends. Cut back growth to 20cm/8in from the base in early spring.

cut out to improve the chances of the new ones.

Also as shrubs grow older, there is a tendency for the stems to become too congested, and one use of pruning is to keep an open shape for those

plants which need light and air to reach the centre. Roses and gooseberries are both best kept with a simple framework and an open centre.

When pruning any plant, a vital consideration is whether

The red-stemmed dogwood, Cornus alba 'Sibirica' (right) is grown for its attractive bark rather than its flowers and so it should be pruned to encourage plenty of young stems. Old stems can be cut almost to ground level in the spring and they will grow to 1.2m/4ft.

The sumptuous, rich magenta flower heads on the buddleja bush (left) have been produced in late summer on the same season's growth. The plant should be cut back every spring to within one to three buds of the old wood. Weak growth can be cut out entirely.

Hydrangea macrophylla (below) suffers from hard pruning in spring. This is because it flowers on last year's wood. For the first few years it requires only cosmetic pruning.

PLANTS WHICH NEED NO PRUNING

Some plants are better not pruned unless it is absolutely necessary. If they are planted with space to develop fully they may never need any pruning. This does not mean that they cannot be cut, say, for flower arrangements in your home. These plants, if left to themselves, provided they are planted in the correct position, will maintain a good shape.

Some care is needed when cutting from conifers, however (firs, pines, cypresses and Leylandii). Cuts made into older wood will not sprout again, and caution is needed to avoid making a gap in the foliage.

- Japanese maple (*Acer palmatum*)
- camellia
- conifers (especially dwarf and low-growing kinds)
- daphne
- witch hazel (*Hamamelis mollis*)
- hebe
- calico bush (*Kalmia latifolia*)
- magnolia
- osmanthus
- pieris
- rhododendron

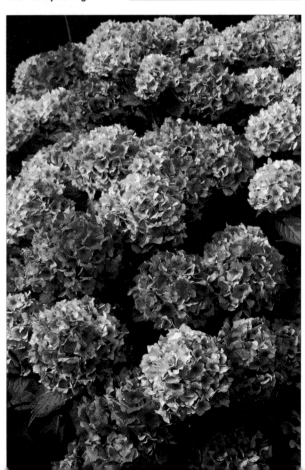

it flowers on the previous or the new season's growth. If you prune a plant which flowers on last year's wood in spring, then you are effectively cutting off this year's flowers. So always check before you start to snip away.

Buddleja, the butterfly bush, can be cut hard down to a framework each spring. Its flowers are then produced at the end of the current season's growth, in late summer. Hydrangeas, on the other hand, flower on the wood they

GARDEN NOTES

WHEN TO PRUNE

Timing is important. You must understand the growing habits of a tree or shrub before you begin to prune it. Many established plants are pruned according to flowering habits, while young shrubs and fruit trees or ornamental trees are often pruned hard at the time of planting. If in doubt, check before you cut.

make in the previous year so prune after flowering. But this is not vital. If left until spring the old flower heads protect the new buds from harsh weather.

Fancy foliage

Sometimes plants are pruned to encourage leaf shoots to grow, rather than flower shoots. This is done where the bark or stems are more attractive than the flowers; they may have vibrant autumn foliage or winter colour. The red-stemmed dogwood, *Cornus alba* 'Sibirica', is pruned this way. The old stems can be cut off just above ground level every spring, and new shoots rise up 90-120cm/3-4ft. (In

winter these scarlet wands are ideal for flower arranging.) The same method is also used for purple or white stemmed willows.

Shrubs which do not have a central trunk should have their stems shortened after planting, to encourage a generous bush with plenty of stems. For instance, newly planted roses are cut down hard to coax lots of low shoots and give the roots time to establish before the bush becomes top heavy.

Heathers are much better looking in later life if the leading shoots have had the tops nipped out from the first year.

A tidy trim

The natural growth of many plants may not be as tidy and attractive as you would like. Pruning can correct this.

Heathers, again, are a good example of plants which are 'prettier' when pruned. If the old flower shoots, which can be as long as 25cm/10in, are cut in early spring, they need

Waves of luscious heather bring warmth and texture to a garden (above). Heathers do not need to be pruned but without a bit of skilful snipping they can look very scraggy.

Dead-head all varieties of heather after flowering by trimming with shears. This will encourage more compact, bushy growth.

The holly tree (above) has acquired its present shape after good pruning over several years. Two basic techniques have been used. Side shoots have been systematically removed to keep one single stem encouraging it into a standard shape. It has also been trimmed into an attractive bushed outline.

PRUNE IN SPRING BEFORE FLOWERING

- lad's love (*Artemisia abrotanum*)
- berberis, if necessary
- butterfly bush (*Buddleja davidii*)
- common heather (*Calluna vulgaris*)
- clematis (late-flowering species and hybrids: *C. orientalis* or *C.* 'Etoile Rose')
- caryopteris
- red-stemmed dogwood (*Cornus alba*)
- bell heather (*Erica cinerea*)
- Cornish heath (*Erica vagans*)
- fuchsia
- *Hypericum* 'Hidcote'
- bay (*Laurus nobilis*)
- tree mallow (*Lavatera olbia*)
- flowering nutmeg (*Leycesteria*)
- honeysuckle varieties
- Russian sage (*Perovskia atriplicifolia*)
- Jerusalem sage (*Phlomis fruticosa*)
- Cape figwort (*Phygelius capensis*)
- potentilla
- roses (hybrid tea and floribunda types)
- rue (*Ruta graveolens*)
- sage (*Salvia officinalis*)
- elder (*Sambucus*)
- cotton lavender

CUTTING QUESTIONS

Q I am just back from holiday and it is the middle of spring. Am I too late to prune my hybrid tea and floribunda roses?

A No, you're not. Seasonal pruning is always better done late than not at all. This applies to spring and summer pruning. In the case of the roses, the flowers may be a little delayed by late pruning, but the bushes will at least retain their shape and vigour.

Q I have just moved into a house with an overgrown and neglected garden. How drastically can I prune to tidy it up?

A Some plants are better not pruned if you can avoid it (see list on p.65). Those which can be pruned will probably stand very drastic pruning indeed – even cutting off at ground level. To stop the garden looking too bare, try doing a section at a time. Spare a thought for your garden wildlife, too.

Q What is meant by 'new wood'?

A It is simply a term to describe this year's stem growth. Past growth is known as 'old wood'. Plants that flower early in the season tend to produce their flowers on the previous year's growth.

PRUNE AFTER FLOWERING

- *Clematis montana*
- broom (*Cytisus* spp.)
- deutzia
- escallonia
- forsythia
- Spanish broom (*Genista hispanica*)
- rock rose
- winter-flowering jasmine (*Jasminum nudiflorum*)
- Jew's mallow (*Kerria japonica*)
- mock orange (*Philadelphus* spp.)
- cherries, plums
- roses (ramblers and old-fashioned shrubs)
- weigela
- hydrangea
- *Buddleja alternifolia*

This cider gum, Eucalyptus gunnii (above) has an abundance of healthy new growth. Coppicing is the best method of keeping it in check for a small garden and encourages plenty of attractive young foliage growth. Cut the whole stem down to ground level each spring.

The cherry laurel, Prunus laurocerasus, does not require regular pruning, but it can be cut right back if it becomes too large. Prune into the old wood after flowering. Left to its own devices, this unsightly specimen (right) has become overgrown.

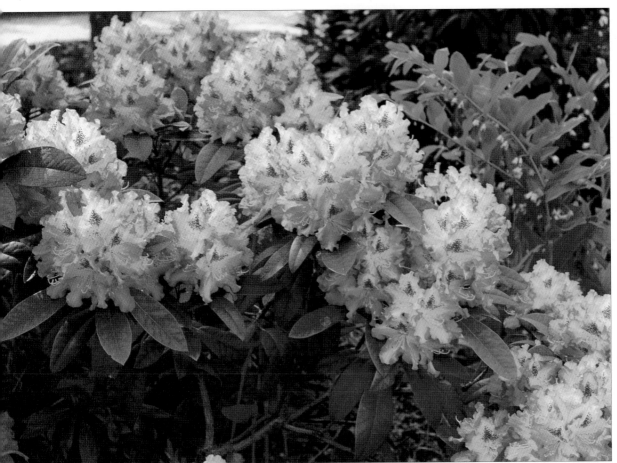

The vibrant hybrid Rhododendron 'Blue Ensign' (left) requires the absolute minimum of pruning. The shrub is naturally bushy and forms a neat, compact shape. Flowers and seeds are produced abundantly. To encourage good, strong shoots, however, dead-heading is advisable.

A stately pair of common yew trees (Taxus baccata) creates an imposing look for the front of a grand house (below). Yew has a neat, tidy growing habit and requires only cosmetic pruning. If the tree grows out of control, it can be cut back. Dead, diseased and damaged growth can be removed at any time of year.

never become straggly. Any large-flowered, vigorous clematis such as *C. orientalis* is also pruned hard in early spring, to relieve it of a mass of old tangled growth. The flowers will appear in due course on the new shoots. If they are not pruned in spring they begin to grow from where they flowered the year before. Soon the plant will become bare at the base with flowers at the top only.

There are, of course, times when a mass of congested shoots looks right. This effect is achieved by clipping.

All shapes and sizes

Naturally dense bushes, like hebe, can have any long rogue shoots cut back to maintain the rounded form. It is worthwhile noting that not all shrubs grow at a regular rate, one section may be more vigorous than another and the result is an asymmetrical shape. To rectify this the weak shoots require hard pruning and the

stronger shoots a light touch; this is because hard pruning stimulates growth.

Often, pruning is simply used to limit the size of a plant. For instance, many which have become just too large for their situation can, of course, be cut right down to start again. This is true of roses, mock orange, hydrangeas, holly, laurel, yew and many others.

A healthy garden

Pruning helps to keep plants strong and healthy, preventing disease as well as curing many ailments. It is vitally important that all dead, damaged or diseased shoots are removed from the plant as soon as they are spotted. They should be burned immediately and should never be added to the compost heap.

The shoots should then be cut back into the healthy wood, to a bud if possible, as this will provide strong, healthy new growth.

A special pruning saw has no back to it and therefore can be used in very tight corners or in dense growth as pictured here (right).

Anvil-style secateurs are used (below right) to prune a mass of dense honeysuckle. This is an ideal tool for rough work. The most important consideration when buying secateurs is that they are comfortable in your hand.

SECATEURS

In the anvil type, the blade is brought down onto a fixed block opposite. Beware though, as blunt blades will crush the stems or fail to cut right through.

In the scissor type (sometimes known as 'by-pass' secateurs), two blades move together. They must be hinged as tightly as possible but still with free movement, if they are to cut cleanly. They are often more expensive, but serve a wider purpose.

When choosing secateurs, go for the simplest-looking mechanism (with safety lock and hinge) and buy the best quality you can afford. A good pair of secateurs, with no gimmickry should last a lifetime.

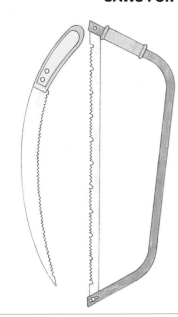

SAWS FOR PRUNING

For smaller cuts in hard-to-get-at places a pruning saw is ideal. It cuts on the pull-stroke only.

For larger branches you will need a bow saw. An excellent choice is a small bow saw with a pointed nose to get into smaller spaces. The blades are easily replaced and inexpensive.

Though long-handled pruners (loppers) are useful where more leverage is needed, a saw is often just as easy, much cheaper and generally more useful.

Use a saw to cut branches thicker than a broom handle. Choose from a Grecian saw (far left) or a bow saw.

There are several different groups of clematis which require pruning in different ways. The intense purple hybrid 'Perle d'Azur' (top) flowers in summer and autumn on the growth it has produced in the same season. In late January or early February the whole of the previous year's growth should be cut back. If this is not done it will rapidly become bare at the base. C. montana *var.* rubens *(above) is from the spring flowering group. It blooms on growth developed the previous summer and so it should not be pruned until after it has flowered.*

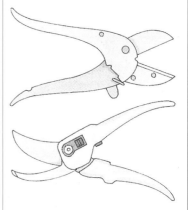

Choose secateurs which are comfortable in your hand and keep them as sharp as possible.

DEAD-HEADING AND DISBUDDING

Dead-heading and disbudding are easy jobs, well worth doing. It pays to know which plants need this treatment and when and how you should do it.

You have probably disbudded plants without realizing it. It means removing, usually by pinching out, new growth buds. This allows the plant to concentrate all its energy on producing fewer, but showier flowers or better fruit.

New buds are produced at the leaf axil (where the leaf stalk is attached to the stem). They can grow into either a shoot or a flower, possibly followed by a fruit.

Controlled growth

In many plants, the development of buds lower down the stem is suppressed by the main growing point of their stem. So gardeners 'stop' plants, pinching out the growing point to enable lower buds to grow freely; this produces a much bushier plant.

Stopping a plant does just that – checking its growth for a while. But after a short delay, it starts into growth again.

You don't have to stop or disbud many plants in the garden; it all depends on your aims. If you are developing an interest in exhibiting blooms, then you will want to stop or disbud certain flowers.

Dead flower-heads are often removed for tidiness, but there are other reasons too.

Many early-flowering herbaceous perennials will give a

fine second display if cut back. Other plants will give a display over a long period if the old, dead flowers are cut off and removed regularly.

In nature, plants flower in order to attract pollinators so that seed can be formed, to ensure the survival and spread of the species. But seed production takes a lot of energy. It should be prevented in the case of bulb, corm, rhizome and tuber-forming plants, because it will affect the following year's display of flowers.

Plants that can produce a continual display of flowers may do so only if you prevent them from setting seed. This stimulates them into eagerly producing more flowers, with the aim of eventually being able to set seed.

Some plants are good at setting seed and spreading themselves around your garden, so you must dead-head these promptly if you want to confine them to one place.

How to dead-head

Certain plants, including the heathers, lavender and herbs, produce flowers on long extension growths. Dead-head them to keep the plant vigorous and to prevent it becoming straggly and bare at the base.

Garden shears or one-handed shears are useful for

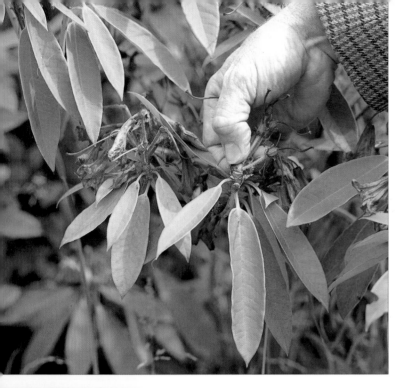

Dahlias need regular care. Three or four weeks after planting, you should stop them by neatly pinching out the main shoots. In time, fading flowers must be dead-headed (below left).

With rhododendrons (left), always dead-head with finger and thumb as secateurs may harm the tender shoots.

Calluna heathers (right) flower in summer and autumn. Dead-heading tidies them up and encourages new growth.

Cerastium (below right) can be safely dead-headed with shears.

trimming heathers and similar plants, and for removing dead flowers from some of the larger herbaceous perennials.

Plants such as pansies are easier to dead-head with finger and thumb. All-purpose scissors are useful for tougher plant stems, and secateurs are best for woody plants.

When dead-heading shrubs, cut back to where another bud arises, which is usually in a leaf axil. If a side-shoot has already begun to grow, cut back to that shoot.

Carnations While garden pinks are dead-headed to produce a long flowering season, greenhouse-grown, perpetual-flowering (florist's) carnations require more attention.

Spray carnations are stopped, but not disbudded. However, single-flowering and early-flowering sprays are not stopped, but are disbudded!

Stop spray carnations by removing the first small pair of leaves, a couple of weeks after planting. This encourages the production of many stems but delays flowering.

Carnation stems are jointed. The two or three joints at the base of the stem are disbudded on single-flowering carnations. Those part-way up the stem are left with buds. Once you can see the main flower bud, you should disbud the six joints which lie below it.

When you cut the main stem and its flower off, you should cut above the joint which still has a bud. You are effectively stopping the plant and the remaining buds will develop healthily into laterals bearing the second flush of flowers.

Chrysanthemums (These are now correctly known as dendranthemums.) Annuals benefit from stopping as this produces bushy plants. They are often used for cut flowers; picking the blooms prolongs their display, which will be a colourful highlight in any border. Hardy perennials just require dead-heading.

The tender chrysanthemums are classified according to flower type, size and season. Only large or medium flower types are disbudded. However, all types are stopped when the plant is about 15cm/6in tall, to induce branching. You then remove one or two side-shoots from each stem every day, by snapping off the shoot with your fingers, until you have the number of shoots that you want. This is around six for garden or cut flowers, but only two or three for exhibition.

The central bud is then removed, because it flowers earlier and is larger than the blooms on sideshoots. If the

SECURING THE CENTRAL BUD

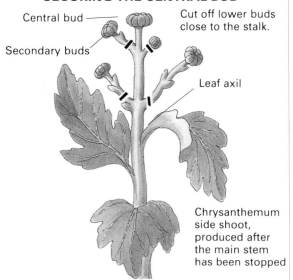

Central bud

Secondary buds

Cut off lower buds close to the stalk.

Leaf axil

Chrysanthemum side shoot, produced after the main stem has been stopped

A chrysanthemum side shoot has a central bud with other buds beneath it. Remove the lower buds to produce one good bloom.

Dahlias Stop them about a month after planting outside, once strong shoots appear.

If you are growing them for exhibition, restrict the number of side-shoots which develop.

Dahlias are classified by flower form and size. Restrict Giants (over 25/10in) to 2-3 stems, Large (20cm-25cm/8-10in) to 3-4 stems, Medium (15-20cm/6-8in) to 5-7 stems, Small (10-15cm/4-6in) to 8-10 stems and Miniatures (up to 10cm/4in) to 10-12 stems.

In addition, if growing pom-pons, pinch out the side-shoots once they have two pairs of leaves. This will produce a mass of 5cm/2in blooms.

When dead-heading dahlias, cut down the stem to a developing side-shoot. This prevents the plants from becoming spindly and top-heavy.

central flower bud has not formed by early summer, the growing tip is pinched out anyway, or flowers on the side-shoots will be delayed.

The remaining flowering stems then produce their own side-shoots with flower buds. These are snapped off as soon as they can be handled so that there is only one flower left on each stem.

Other side-shoots on the flowering stem are also removed as they are produced. Snap off one or two each day.

If spray chrysanthemums, which are not disbudded, show signs of the crown bud (the terminal bud) developing ahead of the surrounding flower buds, then make sure you pinch out the crown bud.

Chrysanthemums (above right) are normally stopped before they reach full height. With a little practice and knowledge, they can be made to produce their best blooms by a certain date, which is invaluable for those who exhibit them.

Dead-heading (right) not only improves the look of a plant but often encourages more flowers.

The leading shoot of a standard fuchsia (far right) is allowed to grow until it reaches the required height. It is then pinched out. Stopping laterals at every second leaf will increase the number of blooms.

PLANTS BEST DIS-BUDDED

Greenhouse perpetual-flowering (florist's) carnations. Dahlias for exhibition. Sweet peas for exhibition. Florist's chrysanthemums – types grown for large blooms.

PLANTS NOT DIS-BUDDED

Dahlias for garden display. Spray carnations and garden pinks. Spray, Korean, cascade and charm chrysanthemums. Annual and herbaceous perennial chrysanthemums. Most garden plants.

Roses Some roses tend to produce two or three buds at the site of a pruning cut and you should rub out these to leave only one bud. If all of them develop, they will grow into weak stems.

If exhibiting hybrid tea roses (now called large-flowered bush roses) you should look for extra flowers that may form on a single stem. Prune them out to leave one main bloom.

When dead-heading roses, prune to the first five-leaflet leaf below the bloom. When dead-heading floribunda roses (now called cluster-flowered roses), ensure that you remove the whole flower truss down to the first five-leaflet leaf on the main stem.

Because the dead-heading of repeat-flowering roses stimu-

GROWING TIPS

PLANTS TO DEAD-HEAD	PLANTS NOT TO DEAD-HEAD
Herbaceous perennials that flower before late summer and will put out a second display, e.g. avens (*Geum*), lungwort (*Pulmonaria*), delphinium and cranesbill (*Geranium*). Sweet peas. Garden pinks. Bulb, corm, tuber and rhizome-forming plants. Bedding plants such as bedding dahlias, African marigolds, nemesia, geranium (*Pelargonium*) and pansies. Roses which repeat flower. Self-seeding plants, e.g. lady's mantle (*Achemilla*), ornamental onions (*Allium*) and columbines (*Aquilegia*).	Those plants with attractive dead-heads or seed or fruit, grown for flower arranging, e.g. honesty, hydrangea and poppy. Most bedding plants. Shrubs which only flower once a year, e.g. lilac, viburnum and mock orange. Cold-sensitive plants in cold gardens, where the old flower-heads give some protection to buds below, e.g. hydrangea. Plants grown for fruit for food, ornament or wildlife, for example firethorn (*Pyracantha*), quince (ornamental and edible types), cotoneaster and varieties of roses with ornamental fruit (hips).

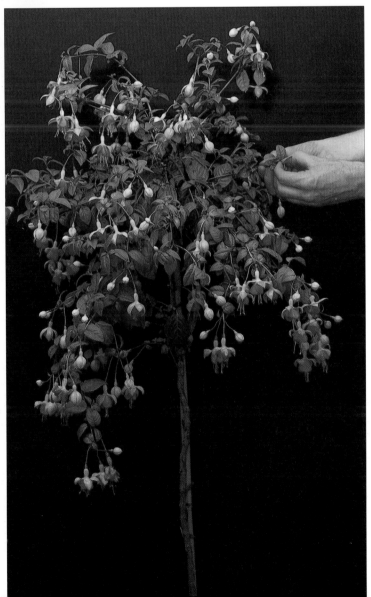

lates new growth, stop dead-heading in early autumn. Otherwise new soft growth can be killed by early frosts. The buds below the dead flowers are best left dormant so that they will grow the following spring.

Sweet peas These need stopping once they have two to four true leaves, because the first shoot usually turns out to be blind (flowerless) after growing about 1m/3ft tall.

If you pinch out the plant it will produce two shoots from the base and these will flower.

Daily care
If you want straight flower stalks and exhibition-quality blooms, you have to grow sweet peas carefully. Only allow one shoot per plant and tie this in to a support regularly. Snap off all side-shoots and tendrils to let the plant's energy go into the flower. You must do this daily for success.

Even if you are content to let your sweet peas scramble up supports with their own tendrils, you must dead-head regularly. Do not let the pods form, because this suppresses further flowering.

STEM CUTTINGS

Taking cuttings is the most cost-effective way of increasing your stock of garden plants – and it's so simple, too. Just follow these basic guidelines.

Have you ever seen a plant in a friend's garden you would love to have and don't know where to find? Have you a particularly successful specimen in your own garden that you would like more of? In fact, it is really quite easy to make more of them – all you need to do is learn the simple art of taking cuttings.

When you take a stem cutting you remove a stem from a plant and encourage it to form roots to support itself as a new and separate plant.

There is nothing difficult about stem cuttings as the basic operation is really very straightforward. What you do need to remember is that there are right and wrong times to take a cutting, depending on the plant. A cutting taken at the best time will always stand a much greater chance of succeeding.

How and when

Some plants will root in a jar of water or straight into the ground. Others need more controlled conditions. Some cuttings need to be taken when the plant is in full leaf and growth, and need careful attention to tide them over that critical period before the formation of new roots. Others can be taken when the plant is dormant, making the process less stressful for the cutting. Different plants respond differently to different methods.

One thing about stem cuttings is certain: they are a very cheap way of obtaining new plants. Often from the purchase of a single plant you can make dozens of cuttings several times a season. Young

When you are in a friend's garden and you see a plant you would like to have in your own garden, ask if you can take a stem cutting (above). You can guarantee that if it is successful it will look exactly like its parent plant. As this chart (right) shows, there are a few basic seasons for taking cuttings. Softwood cuttings taken in spring are ideal for delphiniums, chrysanthemums and dahlias. Take semi-ripe cuttings in late summer with a 'heel' of older wood.

plants from cuttings can make an interesting and lucrative stall at a bazaar – you will find yoghurt cartons are usually quite acceptable as plant pots.

Plant clones

Unlike a plant grown from seed, a cutting has the advantage of being identical to its parent plant. So if you take a liking to a plant variety in a friend's garden, a cutting will give you the same specimen. Plants produced in this way are said to be of the same clone, which simply means that they all stem from identical genetic material.

This is especially useful where uniformity is needed in the garden. For instance, a yew or cypress hedge made from cuttings from one particular plant will give you a hedge of even greenness and density of habit. Hedges from seed-grown plants will always show individual colour and density variation; growth rates will vary, too.

When it comes to cuttings, as with so much else, you get the best from the best. Good strong healthy shoots always produce better plants and root more easily. Of course, you will not want to disfigure a favourite plant or spoil its

shape, but spare a little of it for cuttings as it will pay off later. It is no surprise that in nurseries cuttings are taken from carefully grown stock plants trained to produce ideal cutting material even if they have a poor shape.

Collecting cuttings

When a plant is in leaf and growing strongly, it is best to take cuttings when it is as full of sap as possible – so avoid midday or very hot weather. The day after a heavy rain storm is ideal, as the plants will have had a good long drink. Early morning is another good time, before the heat of the day reduces the moisture level within the leaves.

If you are collecting cuttings from the garden, cut a slightly

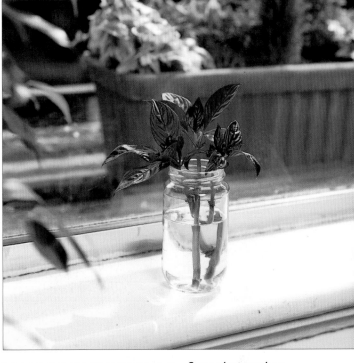

SHORT CUTS

EASY OPTIONS

Some plants are very easy to grow from cuttings. Geraniums or fuchsias will root at almost any time during the growing season. Busy Lizzies and willow will root in a jar of water on a window sill. Roses are worth trying as hardwood cuttings, any time between late summer and the middle of winter.

GARDEN NOTES

HEEL CUTTINGS

Semi-ripe cuttings are often taken with a heel of older wood attached. By pulling rather than cutting off a side shoot, a little of the older wood on the main stem comes away with the cutting. Using a very sharp knife, trim it clean of any damaged tissue (without removing the heel), before rooting it.

Some plants such as the buzy Lizzie (above) are so keen to propagate that they need practically no encouragement. All you have to do is cut off a piece, strip off the bottom leaves and stick it in a jar of water.

To propagate thuja take semi-ripe cuttings with a heel. Instead of cutting through the stem pull off a side shoot taking a little old wood with you (below).

				Spring	Summer	Autumn
Border perennials	(basal)			▮		
	(stem)				▮▮▮	
Bedding plants				▮▮		
Herbs, alpines				▮▮▮		
Shrubs, climbers (softwood cuttings)					▮	

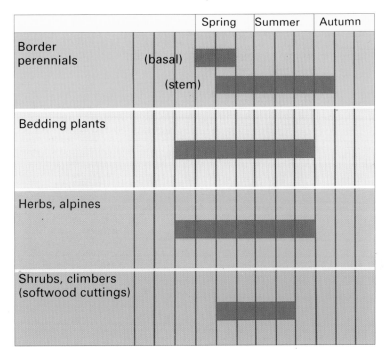

PROJECT LAVENDER FROM CUTTINGS

Lavender is easy to propagate from cuttings, and you can easily make a hedge of it from cuttings taken the previous season. Follow these easy steps to make your hedge. The cuttings will take about three weeks to root. Once this has happened, remove the polythene and gradually reaccustom your plantlets to full sun. Keep them indoors on a cold window sill (or in a cold frame) over winter. In the early spring, pot up the plants individually into 8cm/3in pots and plant them out about two months later, after hardening off. In well-drained soils, lavender flowers from mid-summer to autumn.

1 Use a sharp knife to cut through the base just below a leaf joint; remove the leaves from lower third.

2 Dip the cuttings in a fungicide solution and shake off the excess. Dip stem in rooting powder.

3 Fill a small pot with an equal mixture of peat and sand. Make holes 2.5cm deep.

4 Put about four cuttings into the holes and gently firm them in.

5 Cover with well-ventilated polythene and put in a warm, light place. Turn the polythene inside out regularly.

HORMONE ROOTING POWDER

GROWING TIPS

Hormone rooting powder is best used in the season of purchase. Many plants root perfectly well without it if the timing is right. The process may be slower without rooting powder, but do not let that put you off.

If you only want to produce one plant then experiment with timing, too. It is surprising how often you will succeed with a chance cutting offered by a friend on the spur of the moment.

longer length than you need. You can then trim them up properly on a table indoors. Always keep your cuttings in a closed plastic bag in the shade until you are ready to deal with them, to prevent wilting. Remember to collect a few extra cuttings, too, to allow for a few failures.

Sharp, clean secateurs are best for collecting all cuttings and are perfectly adequate for making the final trimming up of woody cuttings. Softer stems are best cut on a board, using a sharp craft knife.

Take semi-ripe cuttings with a heel and dip them into hormone rooting powder. Plant cuttings in individual pots filled with an equal part of peat and sand. Place the pots in a polythene bag tent to prevent the cuttings from wilting and keep them in a shady spot (below).

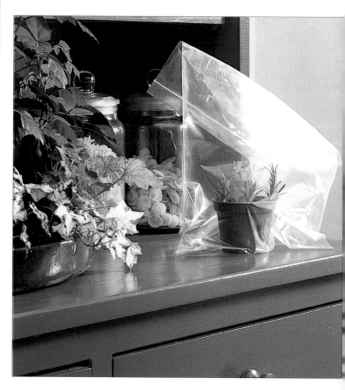

Cuttings have a language all of their own and this may initially be confusing but in the end it all boils down to a few basic seasons for cutting: softwood cuttings are taken in spring, semi-ripe in late summer and hardwood in autumn and winter.

Softwood cutting

Softwood cuttings are made from short sections of new growth in spring. Take them as soon as about 5-10cm/2-4in of stem have developed.

In early spring take cuttings of the new basal shoots of delphiniums, chrysanthemums, fuchsias, achillea, dahlia and perennial salvias. In early summer try tip cuttings (4-6.5cm/1½-2½in) of potentilla, deutzia and cistus.

Softwood cuttings should be cut cleanly to 6.5cm/2½in long at the leaf joint or 'node', using a sharp knife. Remove the lower few leaves by nipping them off with your fingernails or with a knife. Dip the whole cutting in a solution such as benomyl fungicide and shake off the excess. Then dip the bottom inch into hormone rooting powder and push the cuttings 2.5cm/1in into an

Cuttings from a pelargonium are inserted into a growing medium (above). Choose two or three good shoots and strip off bottom leaves.

Make sure cuttings have rooted before transplanting. Pull gently and if it resists it is rooted (below).

equal mixture of peat and sand in a shallow plant pot. Water well. Cover with a clean plastic bag and seal with a rubber band. (Alternatively put the pot in a propagator with an electrically controlled bottom heat at 70°F.) Keep in a light place but out of direct sunlight. Most cuttings should take root within three weeks.

Turn the plastic bag inside out every few days to reduce condensation and so minimise the risk of moulds developing. It also helps if you cut off the corners of the bag, to give just a little ventilation.

Root resistance

To test a cutting to see if it is rooted, first look underneath to see if any roots are visible at the drainage holes. If not, pull the cutting gently. If it resists well, it is rooted.

As soon as the cuttings are rooted, take off the polythene (or remove from the propagator) and give them a few days to re-acclimatize before you pot them up individually.

Semi-ripe cuttings are taken in late summer, when growth is slowing down and the new shoots are slightly firmer. In midsummer try

geraniums, heathers, deutzia, weigela, philadelphus, forsythia, potentilla, and dogwood (*Cornus alba*).

You can often just take a side shoot, and cut it off either at a suitable leaf joint or with a little 'heel'. This means that you pull off your new stem with a little piece of wood from the older stem still attached.

Semi-ripe cuttings are easier than softwood cuttings because the risks of disease are less. They are slower, though, and it will be next year before your new plantlets begin to grow. Side-shoots are taken from the parent plant, from 10-20cm/4-8in long (2.5cm/1in in the case of heathers). Remove the leaves from the lower 5cm/2in of stem which is cut cleanly at a leaf-joint or with a heel. Dip the lower part into hormone rooting powder, and insert the cuttings into a pot of an equal mixture of peat and sand or into soil in a cold frame. Water well.

Stop wilting

A polythene bag tent over the pots will prevent your cuttings wilting, but they will still need shading from bright sunshine. Pots kept indoors on a window sill should root in 3-5 weeks and can be overwintered in a cool garage after their leaves drop, ready for potting up in spring.

Cuttings in soil in pots or a cold frame may not root until well into the winter, and are often best left undisturbed until the following autumn.

Hardwood cuttings are very easy but not all plants can be propagated in this way. In autumn try willows, roses, currants and cypresses. Simply cut off 23cm/9in lengths of good vigorous stem, and insert them into the soil for three-quarters of their length. You can either grow them in their final position or in an unused corner to be transferred the following autumn. Rooting takes place in the spring.

PROPAGATION BY LAYERING

For beginners and experts alike, layering is a method of propagation which is almost guaranteed to provide plenty of plants for the garden or indoors.

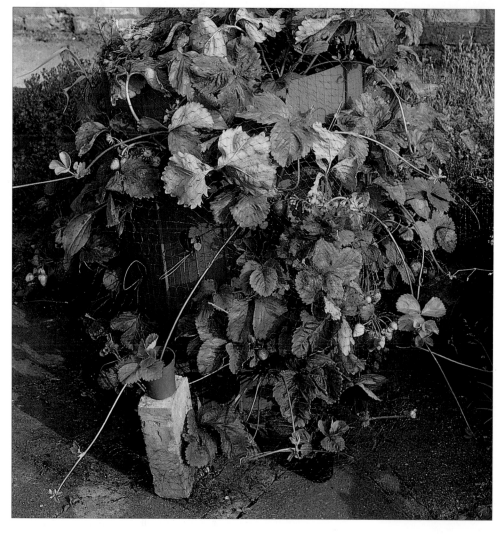

It is easy to propagate strawberries by potting up runners while they are still attached to the plant. When roots have formed, the runner can be severed. Plants in strawberry barrels (above) will produce runners at a variety of heights, so pots often need to be propped up on bricks.

Layering involves rooting a shoot or stem while it is still attached to the parent plant. Unlike the alternative of taking cuttings, there is little risk of the shoot dying before it has formed roots. As the process requires only simple preparation and aftercare, this makes layering one of the easiest and most reliable methods of plant propagation for the newcomer to gardening.

It is one of nature's own methods of propagation. Shoots of brambles, for instance, root into the soil at their tips. The branches of some trees, such as beech, will often take root where they sweep to the ground, and stems of rhododendron will root and form new plants at the point where they come into contact with the soil.

Why layer?

There are many good reasons for layering. The main one is that some shrubs and trees are very difficult to propagate by other means, such as cuttings, but prove easy from layers. Examples include rhododendrons, magnolias, witch hazel (*Hamamelis*), camellias, pieris, elaeagnus and hollies (*Ilex*).

With certain plants, such as strawberries, this is perhaps the only practical way to propagate new stock.

Layering requires very little equipment or expertise and needs no artificial heat (except when layering houseplants).

The usual method for shrubs is simple layering. This is suitable not only for those which are difficult to propagate from cuttings, but also for virtually any shrub or climber whose stems can be brought into contact with the soil.

Carry out layering during the growing season, ideally between mid-spring and late summer. Use young shoots produced in the current or previous season, as old woody ones will fail to root, or will do so only over a long time. If desired, several shoots from each shrub can be layered.

How to layer

First, the surrounding soil should be prepared by digging or forking it over to a depth of

30cm/12in. Mix in some coarse horticultural sand and moist sphagnum peat or coconut fibre. Break the soil down as finely as possible.

The shoot is prepared about 30cm/12in from its tip by first stripping off some leaves to make a clear section of stem. Then, in this area, cut a tongue about 5cm/2in in length by drawing a knife halfway through the stem. Make the cut through a leaf joint (also known as a 'node').

Wedge the tongue open with a small piece of wood or a stone and dust the surface of the cut with a proprietary hormone rooting powder.

The prepared part of the stem is then pegged down into a 15cm/6in deep, saucer-shaped hole in the prepared soil. Hold it in place with a piece of thick galvanized wire bent to the shape of a hairpin, and make sure the cut is still open. The top part of the shoot beyond the cut should be tied vertically to a short bamboo cane so it grows upwards.

Cover the pegged part of the stem with a 15cm/6in layer of soil and firm it lightly. The soil around layered stems should be kept moist until they have formed a good root system.

Gradual growth

Rooting will take place where the cut was made in the stem. Layers should not be lifted until a substantial root system has formed. This process may take as little as a year with some shrubs, such as forsythia, but can take 18 to 24 months with some of the more difficult shrubs. If you lift a layer and find that it has not rooted, replant it straight away and firm it in.

Lift the layers in autumn or early spring carefully, using a garden fork. If well rooted, cut away from the parent plant just beyond the roots. Rooted layers of shrubs should be immediately replanted elsewhere in the garden. Either put them in their permanent positions or, if you have the space, in a nursery bed to grow on to a larger size.

Another technique

Tip layering is even easier and is used for blackberries and loganberries and for other similar hybrid berrying fruits that have long stems.

It is carried out in mid- to late summer, using the current year's stems. Soil preparation is precisely the same as for simple layering.

Simply bury the tip of the stem about 8cm/3in in the soil. If necessary, keep it in place with a wire peg.

Alternatively, tips can be rooted in 9cm/3½in pots containing a peat and sand mix. Sink the pots to their rims in the ground below each tip.

Tip layering a thornless blackberry (above). The tip of a stem has been buried in the soil and will soon root.

Rhododendrons (below) can be layered at any time. A small slit along the stem hastens rooting. Roots take two years to form.

AIR LAYERING

Cut a slit 15-38cm/6-15in below the tip, between growth buds.

Dust the cut with hormone rooting powder. Pack with moss.

Enclose the cut with polythene, securing it at the bottom.

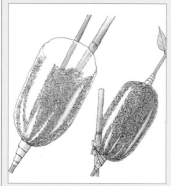

Pack the sleeve with more sphagnum moss and secure it at the top. Roots will grow into the moss. Tie stem to a cane.

In late autumn of the same year, when the tips have rooted, cut them away from the parent plant and plant them elsewhere in the garden. The best place is in a nursery bed where they can grow on.

Air layering

It is impossible to bring the stems of some shrubs and the branches of most trees down to ground level. These can be propagated by a technique known as air layering.

Prepare a young shoot as for simple layering, but hold the cut or tongue open by packing it with a wad of moist sphagnum moss, which you can buy from a florist.

Wrap more moss around the prepared part of the stem, holding it in place with a 'bandage' of clear polythene sheeting. Use waterproof tape to hold the polythene in place, making sure it is firmly attached to the shoot.

You should be able to see when roots have formed. Rooting will take one to two years. Treat rooted layers as already described. Remove the polythene but leave the moss in place; removing it will damage the brittle roots.

Border carnations

Many people are surprised to learn that border carnations can be layered. This is an easier and more reliable form of propagation than the alternative method of taking cuttings.

As the plants soon deteriorate, it is a good idea to propagate border carnations every couple of years or so.

The best time to layer carnations is in late summer, when flowering is over. For success, you must use the current year's shoots before they start to become woody. Several shoots can be pegged down around each plant.

First, lightly fork over the soil around the parent plants, using a hand fork. Then spread a 5cm/2in layer of John Innes potting compost evenly

over the cultivated soil.

Using unflowered shoots, carefully cut off the leaves at the base of the shoots, where they will be pegged down. Then cut a 3.5cm/1½in tongue in each, using the technique described under simple layering. Make the cut through a leaf joint. There is no need to use hormone rooting powder.

Peg down each layer into the compost, keeping it in place with a wire hairpin-shaped peg. The tongue must be kept open. Cover this part of the stem with a 5cm/2in layer of

Air layering is the most successful way of propagating any Ficus shrub. Taking cuttings is a chancy method, not least because they have to be propagated at a relatively high temperature, which can be difficult. Here (above) a cut has been made in a one or two-year-old stem in early to mid summer and rooting is taking place. The whole process, which is a little unsightly, may take two years.

John Innes potting compost.

Keep the layers moist and they should root in about eight weeks. Cut them from the parent plants and leave them in the ground for a few days to recover from the 'shock'. Then lift them with a fork and replant them in permanent positions in the garden. These new plants will start to flower next year in mid summer.

Strawberries

Strawberries are propagated by layering the young plants which form on the ends of runners (creeping stems). Strawberry plants, like carnations, soon deteriorate and should be replaced by young plants about every three years to keep up crop yields.

If runners are not needed for propagation, remove them. Runners can be layered in early or mid summer. Always layer the first plantlet on a runner, removing any beyond

it. Five to six runners can be layered around each plant.

Hold the plantlets in close contact with the soil by inserting a wire peg just behind each one. They can be rooted in the soil or in small pots of John Innes potting compost that have been sunk in the ground. Keep layers moist at all times.

When the plantlets are well rooted, in late summer or early autumn, cut them away from the parents and plant them in a newly dug strawberry bed. Flowering and fruiting will start the following year.

Indoor uses

Layering is not just a technique for garden plants. It is suitable, too, for some houseplants. Air layering can be used for woody or tree-like kinds, such as rubber plants and figs (*Ficus* species), crotons (*Codiaeum variegatum*), philodendrons, and dumb cane (*Dieffenbachia species*).

These are often air layered when they become too tall and need to be replaced with smaller specimens. You can do it in normal room conditions during the spring or summer.

Prepare a stem about 30cm/12in from its tip, as described for simple layering. The cut, which forms the tongue, is made in an upward direction. Dust with hormone rooting powder and then wrap the cut with moss covered by a protective polythene sleeve.

In warm conditions the stem should root in several weeks. Remove the polythene (but *not* the moss) and place the layer in a suitably sized pot, using soilless or soil-based potting compost. If possible, keep the young plants in warmer conditions for a few weeks.

If you wish, you can cut back the parent plant, by about half to two-thirds. It should then form side shoots and make a good bushy specimen.

SERPENTINE LAYERING OF CLIMBERS

Instead of obtaining only one plant per stem, you can ensure several from climbing plants by a technique known as serpentine layering.

Examples of climbers suited to this method are wisterias, clematis, honeysuckles (*Lonicera*), vines and jasmine (*Jasminum*).

This method is a variation on simple layering. Instead of rooting a stem in just one place, a long young stem is pegged down in several places along its length.

Climbers sometimes root more quickly than shrubs – often in as little as 12 months.

It is advisable to mark your layers with canes or plant labels so that you remember where they are. Make a note of the date so you know when to check them for roots.

1 Take a young, pliable outer shoot of the climber – here it is honeysuckle – and lay it out on the ground where you want it to root.

2 With a sharp knife make slanting cuts 1-2.5cm/¹/₂-1in long in the stem. Make the cuts close to nodes. Several cuts can be made.

3 Having added humus and sand to the soil, peg down each cut with a staple of bent wire and cover it over with soil.

4 Shoots layered in early summer should form roots by early autumn. Sever the plants, pot them up and plant out in the spring.

ROOT PROPAGATION

In many cases you can fill a whole border from the roots of a single plant, in a short time. The method is simple and the results very satisfying.

The easiest way to increase your stock of herbaceous plants is to divide their roots. From a single plant, you can build up to a dozen or more in a couple of years with regular splitting. It really is a good, cheap way to fill a border, and groups of plants often look better than single specimens.

As well as dividing the crown of a plant, it is also possible to take cuttings from the roots of some plants. This is easy to do and is usually highly successful if you follow a few basic guidelines.

Divide and grow

The best times to divide herbaceous perennials are autumn and spring. Autumn planting allows just enough time for the new plants to settle in and build up their strength before they face the stresses of winter, while spring planting ensures the plants first face the world in warm weather. On cold, heavy soils, spring planting is generally more successful than autumn. Late-flowering plants such as Michaelmas daisies should also be left undisturbed until spring.

Methods of dividing plants vary according to the type of root system they have. Check what kind of root systems your plants have first as it is important to use the correct method. Looking at the roots will also help you estimate how many pieces your plant will provide.

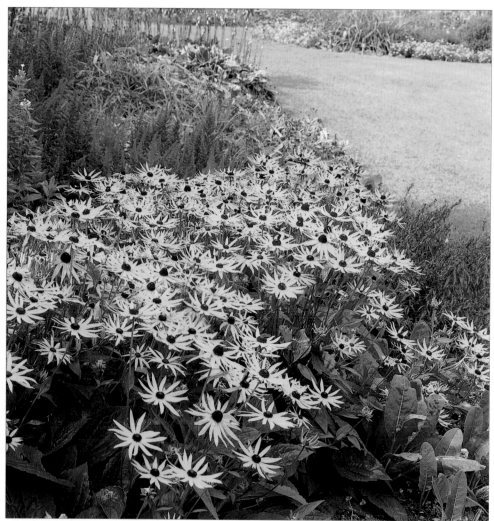

A fork is the best tool for lifting out of the soil any plants you are dividing. You will need to resort to a spade only occasionally for really stubborn plants like hosta and aruncus. Ease up the soil around your plant with a fork until it comes free, with as much root as possible intact. Shake off the loose soil, and you are ready to start dividing the crown.

Fibrous roots

Fibrous root systems are the easiest kind to divide, and they usually break apart very

One of the most prolific herbaceous plants is Rudbeckia fulgida var. sullivantii 'Goldsturm' (above). Its flowers have cone-shaped black centres. Flowering lasts until autumn and the roots grow quickly, making it excellent for root cuttings.

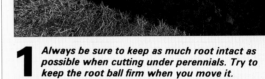

FIBROUS-ROOTED PLANTS

Plants with fibrous roots will give you the greatest number of divisions per plant, especially when divided every couple of years. These include:

- yarrow
- lady's mantle
- pearl everlasting
- Michaelmas daisy
- bellflower
- chrysanthemum
- fleabane
- cranesbill
- avens
- bergamot
- phlox
- cinquefoil
- primula
- pyrethrum
- coneflower

GARDEN NOTES

easily. Simply divide up the crown into small individual pieces with their own roots attached. With some plants like anaphalis, bergamot and primulas, you can do this with your hands quite easily. For tougher subjects you may need a fork, or in some cases two forks, used back to back, as levers. The important thing is to take care of the buds and crown surface, because, although you can use brute force when necessary to divide roots, when you spoil the crown, the work will have been in vain. Replant the divisions straight away before the roots have time to dry out, and water them in well.

Very leafy subjects like pyrethrum can be handled more easily in autumn if all the foliage is cut down to 5cm/2in before you divide. This also stops the plant wilting while it is establishing new roots. This is a useful tip for moving any herbaceous plant. Fibrous-rooted plants will give you the greatest number of divisions per plant, especially when divided every couple of years.

Some fibrous-rooted plants increase rather loosely at the root (Michaelmas daisy, Shasta daisy, *Rudbeckia sullivantii* 'Goldsturm') and these are best divided into small individual shoots, as they will quickly build up again. Side shoots can be lifted without digging up the whole plant but you should lift and divide the whole plant every two or three years to keep it healthy.

Fleshy roots

Plants with fleshy root systems such as plantain lily (hosta), day lily (hemerocallis), red hot poker (kniphofia), and African lily (agapanthus), may be more tricky to separate into small pieces. Slice the crown in half with a spade and then lift just one half for division.

Washing the soil off the roots with a hose may make the crown come apart a little

DIVIDING LARGE CLUMPS

1 *Always be sure to keep as much root intact as possible when cutting under perennials. Try to keep the root ball firm when you move it.*

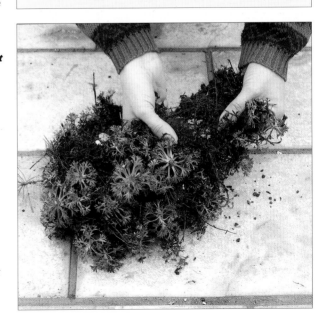

2 *A dense root ball can be divided quite simply by using two garden forks, back-to-back. It is best to ease the clump apart gradually.*

The roots of the day lily (hemerocallis) are so thick and fleshy that it can be useful first to cut the entire clump neatly in half (left). This makes it easier to separate the roots, which should be done sometime between autumn and the following summer.

The rosettes of the saxifrage (right), can be detached and used as cuttings. This is best done in early summer. They will benefit from being grown in a bed of peat and coarse sand, with constant light watering.

DIVIDING IRIS ROOTS

The woody roots of peonies are storage organs, rather like a dahlia tuber. So, similarly, if you want to divide dry dahlia tubers before you replant them in the spring, make sure there is at least one bud to each division.

Rhizomes

Couch grass, ground elder and mint spread by enlarged underground stems, called rhizomes, often becoming invasive and difficult to uproot.

Solomon's seal grows from a much more restrained rhizome, which can be dug up and broken into smaller pieces, each with a shoot, in spring. It should be planted just below the surface of the soil.

The rhizomes of bearded irises live on the surface of the soil, where they can be ripened by summer sunshine to induce flower production. Divide these irises in the summer immediately after flowering. Every three years, lift the clumps and replant the best, strongest rhizomes. Discard the weaker ones and old, central, worn-out portions.

The rhizomes to be replanted should point towards the sun so the root is not shaded by the fan of leaves. The leaves can be shortened

The exotic beauty of an iris (above) appeals to gardeners of every taste. Wait until the flowering season is over before dividing and do not overcrowd the new plantings.

Lift those with fibrous roots with a fork and gently separate the thicker clumps (above) so that the root ball can be more easily handled. But do not strain the weaker roots.

Some irises have rhizomes; these can be pulled apart with your hands (above). Dip stubborn clumps in cold water for a few minutes and the soil will crumble away.

more easily. You can also shorten the roots to 15cm/6in or so. Replant at once.

Woody systems

With old woody hosta clumps, it is easiest to slice up the clump with a spade just as you would cut a cake.

Peonies, goat's beard (aruncus) and astilbes all have woody roots. In spring you will

need a sharp spade to divide old plants. Peonies must have at least one bud to each division, so you will not get very many pieces, even from an old plant. Unless you are especially keen to propagate from them, peonies, like hellebores, are best left undisturbed. Goat's beard and astilbes divide well but can be tough – so be prepared!

This variety of Michaelmas daisy (right) is Aster novi belgii 'Eckingale White'. It has fibrous roots which grow quickly and benefit from being divided into small, separate shoots. If this is not done, the plant may lose much of its vitality.

PLANTS FOR ROOT CUTTINGS:

- Japanese anemone (anemone)
- bear's breeches (acanthus)
- anchusa
- stork's bill (erodium)
- sea holly (eryngium)
- cranesbill (geranium)
- Oriental poppy (papaver)
- border phlox
- mullein (verbascum)
- tree of heaven (ailanthus)
- flowering quince (chaenomeles)
- Indian bean tree (catalpa)
- foxglove tree (paulownia)
- sumach (rhus)
- tree poppy (romneya)
- false acacia (robinia)

GARDEN NOTES

with secateurs to 20cm/8in, to reduce wind-rock until the plant is re-established. The species of iris such as *I. sibirica*, which have grassy leaves and thinner, drier rhizomes, should be split into small clumps rather than individual rhizomes, in early autumn.

Suckers

Plants which spread by suckers include rubus, Japanese quince (chaenomeles), tree of heaven (ailanthus), cherry

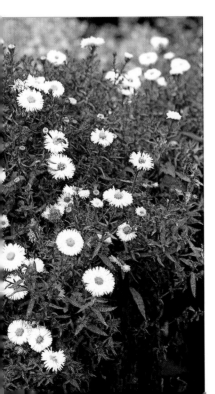

PROJECT   TAKING SIMPLE ROOT CUTTINGS

Taking your own cuttings can be very satisfying. You can use the new plants to add to the stocks in your borders or swap them with friends for their cuttings.

There could hardly be a better choice of a plant to take cuttings from than the drumstick primula (*P. denticulata*). It flowers in colours varying from lilac to rose and deep purple, and looks attractive grown in borders, rock gardens and as an edging to ponds.

Its roots should be cut in winter when they are dormant. Cuttings taken in mid summer will yield either a very low or no success rate.

Always leave about half the roots of each primula around the crown, so that you can replant it in your main display. The half you cut off will be quite sufficient for a good number of successful cuttings. These should be ready for planting by the following summer.

1 Use a sharp knife to remove the thickest and longest roots. Cut the root close to the plant. Leave about half the roots around the crown.

2 Line a seed tray with a mixture of moist peat and grit. These should be used in equal volumes. Firm the mixture down with a tamper (above) or the back of a trowel.

3 Cut the roots into 5cm/2in lengths. The ideal thickness is that of the middle section. The ends, which are too thin for use as cuttings, are shown on the right.

4 Lay the good cuttings on the surface in parallel rows. Cover them with a layer of moist peat and grit. Leave the tray in a cool place while the cuttings root.

5 Wait about a month, until the new leaves are large enough to handle easily. Use John Innes I compost and plant them in 7.5cm/3in pots.

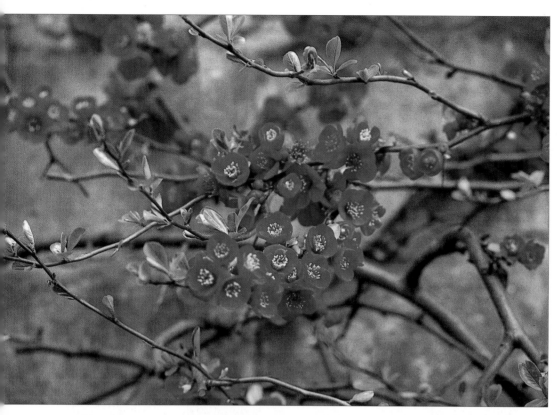

The crimson chaenomeles (above) originates in China and Japan. A hardy, flowering shrub, it grows fruit in autumn and looks attractive when clothing walls.

The cuttings are taken in mid summer and should each be about 10cm/4in long. An alternative, slower method is to cut longer shoots in September. This shrub takes several years to reach its full height.

GROWING TIPS

SOUND ADVICE

Q How often should I divide my herbaceous perennials?

A The real answer is, only when they need it, which means when they begin to lose vigour and flower less well. For some plants, like bearded irises, Michaelmas daisies and Shasta daisies, this means every three years or so. Without division they would become congested, and the centre of the clump would begin to die out.

If you want to increase your stocks of a particular plant, though, it is quite possible to divide most species every year. The best time to divide perennials is early autumn. It gives them time to establish themselves before winter. On heavy, cold soils it is better to wait until spring.

EASY EDGING

The ultra-hardy and vigorous geranium *G. ibericum* is clump-forming but root cuttings could soon provide you with a natural-looking low divider for a cottage garden. It has large flowers and grows to 60cm/2ft high.

In late autumn, lift a strong clump of the geraniums; a plant which has been in your garden for two seasons or more will provide sufficient root material for 20 cuttings. Root in peat and sand mixture and overwinter in a cold frame or sheltered position before planting out. Space them 25cm/10in apart to allow for growth.

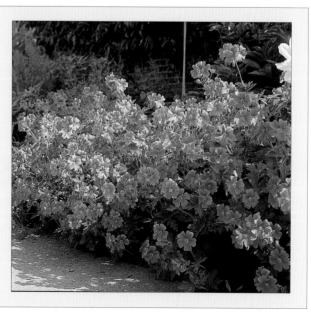

(prunus), lilac (syringa), snowberry (symphoricarpos) and acacia (robinia).

Suckers provide a ready means of dividing woody plants at the root. Separate the root from the parent plant at the point where a shrub has made suckers. This should be done between late autumn and early spring. Plant them as you would a new plant.

Sever the root on either side of the sucker with secateurs, then use a fork to lift the root. Sometimes it pays to sever the root a season before you lift the sucker, to make it fend for itself before you introduce a major upheaval.

Root cuttings

Some plants can produce new plants from cuttings taken from their roots, instead of the more familiar stem cuttings. They tend to be plants with fat, succulent roots which makes the process easier than you might imagine.

It is vital to keep the cuttings the correct way up or they will not grow. So to make this easier, cut the tops at right angles and the bases at a slant, so you cannot be mistaken. Root thickness varies according to the plant you are dealing with, but as a rule of thumb, do not use root sections that are much thinner than a pencil.

Cool places

Place the prepared cuttings 2.5cm/1in apart around the edge of a 12.5cm/5in pot of moist compost or soil, with the top 3mm/⅛in protruding above the compost. There is no need to use any rooting hormones. Cover them with 6mm/¼in of grit and place the pot in a cold frame or plunge it in soil in a shady garden corner.

Shoots should begin to appear by early spring, especially from autumn cuttings. These can be either potted up individually and grown on, or planted out directly into their growing positions.

SOFT FRUITS

Delicious soft fruits such as raspberries and gooseberries are usually grown in utilitarian fruit frames, but can be made part of a decorative scheme.

Although usually grown for their edible fruits, many berries and currants also provide attractive foliage and abundant flowers, making them suitable candidates for inclusion in even a small ornamental garden.

They will not necessarily fruit as abundantly as they would when grown in a more intensive way, but more than make up for this with the decorative, and sometimes practical roles they fill outside the fruiting season.

If grown solely for their fruit, soft fruit bushes are usually planted in straight rows. Those that need support, such as blackberries and raspberries, are grown in a series of lines fixed to strong, utilitarian posts and wires.

In a garden setting, you can use bush or shrub fruits as part of a mixed border, while climbing plants can be grown against fences, arches, cane wigwams or walls.

Herbaceous fruiting plants, such as strawberries, can be used effectively as ground cover under larger trees or as edging for beds and borders.

Some fruits, particularly gooseberries, can be trained to grow as standards with the fruiting stems trailing or weeping. Such a feature will add height to a border.

Raspberries and blackberries make attractive thin hedges, useful as windbreaks or to camouflage an untidy corner of the garden.

Strawberries, with their handsome foliage and pretty white flowers, fit happily into an ornamental garden.

They are essentially ground-covering and mound-forming plants that will keep down weeds, and can be used to make an attractive show at the base of taller, top fruit trees. They are also suitable for edging flower and vege-

table beds in a cottage garden.

In containers such as half-barrels, tower pots and terracotta strawberry pots, you can create a hanging garden of delicious fruits.

For the best summer berries, grow 'Pantagruella', 'Red

Growing several plants in multi-tiered strawberry pots in traditional terracotta or more modern materials (above) makes the most of the strawberry's tumbling fruit and flowers and attractive runners.

KIND CUTS

Learn how to prune each of your soft fruits to get the maximum crop from them. **Blackberries** produce from young canes shooting from the base of the plant, so tie them in when you prune out the current season's fruiting stems.

Blackcurrants fruit on one year-old stems. Cut back a third of each year's fruiting stems when you harvest.

Prune **blueberries** only when they are well-established, about four years after planting. Then, take out a quarter of older wood to ground level or to a good new shoot.

Prune **gooseberries** to produce a strong-growing framework of branches from an open, goblet-shaped centre. This makes it easier to pick them without getting scratched. Prune again in summer, taking all new shoots back to just five leaves. In winter, prune to two buds per stem.

Raspberry plants are pruned according to fruiting time. Autumn fruiters are cut down to ground level in winter, while the others are cut back after picking.

Red and white currants need pruning in summer and winter to get maximum crops.

Gauntlet' or 'Cambridge Favourite'. Some varieties crop right through the summer until the first frosts of autumn. 'Rapella' and 'Aromel' are among the best of these 'perpetual fruiting' varieties.

A variety developed with the ornamental gardener in mind, *Fragaria* 'Pink Panda', bears pink flowers from spring through to summer, and its leaves are semi-evergreen.

The alpine strawberry (*Fragaria vesca*) has smaller flowers and small, albeit very fragrant fruits. It also has a very decorative form with variegated leaves.

Cane fruits

Raspberries, blackberries and a whole host of hybrid berries are usually grown on strong fencing framework supports. They still require this support in an ornamental garden; the trick is to put them where they can perform practical or decorative functions.

Raspberries are the ideal slim-line hedging material for a mixed garden. Use them to make a natural shade screen or windbreak in a mixed fruit and vegetable plot. They can also be planted to hide an ugly

shed or compost heap.

Alternatively, they can make an attractive feature if grown in groups up a cane wigwam or, like pillar roses, tied to a thick central support.

Raspberry canes are bare at the base. To cover their bare feet, plant the area up with low-growing annuals, alpine strawberries or herbs.

To keep up a succession of fruit, plant several canes each of a number of varieties. 'Glen Moy', 'Malling Joy' and 'Malling Admiral' are summer-fruiting and produce red berries, while the autumn-fruiting 'Fallgold' has yellow ones. Delicious red autumn fruits come from 'Autumn Bliss' and 'September'.

Blackberries also need support, but are easier to integrate into your garden. A thornless variety, 'Oregon Thornless' makes a wonderful attraction on an arch into a rose garden, for instance.

You can also use blackberries and various hybrid berries, such as loganberry and tayberry, as fan-trained climbers against walls or to cover a trellis gazebo.

The most vigorous blackberry is 'Himalaya Giant'. Its

canes grow up to 4.5m/15ft long, making it suitable for climbing and rambling through a hedge.

Currant affairs

Blackcurrants are normally grown as quite bushy plants. One or two would make a suitable addition to a mixed shrub

Strawberries are the most versatile soft fruit for use in an ornamental garden. The dense foliage forms low, neat mounds that make the strawberry a suitable choice for edging a border (below).

All gooseberries are green at some point in their development, but extra ornamental interest is provided by those varieties whose berries redden as they ripen, sometimes achieving a rich maroon colour. 'Whinham's Industry' (left) is an adaptable variety, suitable for just about any soil.

Fruit cordons make good seasonal screens, used either as dividers or to hide an ugly wall or fence (below). Here, the foliage cover is provided by a red currant and a gooseberry growing side by side.

A FAN-TRAINED RED CURRANT

Currant bushes can easily be trained to grow into decorative shapes.

After planting, cut back stems to 30cm/12in above ground level. Tie them in to a wall or fence support system of wires and vining eyes. Arrange them in the shape of a fan, and remove any stems that grow forwards or into the wall. Prune the stems a further 10cm/4in to encourage good strong growth in the first year.

Water the plant in well and mulch its base with well-rotted compost.

and perennial border. They can also be pruned to grow as thick bushy hedges.

If you have limited space, you can fan-train blackcurrants to grow against a north-facing wall of the house or patio. 'Ben More' flowers late in spring, usually avoiding last frosts, and has a sharp flavour. 'Ben Sarek' is a relatively low-growing, bushy plant, that suits mixed borders or a short fruit hedge.

Red and white currants fruit on spurs supported by a framework of older wood and can be trained to grow in many styles. They can form tall, thin internal hedges that drip with clusters of jewel-like fruit in season, or you can grow them as half-standards to add height to the centre of a herb knot garden. Fan-trained red or white currants soften harsh, new wooden fencing and produce a good crop.

For an upright bush, choose 'Red Lake'. It produces long trusses of flavoursome fruit in late summer. The summer-flowering 'White Versailles', with its sweet, creamy yellow currants, is the popular choice in white currants.

Gooseberry bushes are so prickly that you may not wish to include them in ornamental planting. If you do, grow in a well-pruned 'goblet' shape to make them easier to harvest.

Playing gooseberry

However, you can also grow them against walls or fencing as fans or cordons. Make a gooseberry hedge by training plants into fan-shapes along a thin wire support. Plant up both sides of the support for maximum fruit.

Gooseberries trained as standards add height to mixed borders and make an unusual avenue in a herb garden. Underplant them with clumps of chives or strawberries.

'Golden Drop' is an upright plant with a neat, compact habit that suits mixed shrub plantings. Its fruits are also delicious to eat fresh.

'Careless' is the variety most often chosen for reliable cropping. It has a spreading habit and could be trained to a fan-shape against a north wall.

Of the maroon-red gooseberries, 'Whinham's Industry' does well in all soils and in shade, while 'May Duke' is

PERFECT PARTNERS

Many soft fruits are eminently companionable and combine well with a wide range of flowering plants. Alpine and ordinary strawberries look attractive grown at the base of bare-stemmed plants such as clematis or with patio roses (above). You can also grow them at the feet of raspberry canes to double the ornamental value of their fruit.

GROWING TIPS

SICK BAY

Virus diseases are carried by insects such as greenfly and leafhopper from plant to plant. In a mixed planting, predators are likely to be present that can pick off the insects.

Always buy Certified Virus-free stock to make a healthy start. If you have to spray to control insects, use selective sprays that will not harm beneficial pollinating insects.

If soft fruits do become infected, you will see this as blotchy markings on leaves or distorted growth. In this case remove and burn those plants that have been infected.

equally good used green in early spring for cooking or eaten fresh in summer after it has turned to red.

Turning blue

Blueberries need an acid soil and full sun. If your garden suits rhododendrons and heathers, then plant blueberries in the open ground.

If your soil is not suitable, grow them in an ericaceous compost in large containers on a sunny, sheltered patio.

The flowers of the blueberry appear in spring and resemble the bell-like clusters of the evergreen shrub *Pieris formosa*. They are succeeded by equally attractive fruit. As they ripen the berries change from green to red, then to a

dark blue with a deep bloom.

Blueberries need plenty of water, especially if you are growing them in containers. 'Blue Crop' is a hardy choice, a heavy cropper with good drought resistance. For very large berries, grow 'Earliblue'.

Buying plants

It is always best to buy from soft fruit specialist growers. Gooseberries, strawberries, raspberries, red currants and some hybrid berries are available as certified stock, free from pests and diseases.

Order early, to give you the best chance of obtaining the varieties you want. Buy bare-root stock if you know you can plant in autumn or spring.

Otherwise choose container-grown stock. It will not suffer any loss of vigour if planting conditions are not the best.

Go Organic!

NONE FOR THE BIRDS

Birds are always a problem at harvest time, when soft fruit is grown unprotected in a garden. To make sure you get your fair share and more of your soft fruit, cover bushes with temporary nets once the berries begin to ripen.

Protect strawberries grown as edging plants with a network of black cotton. Fan and wall trained soft fruit can be saved with netting fixed to a wall-batten, and draped over the fruit plant like a curtain.

Blueberries need a week on the bush after turning blue before they can be picked. Protect them with a net shawl thrown lightly over them.

Many of the hybrid berries, such as tayberry, are vigorous climbers, and can be trained to quickly clothe a pergola or an arch (above left).

The blueberry belongs to the same genus – Vaccinium – as the bilberry, cranberry and whortleberry. It has to have an acid soil, but given that produces a good-looking shrub with fine autumn colour and fruits which change from green to red and then blue – with a soft silver bloom – as they mature. 'Blue Crop' (left) is a reliable variety.

Most strawberries have white flowers, but there are several pretty pink-flowered varieties. Those of the ornamental Fragaria 'Pink Panda' (right) are produced throughout the summer. This variety looks particularly good in a hanging basket (above). The flowers and fruit bring colour, while the runners trail down attractively.

SMALL FRUIT TREES

Exciting new developments have made it possible to grow fruit as part of a creative gardening scheme, even in the smallest garden.

In the past, gardens were expected to produce all the fruit and vegetables for the household. Fruit trees, bushes and plants were an integral part of a decorative and well-stocked garden.

Times changed and fashions in gardening changed with them. The growing of fruit was one of the casualties. There were several reasons for this, lack of space being a major one. Fruit trees were large and modern gardens were not.

Good news

The problem of lack of space is now a thing of the past. Dwarf rootstocks have made available a whole host of fruit trees that will fit happily – and indeed decoratively – into the tiniest of gardens.

Some are even self-fertile, which means you no longer have to plant several trees to get fruit. Even where a pollination partner is required, the dwarf trees are often so compact it does not present a real space problem.

Small trees make useful vertical focal points, and walls may be screened with fruit bearing plants instead of the more usual climbers.

There is no need to set aside space for a fruit patch either, or to grow soft fruits in an ugly fruit cage which clutters up a large chunk of your garden. Fruiting plants can be used creatively to enhance your beds and borders.

Fruiting shrubs and bushes can act as architectural plants, giving shape and sub-stance to a planting scheme. Rhubarb, for example, makes a bold, exciting shape at the back of an herbaceous border at the same time as providing you with a delicious crop.

Many kinds of fruit will live quite happily in containers on your patio, transforming it into a productive and beautiful feature. A dwarf peach or apri-

DON'T FORGET!

A LITTLE CARE

Dwarf varieties of most trees require good soil and good growing conditions.

Prepare ground thoroughly with plenty of organic matter. Feed, water and weed regularly to ensure good crops.

Although fruit-growing has largely gone out of fashion among less committed gardeners, a mature apple tree (above) still earns its place in the garden with drifts of fragrant blossom in the springtime and branches laden with attractive, delicious fruit in the autumn.

PEAR PARTNERS

If your neighbours have apple trees you can usually get away with just planting one of your own; there is no need to supply a pollination partner. Pear trees are grown far less often and neighbours are less likely to supply the pollination partner.

A standard pear tree is too big for the average garden and there is less choice of rootstocks. If you have the room, Quince A or Quince C rootstock will produce trees growing to between 3m/10ft and 6m/20ft high, but remember you will need to accommodate two.

Pear blossom is not as beautiful or plentiful as that of apples, but the fruit, especially the Comice varieties (above), is excellent.

Peaches are rarely considered for gardens in temperate climates, but will sometimes fruit and always make an attractive small tree if grown in a container (left).

Dwarfing rootstocks such as M9 mean that several varieties of apple can be grown in a small area (below).

cot tree looks lovely in the right pot and strawberries grown in strawberry pots are both productive and stunning.

Fallacies

It is widely believed that specialist skill is required to grow fruit successfully. This is simply not true. A fairly basic knowledge of gardening methods is certainly enough to grow many delicious fruits.

Pruning, for example, is not really as mysterious as it sounds and you certainly do not have to be a qualified surgeon to make a decent job of it.

Neither do you need a degree in horticulture to understand the principles of cross-pollination. Some fruits, such as the majority of apples and pears, need to receive pollen from another variety in order to set reliable fruit. All that is required is that another tree, close by, blossoms at roughly the same time as your tree. The partner need not even be in your own garden; a neighbour's tree will do just as well.

Time and money

A further fallacy is that fruit growing is very time-consuming; in fact, it can take up less time than a modest

vegetable patch for a greater reward. It simply depends on what you grow. Figs are time-consuming, but apples, garden blackberries and strawberries are generally not.

Most fruit trees and plants will be productive for years, amply repaying the initial cost of buying your stock. The secret of growing a fruit tree or two to suit your garden lies in the rootstock, which will decide how large your tree will be, how much fruit it will bear and what conditions it will need. It is very important to choose the right rootstock for your purposes.

ROJECT

A PATIO ORCHARD

Apples grown on rootstocks M27 and M9 make excellent trees for pots. Ballerina trees (rootstock MM106) also take happily to containers.

A group made up of a bush, a dwarf pyramid and a compact column would give you a wonderful array of shapes and a delicious selection of fruit.

Add strawberry pots and one or two dwarf peaches and you will prolong the blossoming and fruiting periods as well as varying shape and colour.

All the small trees need to be in wooden or terracotta pots of about 30-40cm/12-15in. Plant in a heavy compost such as John Innes No.3 and stake the trees firmly. You will need to repot every second year.

All container plants need regular feeding and watering in dry, hot weather. Fruit requires a high potash liquid feed from when blossoming starts until shortly before harvest time. Feed fortnightly during this period.

Protect your pots in winter by wrapping them up in insulating material or bring them inside.

Branchless Ballerina apple trees crop well in small areas (above left). Underplanting will help to integrate them into a small garden.

Many soft fruit bushes lend themselves well to a smaller, mixed garden. Smooth-stemmed blackberries such as 'Oregon Thornless' (above) will clamber over a trellis, while currants – black, white or red – can form bushes or be trained to cover a wall with leaves and bright summer berries (right). Raspberries such as the autumn-flowering 'Heritage' (below) grow on canes which can be trained on a cordon or trellis.

A particular variety of fruit can be grafted on to any one of several rootstocks. A Victoria plum tree, for example, is usually far too big for the average garden, but when it is grafted on to a Pixy rootstock it becomes small enough to be accommodated.

Apple trees

Ballerina varieties look delightful as a central feature in a bed, surrounded by bedding plants; they provide a vertical, columnar shape, clothed with blossom in season, which contrasts with the basically horizontal outlines of the rest of the bed. For a more formal effect, you might want to plant an avenue of Ballerina trees leading to a bench, a statue or even a fountain. Their lack of branches means that they cast little

shadow, which makes it possible to interplant them with bedding and ground cover plants. The whole effect will be absolutely stunning, especially in apple-blossom time.

If you prefer a conventionally shaped tree but have very little room, then the unromantically-named M27 rootstock is for you. Trees grown on this reach a height of about 2m/6ft. A pair of such trees planted in wooden half-barrels or terracotta pots could grace a doorway or flank the steps of a patio.

Other trees

Of course, apples are not your only option. Pears are big trees, so container growing is not possible and you will need two for pollination.

Plums may be grafted onto Pixy rootstock or they may be

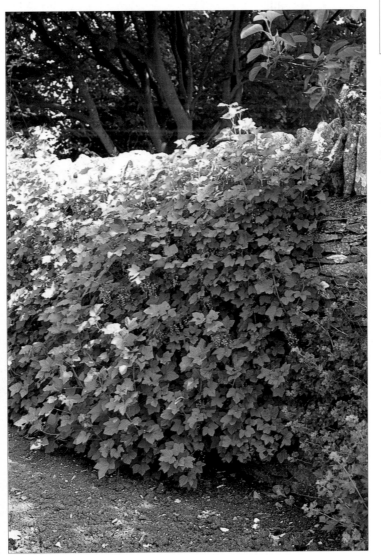

grown as a fan on a south-facing wall. Several fruit trees, including cherries, peaches, nectarines and apricots, may be grown as fans and they make a delightful and tasty alternative to climbing plants.

For all of these, a sheltered, sunny site is essential. Late, unexpected frosts may make some years fruitless but the joy of picking your own succulent exotic fruits in good years makes growing them worth the risks. Besides, whether they fruit or not, fans are an attractive, decorative, garden feature.

Soft fruits

Bush fruits, such as raspberries, gooseberries, and red, white or black berries, may be incorporated into the backs of borders to add shape, colour and bulk to a design, and some may also be grown along cordons to act as a kind of living fence or trained along tellises to divide up your garden.

Strawberries can be planted in containers for the patio or as edging plants for a border.

SHRUBS

Shrubs are the backbone of garden design but they can also be some of the most beautiful feature plants – so choose them with care.

Shrubs are hard-working garden plants that can be ornamental features as well as practical attributes in your garden. They are part of the permanent framework of the garden and, once they are well established, there is little extra maintenance that you need to perform to keep them healthy and flourishing.

Average soil conditions will suit most shrubs which will grow well in sun or shade. Except in severe drought conditions, or when newly planted, they do not need regular watering. Some may need a little pruning to make them flower well but apart from that they offer much decorative value for little effort on your part.

What is a shrub?

Shrubs have tough, woody stems that do not die back in winter. The many stems or branches grow from near ground level and provide an overall bushy shape to the plant. There is no central or dominant, leading stem.

When you set out to buy shrubs from a garden centre in winter or spring when some of them may be bare and leafless, look for their unmistakable well-branched outline.

Decorative displays

Some shrubs are evergreen, with leaves all year round. While others are deciduous and lose their foliage in winter. Some, like forsythia, burst into flower early in spring. Others will dazzle you in autumn with russet coloured foliage. Many produce coloured fruits that are decorative and

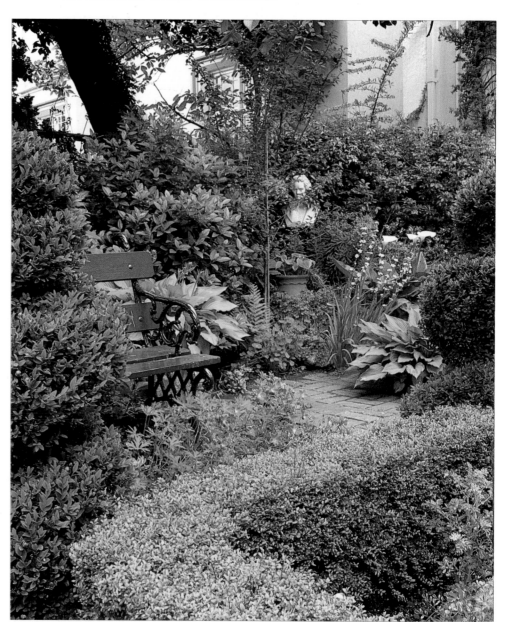

attract birds too.

Shrubs are the backbone of a good garden plan. They clothe and shape it, softening edges and adding colour and fragrance. A garden quickly looks established once the shrub framework is planted.

Best of all, they provide their attractive flowers, foliage, or their autumn fruits with the minimum of routine care. Some simply need removal of dead and damaged wood and a light pruning to keep them within bounds before the beginning of the growing season in spring, while

Shrubs form the framework of good garden design. Use them to create a layout to which you can add your personal stamp – choose colours, textures and even statues to complement the shapes and shades of the shrubs.

If you have a sheltered, sunny spot fill it with a Choisya ternata – Mexican orange blossom (left) – and lose yourself in the wonderful aroma of the white flowers which first deck the dark,glossy leaves in late spring and again in autumn. It is a slow growing shrub which is easily kept in check, making it suitable for all gardens.

Although often similar in height, dwarf conifers are trees not shrubs. They have one central trunk while shrubs have many branching stems. Shrubs and conifers make an extremely attractive display (below) and it can be remarkably colourful. Ranging from smoky blue-green to bright yellow-green and maroon they are lovely on their own, but mix them with a few well chosen flowers and the whole ensemble really comes to life.

WHAT IS A SHRUB?

GARDEN NOTES

Shrubs have tough, woody stems that do not die back in winter. They differ from trees in that they are generally not as tall and they do not have a central trunk. All their branches grow from near ground level, and create a bushy shape.

others need special pruning to make sure that they produce a mass of beautiful flowers.

Because shrubs are such popular and useful garden plants there are many that are easily available at garden centres and nurseries. Their popularity means that they are usually inexpensive and you can be sure that you are buying healthy, reliable and garden-worthy plants.

You may, however, wish to include in your garden shrubs that are not so widely available. They may be expensive and you would find them at specialist nurseries, but make sure they do not require too much extra attention or special situations that you cannot easily provide.

Shrub or tree

While the growth habit of trees is usually dominated by a central leading stem (the trunk or bole) with a head of branches sprouting from the top, shrubs do not develop this central stem. Instead their many stems branch at different angles to the ground and make a rounded shape.

There is, however, an area of overlap between shrubs and trees. Holly, hazel, hawthorn and some willows may develop into trees or into shrubs depending on how you prune and maintain them. Beech, for example, is often grown as a hedge. Similarly, Leyland cypress is clipped into shrub-like shapes to make hedging.

The other difference between shrubs and trees is in

Lighter than air, the arching branches of the Tamarix ramosissima 'Pink Cascade' (above) seem coated with a fine pink dust which looks as if it might be blown away in the slightest breeze.

Some shrubs have a prostrate habit and are excellent as ground cover. Photinia davidiana var. undulata 'Prostrata' (below) has white flowers in summer and berries in winter.

height. Trees may offer as much ornamental value as shrubs, but most take up a great deal of space when they reach maturity. They may take many years to reach full height (this can range from a couple of metres up to 40m/100ft or more), so seem to have shrub-like proportions at first. Once they are mature they are likely to be too big for your garden; they may block out light and will certainly be dif-

ficult to underplant successfully, as they drain the soil of moisture.

Shrubs can grow tall and wide, but they do respond well to pruning and maintenance, so you can control their ultimate size. They will not attain the height of some trees, but can range from under 30cm/1ft up to 6m/20ft.

Shrubs in the garden

Shrubs can be purely ornamental features for you to admire and use in the garden. Flowers are their most obvious advantage. Shrubs flower over a long period from spring through to late autumn, and some even flower in winter, making them essential to keep year-round colour in a garden.

Coloured bark or stems, evergreen foliage or variegated leaves, autumn leaf colour, coloured fruits or berries and a pretty fragrance are among the decorative charms that shrubs bring to the garden. Additionally, many shrubs will do well when planted in containers on balconies and patios. Pieris, camellias, formosa and lavender are included among these.

Beyond the purely ornamental, shrubs can be used to define the space in your garden. They introduce changes of height in a border or terrace

area, and can also be used to enclose parts of the garden. In a large garden you can use shrubs to guide your eye to particular views or vistas.

Shrub screens

They also work well, if planted in groups or straight rows, as hedges or windbreaks. In a small garden, they are ideal plants to make screens around unsightly sheds or utility areas. Some shrubs grow very low and scramble across the ground. These can be used to a gardener's advantage too, as they will stabilize and decorate banks that may be difficult to maintain under grass.

Many shrubs hold their foliage throughout the year, offering you permanent colour and shape. Evergreen shrubs

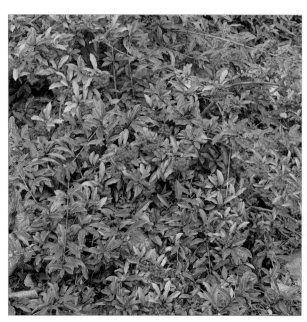

Lithodora diffusa (right) is another shrub with a spreading, prostrate habit. It looks like an alpine, proving that shrubs are an extremely diverse group of plants. Some look like trees and others, like this one, are small enough to grow in rockeries. It has a height of 15-30cm/6-12in and spread of 60cm/2ft. Masses of vibrant, violet-blue, star-shaped flowers are produced in summer. This species likes a soil that is slightly acid.

are most suitable for hedges or screens, as they offer permanent cover or privacy. They do drop some leaves, usually in spring, but not on as large a scale as deciduous shrubs.

The leaves of evergreens are usually glossy and there are many evergreen shrubs with golden and white variegations that will offer you added colour. Although decorative in their own right, evergreen shrubs also provide a useful backdrop for many other garden plants.

Deciduous shrubs

These plants look bare and twiggy in winter, when they lose their leaves, but their soft and fresh spring shoots and leaves, followed by flowers and possible autumn leaf colour, more than make up for this seasonal lack of beauty.

Some shrubs, including many of the dogwoods, have exceptionally beautiful stems that create an eye-catching winter feature.

Hardy or tender?

Hardy shrubs will not need any protection during winter or outside the growing season. Some, like *Convolvulus cneorum*, a shrubby bindweed that is not invasive, and abelia (*A. grandiflora*) are hardy in most situations, but in very cold districts they may need a sheltered position.

Tender shrubs are those that need protection in winter, either by mulching their roots with straw or by placing a seasonal barrier of protective netting or insulation around them. Some may have to be kept inside or in a conservatory over winter.

On the borderline are shrubs such as the pretty yellow-flowered wall plant, *Fremontodendron* 'Californian Glory'. It will need a sheltered or sunny position to survive in very cold areas.

Sub-shrubs

This term is applied to plants that have a woody base and soft stems. They are perennials whose soft stems die back in winter. Like shrubs they have bushy shapes, but are generally low-growing.

Included in this group are the low-growing rock rose *Helianthemum alpestre,* and the lovely little rockery plant *Lithodora diffusum*.

Conifers are usually classified as trees, but many of the compact, slow-growing specimens are used as shrubs in garden situations. True dwarf conifers are valuable additions to the shrub repertoire.

They do remain small and are genuinely slow-growing,

but they may revert back to their true type and grow too tall for your purpose. If your rockery dwarf conifer starts developing vigorous shoots, cut them back before too much growth is made.

Size and scale

Most garden centres and nursery catalogues estimate the size a shrub will reach either when mature or up to ten years after planting. In a

Many tiny shrubs, like the Helianthemum oelandicum *ssp. alpestre or rock rose, look more like little alpines. The rock rose (above) loves a well-drained, sunny spot and is ideal for brightening up a rocky patch or a dry bank. Its open-faced, five petalled, bright yellow flowers appear from early to mid summer.*

EARLY FLOWERS

Some early flowering shrubs that offer delightful flowers and do well in most conditions include the following:
● Quince (*Chaenomeles × superba*) provides cup-shaped flowers on bare stems in early spring, with edible fruits in late summer. Grow it against a sunny wall. After flowering, prune it lightly but do not cut away all the fruiting stems. (1.5 × 1.5m/5 × 5ft)
● Winter hazel (*Corylopsis pauciflora*) offers attractive, delicately scented yellow flowers that seem to drip down from its bare stems. The flowers need protection from early sun. (0.9-1.5 × 0.9m/3-5 × 3ft)
● Mahonia japonica is a huge evergreen shrub with decorative spiky leaves and long trails of yellow scented flowers in late winter, early spring (up to 2 × 3m/6½ × 10ft).
● Laurustinus (*Viburnum tinus*) is an evergreen with bouquets of small white flowers in spring. (2.7 × 1.8m/9 × 6ft)

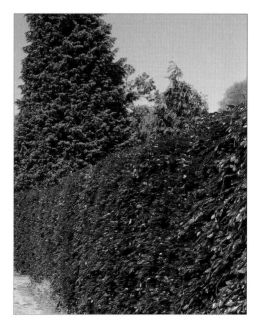

As well as being extremely decorative, many shrubs have very practical applications. Fagus sylvatica 'Purpurea' (right), better known as the purple beech, makes a perfect hedge. Beech is one of the borderline shrubs that doubles up as a tree. When trained into a hedge it is a shrub but when allowed to grow tall and straight it is a tree. When kept clipped, these hedges do not drop their dead, brown leaves in winter but remain densely covered in foliage.

The beauty of shrubs is that they are generally hardy. The frosted plants (left) look magical and the colours are tinged with blue. Libertia formosa, Nandina domestica and euonymus have been used here.

Skimmia japonica (below) is a very versatile shrub. From early until late spring it produces abundant clusters of star-shaped white flowers. The rich green foliage is highly aromatic throughout the year and bright red fruits are produced in autumn.

small garden you need to know the ultimate size the shrub will reach: you do not want to have to uproot an expensive and cherished plant because there is no room for it.

You can control the size and shape of most shrubs by careful pruning or keeping them in bounds when they do get overly large. Do this on a regular basis, rather than making a severe cut-back when the shrub is well-established.

Most shrubs will grow in average garden soils but to grow vigorously and flourish they should be planted in a site which is well prepared and has good drainage. The planting hole should be well dug to a depth of up to 30cm/1ft to allow for the plant's root system. Early spring or late autumn are generally the best times to plant shrubs. Apply a little fertilizer to the planting hole along with plenty of good garden compost and a handful of bonemeal. Water the plant in well and keep it well watered, especially in drought conditions and in the first year of its planting.

PRUNING SHRUBS

● Many shrubs need pruning to increase their flowering capacity. Deciduous spring and early summer flowering shrubs should be pruned immediately after flowering. Cut back old wood with faded flowers to encourage new growth. Flowering currant (*Ribes sanguineum*), forsythia (*Forsythia spectabilis*) and mock orange (*Philadelphus*) are included in this group.

After pruning, new growth will quickly appear and it is on this new wood that the buds for next year's flowers will be made. If the plants bear fruit later in the season prune lightly after flowering and enjoy the fruits.

● Prune most late summer flowering shrubs in spring. They produce their flowers on shoots grown immediately after pruning. Cut them back hard so that they make plenty of new wood in spring to carry their flowers. Included in this group are the butterfly bush (*Buddleja davidii*), pheasant berry (*Leycesteria formosa*) and the tamarisk tree (*Tamarix ramosissima*). Winter-flowering shrubs simply need pruning to tidy up any dead or diseased branches after flowering in early spring.

GARDEN NOTES

Another plant with attractive berries is Mahonia japonica (right), but these appear in summer. Sprays of pretty yellow flowers decorate the spreading branches from mid winter until early spring, introducing a touch of summery colour to your garden in the wintry months. These shrubs are excellent as specimen plants as they are sure to provide year-round enjoyment. This particular species grows to about 2m/6½ft and has a wide spread of approximately 3m/10ft so make sure it has enough room.

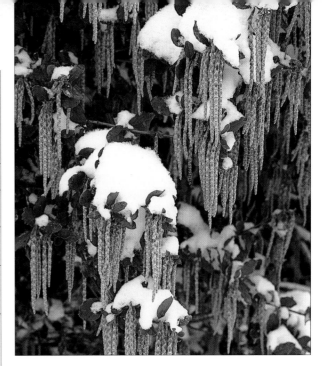

SHRUB CHOICE

Shrubs, whether evergreen or deciduous, are a good choice for a new garden, to fill empty space and make an immediate impact. They create an excellent background for bedding plants and, if well chosen, provide year-round interest. Here is an attractive selection.

PLANT NAME	ATTRACTION	SIZE
abelia *Abelia grandiflora*	fragrant flowers in summer	height and spread up to 1.5m/5ft
common camellia *Camellia japonica*	spring flowers and evergreen leaves	bushy, up to 3m/10ft high
Californian lilac *Ceanothus 'A. T. Johnson'*	beautiful blue, showy spring flowers	1.5-3m/5-10ft high
Mexican orange *Choisya ternata*	slow-growing, shade-tolerant bush with orange-scented flowers in spring and autumn	up to 3m/10ft but can be pruned hard after spring flowering
mezereon *Daphne mezereum*	early spring flowers, purple-red and scented, on leafless branches; berries in autumn	up to 1.5m/5ft
silk tassel bush *Garrya elliptica*	fast-growing, with grey-green catkins in winter and spring	up to 3m/10ft but can be pruned
griselinia *Griselinia littoralis*	fresh green leaves; makes very good hedging in coastal areas	up to 2.4m/8ft wide and tall but can be kept in bounds if trimmed regularly
Oregon grape *Mahonia aquifolium*	evergreen with fragrant yellow spring flowers and grape-like fruits; shiny dark green leaves turn reddish-purple in autumn	90cm-1.8m/3-6ft tall
Jerusalem sage *Phlomis fruticosa*	grey foliage; whorls of yellow summer flowers	low-growing, up to 1.2m/4ft
pieris *Pieris formosa 'Wakehurst'*	new leaves have a red blush of colour; white flowers appear in late spring	height 1.2-1.5m/4-5ft or more
firethorn *Pyracantha rodgersiana*	good wall or screening shrub, with clusters of white flowers; orange berries in autumn	erect; 2.4 × 2.4m/ 8 × 8ft, but depends on how it is pruned
rosemary *Rosmarinus officinalis*	a culinary herb with aromatic leaves and pretty blue flowers in early spring	bushy, up to 90cm/3ft
viburnum species	many have good flowers, some scented, in early spring and through the year	up to 3m/10ft but can be pruned

Some shrubs enjoy particular soil conditions. Azaleas, rhododendrons and camellias, in particular, prefer a lime-free or acid soil. To provide the right conditions you may need to make an acid bed or plant them in containers with ericaceous compost.

It is less work and less expensive if you grow shrubs that thrive in your particular region. Otherwise you might have to give them extra attention to make sure they do well in a climate or soil that does not quite suit them.

The catkins, weighted down by a fresh new snowfall, droop heavily from the Garrya elliptica (above) in winter and spring. It prefers a sheltered spot as long severe frost may damage the plant. Generally they are frost hardy.

Viburnum tinus, a winter flowering viburnum (below) is an evergreen. Pretty pink buds open into white flowers. Some varieties have pink-flushed flowers. This is ideal as a specimen shrub.

HERBACEOUS PERENNIALS

Lovely herbaceous perennials are the backbone of many gardens, providing long-term colour and blending well with annuals and existing shrubs.

Herbaceous perennials are hard-working, decorative plants that can generally be left undisturbed for many years. Once you have planted a selection of them you can sit back and enjoy the display with just the minimum of maintenance in the future.

The term 'perennial' is the name for a large group of very diverse plants that live for many seasons. You do not have to replace them or sow fresh seeds each year. Most of them take a rest from above-ground activity in winter, but when they spring into action in the growing season they provide a fine display of colour.

Herbaceous perennials are essential foundation plants in a garden as they provide much ornamental value for relatively little outlay. Most are tolerant of average conditions, but if you have a particularly dry or damp garden it is wise to choose those that will suit it.

Herbaceous perennials come in a range of shapes and sizes and differing flower colours, but their general behaviour is similar. They live for many seasons, producing flowers with consistent vigour, and in autumn most of them lose their stems and leaves. Underground, their root systems continue to live and many increase in size, spreading into clumps from the roots.

Garden value

Perennials are great value because they have long flowering periods. They come in a wide range of heights and are therefore versatile plants in any garden layout. They are relatively inexpensive to buy and they grow in size, providing you with extra plants over the years. Some herbaceous perennials form clumps and mats of vegetation that make good ground cover in a border, suppressing weed growth.

Some border perennials have green leaves during winter and these are the ones that will fill the gaps in the garden left by perennials that die back. Hellebores, including Christmas rose, have flowers and leaves through the year. Epimediums, too, hold their lovely autumn leaves until spring when delicate flowers dance above the new foliage.

Reliability

For gardeners the main attraction of herbaceous perennials is their general reliability and adaptability to a wide range of garden conditions.

In spring, when the soil is beginning to warm up and the growing season begins, herbacious perennials are on sale at garden centres, but they hardly look their best at this stage. All you can see in the pot is a few shoots and a clump of leaves. It is hard to believe

A border of herbaceous perennials, showing the variety of height and form that can be achieved. In the foreground are low-growing, mauve asters. In the centre is bright red montbretia. At the back are hollyhocks in two colours and the tall spikes of bear's breeches (Acanthus).

PLANTING OUT FROM POTS

Container-grown plants can be put out at any time of the year but between spring and autumn is usually the best time. Dig a hole sufficiently deep and wide to allow a full spread of the root system. For a large plant, mix some moist peat and some bonemeal with the soil in the planting hole. Ease out the roots from the pot, keeping the soil ball as complete as possible, and set in position. Depress the soil around the plant slightly to help it collect moisture, and water.

that this Cinderella will turn into a choice garden plant. In autumn, also a good planting time, there is little to see on most herbaceous perennials.

Are they hardy?

Most herbaceous perennials are hardy and will survive the winter without any frost protection. A few, such as red hot pokers, may need the crown

protecting in cold areas, with a layer of straw or bracken, or even a layer of weathered ash. Just a few, like dahlias, are tender and will be killed by frost; these must be lifted and given winter protection (as stored tubers in the case of dahlias), then replanted the following year.

From autumn to early

spring is a good time to take root cuttings. Pot them up and keep them frost-free. Plant them out next autumn.

Some people feel that perennials leave too many gaps in winter when the majority die back. You can minimize this by clever planting with a few that do not die back, or with spring bulbs and winter flowering perennials. Today, most perennials are planted into mixed borders rather than in borders solely devoted to perennials, so gaps are not likely to be too noticeable. One of the

---

CHOICE PERENNIALS

- *Hellebores* grow to about 60cm/2ft and flower in winter or spring. Leave them undisturbed if possible. Hardy and evergreen.
- *Pulmonaria* (lungwort) has speckled foliage, is evergreen and hardy, flowers in early spring to early summer, does well in shade and is good ground cover. A useful front of border plant.
- *Sedum spectabile* has fleshy leaves and flowers late in autumn. It does well in hot and dry conditions and makes good ground cover in the middle of a border.
- *Aquilegia* (columbine) is not always very vigorous but is easy to replace with seedlings. The flowers are very graceful.
- *Rudbeckia* makes a splash of strong colour in late autumn and does well in sunny or shady sites.
- *Dianthus,* (which includes pinks and border carnations) provides a good show at the front of a border.
- *Lupins, hollyhocks* and *delphiniums* are favourite choices for the back of a border, or to give an island bed height. They need staking and may need replacing if they lose their flowering vigour.
- *Crocosmia* (montbretia) provides orange or red flowers in late summer. It will need dividing as it spreads quickly.
- *Japanese anemones* are excellent border perennials, providing dainty pink or white flowers on long stems that are self-supporting.

Two choice perennials that will add colour to any flower bed. The bright pink of Sedum spectabile *'Autumn Joy' (above) and the bi-coloured flowers of the aptly-named* Dianthus *'Snowfire' (below) which can be grown as an annual.*

pleasures of these plants is the discovery of new shoots and leaves starting into growth after a dormant period.

Height and shape

When you decide to plant perennials there are a number of

factors you need to consider. First you should choose plants to suit your particular colour plans. Knowing their eventual height and shape is also important. If a plant is going to spread into a large space, it is no use planting anything too close to it. On the other hand, you do not want unsightly gaps in the soil, so spread is a necessary dimension to know.

Perennials vary greatly in height. Some, including delphiniums, traditional border giants, grow to 1.5m/5ft or more. They should be planted at the back of a border. There are many perennials that grow to medium heights (between 90cm/3ft and 1.2m/4ft), including Japanese anemones and day lilies *(Hemerocallis)*. Then come the vast majority that are up to 60cm/2ft high. For the front of a border or for growing on rockeries there are many perennials that do not grow taller than 15cm/6in, but they spread out wide to form ground-covering mats of flowers and leaves.

Good company
Perennials used to be planted in traditional one-sided borders that backed onto walls or hedges. Although glorious in the summer growing season, they were a depressing sight in winter. Today, perennials are usually combined with shrubs, bulbs and bedding plants in mixed borders that can give all-year pleasure.

Island beds, that can be seen from all angles, are popular for perennial plantings. Such beds offer all round light and good airflow. They are often very informal in style. Remember, though, when planting such a bed, that it will be seen from all directions. You can avoid using stakes by selecting varieties that are strong enough to support themselves, or will prop each other up.

Where to plant
The best site for most perennials is an open sunny position where their leaves can have as much light as possible. This makes it easier for them to make the food necessary for growth and flower production.

They need a well-drained soil but will want watering in extremely hot conditions. There should be a good flow of air around the perennial border to avoid a build up of pests

and diseases. However, exposed and windy sites are not suitable for these ornamental plants. The best soil to grow a wide range of perennials in is a medium loam that has been enriched with well-rotted compost or fertilizer. Whether you plant two or ten perennials in a border, they will all be competing for the sun, moisture, air and soil – so you should ensure that there is enough to go round when you plant them out. Space them out well.

General care
Although herbaceous perennials are not particularly demanding plants, they do need

The show of colour produced by an imaginative planting of herbaceous perennials in a mixed border (above) can be quite stunning. This picture was taken in late summer when the chosen flowers were at their best. They contrast pleasingly in height, form and colour with the clumps of ornamental grasses.

Almost anything that will keep the frost away can be used to protect delicate perennials. Here (below) dry leaves and stems are being placed on a wire frame over the crowns.

PROJECT
DIVIDING PERENNIALS

Every three or four years you should rejuvenate perennials by lifting them in autumn and dividing them. When the plant is out of the ground, place it on a sheet of plastic and use two forks to lever it apart. Replant the sections of the root on the outer edge of the plant. Add a little slow release fertilizer and water them in. In spring you will have the bonus of extra plants.

The older roots at the centre of the plant will be less vigorous (producing fewer leaves and blooms if left to grow) and should be discarded.

some care and attention. You will need to feed your perennials with a general compound fertilizer in early spring when growth begins, and then again in mid-summer.

A mulch of organic material soon after the first feed helps to conserve moisture and discourages weeds. Apply the mulch thickly to a depth of 7.5cm/3in. Perennials in mulched beds usually need watering only in exceptionally dry conditions, when they will need the same attention from sprinklers and hoses as your other garden plants.

In late summer and early autumn it is usually necessary to cut back dead flowers and dying stems and leaves from some of your more unsightly perennials. You can tidy up beds and borders at the same time, hoeing out any weeds.

A bonus with some early flowering perennials, such as lupins and delphiniums, is that they will flower again in later summer if they are dead-headed as soon as their first flowers fade.

Problem perennials

A few perennial plants do present problems, but you can find ways to avoid these. Some, for example, do much better than others and become garden thugs, swamping and overwhelming slower and gentler-growing plants. Avoid perennials such as *Achillea ptarmica* 'The Pearl' as it is a very invasive plant. To keep it under control you will have to divide it every year.

Some older varieties are prone to diseases such as rust and mildew. Michaelmas daisies, in particular, are affected by mildew, but this can be largely avoided by buying new varieties that are disease resistant. Some perennials lose their vigour after a few years and so are not such good value.

GROWING FROM SEED

Some perennials can be grown from seed but it is a lengthy and often challenging process. If you think it is worth growing from seed, you are wise to buy from a reliable seed merchant or your plants may be of uneven or poor quality. Sow indoors or under glass from mid-winter.

GROWING TIPS

Tall-growing hollyhocks (far right) are fairly sturdy but should be staked unless in a sheltered site.

Tall perennials will need staking against rain and wind damage. Whatever form of support is used it should be put in place early to avoid damaging the plants. There are several options. Ready-made frames can be bought from garden centres. A framework of twiggy pea sticks, carefully inserted in a clump to a height of 90cm/3ft, will soon be covered by foliage. Single tall spikes can be staked with a bamboo cane, but the best option for groups of flowers is to form a 'cage'. Insert three canes and circle them with wire or garden twine (right).

The epimediums form excellent ground cover. Epimedium × perralchicum (right) has evergreen heart-shaped leaves and produces yellow flowers in spring.

Lupins, for example, should be replaced every few years. Hollyhocks get rust spots on their leaves: this can be controlled by spraying but it may be simpler to replace with new plants.

Tall perennials need staking to prevent them flopping over in winds or after rain. Some of medium height also need staking and this can be time-consuming and a bit unsightly in the middle of an ornamental border. Avoid perennials that are too tall or choose varieties that are known to be self-supporting, such as the Belladonna hybrid group of delphiniums rather than those with very tall spikes. Try *D. belladonna* 'Blue Bees'.

BULBS, CORMS, RHIZOMES AND TUBERS

Bulbs, corms, rhizomes and tubers are types of food storage organs developed by plants for their survival from one growing season to the next.

Bulbs

Onions, daffodils, tulips and fritillarias all grow from bulbs. A bulb is a modified shoot, with its very short stem enclosed by layers of fleshy leaves.

In the first year, the food manufactured by the leaves is moved to the base of each leaf. These bases become the fleshy layers of the bulb. They are the part of the onion that we eat.

The following year, a bud within the bulb springs into life and produces new leaves, which in turn make food and store it in their bases.

Once the bulb is large enough (and the exact size depends on the plant) a flower bud is produced and this grows in the following year.

Corms

Corms are swollen stem bases. Examples are crocus, freesia and gladiolus. The first year's leaves make and then transport food down the stem to form a corm.

This lies dormant until the next growing period, when the terminal bud uses the stored food to grow. The roots then develop and flowers and leaves are produced.

More manufactured food is transported to the bottom of the stem where a new corm is formed on top of the old one, which eventually shrivels. Cormlets (small corms) are also produced. These can be separated from the parent corm and replanted.

Rhizomes

A rhizome is an underground stem which does not necessarily store food. Examples of food-storing rhizomes include iris

MAINTENANCE

Bulbs need moisture so they can elongate rapidly during their short growing season.

Keep the area where they are planted well mulched with leaves, leaf mould or garden compost. Or you can use a mulch of coir, bark or coco shells. Top the mulch up when the bulbs are dormant.

Resist the temptation to tidy up foliage by tying it off. The foliage is only present for a short time and has to manufacture food for storage underground.

The plant needs this food to send up next year's leaves and flowers.

Bulbs grown in lawns must be left until the foliage has yellowed before mowing.

You can help the leaves manufacture the maximum amount of food by applying a fertilizer. Spread or water on a general purpose fertilizer, or, better still, bone meal or another high phosphorus fertilizer. Then you will have a beautiful display, year after year.

The white flowers of Ornithogalum nutans (above) grow from bulbs.

At near left is a bulb, then two tubers, three corms and two more tubers (right).

Bulbils (mini-bulbs) grow from the stems of lilies and the onion family (top).

and arum. The leaves manufacture food which is transported to the rhizome and to any lateral buds.

The main rhizome increases in length each year. One or more branches may develop off it and they, too, will grow longer. In spring, food is transferred to aerial shoots which develop into the plant's new leaves and flowers.

Tubers

A tuber is a thickened, fleshy underground root (as in the dahlia) or stem (a potato, for example), which helps the plant survive periods of cold or drought. Many popular plants have tubers, including arum lilies, dahlias and many types of begonias.

Once the plant is dormant, the tubers can be lifted and cut up, with at least one 'eye' or bud on each piece, which is then replanted.

Planting depth

As a rule of thumb, plant bulbs, corms and tubers at least twice as deep as their diameter. Gardening books give detailed information about particular species.

Some plants which are not completely frost-hardy have a better chance of survival if buried deeper than the rule of thumb suggests. Further insulation can be provided by mulching the ground.

Rhizomes are not usually planted as deep as bulbs and

corms. Iris rhizomes are planted very shallowly, with their tops visible on the soil's surface, so that the sun can ripen each year's growth.

What to lift

You only need to dig up (lift) bulbs, corms, rhizomes or tubers if they are not winter-hardy. They should be brought into a frost-free place to ensure survival. The only other time to lift them is when dividing and replanting (see box).

However, garden tulips (but not species tulips) benefit from being lifted and moved to another part of the garden each year, in order to prevent disease problems.

The other situation where you may want to lift bulbs, corms, rhizomes or tubers is where you grow spring and summer bedding plants. When you pull up the spring bedding to make way for the summer plants, the bulb foliage may still be present, or the bulbs may be too near the surface for you to plant above them.

In this situation, you can lift all the bulbs, but you must replant them elsewhere straight away, so that they can complete their growth cycle and die back naturally. Otherwise the bulbs will not receive a top-up of nutrients and next year's flower bud may not form.

Bulbs, corms, rhizomes and tubers are liable to damage and drying out, so try to buy

them as soon as they are delivered, healthy and intact, to the shop or garden centre.

Avoid shrivelled up material (but remember that corms are often very dry and shrivelled). Do not buy very soft, bruised or otherwise damaged material. Also to be avoided are those with shoots or roots.

Replanting

Bulbs, corms, rhizomes and tubers are sold in a dry state for convenience. You can, though, dig up and replant them while they are in leaf, providing that you do not allow the roots to dry out.

In fact, snowdrops are more successfully established 'in the green' – that is, with their leaves on. Specialist nurseries sell these by mail order or you can beg some from friends. Wait until the flowers are over, because the flowers will wilt if you move them and you will not have the pleasure of their display.

Snowdrop bulbs dry out too much indoors, which is why shop-bought bulbs are often unsuccessful. Grape hyacinth

PLANTS FOR DRY SHADE

Name	Type	Flower
Chionodoxa forbesii	Bulb	Spring, blue
Colchicum speciosum (meadow saffron)	Corm	Autumn, pink, purple, white
Corydalis solida	Tuber	Spring, purple
Crocus tommasinianus (crocus)	Corm	Early spring, lilac
Cyclamen hederifolium (cyclamen)	Tuber	Autumn, pink
Eranthis hyemalis (winter aconite)	Tuber	Early spring, yellow
Galanthus nivalis (snowdrop)	Bulb	Early spring, white
Hyacinthoides non-scripta (English bluebell)	Bulb	Late spring, blue
Narcissus pseudonarcissus (wild daffodil)	Bulb	Spring, yellow
Ornithogalum nutans	Bulb	Spring, white
Scilla bifolia (squill)	Bulb	Spring, blue

PLANTS FOR VERY MOIST SOIL IN SHADE

Name	Type	Flower
Nectaroscordum siculum (previously *Allium siculum*)	Bulb	Early summer, purple/green
Camassia leichtlinii (quamash)	Bulb	Early summer, blue
Lilium pardalinum (panther lily)	Bulb	Summer, red/orange
Lilium superbum (swamp lily)	Bulb	Summer, red/orange
Trillium spp.	Rhizome	Spring, various

(*Muscari* spp) bulbs are also prone to drying out so they should be bought soon after being delivered to the shop. These are not often sold 'in the green', but they are so common in gardens that you can probably beg some from a friend.

Growing conditions

Those bulbs, corms, rhizomes and tubers that need full sun require it in order to ripen and produce good growth and flowers the following year. Few will tolerate extremely dry soil, however.

Moisture is necessary to start them into growth and to help elongate the flower stalks of the taller types. You may have noticed how a clump of daffodils produces shorter flower stalks in dry years.

Our spring-flowering bulbs are adapted to grow in woods. They thrive because they complete their growth before the trees begin theirs. The trees are still dormant when the bulbs need moisture. Sun and rain can penetrate to the ground because the trees' leaves are not yet open. By the time the full leaf canopy is out, the ground level show is over.

A garden is less natural. It often has evergreen trees, hedges and shrubs, which are a barrier to sun and rain and are competing for moisture.

Several of our most popular spring flowers grow from bulbs. They include bluebells (left) and daffodils (below left).

Iris rhizomes (opposite bottom) are usually divided and planted out after flowering. They can take a time to become established and often do not flower until the second season.

After lifting in autumn these gladioli corms (below) must be dried out before being stored in a cool, frost-free place.

PLANTS FOR FULL SUN

Name	Type	Flower
Agapanthus (African blue lily)	Tuber	Summer, blue
Allium aflatunense	Bulb	Late spring, pink/purple
Allium moly (golden garlic)	Bulb	Late spring, yellow
Arum spp.	Tuber	Spring, yellow or black
Brodiaea spp.	Bulb	Late spring, blue/violet
Gladiolus	Corm	Summer, various
Hyacinth	Bulb	Spring, various
Iris spp.	Rhizome or bulb	Spring, summer, various
Nerine spp.	Bulb	Autumn, pink
Oxalis spp. (sorrel) (most)	Rhizome or tuber	Late spring, various
Tulipa spp. and hybrids	Bulb	Spring, various

To naturalize bulbs in grass or woods plant them in random groups and singly.

When planting in flower beds, plant them near other plants which will grow up and disguise the bulb foliage when it is dying back. You can also plant them beneath deciduous shrubs and among shrubs with a short flowering season, to brighten up a dull area.

Sources of bulbs

The demand for bulbs, corms, rhizomes and tubers from gardeners has resulted in wild populations of plants being robbed. Although garden hybrids are bred and grown by commercial nurseries, species such as cyclamen, snowdrop and snowflake may not be.

Unfortunately, once dug up from the wild, they are not kept for propagation, but sold. This is happening particularly in Turkey. If possible, buy stock from cultivated plants of endangered species such as cyclamen.

PLANTS TO LIFT BEFORE FROSTS

Name	Type
Agapanthus spp. (hybrids are hardy) (African blue lily)	Tuber
Anomatheca laxa (Lapeirousia)	Corm
Caladium spp. (angel's wings)	Tuber
Chlidanthus fragrans (perfumed fairy lily)	Bulb
Clivia spp. (kaffir lily)	Rhizome
Eucomis spp. (pineapple lily)	Bulb
Freesia spp.	Corm
Gladioli	Corm
Haemanthus spp. (blood lily)	Bulb
Iris orchioides (one of the Juno irises)	Bulb
Sauromatum venosum (voodoo lily)	Tuber
Sparaxis tricolor (harlequin flower)	Corm
Tigridia pavonia (tiger flower)	Bulb
Tritonia spp.	Corm
Watsonia spp. (bugle lily)	Corm
Zantedeschia spp. (arum lily)	Tuber

Make sure that the soil in which you plant the bulbs will be moist (but well-drained) at the critical growing time.

You may have to add garden compost to the planting area to increase moisture retention. Water the area well in order to encourage growth.

Many bulbs, corms, rhizomes and tubers, such as anemones, can be started off by soaking them before planting. If you soak the ground, too, they will have a good chance of becoming established.

Plant bulbs in clumps for a splash of colour, or plant them in drifts to flower through other plants or between rocks.

WHEN TO PLANT

Spring: summer-flowering bulbs.

Early autumn: madonna lilies, colchicums, autumn-flowering crocus, daffodils, winter aconites and snowdrops.

Late autumn: tulips.

CLIMBERS AND CREEPERS

A climbing plant can do far more than just scale a wall. It is equally at home trailing from a tub, cascading over a bank or softening the outline of a garden ornament or statue.

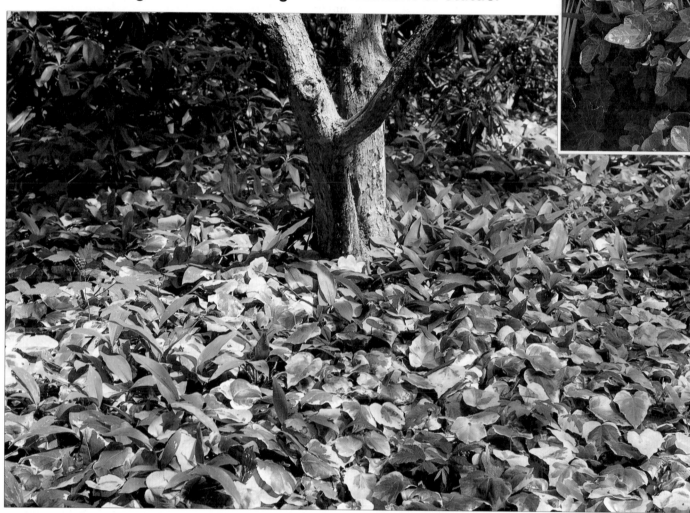

Climbers are most commonly used to festoon trellises and pergolas with glorious summer flowers, or to embroider walls with leaves that develop rich autumn tints. Yet they can also play other exciting roles in a garden, if you don't think of them simply as 'climbers'.

In the wild, these plants sprawl and scale their way through life, greedily taking advantage of whatever support is available. In the garden, however, climbers are usually provided with a support that both enables them to climb and contains their desire to wander further.

Spreading creepers

When a garden climber is not given support, it will either creep in search of something to climb up or will develop a sprawling and bushy nature. Some climbers, especially ivies, are quite happy to creep along the ground while those with a woody nature usually spread outwards.

Climbers without supports have an unruly nature but they can be trained and used in many different ways, including carpeting an area under a tree, brightening a steep bank or clothing an unsightly tree stump.

Tubs and troughs

When grown in large tubs, climbers are free to trail and cascade, but not to spread or

Cloak a bank in a dense blanket of Persian ivy (above), which will spread on the ground to create a carpet of variegated colour. This Hedera colchica 'Dentata Variegata' has glossy green leaves with golden tinged edges.

Common ivy has been used to frame this statue (above right). Naturally it will creep horizontally and when something crosses its path, it will climb.

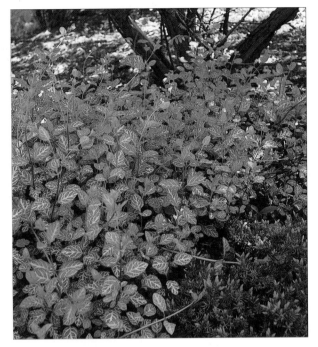

talis) at the tub's base, so that the blue or violet-blue flowers of the clematis grow down through the small, green leaves of the cotoneaster.

The orange-peel clematis (*C. orientalis*) should be planted in a large tub and the stems should be allowed to sprawl and cascade into nearby plants. It creates a spectacle of yellow, scented, bell-shaped flowers during late summer and early autumn. *Clematis tangutica* is similar, and also at its best when spreading into other plants.

Japanese honeysuckle

Japanese honeysuckle, *Lonicera japonica* 'Aureoreticulata', is eye-catching in any container, with its variegated green leaves with bright yellow veins and fragrant pale yellow flowers. Unfortunately, this evergreen plant is not suitable for extremely cold gardens.

On a smaller scale, trailing and sprawling annuals are superb for softening the silhouettes of troughs and window boxes. There are many trailing forms of climbing and upright annuals, including nasturtiums, lobelias, and begonias. These can be raised

wander unduly.

Few climbers are more suited to this than Chinese clematis, *C. macropetala,* which normally grows to 3m/10ft when climbing up a trellis. In a tub, where its height is restricted to about 1.2m/4ft, its trailing stems will spread around the base of the container, softening the outline. The nodding, violet-blue, early summer flowers are followed by fluffy seed heads. The variety 'Markham's Pink' (also known as 'Markhamii') is less vigorous and ideal both in smaller tubs and for trailing over low walls.

Terracotta jars

Tall terracotta 'olive' jars are particularly suitable for growing clematis, enabling the plant's stems to trail freely and producing a very attractive display. Because clematis generally likes to have cool roots, position your container with an easterly or westerly aspect rather than one facing directly south.

The types of clematis best suited for containers are those with a cascading nature and a mass of stems. *Clematis alpina* is suitable but can look sparse unless grown with another plant. Try growing fish bone cotoneaster (*C. horizon-*

Honeysuckle may seem an unusual choice for ground cover but it creeps along horizontally just as well as it climbs. Lonicera japonica 'Aureoreticulata' (above) is an evergreen variety.

If you plant a small growing clematis such as C. macropetala 'Maidwell Hall' (left) in a big stone jar and give it no support it will soon cascade over the side.

With its attractive herringbone shape and year-round display of colour, Cotoneaster horizontalis (left) provides a particularly effective covering for bare walls or banks. In early summer small pink flowers appear, followed by the characteristic rich profusion of bright scarlet berries. In late autumn the glossy dark green leaves turn a warm and glowing red. If you site this climber against a shady, sheltered wall, it can grow up to 2.5m/8ft high.

each year from seeds. If you have troughs on high walls or along the tops of flat-roofed garages or porches, these plants are a must. They will unify your display and hide the containers.

Cloaking walls

Low walls around front gardens can be stark and featureless unless partly covered with a few plants. Flowering shrubs that can be pruned to shape, such as forsythia and bridal wreath (*Spiraea × arguta*), are ideal for softening the outlines of garden gates, but low walls benefit most from cascading and trailing plants. The variegated greater periwinkle, *Vinca major* 'Variegata' (sometimes sold as 'Elegantissima'), has a vigorous sprawling and trailing habit that enables it to clamber over low walls, but for a more dominant yet still cascading nature the deciduous fishbone cotoneaster, *C. horizontalis,* is better. Although not classified as a climber it has a cloaking nature, spreading horizontally or vertically.

Garden steps can be improved in appearance by planting sprawling climbers at their sides. Common ivy (*Hedera helix*) is the easiest form to grow and forms a dense carpet of evergreen leaves and is suitable even if the area is heavily shaded. If your steps are in a sunny spot, however, you have far wider more colourful choices.

Variegated ivies are bright and include the Persian ivy (*Hedera colchica* 'Dentata Variegata'). If you have steps which pass through an arch as they connect two levels of the garden, this ivy will soon clothe the entire feature with green leaves edged creamy-yellow and with white overtones. The Canary island ivy (*Hedera canariensis* 'Gloire de Marengo') is also very attractive, with leaves variegated silvery-grey, creamy-white and green.

Ground cover clematis

Several clematis varieties are ideal for cloaking the ground, especially *Clematis × jouiniana* 'Praecox', a shrubby

Common ivy, Hedera helix (right), is one of the most useful climbing plants and can easily be grown as either a creeper or a bush. The young runners have aerial roots along the stem and will attach themselves to any surface you give them. When the runner reaches the top and cannot grow upwards any further, it will begin to form a bush with yellow-green flowers and black berries.

Ivies make wonderful ground cover and do an excellent job of filling in gaps and softening the appearance of straight edges. A sunny flower bed with plenty of light provides the perfect spot for the variegated 'Goldheart' (below), one of the many varieties of Hedera helix. Dark green ivies, on the other hand, will grow quite happily in dark areas of the garden.

climber with azure-blue flowers in late summer. Others include *C. tangutica,* one of the prettiest of the yellow-flowered clematis, which has brightly-coloured, lantern-like flowers from midsummer to early autumn, followed by fluffy silver heads, and *C. flammula* which bears white, fragrant flowers from late summer to autumn.

Highlighting statues

Positioning statues and ornaments in a garden is an art and one that should not be rushed. Large ornaments need to be seen from a distance, whereas small and delicate ones can create a surprise in a small garden, perhaps becoming apparent only after turning a corner.

Small statues can be enhanced by creating sympathetically coloured backgrounds.

Hedera helix 'Buttercup' (above) has light green leaves which turn a beautiful rich yellow in full sunlight. It is resistant to frost and makes an eyecatching splash of colour against a plain wall or among other evergreens.

The Japanese crimson glory vine, Vitis coignetiae (below), is a magnificent ornamental creeper. In the autumn its large green leaves turn all colours from yellow through orange and red to purple and crimson.

CLOAKING TREE STUMPS

Cloak an old tree stump in a climber. Here are a few from which to choose:
● Persian ivy (*Hedera colchica* 'Paddy's Pride') is evergreen with large leaves.
● Canary island ivy (*Hedera canariensis* 'Azorica') is a vigorous evergreen.
● Japanese climbing hydrangea (*Hydrangea petiolaris*) is deciduous.
● *Clematis viticella* is excellent for trunks over 60cm/2ft high.

BRIGHT IDEAS

1-4ft high, then plant a climber to cloak it and turn it into a pretty feature.

Do not plant the climber too close to the stump, as the soil around the trunk will be impoverished and dry. A planting distance of 45-60cm/1½-2ft is about right.

As well as climbers, many roses are superb for smothering tree stumps with summer flowers. 'Aloha', for example, is a modern shrub rose with fragrant, double, rose-pink flowers. It will grow to a maximum height of 1.5-2.1m/5-7ft. 'Juno' is a centifolia type bearing large, blush-pink fragrant flowers, while 'La Ville de Bruxelles' is a damask rose with large, rich pink and very fragrant flowers. Both of these varieties grow to a maximum height of 1.5-1.8m/5-6ft.

Bank and walls

If your garden has a steep bank, you may find it difficult to cultivate. The soil is probably prone to being washed away by summer storms and, even if grassed over, you may find it awkward to mow. A

For instance, bright white statues can be too dominant amidst green plants, but when cloistered with a light-coloured background, and a white-flowered climber tumbling from a wall, they can create an aura of peace and tranquility.

Weathered statues are ideal when positioned against dark green plants such as yew. Alternatively, position them to be highlighted by the sky, with trailing plants around the base to soften the edges and to unify it with the surroundings. Do not use bright, variegated plants, as these detract attention from the statue.

Clothing tree stumps

Digging up an old tree stump is laborious. It is a task, however, that can be avoided. Leave the stump where it is, cutting it down to 30cm-1.2m/

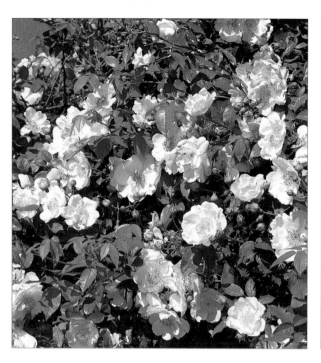

ROSES TO SMOTHER THE GROUND

GROWING TIPS

Many roses are superb as ground-cover, but do not grow them beneath densely-leaved trees or evergreens.
● 'Max Graf' has a spreading and low-growing nature. It rarely grows taller than 30cm/1ft. It has pink apple-scented flowers.
● 'Nozomi' grows to 30cm/1ft high and has a 1.5/5ft spread. It bears small, pink and white flowers.
● 'Snow Carpet' grows about 30cm/1ft high and has a 90cm/3ft spread. It has double, snow-white flowers.

If you're looking for ground cover but perfer the idea of fresh summer blooms to an ivy or vine, then a ground-sprawling rose could fit the bill. The delicate blush-pink flowers of 'Scintillation' (above) bring a fairytale feel to the garden while at the same time solving the problem of that awkward-to-mow area. Rambling and climber roses are not difficult to grow. Several species are so vigorous and thickly-flowering you can use them together with ivy or a vine to grow up the walls of your house.

sprawling or creeping climber could be the answer to your problem. A ground-sprawling rose, for example, will create a breathtaking feature which is also labour saving.

Roses that happily sprawl over banks and walls include 'Félicité et Perpetué' (creamy flowers with a primrose fragrance), paulii rosea (pink and white centres) and 'Scintillation' (blush-pink).

Old, weathered brick walls, perhaps already rich in shades of red and brown, can be further enriched by training a honeysuckle along the top so

that the colourful clusters of summer flowers cascade at eye height. Plant the honeysuckle on the sunny side of the wall, preferably where the setting sun can light up the flowers during the evening. Fix supporting wires 10-15cm/4-6in from the top of the wall.

Rambling romance

If you have a rambling and informal garden, with perhaps an old brick shed or garage which has partly fallen down, do not write it off. It can probably be turned into a whimsical and unusual feature when

draped with trailers and other plants. Paint the walls white and plant white climbers such as the densely-flowered and extremely vigorous mountain clematis (*C. montana*) to trail and cascade from the top. *Clematis armandii* 'Apple Blosssom' is also spectacular, less densely flowered but with the bonus of attractive leaves. If it is practical, plant your clematis on the opposite side of the wall, so that they appear to cascade over the top. Large areas of white wall tend to dominate the delicately-shaped, blue or violet-blue flowers of *Clematis alpina* 'Frances Rivis', so it is best to plant this variety against a grey background.

Long stretches of wooden fencing, especially when ageing, can be dull and uninteresting. Grow the vigorous climber 'mile-a-minute' vine (*Polygonum baldschuanicum*) to create a cascade of frothy, white flowers from the top of the fence from mid summer to

PERFECT PARTNERS

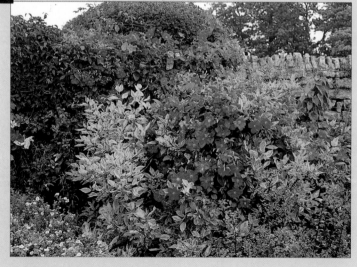

A swathe of clematis falling over a stone wall provides bright summer colour, set off by the *Cornus alba* 'Spaethii', commonly known as dogwood, planted in the bed at the foot. This attractive shrub with its golden variegated leaves gives support to the clematis in summer. In winter, its brilliant red bark stands out against the grey stone.

autumn. It is so vigorous – up to 3.6m/12ft of growth each year – that it can be planted at one end and allowed to scramble right along the length of the wooden fence.

Brightening hedges

Hedges that have become old and perhaps unsightly can be brightened by allowing the mountain clematis (*C. montana*) to sprawl over it. The white flowers, about 5cm/2in across, appear during spring.

Vigorous climbers can also look spectacular when clambering up the trunk and through the branches of a deciduous tree. Choose a climbing rose such as 'Cécile Brunner' with its thimble-sized, shell-pink, slightly scented blooms, or 'François Juranville', whose glowing pink flowers are tinted with gold and are gloriously apple-scented. The Japanese glory vine (*Vitis coignetiae*) has large leaves that turn rich shades of orange, red, yellow and purple in autumn.

Honeysuckle (above), or woodbine as it is sometimes known, is one of our best-loved wild plants. In summer it bears pale yellow flowers tinged with purple-red, followed by bright red berries.

Rambling and climbing roses come in all shades and, trained over a pergola or tree (above right), will smother the bare wood in a frothy cascade of sweet-scented flowers to give your garden a delightful touch of old-world charm.

Quick-growing and easy to cultivate, clematis is one of the most popular climbers. A luxuriant fall of the spring-flowering Clematis montana *var.* rubens *(right), transforms a featureless strip of plain board fencing into a mass of pale pink stars.*

Gardening on a small scale need not be a restriction. With the ingenious use of containers, many harmonious effects can be achieved in the minimum of space.

CHAPTER TWO
Container Gardening

HANGING BASKETS

Create a lovely visual effect with a beautiful basket that can be hung wherever you need a splash of summer colour. You can buy ready-planted baskets from a garden centre, but it is much more fun to plant your own.

anging baskets can be used to brighten up a bare wall, giving a view of flowers and foliage from windows that would otherwise face only bricks. They can make a 'garden' on the side of a house or dreary back yard where there is no room to grow any plants at ground level.

Hanging baskets can be suspended from a pergola to give a floral walkway down a garden path or across a patio. They are especially good in this instance, to add summer colour when the climbers grown on the pergola flower early or late in the season and have little to offer except foliage in high summer.

What sort of basket?

Traditionally, hanging baskets were made from galvanized wire and would be lined with sphagnum moss. Nowadays black polythene is often used instead of, or together with, the moss. The major advantage in using moss is that it is more attractive than black plastic.

A third alternative is to buy ready-made moulded liners of compressed peat and fibre which can be placed straight into your basket.

The basket itself is usually made from plastic or wire and can either be meshed or solid. The main advantage of mesh baskets, is, of course, that plants can be inserted through the gaps, making a spectacular display. Solid baskets,

Basketworks: enliven a wall clad with green leafy climbers (above) by adding a softly coloured basket arrangement; use a riot of red against pale brickwork (above left); a porch is the perfect place to hang a showpiece basket (left).

PLANTS FOR BASKETS

For the best effect, plant trailers such as ivies around the edge, and slightly taller plants in the centre. Here are some examples of suitable plants:

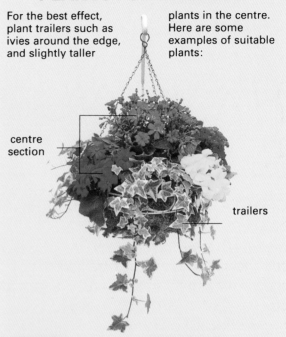

centre section

trailers

CENTRE SECTION

calendula (marigold)
fuchsia (non trailers)
petunia
French marigold
tobacco plant
pansy
begonia
geranium
cineraria
lobelia (non trailers)
dwarf snapdragon
busy Lizzie
coleus
calceolaria

TRAILERS

lobelia (trailing varieties)
small leaved ivies (variegated and non-variegated)
Helichrysum petiolatum (semi-trailer)
ivy-leaved geranium
nasturtium
fuchsia (trailing)
dwarf sweet peas
Verbena hybrida
petunia
mimulus
Campanula fragilis

though slightly easier to plant, are often not quite so effective. The solid plastic versions are like large flower pots and usually have rigid plastic wires and a drip saucer attached to the bottom. Others are made from fibre and resemble heavy-duty versions of

the peat and fibre liners. These will only last for a couple of seasons, but are inexpensive, look natural and are extremely easy to use.

Making an impact

A wide selection of both flowering and foliage plants make much more of an impact than just two or three plants of different varieties.

Conversely, try just one kind of plant in a single colour for a really striking effect. Some of the best plants for this are petunias or fibrous-rooted begonias for a sunny position and busy Lizzies or fuchsias for a shady site.

Plan your baskets with your window boxes or other containers in mind; either match them in colour and texture for a harmonious effect or contrast them completely for an equally attractive and very arresting design. Try matching your baskets to complement their surroundings, picking up

WATERING TIPS

● Put a few lumps of charcoal into the moss base of your basket to keep water fresh.

● Fit an adjustable spray to the end of the hose for fine watering.

● A bamboo cane tied in several places along the end of a hosepipe will keep the pipe rigid, making watering a high container much easier.

LONG-LASTING

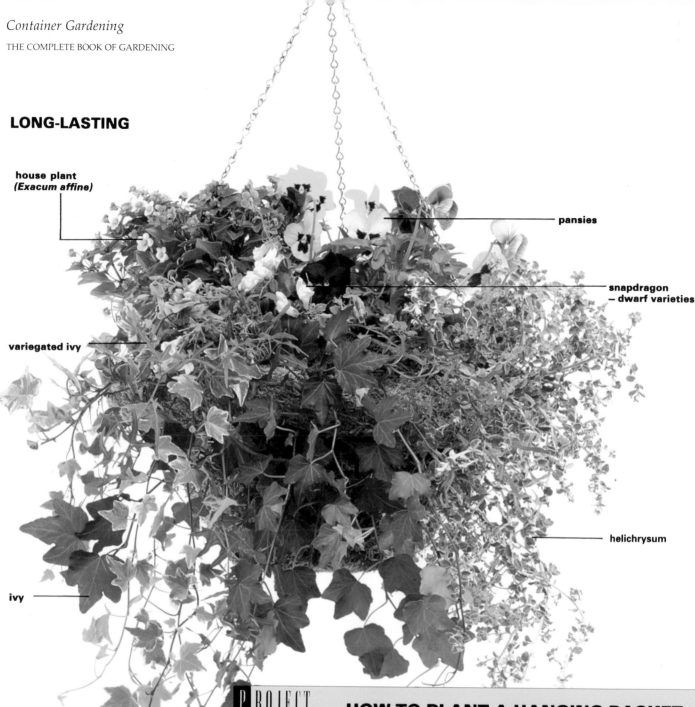

house plant
(*Exacum affine*)

pansies

snapdragon
– dwarf varieties

variegated ivy

helichrysum

ivy

Long-lasting Basket

To fill a basket 25-30cm/10-12in in diameter, you will need approximately four pansies, six ivies (some plain, some variegated), one or two dwarf antirrhinums and three helichrysums.

Choose reasonably mature plants so that you will not have to wait too long for the basket to 'bush out'.

While you are waiting for plants to spread, fill any gaps with small, potted plants that can easily be removed. This *Exacum affine* is really pretty, but tender, so place in an outdoor arrangement only in very mild or sheltered conditions.

This basket will look good all summer long and last well into autumn, until the first frosts.

PROJECT — HOW TO PLANT A HANGING BASKET

Planting Guide

Stand the basket on an upturned pot to help steady it as you work.

The sphagnum moss should be damp; position it with the greenest parts facing outwards.

Before adding special potting compost, you may like to place an old saucer or a circle cut from a plastic bag in the base of the basket as a further aid to moisture retention and a few lumps of charcoal, which helps to prevent water becoming stagnant.

Firm the roots of plants into the compost as you work. When you have finished planting, stand the basket in a large bowl or container of water until it is thoroughly soaked. Soak once a week thereafter, and water daily using a can with a fine rose.

1 *Place basket on a plant pot and line with damp sphagnum moss. Push trailers through sides.*

BOLD AND BRIGHT

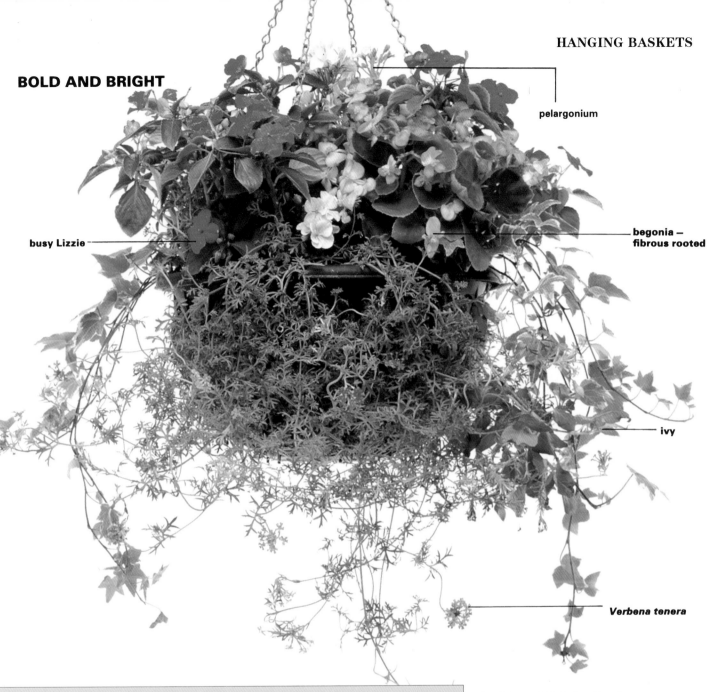

pelargonium

begonia —
fibrous rooted

busy Lizzie

ivy

Verbena tenera

2 Cut a circle of plastic for the base of the basket to aid moisture retention. Arrange the outer rim plants and firm in.

3 Position the central plant, which should stand taller than those surrounding it. Firm in, water the basket and allow to settle and drain before hanging in your chosen location.

Bold and Bright Basket

This basket displays bold and pastel coloured plants in greens and pinks. The two-colour theme makes just as great an impact as baskets with a mass of colours. This selection of plants fills a 25cm/10in basket with a beautiful array of foliage and leaves.

You will need three or four busy Lizzies and the same number of begonias, two small pelargoniums, about six verbenas and three or four ivies.

Arrange the plants on the surface of this basket before putting in their final positions to show off a balanced display.

Plant the verbenas first, ensuring that they are evenly spaced around the basket, their trailing stems poking through the sides. Follow these with the different ivies.

Finish your basket by planting the busy Lizzies, begonias and geraniums which will form a bushy mass of flowers and foliage on top.

on the colour of your garden pots for example.

A basket filled with moist compost and well-developed plants weighs a considerable amount. It must be hung from a very strong support, on chains, from a bracket screwed either to a wall or to the sides of a doorway, or hung from the underside of a porch, balcony, arch or pergola. You will need to use a drill with a masonry bit to plug the wall before screwing anything to it.

Watering ways

Compost in hanging baskets dries out rapidly in hot weather and needs watering once or even twice a day. An effective way of doing this is to take down the basket and stand it in a bowl of water for 15 minutes or so until the compost is thoroughly damp. This will quickly revive a flagging display. You should not do this, however, if the basket is too heavy or it contains trailing plants which could easily be crushed in the process.

There are special devices available which allow baskets to be lowered on a pulley for

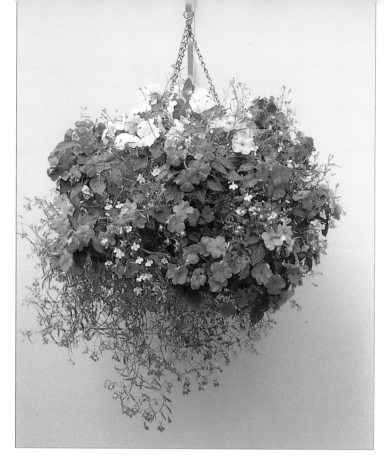

A basket (right) full of lobelia and busy Lizzie in brilliant shades of pink with just a few touches of white makes a most attractive, colour-coordinated display.

Make the most of the smallest of garden spaces with lots of flowering baskets. Creating a theme makes a bold statement, such as here, where trailing basket pelargoniums link prettily with the tub pelargoniums beneath.

easy access. Alternatively, a pump can with a two litre bottle and long tube makes watering easy without lowering, and so does a watering lance fitted on to the end of a garden hose – or try an old washing-up liquid bottle as a cheap option.

Even after heavy bursts of rain baskets may need watering as plant growth may have prevented rain reaching the roots, or house eaves may have kept the rain off all together.

Keep them sweet

When you water your basket, take the opportunity to cut off

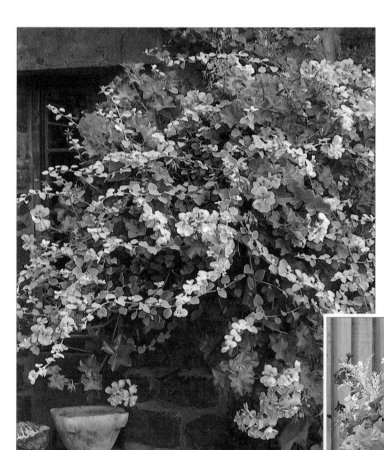

This simple but effective planting scheme uses foliage as much as flowers for its impact. Soft pink trailing pelargoniums and silvery helichrysums show up particularly well against a dark brick wall.

HANGING TIPS

DON'T FORGET!

● Do not hang a basket where it could hit a tall person's head as they pass.

● Avoid areas where drips of water or falling leaves or soil could be a nuisance.

● Wait until all risk of frost is past before hanging out a basket containing tender plants.

● Do not site baskets in exposed places, such as where they could be damaged by wind or rain.

A newly erected fence can look a bit stark while you're waiting for plants to grow up against it. Just the place to have a hanging basket (left), or even two or three.

GOING AWAY?

This short-term measure will keep plants happily watered for a few days at most. If you are on holiday for a longer period, a neighbour will have to 'plant-sit'.

● Take the basket down and put it in a shady spot.

● Fill a bucket with water and stand it either on a shelf or raised on bricks above the basket. Suspend a length of bandage or long strip of capillary matting between the bucket and the basket, which will conduct water to the soil. (A stone or brick will keep the bandage firmly in place.)

the dead heads from flowering plants and, as the season progresses, pinch back any very vigorous plants, such as *Helichrysum petiolatum* or nasturtiums, as they can smother their neighbours if left to grow unchecked.

You may need to remove plants that have died or finished flowering. Rather than leave gaps in the basket, ease some small plants such as fibrous-rooted begonias or violas into the spaces left behind.

Little pests!

Keep a watch out for weeds and remove them at once. You can deter birds from pulling out young plants by pushing a number of short twigs into the compost, then winding black thread, lattice-fashion, around them to create 'netting'.

Aphids (green or black fly)

are the most common pests you are likely to encounter. They must be dealt with quickly otherwise they will soon multiply. To avoid using insecticide, spray the aphids forcefully with soapy water and repeat the treatment as necessary.

Bloomin' beautiful

Colour scheming does not have to be confined to the house. Just as you match the colours of carpets, curtains and cushions, let your imagination flow and indulge your creativity by planting baskets which reflect the colours of your garden. Most small plants which will flourish in a container will grow happily in a hanging basket – so use them to the full.

For something really different try growing fruit or vegetables in a basket. Use dwarf or

mini tomatoes, or Sweetheart strawberries to make a vibrant display of red and green. Make a herb basket and hang it by the kitchen door so that your fresh supply is near at hand. Fill it with parsley, a mix of silver, gold and green thymes, purple and gold sages and other colourful herbs. Add bright nasturtiums and remember the leaves, flowers and seeds are edible.

Hanging baskets need not be banished in autumn and winter. If kept in a sheltered spot, replace summer displays with small leaved variegated ivies or euonymus. Plant early bulbs like crocuses and snowdrops to welcome the spring and replace these later with coloured primroses, pansies, pot-grown hyacinths or dwarf daffodils – to take you into summer.

SHRUBS IN TUBS

If it's a formal look you're after, clipped bay trees by the front door, shaped yew on the patio, and upright conifers on the balcony will add a touch of class to even the smallest garden.

Formal shrubs in tubs do not belong only in grand gardens. They are often at their most effective in relatively modest spaces where they have lots of impact. In a very small town garden, a patio, balcony or roof garden, a few formal container shrubs will add welcome greenery and real character.

Many informal shrubs – those with a loose outline or spreading profile, such as Japanese maples and false castor oil plant – make excellent container shrubs. It is the crisp, geometric outline of formal shrubs, however, that makes them especially useful as focal-point plants or for creating a sense of design and structure in a garden.

Bold statements

You can, of course, grow formal shrubs in the ground, but planted among other shrubs they often lose some of their impact, and you cannot move them around at will, as you can when they are in containers.

You can place these potted shrubs where their very unexpectedness is an attraction – by the front porch, or on a balcony for instance.

Pot panache

The containers, too, make a vital contribution. By raising a shrub off the ground and presenting it in splendid isolation, they actually enhance the plant. As formal shrubs are usually evergreen, and most will be grown for foliage effect, a container that has a bold or intricate design will add another element of interest.

Clay pots (far left), painted to match the front door, make ideal containers for the variegated Aucuba japonica 'Maculata'. The effect is stylish yet unimposing and provides the finishing touch to an enclosed porch.

These bay trees (right) have been trained into tall columns and are being used to frame an unusual arched window. The stylish elegance is reflected in the smart white painted wooden 'Versailles' tubs.

For a less constrained, yet still formal approach, this bay tree has been left to grow naturally. The softer outline complements the country charm of the cottage.

own (which is much cheaper), buy a tall-growing variety. 'Handsworthensis' is a good one, or choose the variegated 'Aureovariegata' for a lighter, more colourful look.

Privet is cheap, tough, and quick-growing – all of which makes it a good one to try if you want to start training your own plants. You will need to clip it frequently as it can become unruly, and it lacks the elegance that some of the more 'classic' plants possess, but a golden privet will bring colour to a dull corner in a way that other traditional green formal shrubs cannot.

Shrubby honeysuckle (*Lonicera nitida*), not to be confused with the climbing group of honeysuckles, is another inexpensive plant that clips well to a formal shape. It is unlikely that these will be available as ready-trained specimens, but they are widely sold as hedging plants, and it is easy to clip them to almost any shape. There is a golden form that is particularly attractive, 'Baggesen's Gold'.

Cutting style
Yew is a favourite topiary plant, but it does not generally do so well as a container plant. You can, however, sometimes buy ready trained container-

For quick and dependable results, keep to widely available, reliable plants to achieve the desired effect.

What to grow
Bay (*Laurus nobilis*) responds well to formal clipping, and is ideal to use in pairs by the front or back door. There is also the bonus of bay leaves for the kitchen – but do not raid the plant too often or you will spoil its shape.

There is just one major drawback with bay; it is not reliably hardy. In mild areas, it will survive most winters unharmed, but it is not a good choice in cold districts, especially as container plants are more vulnerable to frosts.

Box (*Buxus sempervirens*) thrives on formal clipping, and is really tough. You can buy ready-clipped pyramids from good nurseries and garden centres, though you will still have to keep it trimmed.

If you want to train your

It is worth standing a particularly fine specimen of a tender shrub such as this Schefflera arboricola 'Variegata' (above) on the patio for the summer. Keep such plants indoors during the winter months or they will be killed by frosts. A sleek conifer (right) with its tall, narrow shape creates a distinctive focal point near a window or doorway. This easy-to-care-for shrub makes it a practical choice.

grown topiary specimens.

If you want to experiment, and save money at the same time, start with something easy to train like a holly or the winter-flowering bushy evergreen *Viburnum tinus*.

You are unlikely to buy these ready-trained, but if you do not mind waiting a few years, the results will be impressive (hollies in particular can be very slow growing). Both of these plants are widely available in garden centres.

To keep faster growing formal shrubs in shape, clip them with shears as frequently as necessary – this may be as much as several times in one growing season.

Plants with larger leaves

Box (left) is the ideal shrub for clipping and this one has been trimmed into a lovely ball shape. The simplicity of the pot complements the rounded outlines. Similarly, this beautiful bay (right) has been trained into an ellipse and its formal oval outline contrasts well with the easy country charm of a wooden barrel.

Cupressus macrocarpa (below) is an excellent choice as a container shrub. Fast growing and aromatic, it does not require frequent clipping.

The beauty of this Euonymus fortunei 'Emerald and Gold' (left) lies in its delicately patterned foliage. Colourful all year round, it is the perfect addition to a patio, path, balcony or any area that needs brightening up. It can be trimmed into shape using shears if a more formal look is desired.

FIVE FAVOURITES

- Box (*Buxus sempervirens*). Small, leathery, dark green leaves. Variegated varieties available. Easily clipped.

- Bay (*Laurus nobilis*). Large, leathery green leaves. The beauty lies in the formal shaping. Trained specimens are widely available.

- Privet *(ligustrum)*. Try a golden variety for a brighter look. Easily clipped to shape.

- Shrubby honeysuckle *(Lonicera nitida)*. Small green leaves, and quick growth. Easy to train; but requires frequent clipping.

- Yew *(taxus baccata)*. Tolerates close clipping.

should not be clipped with shears, however.

The least expensive choice for a grow-your-own formal container plant is a conifer. Many grow naturally into an attactive oval or cone, without any trimming. Because many are relatively quick-growing, they are also usually inexpensive. You can buy fairly large container-grown specimens for much less than you would pay for other trained evergreens of similar size. They need not be boring either: try golden forms, or those with unusual blue-grey foliage.

Not all conifers do well in containers, however. Some cannot tolerate dry roots, which is a hazard for container plants if you forget to water regularly in dry spells.

Choosing containers

A generous amount of good compost is essential if your shrub is to thrive in a container. Similarly good drainage is a must. Some plastic shrub tubs come with areas of

SHAPING UP

Pencil column

Pyramid shape

'Lollipop'

Oval outline

Buy plants ready-trained for stunning effects. Use shears for small leaved plants and secateurs for larger leaves.

thin plastic that have to be punched out to create drainage holes. Any container which is less than 30cm/12in in diameter is unlikely to be suitable for a tree or shrub; ideally 45cm/18in is the minimum size unless the plant is still very small.

Plastic tubs are practical and inexpensive but generally do not look very imposing.

Imitation stone (sometimes known as reconstituted stone) is very impressive and an ornamental pot or urn, perhaps with some ornate decoration, or standing on a plinth, is just right for a plant such as a formal clipped bay or a neat specimen conifer.

Frost-proof clay or terracotta pots come in wide variety of shapes and sizes and are ideal for shrubs cut into 'lollipops' or similar shapes as their simplicity will enhance rather than detract from the overall effect.

Wooden 'Versailles' tubs, square in shape, are elegant and look especially good containing bay pyramids. Some plastic versions can look very convincing.

Half barrels make ideal shrub tubs. Before you plant anything in them ensure that they have suitable drainage by

POT TRAINING

Q I have had a clipped bay for several years but some of the leaves look brown at the edges.

A The brown leaves are probably the result of winter cold or wind burn if it stands in a windy or exposed position. Move it to a sheltered spot, especially in winter.

Q I have a conifer in a pot and would like to add some seasonal colour. Can I plant something else in the container?

A Try a few small spring-flowering bulbs such as crocuses or grape hyacinths, and a small trailing variegated ivy. Unless the pot is very large, however, summer bedding plants may be deprived of moisture so water daily. Dead-head flowers for a long summer display.

drilling a few large holes in the bottom. You may like to paint them white, maybe with black hoops. These make attractive containers for most formal shrubs.

PROJECT PLANTING A SHRUB

1. Place a thick layer of crocks or large gravel in the bottom of the container to improve drainage, remembering that it must also have drainage holes.
2. Add a good loam-based compost to a depth that will bring the root-ball to within about 5cm/2in of the rim of the container. Don't depend on the garden soil. Container plants use a lot of nutrients and the soil probably won't have enough to feed the plant.
3. Remove the shrub from its container, tease out a few large roots, and trickle compost around until it is level with the top of the root-ball. Water well.

To prevent weeds, sprinkle a layer of gravel around the top.

ALPINE SINK GARDEN

A miniature alpine garden is easy to make and will last for years. Neatly contained, it makes a charming focal point.

All you need for a really individual container garden is a stone trough or an old sink. An alpine sink garden looks good in almost any setting, takes very little time to make and requires the minimum of care and maintenance – just regular watering during the growing season.

First, find your container. Alpine troughs made from reconstituted stone are available from most garden centres, but at a price. Better still (and cheaper), use an old-fashioned porcelain sink. If you are willing to scavenge from derelict houses, factories or even an old hospital, you may be lucky enough to discover a discarded porcelain sink ready for the taking. Such finds, though, are rare. You may be better advised to ask a local builder who renovates old houses to look out for one for you. Junk yards and architectural salvage companies are further possible sources, but they may charge you more.

An 'antique' sink

Giving an old porcelain sink an 'antique stone' finish is a simple process. After scoring the smooth surface by chipping it with a hammer or using an electric drill fitted with a coarse carborundum disk, paint it with a bonding agent. When this is tacky, slap on a mixture of equal parts of sand, cement and peat, building it

up to a layer approximately 1cm/½in thick. Leave the sink for a few days to dry completely, before planting.

The sink will soon take on a weathered appearance, but this can be accelerated by painting it with liquid manure, boiled rice water or natural yoghurt, which encourages the growth of algae and moss.

Site your sink

Once you have found your sink, decide where you want to site it: on the patio, perhaps, under a window or in the corner of your lawn? You should also decide whether you want to leave it as it is or – particularly if it is cracked or chipped

A LANDSCAPE IN MINIATUR[E]

A patio or paved area provides the ideal location for a sink garden

Encourage lichen to grow on the trough, for an 'antique' effect

When selecting the planting positions make sure plants will have enough room to spread

Some plants, like this *Sempervivum grandiflorum*, will grow happily in the compost-filled crevices of rocks

A layer of grit or shingle around the base of the plant looks attractive and is essential to prevent rotting and to conserve moisture

---

PLANTING POINTS

Before and after:
● put your sink or trough in its permanent position before filling
● provide good drainage to stop rotting
● be prepared to water frequently in summer
● choose plants carefully (see list)
● do not cram in too many plants – give them growing space
● feed plants regularly with fertilizer in the growing season
● never fertilize in bright sunlight or on dry soil
● use good quality soil or John Innes No. 2 potting compost

DON'T FORGET!

A sink garden provides you with the ideal opportunity to exercise your creativity. Here (above) a wonderful selection of dainty alpines, dwarf conifers and succulent, fleshy plants have been carefully selected to flourish on and around a few well-chosen rocks. The resulting effect is one of a harmonious landscape in miniature.

– whether you wish to 'antique' the outside to resemble an old stone trough. Move the sink to its permanent position now as it will be too heavy to move once it is filled with compost.

Good drainage, the correct soil or compost mixture and carefully chosen plants are the most vital considerations. If you begin with the best ingredients you will keep your sink garden looking happy and

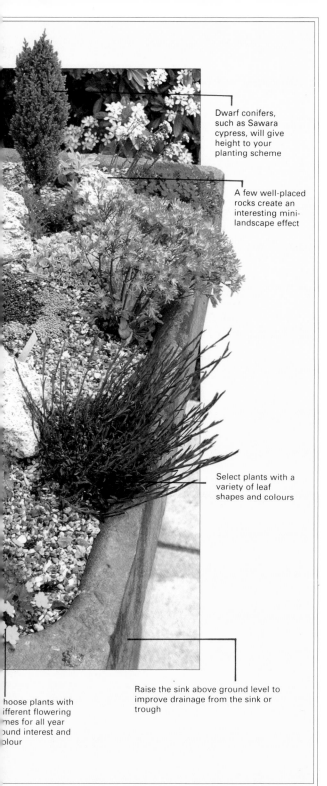

Dwarf conifers, such as Sawara cypress, will give height to your planting scheme

A few well-placed rocks create an interesting mini-landscape effect

Select plants with a variety of leaf shapes and colours

Raise the sink above ground level to improve drainage from the sink or trough

Choose plants with different flowering times for all year round interest and colour

Instead of selecting lots of different plants to fill your trough garden, select just one variety for a stunning and full effect. The dazzling white saxifrage (right) 'Tumbling Waters' cascades gracefully over the edge of the trough softening the edges as it grows. This plant thrives in a well-drained trough but the roots must not be allowed to dry out. Water daily, if necessary, in dry conditions.

the hole with a piece of folded small-meshed netting.)

Put a layer of coarse gravel or broken clay pots (crocks) in the bottom, to a depth of at least 2.5cm/1in. Cover this with a 5cm/2in layer of well-rotted garden compost or composted tree bark.

Compact compost

Fill the sink to within 6mm/½in of the rim with good quality soil or John Innes No 2 potting compost. Create a slight mound in the centre to prevent the soil from 'dipping' when it is first watered and

to improve drainage.

For the best results, buy compost from a garden centre or nursery. Most garden soil does not contain enough nutrients to keep container-grown plants happy and healthy. Garden soil has a different texture too and is also more likely to set in a solid lump after it has received a good soaking.

As you put the compost into the sink, press it down fairly firmly. This will allow the plants' roots to become firmly anchored and also ensures the compost level will not settle

healthy for many years.

Drainage is very important: container plants need frequent watering but if water cannot drain away, your plants will soon become waterlogged. To prevent this, first stand your sink or trough on a stable base of bricks or blocks.

If you are using a sink, cut away the wastepipe but leave the strainer over the plug hole. (If the plug is missing, cover

Troughs come in all shapes and sizes and this oval one (right) has been sunk into a border. Here, several different varieties of the same plant have been chosen in complementary colours.

Sempervivums come in deep, dark red and fresh, bright green. Some types display contrasting colours on the tips of their succulent leaves.

A profusion of piercing blue contrasts splendidly with the stark grey rocks and gravel (left). Spring gentian (Gentiana verna) loves the environment created by a sink garden, as long as it is well drained. The dainty flowers emerge in early spring, their five petals are joined to a white, tubular neck and are borne on short upright stems.

too much after watering.

Before planting up, lay your chosen plants on the surface and rearrange them until you are happy with the total look of your miniature garden. Attention to height and colour is particularly important with such a small area to design. Do not be tempted to cram in too many plants or they will not have space to settle and spread.

Large rocky stones, specially for alpine gardens, can be bought from garden centres. Called 'tufa', it is a porous limestone on which many alpine plants can thrive. Try to create a natural effect with the stones sloping gently and most of the undersides buried in the compost.

Once you have planted up the sink, cover the exposed soil between the alpines with a 6mm/½in layer of gravel, small pebbles or fine shingle. This is not only attractive but helps to stop the container from drying out too quickly. It also keeps the plants' leaves away from the damp soil which prevents them rotting. Water in well after planting.

After a while – it could be months or years – you may decide you have not achieved the desired effect. Do not despair; it is easy to replace individual

WHICH PLANTS?

Here are a dozen rockery perennials which are ideal for sink gardens. Make your own selection, contrasting shape, colour and foliage.

- common houseleek *(Sempervivum tectorum)* — rosette-shaped succulent with rosy-purple flowers. Evergreen perennial
- stonecrop *(Sedum spathulifolium)* — low-growing evergreen with grey-green leaf rosettes that form dense mats; yellow flowers
- stonecrop *(S. spurium)* — creeping evergreen with mid-green leaves and red stems; pink, white or red flowers
- aubrieta *(Aubrieta deltoidea)* — spreading, mat-forming plant with crimson, purple or pink flowers; can be invasive
- glory of the snow *(Chionodoxa lucilae)* — spring-flowering bulb with narrow leaves and sprays of blue and white flowers
- saxifrage *(Saxifraga species)* — low-growing plant forming compact hummocks; red, pink, white, yellow or purple flowers
- rock phlox *(Phlox douglasii)* — carpeting semi-evergreen with white, pink or lavender starry flowers and oval leaves
- spring gentian *(Gentiana verna* 'Angulosa') — lime-loving plant forming tufts of spiky leaves with bright blue flowers
- rock pink *(Dianthus* 'La Bourbille') — dwarf cousins of the border pink, hardy, with showy pink flowers
- Sawara cypress *(Chamaecyparis pisifera* 'Nana Aureovariegata') — dwarf conical evergreen with a golden sheen
- Lawson's cypress *(C. lawsoniana* 'Minima Aurea') — dwarf rounded evergreen
- common juniper *(Juniperus communis* 'Compressa') — dwarf juniper with needle-like aromatic leaves

PROJECT   **PLANTING**

1 *Place a 2.5cm/1in layer of crocks in the bottom of the trough to help drainage. Add John Innes No. 2 compost.*

2 *Fill to within 6mm/½in of the ri. Press compost down firmly to prevent it settling when watere and to give plants a good anchorage.*

5 *Arrange the plant pots before planting to make the most of colour, height and texture.*

6 *Remove each plant from its container, tease out the root bal gently and set in position.*

plants or even to start again from scratch. Slow-growing plants, for instance, may eventually become too large for your sink. Choose carefully, as many plants will last for as much as five years or longer.

Bit of a boost

When replacing individual plants, remove as much soil as possible without disturbing the other plants and replace it with fresh soil or compost, to give the whole container a boost. This technique is known as top dressing. If you are re-planting completely after some years, replace all the compost to give new plants the best possible chance.

All container-grown plants need generous feeding as the nutrients in the compost can become exhausted after only a few months. As a general rule, feed fortnightly with a balanced liquid fertilizer during the growing season. Always apply fertilizer after watering and never feed plants in hot sun as they may scorch.

During a hot summer you may need to water your sink garden once or even twice a day. The compost should never be allowed to dry out completely and always give enough water to soak right through to the container's base.

ALPINE SINK GARDEN

3 Arrange attractive stones or special alpine rocks, positioning them carefully to create maximum impact.

4 Plants which require good drainage should be set at the edges of the sink, where water drains well.

7 Cover all the exposed soil with gravel, small pebbles or fine shingle to a depth of 6mm/½ in.

8 Give the sink a thorough soaking using a watering can with a fine rose. Regular watering is vital.

CRAFTY CONTRASTS

A miniature garden like this is the perfect outlet for your creativity. A few well placed pebbles will enhance the shape, texture and colour of the plants.

Look for seaside treasures the next time you visit the beach. Shells and driftwood can provide a lovely contrast to delicate little alpine flowers.

This stonecrop, Sedum spathulifolium (above), is a carpeter which has rosettes of succulent silvery-green leaves. Small clusters of yellow star-shaped flowers appear intermittently creating an interesting mottled effect.

Saxifraga moschata (below) forms a neat hummock of olive green, spiky rosettes. Graceful flowers in all shades of pink sit on elegant red stems.

TOMATOES

The humble tomato is one of the most decorative of edible plants and can be grown in any small, sunny corner of the garden – even in hanging baskets or on a windowsill.

A tub full of tomatoes will be a really tasty attraction in your garden. Not only will this 'Totem' bush tomato (left) provide you with plenty of fruit, it will also add a splash of colour to the patio.

Tumbling varieties of tomato are ideal for growing in a hanging basket. The ruby red fruit of this 'Tornado' (below) stand out against the deep green leaves. Keep hanging baskets well watered to ensure a good crop.

G rowing your own tomatoes is not only economical and fun – they taste better, too. Fruits that have ripened on the plant have a far better flavour than those picked half ripe to survive the long journey from producer to consumer. By growing your own, you can also cut down – or cut out – chemical fertilizers and pesticides and choose organic alternatives instead.

You can grow yellow tomatoes, striped tomatoes, strings of tiny redcurrant tomatoes as well as the more familiar cherry, beefsteak and common round ones. There are low tumbling varieties that grow happily in hanging baskets, tubs or growing bags on the patio: bush varieties, ideal for a sunny corner of the garden surrounded by flowers; and dwarf varieties to grow as pot plants on a window sill.

Making a start

When you buy tomato plants from a garden centre or nursery, choose healthy looking ones with deep green leaves, and check carefully for signs of greenfly and whitefly. Reject any with blueish leaves – a sure sign they have been kept too cold – or dead, yellow or broken leaves.

For growing out of doors, do not attempt to plant before the end of spring when there will be risk of frost. Even low temperatures can retard growth and delay the crop, so ideally you should wait until summer which is the best planting time for most areas. If you have bought plants earlier, keep them indoors on a sunny window-sill and water with a weak liquid tomato feed.

Tomatoes from seed

Many people prefer to grow their own tomato plants from seed which takes around nine weeks from sowing to planting out. Seed gives you a bigger choice of varieties, as garden centres stock only the most popular plant varieties. The drawback is that, without the right conditions, you will get poor results. Tomato seedlings need lots of light and constant heat to grow well, so a warm, brightly lit window-sill is essential, as is central heating that does not go off at night.

Sow seed at the beginning of spring. Fill a pot loosely with good seed compost, and flatten it slightly with the base of another pot. Scatter the seeds so they are evenly distributed over the surface. Then sprinkle a little vermiculite over the top, just to cover the seeds. (Vermiculite is a mineral which aids rooting).

Water by standing the pot in a bowl of tepid water till the vermiculite becomes damp. It will darken in colour. Lift the pot to drain out excess water,

Tomatoes make an ideal addition to a container garden. Taller growing tomatoes will require larger tubs; the half-barrel used here (left) is ideal. Simple cane trellis helps to support the dense foliage which blends in beautifully with the lush background. For the best flavour, wait until the fruit ripens to a deep red before picking.

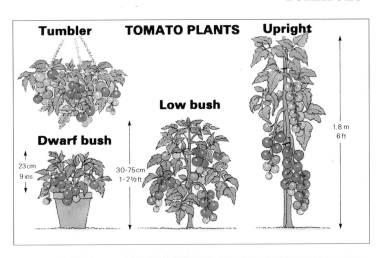

TOMATO PLANTS

Tumbler

Dwarf bush — 23 cm 9 ins

Low bush — 30-75 cm 1-2½ ft

Upright — 1.8 m 6 ft

Grown in a container on a balcony, this variety (right) is called 'Pixie'. It is by nature a tumbler but here it has been trained up canes to form a fan shape. Tender varieties like this 'Florida Petit' (below right) are best grown indoors on a window-sill. It tumbles over the side of the pot in a cascade of fruit.

then stand it in a polythene bag with the top loosely tied. Place on a shelf in the airing cupboard for a few days until the first seedlings appear. As soon as they show, take the pot out of the bag and stand it on a warm window-sill in good light but not strong sun.

Pricking out

When the first pair of leaves open fully and the seedlings are just big enough to handle, gently lift them out with the tip of a pencil, loosening the compost to get the whole root without damaging it. Move each seedling to a pot of its own. Use 9cm/3½in plastic pots loosely filled with fresh seed compost. Make a hole with the point of the pencil, and place the seedling in so its lower leaves rest just above the level of the compost. Firm the compost gently, and water by standing the pots in shallow tepid water until the surface of the compost feels moist. Repeat whenever it starts to dry out (check daily by touching the compost with a finger).

Lots of sunshine

As the seedlings develop, they need more light so gradually increase the amount of sun they get. They should not, though, be exposed to sun during the hottest part of the day.

After they have been in pots for four weeks, start feeding them with liquid tomato feed, following the manufacturer's

RECOMMENDED VARIETIES

- 'Gardener's Delight' is tall and upright, producing red cherry-like fruit with a superb sharp flavour.
- 'Sweet 100' is tall and upright, producing fruit, cherry red in colour with a sweet taste.
- 'Mirabelle', also tall and upright, produces cherry yellow fruit with a superb sweet flavour.
- 'Tigerella', a tall, upright plant, produces medium striped fruit with a very good sharp flavour.
- 'Super Marmande', a tall, upright plant, produces red beefsteak tomatoes.
- 'Golden Sunrise' produces medium yellow fruit on a tall upright plant.
- 'Tornado' is a tumbler with small red fruit.
- 'Pixie' is another tumbler that produces small red tomatoes.
- 'Tumbler', as its name suggests, has a tumbling habit and produces very good red cherry tomatoes.
- 'Alicante', a tall upright plant, has medium red fruit.
- 'Ailsa Craig' is also a tall upright plant with medium red fruit.
- 'Harbinger' is yet another tall upright plant with very good medium red fruit.
- 'Totem' is a low bush with small red fruit.
- 'Outdoor Girl' is a bushy plant with small red tomatoes.
- 'Minibel' is a dwarf bush that produces tiny red fruit.
- 'Mixed ornamental' is a mixture of red and yellow, pear, plum and redcurrant shaped tomatoes that are particularly ornamental as well as being edible.

Beefsteak tomatoes (left) are large, firm and bursting with flavour. This variety, 'Marmande', produces rich red fruits on a tall, upright plant which will need the support of canes. Plant in a sheltered sunny spot for the best crop. When harvesting make sure the leafy green calyx is still attached to the fruit as this ensures the tomatoes remain fresh for a longer period.

Produced on a tall, upright plant this unusual yet delicious variety, 'Golden Sunrise' (left), has a profusion of bright yellow fruit.

The tiny redcurrant tomatoes (below) are particularly ornamental as well as being full of flavour. This variety, 'Yellow Currant', has a translucent quality and the fruits look wonderful in a mixed summer salad.

instructions. When the first bunch of flowers appears and the pot is filled with roots (which you will see though the holes in the bottom), they are ready for planting, providing there is no risk of frost.

Planting out

Whether you buy plants or raise your own from seed, it is important to introduce tomato plants to outdoor temperatures gradually. For two weeks before planting out, stand them outside in a sheltered, sunny spot during the day and bring them in at

Tomatoes come in all shapes, sizes and colours but this stripy variety (left) is one of the most unusual of them all. 'Tigerella' (also known as 'Mr Stripey') is a tall, upright variety which produces medium sized fruit with a particularly good, sharp flavour.

Tall upright varieties need support. Tie the stems to canes as they grow, and nip out any sideshoots (shoots growing where a leaf joins the main stem of the plant) between thumb and forefinger while they are small. Cut off the growing tip of the stem after four bunches of tomatoes have formed on upright varieties. This encourages fast development. Bush tomatoes and tumblers should not have their sideshoots or tips removed, but use a few short sticks to hold the plants up and stop the fruit touching the ground.

Holiday plans

The safest method is to ask a neighbour to pop in daily to feed and water your plants, in return for ripe pickings. For short breaks away, you could buy one of the semi-automatic watering devices now available. These have a reservoir of water from which tubes slowly drip water to each plant. You can improvize this by using an old plastic lemonade bottle with pin holes in the bottom, pushed in next to a plant and filled with water which seeps out very slowly. Both systems need refilling every few days.

Sink pots and hanging baskets into the soil in a sunny part of the garden, and thoroughly soak the surrounding soil with a hosepipe before you go. This should keep plants going for up to a week.

Picking the crop

Tomatoes can be picked and eaten from the time they turn orange, but the flavour develops more if you leave them to night. Wait for a spell of mild weather to plant them out.

Tomatoes need lots of sun and warmth, so choose the most sheltered corner you can for them. Patios are perfect, as the reflected heat from the walls and paving helps create their favourite climate. Tomatoes in hanging baskets need a place out of the wind. If you grow dwarf varieties on a windowsill pick the sunniest spot available.

Potted tomatoes

Fill your container with a good quality potting or multi-purpose compost. The peat-based kind is perfect for tomatoes – never use garden soil. If using a growing bag, cut the bag open and plant following the maker's instructions.

Water as often as neccesary to keep the compost just moist – not waterlogged, and never bone dry. Water daily in warm weather but in very hot spells, water morning and evening. Feed regularly, too. Use a special liquid tomato feed and follow the manufacturer's directions on the bottle.

PROJECT — BAGS OF TOMATOES

1 *Open the growing bag according to the instruction. Remove the tomato from its pot, being careful not to disturb the rootball.*

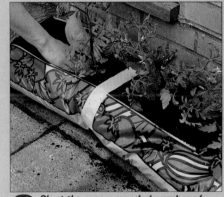

2 *Plant the recommended number of tomato plants and water well. You can grow several different varieties in the same growing bag.*

3 *If you plant tall growing varieties you should insert stakes at this stage. Loosely secure the stems of the plants to the stakes.*

4 *Make sure you water the tomatoes once a day, or more in very warm, dry weather. Feed regularly with a special tomato fertilizer.*

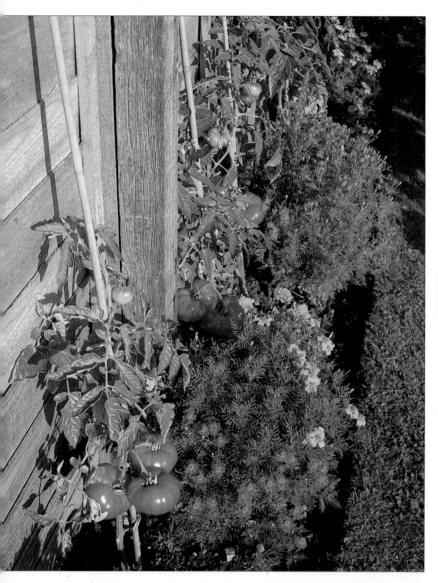

SETTING FRUIT

When growing conditions are not ideal, tomato plants may produce plenty of flowers, but not fruit, or only very tiny fruits which never really develop. This is caused by lack of pollination, and can be a problem with plants grown out of doors, especially when the weather is cold (as it can be in early summer). To avoid this, there are several ways you can encourage fruit to 'set' so that the flowers pollinate and develop fruit. Except in a very bad summer, you will normally only need to assist pollination for the first few weeks when the plants start to flower.

- **create high humidity**: spray plants and flowers with a jet of water on sunny days

- **shake flowers**: tap plants lightly every day with a cane to distribute the pollen

- **set spray**: spray flowers with a special spray, available from garden centres. The resulting tomatoes will have no seeds, but this is quite normal

A combination of fruit and flowers can look very pretty especially when the colours complement each other as well as in this border (left). Positioned near a sheltering wall the tomatoes will thrive and produce an abundance of fruit. Surround them with low growing French marigolds in sunny yellow and orange.

are greenfly or whitefly which will suck the sap of plants. Pick them off if you can or, if there are too many, spray them with warm soapy water or with pyrethrum.

Healthy plants resist diseases so ensure you feed them regularly and water daily. If you are vigilant this regime will see off problems like blossom end rot (black spots on fruit), greenback (unripe patches), half ripe fruit, blotchy ripening, wilting and fruit that split on ripening.

ripen fully on the plants. Before picking, wait till they are a good deep red (or deep yellow in the case of yellow-fruited kinds; bright red and orange striped for 'Tigerella').

To pick tomatoes, look for a 'knuckle' – like a bent finger joint – on the stem just above where it joins the tomato. If you put your finger on top of the bend and press it down flat, the fruit will snap cleanly away leaving the green leafy calyx attached to the fruit. Picked this way, tomatoes stay fresh for several days. If you pull them off the plants without the calyx, they wrinkle and go soft very quickly.

Pests and diseases

Look out for tiny green, brown, pink or white insects. These

HARVESTING YOUR CROP

The beauty of growing your own tomatoes is that you can pick them just how you like them. Green tomatoes are excellent for chutney; when ripe but still firm they are delicious in crisp salads; while ripe, soft tomatoes are delicious in soups and sauces.

In a cold summer your crop may not ripen and you will be left with an abundance of green tomatoes. Pick them with the calyx attached and wrap them in tissue paper. Store in a dark place with one or two red tomatoes or an apple. The gas given off by the ripe tomatoes (ethylene) will help the others to ripen more quickly. Check every day and remove the red ones.

WINDOW BOXES

With a little imagination you can improve the look of your place – from inside and out – by adding a window box of flowers or delightful foliage plants.

The most memorable window boxes are those that appear to cascade with colour and detail, with the container so hidden by foliage and flowers that it looks as if the plants are growing in the air.

To achieve this sort of effect you actually need to exercise restraint. When you first plant it the box will look a little sparse – but give it just a few weeks (and some water and fertilizer) and the plants will develop well.

Lobelia, verbena and trailing pelargoniums are some of the best choices for cascades of colour and texture. For height and spread use petunias or pansies. Tiny blue kingfisher daisies (Felicia bergeriana) add a delicate touch to such a scheme with their feathery foliage. Trails of silver-leaved helichrysum or variegated ivy will complete the picture.

Whatever you choose to fill your window box, make sure that the box itself is secure on your window sill. If the sill slopes downwards, place two or three wooden wedges under

Twin white window boxes perfectly set off this arrangement of red, white and pink flowers, amid varying shades of green foliage. This late summer display is dominated by the large red floral clusters of pelargoniums. The ivy will provide year-round interest.

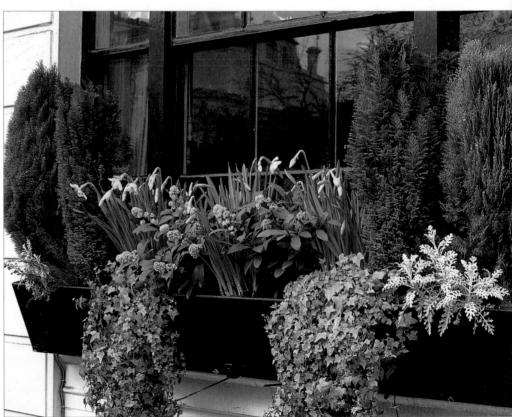

box to prevent it slipping.

If your windows open outwards you will need to fix the window box below the window sill. Fix it at least 30cm/12in lower than the sill, so that tall plants will keep their heads when the window is opened.

Materials

Window boxes are available in a range of sizes and different materials.

Terracotta boxes look very attractive but you must be sure that they are frost-proof if winters are severe in your area. They lose water very quickly, so you must be prepared to check regularly that the soil hasn't dried out: in hot weather this may mean twice a day. They are relatively expensive.

Wooden boxes need to be treated against rot. Choose a wood preservative that will not be harmful to the plants in the box. As an extra precaution, line the sides of the box with plastic to prevent water getting into the wood from the inside.

Plastic window boxes are

Crocuses (above) provide early spring colour. Narcissi (below) produce another dash of spring colour in a box that will have looked good all winter, with its mix of evergreens.

the front of the box, to level it. To be absolutely sure that the box is safe you should fix brackets to the wall on either side and one underneath the sill. Each bracket should protrude across the front of the

WINDOW BOX WATCHPOINTS

● Make sure the window box site is accessible so you can plant and maintain it through the year. Once a window box is planted up it will be too heavy to move.

● If you are working from inside the house, lay down newspaper on the floor inside the window and have ready a rubbish bag for any prunings, dead plants or waste compost.

● Always check that the compost is well watered, especially in summer.

● Feed window box plants with a liquid fertilizer during their flowering seasons.

● If there is no one to water your plants, when you are away, trail a capillary mat from a bucket of water and bury the other end in the compost. Water will be taken up gradually by the plants. Water the box well, so that the matting is drenched.

DON'T FORGET!

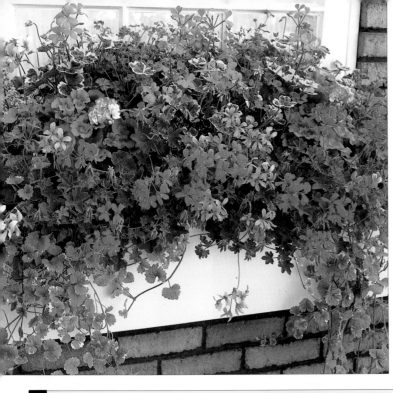

Pink and red pelargoniums in full summer bloom (left) produce a lovely mound of eye-catching colour. Like all such arrangements, they look their best when set off by a neatly painted window box – white is always a good choice. A regular wash or a wipe with a cloth will keep the box and the window frames looking good.

probably the best buy for all-year use. Modern plastics are durable – they don't crack in sunshine and are frost-proof. Once again you must keep an eye on the plants and water them frequently. Drainage holes are usually marked on the base of the box, but you will have to open them using a hand drill. Drip trays are usually bought separately. They hold excess moisture and stop water draining down over your window ledge.

Window box maintenance
To make your window box plants perform well, *you* have to do a bit of work. In the

PROJECT

PLANTING A SPRING BOX
Choose from your favourite spring flowers and create a winter-into-spring window box plan (right).

1 *Drainage is important, otherwise plants will rot. If you are using a container without drainage holes, such as a plastic trough, bore holes in the base of it.*

2 *Add a layer of crocks to the bottom of your window box to improve drainage. Broken flowerpots are ideal. Since water passes quickly through them, plants will not be sitting in a pool of stagnant water. Crocks also prevent compost from blocking the drainage holes.*

3 *On top of the crocks add a loamy, soil-based compost. If your window box has no drainage holes, a bulb compost, designed for such situations, can be mixed in with the main compost. For the best results, window boxes should be re-filled each year with fresh compost.*

4 *Before planting up, remove any dead or dying leaves from your plants. Plant ivies in the front of the box to provide different shades and textures of green in winter and daffodils behind for early spring flowering. Water the box well.*

WINDOW BOX THEMES

● **Herb box**: Upright rosemary, sage, thyme and salad burnet offer a good range of colour, shape and flowers.
● **Salad box 1**: 'Tom Thumb' lettuce, clumps of chives and 'Pixie' tomatoes will provide shape, colour and produce.
● **Salad box 2**: Sow cut-and-come-again red and green lettuce in the front of the box and 'Pixie' tomatoes at the back.
● **Spring box**: Plant *Alyssum saxatile* in front to trail over the edge of the box; grape hyacinth bulbs in the next row and dwarf tulips such as *Tulipa greigii* hybrids at the back of the window box.
● **Cascade box**: Trailing fuchsias, ivy-leaved pelargoniums, variegated ground ivy, verbena and trailing lobelia.
● **Up-and-down-box**: For a cascade combined with an upright effect, grow 'Knee-Hi' sweet peas at the back of the box with trailing ivy-leaved pelargoniums in the middle of the box. For trailing foliage use ivy.

ground a plant's roots search for water and food, but in a container the amount of water and nutrient in the soil depends on you. You need to replenish the water constantly, particularly in very hot weather and if the window box is in full sun all day.

Nutrients must be given fairly often. Give your plants a good start by setting them into a loamy, soil-based compost such as John Innes No 2. Peat composts dry out very quickly and have little nutrient material in them. During the growing and flowering season water the box with a liquid fertilizer every fortnight.

When you are planting up the box place a layer of stones or terracotta crocks in the base to improve drainage. The deeper your box, the taller and larger the plants you can grow

in it. For best effects, and if your window sill will hold it, a box 90cm/3ft long x 22cm/9in deep x 25cm/10in wide, is a good size to work with.

A choice of plants

There is a huge variety of plants that you can choose for window box planting schemes. Obviously you can't grow every garden plant in a window box, but you can have a good deal of creative fun choosing the style, colour scheme and shape that your window box collection will have.

With window box gardens you can dress your windows throughout the year with sea-

If your walls are covered with ivy or Virginia creeper, these plants will provide the ideal backdrop for a bright display in a window box. Pink and white petunias have been used (above) to good effect.

A single-colour theme, using various plants, can be very striking. Taking yellow as the theme, this window box (below) has been planted with chrysanthemums, broom (Cytisus) and variegated ivy. Other single-colour arrangements can be equally effective.

sonal favourites that can be removed when they are past their best, replacing them with choice flowers and plants from the following season.

For a permanent framework use evergreen foliage plants and conifers. Variegated ivy, available in a wide range of creamy white and yellow-green combinations, will provide trailing swags of background colour. The ivy trails will also soften and diguise the look of the window box.

Euonymus fortunei 'Emerald Gaiety', an evergreen, upright and bushy shrub, offers cream and green foliage that takes on a rosy tint in autumn. Dwarf conifers come in a range

POSSIBLE PROBLEMS

● Brown or shrivelled leaves are signs of lack of water or of wind burn in winter. In winter, water only sparingly, as the compost will not dry out so quickly.
● Aphids can cause trouble. Spray the plants with soapy water from time to time when you see signs of insect damage.

of silver, grey and golden colours. They add height and shape to a display.

Brightening it up

In between these framework plants you can add winter and spring colour by planting winter-flowering pansies and spring-flowering bulbs and primulas. When the bulbs and spring flowers are finished, remove them and add your favourite summer bedding plants. With such a planting scheme your box always has a basic shape and height, with bright colours each season.

A herb garden in a window box is both useful and attractive. It can be planted up (right) with such herbs as mint, parsley, chives and fennel. Nasturtiums and violas will add colour, while mint and chives can be left to flower.

PLANTS FOR WINDOW BOXES

Flower	Colours	Height	Season
Crocus	yellow, purple cream	8cm/3in	spring
Grape hyacinth (Muscari)	blue, white	18cm/7in	spring
Heathers (Erica carnea)	purple, pink, white	25cm/10in	winter
Pansies	mixed colours	15-20cm/6-8in	summer or winter
Swan river daisy	blue	20-25cm/8-10in	summer/autumn
Busy Lizzie (Impatiens)	red, pinks, striped	15-25cm/6-10in	summer
Tulipa greigii	red, yellow, cream	25cm/10in	late spring
Petunias (dwarf varieties)	pastels, deep reds, blues, doubles	20-30cm/8-12in	summer/autumn
Wallflowers (dwarf varieties)	yellows, orange, dark red	30cm/12in	spring
French marigold (Tagetes patula)	orange, yellow, red, mahogany	15-30cm/6-12in	summer/autumn
Sweet Pea 'Bijou mixed'	mixed	30cm/12in	summer
Trailing plants			
Lobelia	blue, white, mauve	15cm/6in trailing	summer/autumn
Alyssum saxatile	yellow	20cm/8in cascading	spring
Verbena	mixed	25cm/10in trailing	summer/autumn
Ivy-leafed pelargonium	pinks, mauves, some with variegated foliage	25cm/10in trailing foliage	summer/autumn
Nasturtium 'Alaska'	orange, yellow, cream-variegated foliage	30cm/12in trailing	summer/autumn
Nasturtium 'Gleam hybrids'	orange, yellow	30cm/12in trailing	summer/autumn
Foliage plants			
Ivy	green, white, creamy yellow	trailing	all year round
Helichrysum	silvery foliage	trailing	all year in mild areas
Ground ivy	variegated green and white	trailing	all year in mild areas

You can make an all-year herb window box. For the framework of permanent plants, use perennial herbs like sage and thyme. Add nasturtiums and marigolds in summer for colour. (Their petals can be added to summer salads.) Chives and salad burnet also have attractive flowers and their leaves are invaluable in salads.

For an aromatic window box, use lavender or hyssop. Harvest the flowers and leaves of lavender to use in pot pourri or in fragrant drawer bags. You can use the hyssop leaves to add aromatic oils to a bath or as a herbal tea.

Single-colour schemes work well in a window box. In winter use white or purple heathers planted closely like a miniature flowering hedge. Keep them in their individual pots (they like acid soil conditions) and plant bulbs of complementary colours around the heathers. In spring you will then have a fresh look for the window box. Later you can remove the heathers and bulbs and replant the whole box with a summer scheme.

Creating a natural look

Bring a natural look to your spring window box by using alpines and bulbs. *Alyssum saxatile* grows to form a grey carpet and is a perfect companion for a mass of crocuses.

WINTER WINDOW BOXES

Cold weather need not bring your window box displays to an end. Arrangements of colourful foliage and flowers will brighten up winter window sills.

GARDEN NOTES

TIMING PLANTING

There is a temptation to keep summer-flowering plants in place while they are still colourful. However, a winter box should be planted up by mid-autumn, otherwise the contents have little time to become established before the cold weather arrives.

There are a number of ways of achieving successful winter displays. One of the simplest is to use box liners that you can slip in and out of your window box. These liners, usually made of recycled cellulose, allow you to prepare an attractive arrangement of plants in advance.

You can plant up box liners with winter-flowering bulbs, pansies or primulas. As soon as summer plants are past their best they can be removed and can be replaced by the already planted and partially established winter containers. Use two or three to fill a box; a larger size would be too heavy to move when planted up.

At the end of the flowering season the liners can be placed in a less obvious part of the garden to allow bulb foliage to die back naturally.

An arrangement of evergreens (above), enlivened by the deep pink blooms of cyclamen. The small shrub with leaves dotted yellow is spotted laurel (Aucuba japonica), a versatile permanent plant for window boxes. Grow both male and female plants if you want red berries from autumn to spring. There are a number of varieties.

Another option is to include in your window box some permanent plants that look good the whole year round.

Permanent framework

A design based around evergreens allows you to fill in the spaces between them each season with appropriate colourful flowers. Heathers, ivies and miniature conifers and evergreen shrubs are ideal permanent plants.

Foliage need never be dull. Conifers and heathers have foliage in shades of green or in red, gold or bronze. Many evergreen shrubs and ivies have colourful variegated leaves.

Conifers come in a wide variety of shapes, from slim spires to globes. Some form squat cushions and there are ground-covering forms that hang over box edges. Together with low, spreading heathers and trailing, evergreen creepers, there is no shortage of shapes to choose from.

Creating a skeleton design from evergreens keeps work and expense to a minimum.

Evergreens in pots

If you prefer to remove all the summer plants and replace them at the onset of winter, grow a few evergreens in pots. Sink them into the compost in your box and plant bulbs and flowering plants around them.

A simple design (above left) of upright blue-green conifers with variegated Euonymus fortunei and ivy. If you have little or no window-sill, a window box should be attached securely to the wall just below the window.

The window box itself can add a splash of colour (above right) to brighten up a window-sill. This one has a black steel framework with red ceramic tiles.

The white flowers of heather and viola (below) complement a cream and green hebe and contrast well with the dark greens of a cypress and ivy.

Working to a shape creates the best effect. If the view from your window is pleasing use a swag arrangement to provide a decorative frame.

Designing a shape

Suitable plants for the box ends would be too slim, column-shaped conifers, such as young *Chamaecyparis lawsoniana* 'Ellwoodii', which has attractive grey-green foliage.

A compact, globe-shaped *Cryptomeria japonica* 'Compressa', which has green foliage, tinted red-purple in winter, could go next. Plant winter-flowering heathers in the centre, with ivy or periwinkle trailing over the edge.

If you prefer a less symmetrical design, place two tall, slim conifers at one end. *Picea glauca* var. *albertiana* 'Conica', for

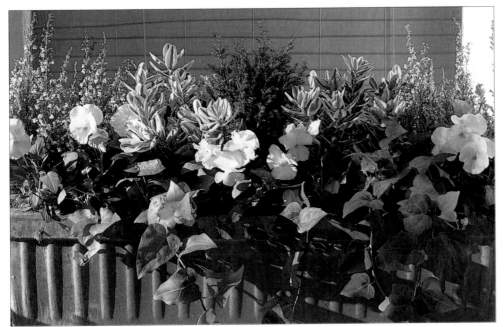

instance, makes a compact green pyramid. Then add smaller, dome-shaped types towards the centre and include one medium-sized spherical conifer at the opposite end.

Partially hide an ugly view with variegated ivy trained on wires fixed across the lower half of the window. In summer, add flowering climbers like nasturtiums or the unusual canary creeper (*Tropaeolum peregrinum*).

If you want to use tall plants in a box without obstructing the view, you should fix the box to the wall below sill level.

Colour schemes

As winter-flowering window box plants are seen in the main from inside the house they look most effective if they tie in with the room's decoration. Alternatively, go for a

An attractive terracotta box (right) sets off the cascading stems of a variegated ivy. White violas add floral appeal.

contrast by choosing sunny colours against the background of a room with a cool white, green or blue interior.

A golden scheme can be based around the gold-tinted conifers shown in the chart. Add yellow-flushed ivies like *Hedera helix* 'Goldheart', which has yellow centres to its leaves, or *H. h.* 'Buttercup',

SLOW-GROWING CONIFERS

Type and habit	Foliage colour	Approx maximum size
Ground cover forms		
Juniperus × *media* 'Pfitzerana Aurea'. Low prostrate form	golden	150cm/ 60in spread
J. conferta. Carpeter	silver on underside	90cm/36in spread
J. squamata 'Blue Star'. Forms compact mound	silvery blue	60cm/24in spread
Pyramid forms		
Chamaecyparis obtusa 'Nana Aurea'. Foliage in twisted whorls	golden	60cm/24in height
C. pisifera 'Plumosa Pygmaea'. Cone-shaped bush	golden	90cm/36in height
Juniperus communis 'Compressa'. Compact spire shape	grey-green	45cm/18in height
Picea glauca 'Nana'. Bush shape	grey-blue	90cm/36in height
Thuja occidentalis 'Rheingold'. Fine, feathery foliage	soft gold turning bronze in winter	100cm/ 40in height
Globe-shaped forms		
Chamaecyparis pisifera 'Compacta Variegata'. Low bun shape	golden	60cm/24in height
Thuja occidentalis 'Globosa'. Small dense globe	strong green	45cm/18in height
T. orientalis 'Aurea Nana'. Egg-shaped bush	bright gold-green turning bronze in winter	60cm/24in height
T. orientalis 'Minima Glauca'. Miniature globe	blue-green	30cm/12in height
T. orientalis 'Rosedalis'. Upright oval	summer:green/winter: purple/spring: yellow	60cm/24in height

NOTE: Most of these conifers will only grow 1-2cm/½-1in per year.

COLOURFUL PANSIES

The pansy is one of the best winter-flowering plants. Universal pansies come in a huge range of clear plain colours and in two-colour effects, as well as in white.

The garden pansy *Viola* × *wittrockiana* comes in winter-flowering as well as summer-flowering types and will flower through the winter in milder areas.

BRIGHT IDEAS

which has new leaves of bright yellow that soften to pale green later.

Choose bulbs like winter aconite (*Eranthis hyemalis*) which, in late winter, has buttercup-coloured flowers surrounded by a ruff of green bracts. Or you could plant the yellow, early-spring-flowering crocus, *Crocus chrysanthus* 'E.A. Bowles'.

For a silver and white scheme, pick variegated *Euonymus fortunei* 'Silver Queen', a shrub with green leaves edged in creamy white. Add white heathers, particularly the varieties of *Erica carnea* (also sold as *E. herbacea*). *E. c.* 'Cecilia M. Beale' blooms from early winter, while *E. c.* 'Springwood White' flowers vigorously from late winter.

Among the many ivies go for *Hedera helix* 'Silver Queen' with its green and silver leaves, or, in a sheltered situation, *H. h.* 'Eva' which has delightfully small, grey-green

Skimmias are hardy, evergreen shrubs, ideal for winter window boxes. They are usually grown for their bright clusters of red berries (above). One variety has red-brown flower buds (top right) in autumn and winter, which add subtle variety to this box of evergreens and colourful cyclamens, though this type of cyclamen is not frost-hardy.

leaves edged with cream.

There is little to rival the heart-warming emergence of snowdrops. *Galanthus elwesii* has large flowers that appear in late winter.

A blue and pink scheme could include the blue-green conifers and the ivy *H. helix* 'Tricolor', which has white-bordered leaves that turn a deep pink in autumn.

Several varieties of frost hardy cyclamen flower in autumn, winter or early spring.

The bright pink flowers of *Cyclamen coum*, for instance, appear in early winter. There are also many different pink heathers to choose from.

Winter care

As most window boxes are sheltered from the rain by the house wall, they will need watering often, even in winter. Conifers, in particular, require moist conditions, as do pansies and primulas. If frost is expected, do not water until conditions turn warmer.

Winter-flowering plants need feeding but for most plants winter is a time of rest. Feed the plants in your winter box once, a few weeks after planting, then just once or twice in spring.

Extreme cold winds can damage the foliage of even hardy plants. It is worth protecting your box in severe frost or snow with a covering of sacking. House walls offer some protection. In extreme cold, the city dweller, surrounded by warm buildings, has the advantage over those living in the country.

POT-GROWN HERBS

Herbs do best in sunny, well drained, relatively infertile situations. In pots you can create these conditions and produce attractive displays.

Many favourite kitchen and cosmetic herbs grow well in containers – and there are several practical advantages to growing these popular, useful plants in pots.

You may not have space in your garden for a special herb area: a single container with the herbs you use regularly will solve the problem. Some herbs, such as mint, spread rapidly in the garden; in a pot you can control their growth. And in winter you can move containers nearer the kitchen or even indoors, so you have herbs at your fingertips.

Best conditions

Herbs do best in well-drained, sunny sites. Pots drain well and can be placed in the sun-niest part of the garden or on a window sill.

Most herbs will grow well in containers. Tall-growing plants, such as fennel, will need staking. You will need to renew the compost annually in your herb pots and repot the plants into larger containers, dividing them if necessary. Water your herbs regularly, especially in very dry conditions, or they will wither.

Herb collections

Herbs are not only useful but also ornamental and decorative. You may wish to grow a collection of different types of one herb, such as thyme.

There are several different varieties of thyme, with slightly different growth habits,

Pots of healthy herbs (right) look quite as attractive as any other foliage plants. When left to flower or combined with flowering plants they can be very eye-catching. The mauve flowers of chives are particularly charming. Terracotta pots enhance and set off nicely the many shades of green.

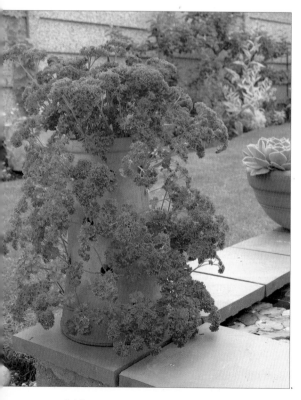

A tall terracotta parsley pot (left) looks elegant wherever it is situated. Here it graces the corner of a raised pond.

A mixed pot (left) of green sweet basil (Ocimum basilicum). The two contrast pleasingly. They flower in late summer and if you are growing them for their leaves you should pinch out the flowers as soon as possible. Basils are generally pest and disease-free but need a sunny site.

A line of pot-grown herbs flanks the steps (below) in a garden richly scattered with potted plants. Left to flower, the chives and several different kinds of mint will add to the colour generated by the pelargoniums, fuchsia and other flowering plants.

GROWING TIPS

IN THE SHADE

Most herbs prefer full sun but some, including chives, parsley, mints, borage, fennel, lemon balm and salad burnet, won't mind a little shade during the day.

different flower colours and leaf variations. Grow such a collection in a uniform row of terracotta pots to make an interesting foliage or flowering feature throughout the year. Most varieties of thyme are hardy evergreen plants.

You can build similar one-herb collections using rosemary or sage. Both will develop into sturdy, shrub-like plants in pots. Harvest them regularly and you will keep them in trim and prevent them growing too woody.

Mints are another good subject for a collection. Apart from their many tangy culinary uses, they offer ornamental interest with varying foliage shapes and textures, as well as a wide range of aromatic fragrances. Mint flowers add to their ornamental value.

Site the collection of mints where it is easily accessible — crushing mint leaves to

WATERING TIPS

Keep pot-grown herbs well watered but do not overwater sage, thyme, rosemary, bay, marjoram, tarragon, curry plant or lavender. Don't let chives, parsley or mint dry out – they do like extra moisture.

Make sure there are adequate drainage holes in the container and place a layer of clay shards or gravel in the base as a drainage layer. Cover this with a coarse mix of compost that won't wash away when watered.

release their fragrance is one of the pleasures of gardening.

Scented pelargoniums can be grown outdoors in potted collections but must be brought indoors in winter, as most are too tender for harsh weather.

Table-top herbs

The low-growing habit of many herbs is suited to a shallow, wide container, such as an old sink or a terracotta bowl. Such displays are most effective when raised above the ground. Place the bowl or sink on a patio wall or on a sturdy patio table.

Creeping thyme *(Thymus pulegioides)* or Corsican mint *(Mentha requienii)* will produce a mat-like 'lawn'. Prostrate rosemary *(Rosmarinus officinalis* Prostratus Group, also known as *R. lavandulaceus)* will also spread and will trail over the container's edge, offering a flush of bright blue flowers in spring. It needs protection in winter.

For a bonsai-like effect, create a Mediterranean landscape in the container with small rocks and gravel. Use a scented and shrubby herb, like lemon-scented pelargonium *(Pelargonium crispum)*, as a 'tree' in your planting scheme.

Herb baskets

A hanging basket of pretty and useful herbs can give you year-round pleasure. Sage, thyme, variegated mint, a strawberry plant, chives and trailing nasturtiums are all suitable for inclusion. Keep them in order by snipping them to use through the summer, flowers and all, for delicious salads.

Containers

Terracotta containers are probably the most visually satisfying. They are also very free-draining, providing one of the basic requirements for good herb growth. But you will need to keep your herbs watered regularly, as terracotta dries quite out rapidly.

To prevent compost drying out too quickly, line terracotta pots with black polythene, punctured with drainage holes. Plastic, imitation terracotta looks almost as good, is lighter in weight and is less expensive.

Specially-shaped containers, such as towering terracotta parsley pots or strawberry pots, make useful homes for herbs where space is limited. A wooden half-barrel provides an excellent permanent home for a herb collection.

Herbs grown in pots can be trained or cut into shapes that make them a focal feature on a patio or verandah.

Fancy shapes

Cuttings of upright rosemary *(Rosmarinus officinalis* 'Miss Jessopp's Upright') can be trained around a wire hoop to make a circular living rosemary wreath. You can also clip them, when established, into a pyramid shape.

Bay trees, suitable for front door decoration, can be clipped into similar conical shapes, or into graceful, ball-shaped trees. Lavender plants can be trimmed over two growing seasons into ball shapes, as can scented pelargoniums.

Mixed planting

In a large container, such as a half-barrel, you can use herbs as part of a mixed planting. The silvery leaves of artemisia or southernwood make a good contrast to the feathery leaves of both bronze and green fennel in the background. Cotton

A hanging basket (left) bursting with herbs contains an interesting variety of plants. Contributing to the rich foliage are sage, mints, parsley and caraway. Ideal for picking for the kitchen, they are also attractive in their own right.

A contorted standard bay tree (left) is certainly a talking point. It has been trained to grow like this. Such trees can be bought from garden centres but will be expensive. With patience you could train one yourself.

Pretty enamelled pots add to the enchantment of a herb collection, setting off the foliage of caraway, broad-leaved parsley and thyme (above).

POT SIZES

Rosemary, sage and bay are best grown in large containers as they grow into fairly substantial plants. Chives, thyme, chervil, parsley and savory suit smaller containers. Start cuttings of rosemary, sage and bay in small containers, re-potting them when their roots fill the container.

The plastic column (right) is a 'portable garden', available from garden centres. Fast-draining, it is an ideal way of growing herbs for those with limited space.

Common thyme (left) forms a low bush up to 30cm/1ft high. Flowers vary in colour but appear in early to mid-summer.

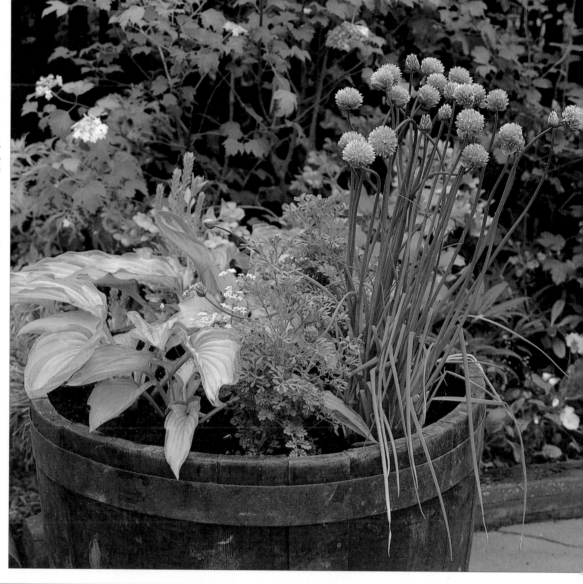

A wooden half barrel makes a fine permanent container, but bear in mind it will be too heavy to move when filled and planted up. Here (right), chives in flower and the delicate foliage of rue are set off by the leaves of hostas. Rue should be planted with care and is probably best avoided if you have children. It can cause severe dermatitis, especially if you get the sap on your skin and it is then exposed to sunlight.

The bright green leaves of lemon balm (top, far right) smell strongly of lemon. It is a hardy perennial whose roots can be invasive. Planting it in a pot will contain it. It likes a sunny position. Pinch out the flowers for maximum leaf production. The leaves complement stewed fruit, fish and poultry.

ℙROJECT   A MINI KNOT GARDEN

The base of a mature standard bay tree looks bare and there are few things suitable for underplanting. The right herbs, however, can turn it into a mini knot garden, with a formal look reminiscent of a box hedge around a traditional herb garden.

At each corner of a rectangular terracotta planter set a variegated thyme, *Thymus* 'Silver Posie'.

Along the sides and in diagonals from each thyme, plant dwarf lavender or cotton lavender. Clip the thyme plants into little pom-pom shapes and keep the lavender or cotton lavender trimmed into a mini-hedge.

lavender and curry plant offer silvery leaves and a low-growing form for the front of the container.

Mixed scented pelargoniums and summer bedding pelargoniums with fuchsias for a central floral and foliage effect.

Colour themes

Choose a colour – gold or purple, for example, – and you will find there are herbs to suit. Golden thyme, golden marjoram, golden sage, variegated lemon balm and ginger mint, combined with variegated rue, will produce a splash of warm colour to brighten the view.

For an entirely purple planting choose variegated purple sage, purple-flowered sweet violets, purple-flowered thyme, purple orach, purple basil, eau de cologne mint and violas.

Basil, incidentally, is only half-hardy and should not be

PRESERVING HERBS

AIR-DRYING HERBS

1. Cut herbs to dry in spring and summer. Mint, sage and thyme should be cut before they come into flower, when their stems and leaves are rich in essential oils. Pick herbs early in the day after early morning dews have dried.

2. Spread the herbs in a single layer on a flat tray or tie them together in small, loose bundles. Place the tray on a shelf in a dark airing cupboard or hang the bundles from the slats of the shelf.

3. They need persistent warmth, 90°F/32°C for the first day, and 75°F/24°C subsequently, and no moisture (steamy bathrooms are out). The time depends on the sappy nature of the herb and the amount of heat – up to four days at the above temperatures and up to two weeks at lower temperatures.

4. Herbs are ready to store when the leaves are papery dry and crumble when touched. Keep them whole when you bottle them, crumbling them just before use.

MICROWAVE DRYING

Herb leaves and flowers can be dried in a microwave and will keep their colour and flavour, but may lose some of their medicinal properties.

Strip leaves off the stems and place them in the microwave on a sheet of absorbent kitchen paper. For extra safety place a small bowl of water in the microwave. Cook on high for 1 minute. Turn the leaves over and cook for a further 1-1½ minutes. When dry they will crumble. Store in an airtight jar in the dark.

FREEZING HERBS

Parsley, basil and herbs with delicate leaves, such as fennel, all freeze well. Freeze them on trays or in polythene. Pack them in old margarine tubs for storage in the freezer. When defrosted and used in cooking they will retain plenty of their flavour.

This earthenware chimney-like container (left) blends well with the brick path in which it is set. It has been planted with thyme in the top and around its base.

put outside until all danger of frost is over. It needs a sheltered, sunny position.

Pot aromatics

One of the most delightful herbal features in a garden is an aromatic path made from creeping thyme or chamomile. If you plant up just one terracotta pot of chamomile and one of thyme you can create a simple equivalent. Rub your hands over the pots of herbs and their enticing fragrance will waft towards you, just as if you were walking down a scented country garden path at the height of summer.

ROOF GARDENS

A roof garden can be an enchanting haven in a built-up area. If you have a strong roof and can protect it from winds, almost anything is possible.

Many gardeners gain inspiration for roof gardens from the colourful examples on modern office blocks. These are usually on strong roofs, supported by a steel and concrete framework.

Unfortunately, most flat roofs on houses are not structurally strong enough to support the weight of surfacing materials, containers, plants, compost and people.

Assessing the roof

Flat roofs on houses are usually formed of several layers of bitumen-felt covered with fine shingle with a slight slope for drainage. Repeatedly treading on this surface damages it.

If you want a roof garden get an opinion first from an architect or a structural engineer. They will tell you what is possible, the cost, and how to gain access to the roof from the house – perhaps by converting a window into a door.

Planning the garden

Plan your roof garden in detail and to scale on graph paper. If no view is pleasing, surround the roof with a fence and create your own vista using shrubs and climbers. A bench and cluster of plants in pots, surrounded by a screen forming a flowery arbour drenched in scent, will quickly capture the senses.

All-weather flooring is essential, enabling plants in tubs and troughs to be tended throughout the year.

Bitumen-felted roofs must be overlaid with a framework of 7.5-10cm/3-4in square timbers spaced 75-90cm/2½-3ft

This charming roof garden (above) relies on simplicity for its effect. Wooden boarding, garden furniture and a few well-chosen container plants do the trick.

Foliage plants dominate the scene in this tiled roof garden (left), cleverly giving the illusion of permanent planting.

On an inner-city roof garden, multi-layered planting can create a glorious profusion of colour (above right) and also hide an unsightly view. Stone urns, however, need the support of a very strong roof, although moulded plastic models can make a good substitute.

On roof gardens, trellis (right) is not only attractive but acts as a filter for strong winds and sun. It also serves as a support for hanging baskets of nasturtiums, petunias and lobelias. Foliage plants add interest to the colourful container-grown display.

BUILDING REGULATIONS

Check with your local council to ensure planning and building permission are not required, especially if you want a screen around part or all of the roof.

Some authorities do not allow the construction of any screen that can be seen from the road, or which obstructs the views from other houses. Without a strong surround a roof garden becomes unsafe for children, as well as too exposed to storms.

apart and covered with strong, wooden boarding.

Concrete surfaces, however, can be covered with light-weight and weather-resistant tiles. Avoid slippery surfaces and heavy concrete slabs. Lightness is the key.

Protecting plants

Wind soon decimates plants on roofs – warm summer breezes dry them while winter gales 'wind-burn' tender shrubs, so

KEEPING COMPOST DRY IN WINTER

Compost in tubs can be protected by covering it with a sheet of plastic in early winter. Remove this in early spring. Use scissors to cut a plastic sheet to its centre, then slip it over the tub.

Draw the two cut sides together and, using string or wire-centred 'twisty' ties, secure the sheet to the central stem. Fix it at a point higher than the tub's rim to ensure that water runs off and not back into the compost. Two or three bricks or pieces of thick wood around the plant's stem usually raise the level sufficiently.

Use strong string to tie the overhanging plastic to the tub, and trim its edge with scissors. From time to time, check that the compost is not absolutely bone-dry.

make sure that your plants are properly sheltered.

Solid walls and fences do not solve this problem as they produce swirling eddies on the lee side. A lattice-work screen that filters wind is best.

Screens that appear solid, but actually filter the wind, can be created by nailing 15-23cm/6-9in wide boards horizontally to both sides of strongly secured upright posts – but stagger the boards on either side so that they overlap by about 2.5cm/1in.

Most plants on roof gardens are grown in tubs, troughs, window boxes and hanging baskets, or in half-baskets attached to walls and fences.

One advantage of container plants is that masses of spring and summer colour can be created from a small (lightweight) amount of compost. Use a peat-based compost with moisture-retentive materials such as vermiculite.

Permanent planting positions can be created if the surface is strong enough to take the weight of a bulk of compost at least 50cm/20in deep and 75-90cm/2½-3ft square, and often twice that size.

In permanent planting positions, especially for shrubs and small trees, use loam-based composts.

Container care

All plants in containers need watering at least once a day in summer. Hanging baskets

QUICK CHANGES

The way to create instant displays – to replace ones that are fading – is to have several inner containers for each window box and trough.

Faded displays can then be removed and replaced with established ones. For instance, as soon as spring-flowering plants have faded, lift out the inner container and replace with summer-flowering plants.

Make a feature of half-wall baskets by hanging them from a trellis (above). These are brightly planted with, among others, helichrysum, impatiens, tagetes and glechoma.

Be imaginative in your choice of container plants. The unusual Juniper horizontalis (above far right) is an ideal roof-garden plant since it is fully hardy.

Roof-top containers are exposed to the full rigours of winter. Protect their compost with plastic sheeting (above right).

Split-level, lightweight containers planted with petunias and pelargoniums and with the miniature rose 'Little Buckeroo' (right) create a strong splash of colour on this roof-top corner.

suspended high up can be watered by tying the end of a hose pipe to a short cane.

Feed summer flowering plants in troughs, window boxes, hanging baskets and half-baskets every two or three weeks from when flowers appear. Shrubs in tubs also need regular feeding, but not after late summer as this encourages the growth of soft shoots and stems that may be damaged in cold weather.

Winter care

In early autumn, reduce the amount of water given to shrubs and trees in tubs, as well as those in permanent planting positions. It is vital that compost is not saturated in winter, as it may then freeze solid.

Move shrubs and conifers in tubs and pots to a sheltered part of the roof if possible.

Because roof gardens are exposed to the full rigours of winter, selecting the right plants is important.

Selecting plants

There are two ways to ensure success. First, choose permanent plants for their hardiness and diminutive size. Second, grow seasonal plants (temporary plants that are grown for their bright displays in spring or summer) in containers.

There are several ways to create a colourful roof garden. Try planting biennials and spring-flowering bulbs during the late summer and autumn in troughs or window boxes in the garden. Move them to the roof in early spring, just as flowers appear.

Bulbs such as daffodils, hyacinths and compact, short-stemmed tulips (early double types and species like *Tulipa fosteriana*, *T. greigii* and *T. kaufmanniana* hybrids) are suitable, as well as biennials like forget-me-not, double daises, pansies and dwarf wallflowers.

Some small spring-flowering bulbs, such as crocuses, *Iris danfordiae* and *I. reticulata*, make attractive displays in window boxes and troughs.

For summer colour in containers there is a wealth of half-hardy annuals. Plants to use include ageratum, alyssum, *Begonia semperflorens*, busy Lizzies, lobelia, French and African marigolds, petunias, salvias and verbena.

For plants left permanently on the roof, use shrubs with hardy constitutions. Prostrate or low-growing plants with a domed outline are less likely to be damaged by strong winds than tall ones. Variegated evergreen types include *Aucuba japonica* 'Variegata'.

Conifers and roses

Several conifers with a low or domed growth habit are suitable for tubs. These include *Chamaecyparis lawsoniana* 'Aurea Densa', *Juniperus horizontalis* and *Juniperus squamata* 'Blue Star'.

Miniature roses in window boxes or troughs can be planted and grown at ground-level, then moved to the roof when flower buds open.

PROTECTING TENDER DECIDUOUS SHRUBS

Shrubs in tubs that are left in place during winter may need protection from cold winds. Insert four or five canes into the compost and create a wigwam. Tie their tops together.

Wrap straw around the canes to protect the plant, tying it with string.

This method is better than a complete wrapping in plastic, as it allows air to circulate freely around the stems and leaves.

Planning the style of your garden is almost as much fun as actually realizing your dream.
Allow your imagination to roam, and you may find it easier than you think to
lift your garden out of the ordinary.

CHAPTER THREE
Gardening with Style

LANDSCAPING

By applying a few simple principles used by landscape gardeners, you can turn a dull plot into something really special, full of interesting shapes and surprises.

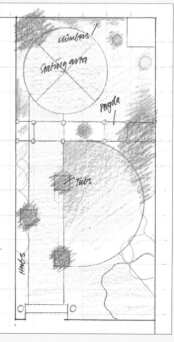

Few of us can afford the services of a professional landscape gardener. However, by applying the basic principles they use, and maybe putting in a bit of hard work at the start, you can make your garden infinitely more interesting, whatever its size. A typical town garden with a rectangle of grass surrounded by straight flowerbeds and raw-looking fences can be improved out of all recognition by redesigning its basic shape.

If you are starting a new garden, either from a bare patch left by the builders, or from an overgrown or neglected old plot, thinking on landscape gardening lines right from the start will stop you making mistakes that take time and money to put right later on. A well-designed garden will be easier to manage and can be perfectly attuned to your specific needs.

Design principles

The ground rules that professional landscape gardeners follow are basically simple, and can be learnt by studying other gardens, either on the ground or in photographs. A visually pleasing garden always has plenty of curves – lawns and beds have gently undulating edges, and paths wind away into the distance.

Strategically placed focal points – a sundial, bird bath, large flower tub or specimen tree – draw your eye onwards and provide extra interest. If there is an interesting feature or pleasant view beyond the garden, this will be framed in foliage to accentuate it.

The garden will probably be designed so that you **cannot** quite see how far it extends, or exactly what happens when

Even a small yard garden can be landscaped (left); the same principles apply. Where a lawn was the feature of the similarly-shaped, slightly larger garden on the opposite page, here wooden decking has been used to provide slight changes of height, a pathway through the garden and a seating area. As the site is rather dark, foliage plants in containers and borders provide growing interest, while the narrowness of the garden has been made an advantage by laying wooden beams from wall to wall to create an arbour.

Dividing a garden up into small areas is a necessity for a long narrow plot. A wooden trellis (above) is perfect for this. It both screens and reveals, and acts as a windbreak and a support for climbers.

As an alternative, a smaller area can be divided up with paths; paving (below) creates strong geometric shapes, while other materials such as grass or gravel can make curved or serpentine edges.

you get to the end – it invites you to explore. This can be done quite simply by partially blocking the view with a trellis and an arch, or inserting a bed running crossways that is planted with tallish shrubs.

However lavishly planted, even wild, the garden may seem at first, it will always consist of clearly defined areas. Lawns, flowerbeds, paths and a paved sitting area are the most common features, but there may also be a vegetable garden, children's play area, a pond – as many different areas of interest as the size of the plot can comfortably take.

Changes of level are also built into the design – terraces, steps and grassy banks in a large garden, raised beds or a rockery in a smaller one. Even if the garden is actually flat, the planting will provide eye interest at different levels – ground cover, herbaceous plants, taller shrubs, climbing plants and trees.

Changes of texture are equally important – a close-

clipped lawn sets off a luxuriant herbaceous border; hard paving contrasts with soft delicate flowers; smooth, still water reflects rugged stone.

Providing privacy is an important part of the landscape gardener's brief. Boundaries will be designed to provide this unobtrusively, without creating a prison-yard feeling.

The first step in redesigning your garden is to decide to what use you are going to put

A well-planned garden has something for everyone. A sandpit (above) encourages young children to use the garden and provides the garden with a focal point. It can be converted into a formal pond later.

Remarkable effects can be obtained by reversing the usual order of things (below). Here a raised central lawn is encircled by a water feature, with more conventional beds filling in around the edges.

it. Is it to be an outdoor room, used mainly for relaxation? Or do you have time to care for lots of flowers and a lawn? Will it need to cater for children playing? What about special features like a pond, rockery, sunken garden, barbecue, or easy-to-maintain raised beds?

Shapes and sizes

The next step is to measure your plot on all sides, to see if it is actually rectangular, or whether it tapers or is irregularly shaped. Make a note of any slopes, and find out which parts of the garden are in sun or shade at which times of day. List features you wish to keep, like established trees or shrubs, and those you want to get rid of, like piles of rubble or dilapidated sheds.

Draw a scale plan of the garden on squared paper. Include the position of the house and anything you are quite certain is going to stay, like a large tree or paved area.

Get several photocopies made, and use one to draw a plan of the garden as it is. Use the others to see how you can create the garden of your dreams. Rough out the broad concept first – in pencil to allow for changes of mind – leaving details of planting and so

on until later.

Do not try to cram too many features into a small garden. Drawing your ideas to scale on paper will make you realize what you can and cannot get into your particular plot.

Paths need to be at least 60cm/2ft wide for easy movement. However, paths are not essential; unless the ground is very boggy, close-mown grass can take their place.

A large lawn that fills most of the width makes a small garden look bigger – like fitted carpet in a small room. The depth of the flower beds should ideally be in proportion to the size of the plot.

Long and narrow

Make the most of a typical long narrow plot by including features that run across the garden – beds with tall planting, internal hedges or trellis work – at intervals on alternate sides. Another way of creating the illusion of width is to set the lawn at an angle of 45° to the house.

A small, square garden looks best with interest in the centre – a round lawn or a central pool or tree. Take away the squareness with curved beds in the corners. An irregular shape lends itself to the

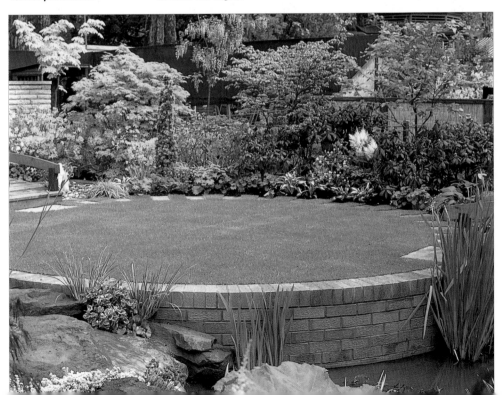

LABOUR-SAVERS

- Have mowing stones round the lawn to reduce the edging chore. Do not have island beds.
- In a small or front garden, get rid of the grass and have a gravel garden instead.
- A pond, once installed, is labour-saving as there is almost no weeding.
- For almost zero maintenance, pave the garden and plant dwarf conifers, heathers, no-prune shrubs and bulbs.
- Cut down weeding by planting plenty of smothering ground-cover plants.

GARDEN NOTES

Ugly but functional buildings need covering up (above). This unsightly garage has all but vanished under a Boston ivy (Parthenocissus tricuspidata).

By introducing steps into your garden, you create changes of height and divide up the garden (below). They are also a handy place to put container plants.

DISGUISES

Some unsightly features can be disguised or totally transformed by planting.
- Dead tree. Grow honeysuckle or a clematis up it and put a circular seat round the base, or cut the top level and turn it into a bird table.
- Cracked concrete. Plant creeping plants like thyme in the crevices. Enlarge broken areas, fill with compost and plant alpines.
- Ugly outbuilding. Clad concrete walls with weatherboard. Fix horizontal wires to timber and plant an evergreen honeysuckle. Russian vine or *Clematis montana* will soon cover both walls and roof.
- Straight concrete path. Soften edges with tumbling, low-growing plants.

BRIGHT IDEAS

creation of several distinct 'mini-gardens', divided by internal hedges or screens.

Some gardens taper off very unsatisfactorily into a triangle at the bottom. Depending on its size, you can cut this off with a big, ground-hugging evergreen shrub, or screen it off with trellis and climbing plants. Create a secret garden in the enclosure – or use it as an area in which to tuck away the shed or compost heap.

Treat a minute garden or walled yard like an outdoor room, with attractive paving, lots of pretty plant containers, raised beds and garden ornaments. Train climbers up the walls for vertical interest. High walls often mean deep shade – paint them white to a height of 1.8m/6ft (so frequent repainting is easy) for maximum light reflection, and choose light-coloured paving. A sunny walled yard, warm and sheltered, is an ideal site for a scented garden.

Once you have roughed things out on paper, get outside and see how it will look in three dimensions. Use bamboo

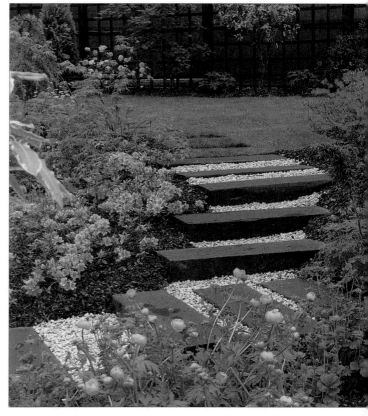

canes to mark the position of any tall features or partitions; pegs and string to map out possible new paths; and a hosepipe or rope to experiment with curves in a flower bed or lawn.

Making it work

Check that the features you planned on paper will work. Herbaceous borders need a sunny spot to flower really well. A pond should get a reasonable amount of sun and be

away from trees. Although a patio is usually sited close to the house, if it is on the shady side of the building think about putting it elsewhere.

A lawn needs sun for at least part of the day to flourish – but you can buy special seed mixes for shade. Use the least sunny parts of your garden for shade-loving shrubs, ground cover plants, and utilitarian items like sheds and compost bins, screened if necessary.

Slight slopes are manageable, but on sharp ones soil gets washed to the bottom, and grass is difficult to mow. Some form of terracing is the answer to this problem.

Sometimes the problem can be solved by dividing the slope into two or more terraces by inserting shallow log steps, and confining the soil with peat blocks, old railway sleepers or low drystone walls. On sharper slopes the downward pressure is much greater and solidly built masonry walls and steps will be needed – this is almost certainly a job for a professional.

Another way of dealing with

Paths that wind off out of sight always add to the sense of space in a garden, and give it an air of intrigue and mystery (above left), though this is not always easy to appreciate when seen from above. It is always a good idea to try and visualize how a new garden scheme will look from the ground as well as from the house.

Although bricks and paving are the usually favoured material for making steps and paths, there are other possibilities (above right). Railway sleepers are strong and weather resistant and will take a dark wood preservative, enabling you to make a flight of steps with contrasting gravel 'treads' and wooden 'risers'.

a slope is to turn it into a rock garden by building rocks into it. However, this is heavy work and may prove expensive; stone is costly, and what looks like a lot does not go very far once half-buried in the ground.

Getting help

Nasties like crumbling concrete or tarmac hardstanding, disused sheds and ancient rubbish tips cannot be designed round or lived with – they must be swept away. Hire a skip if you can manage the clearance yourself, or look in the Yellow Pages under garden services and get some idea of cost.

Garden labourers are also invaluable if you have a totally overgrown plot needing rotovating, an old hedge or dead tree trunk to be grubbed out, earth to be moved or a pond dug. Alternatively you can hire rotovators, hedge-cutters, heavy-duty mowers and flame guns by the day or weekend.

If you have a big tree that needs thinning, look in the Yellow Pages under tree work – never tackle it yourself.

COTTAGE GARDENS

Bring a touch of the countryside to your garden with an informal bank of cottage-style blooms, and have a flower-filled display all summer.

HOW TO ACHIEVE THE LOOK

A profusion of colour, agreeable informality and natural charm are the hallmarks of a traditional cottage garden.

Select old-fashioned favourites (roses).

Let plants spread, providing ground cover.

You don't have to live in a thatched cottage to copy the 'look' of a cottage garden, with its overflowing beds of pretty, perfumed flowers. The cottage garden look is something you can achieve wherever you live and whatever the size of your garden.

You may not want to change the look of your whole garden, but you could choose a few cottage-garden plants that appeal to you and devote a small area of your garden to them, or simply add them to your existing flower beds. As well as looking pretty, a mixture of scented species near the house can fill the air with a wonderful heady fragrance on summer evenings. In a real pocket handkerchief sized plot, you can create a very authentic cottage garden look just by filling every scrap of space with flowers and you will find that this weed-smothering style is easy to maintain.

What is a cottage garden?

Centuries ago, a typical cottage garden would have been very different to our image of it today. A 'real' cottage garden would have been more like a smallholding; with vegetables, herbs, fruit trees and livestock – hens, ducks and geese, rabbits and a pig or perhaps even a cow. Flowers – if there were any – would have been limited mainly to wild plants that found their way in from the surrounding countryside. Basically, the true cottage garden would have looked a bit of a mess!

By Victorian times the 'cottage garden' had become very fashionable, and the typical example bore little relation to its original predecessor.

Today's cottage garden is likely to be a charming and rather disorderly blend of flowers and herbs spilling over brick or gravel paths and daisy-studded grass, with plants arranged to give a wild, natural look as though the garden just 'happened'.

Old-fashioned roses

A cottage garden relies on a mixture of flowers, including roses, for its effect. While modern varieties of rose can look perfectly in keeping in a cottage garden, if you really want to be authentic it pays to choose the sort that are nowadays called old-fashioned. A modern hybrid tea rose, for example, would never look right, but an old-fashioned, rambling

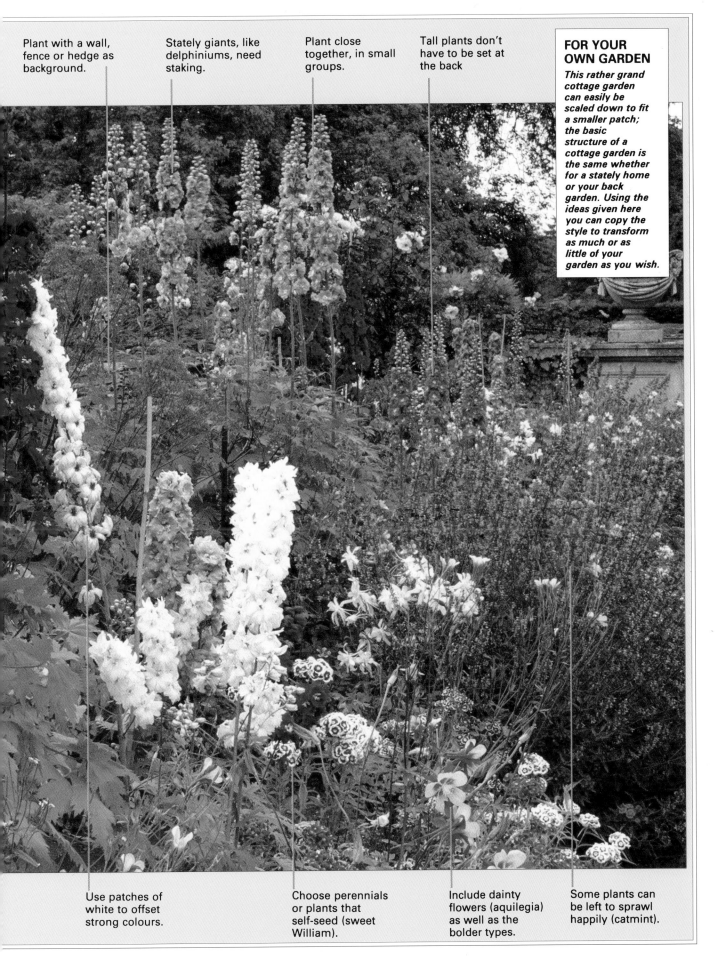

Plant with a wall, fence or hedge as background.

Stately giants, like delphiniums, need staking.

Plant close together, in small groups.

Tall plants don't have to be set at the back

FOR YOUR OWN GARDEN

This rather grand cottage garden can easily be scaled down to fit a smaller patch; the basic structure of a cottage garden is the same whether for a stately home or your back garden. Using the ideas given here you can copy the style to transform as much or as little of your garden as you wish.

Use patches of white to offset strong colours.

Choose perennials or plants that self-seed (sweet William).

Include dainty flowers (aquilegia) as well as the bolder types.

Some plants can be left to sprawl happily (catmint).

A mixture (right) of sweet William, campion, crane's bill, daisy-like chrysanthemums, pansies and cornflowers provides a profusion of small-petalled blooms.
Having such a packed flower bed not only fills the garden with colour, but has the added advantage of suppressing weed growth.

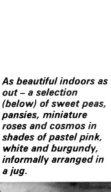

As beautiful indoors as out – a selection (below) of sweet peas, pansies, miniature roses and cosmos in shades of pastel pink, white and burgundy, informally arranged in a jug.

finished blooming.

If it is important to you to have plants with a long flowering season, then choose bourbon or hybrid perpetual roses. These varieties can be relied on to produce flowers, albeit gradually fewer, during the later summer months and into autumn after the main flush of flower is over.

Essential plants

Although a mixture of different plants is an important factor of the cottage garden look, some plants are a 'must' and almost guarantee the romantic effect you are trying to achieve. Delphiniums, poppies, foxgloves, wallflowers, columbine and pot marigolds are prime examples.

Another 'classic' component of the cottage garden is a climber. This will give an appropriate look of unruliness and fullness to your cottage garden bed or border. Pretty examples are winter jasmine, climbing roses or honeysuckle. Train any one of these on to a wall, fence or trellis, or around the front door or porch. Clematis, too, has a suitably random appearance, and grows at an astonishing and satisfying rate. You may prefer to train one of these climbers over an arch made from wood or wire for a truly rustic effect.

Fruit and vegetables

Fruit trees – especially apples – always had a place in a real cottage garden. Nowadays

rose with delicate, flat-faced, pale-toned flowers would be ideal. Old-fashioned roses have the added advantage of usually being quite strongly perfumed.

Old-fashioned roses are easy to grow. They rarely need pruning, and suffer much less from disease than modern varieties. They have a shorter flowering period than hybrid teas however: sometimes only four to six weeks in the middle of summer. This is why they are usually grown amongst other old-fashioned flowers, chosen specially to carry on flowering when the roses have

PROJECT PLANTING PLAN FOR A COTTAGE GARDEN BORDER

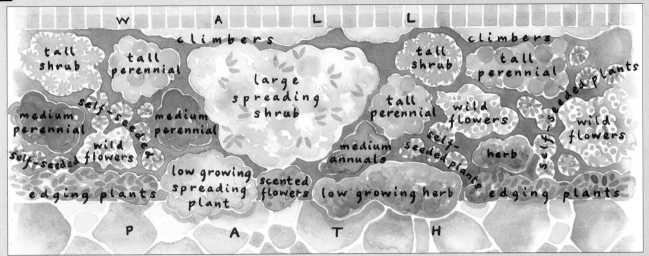

Climbers, tall shrub, tall perennial, large spreading shrub, medium perennial, self-seeders, wild flowers, edging plants, low growing spreading plant, scented flowers, low growing herb, medium annuals, herb

Climbers –clematis, climbing rose, fan-trained fig, apricot, peach or apple tree
Edging plants – dwarf box, lavender, thyme, London pride
Large spreading shrubs – lavatera (mallow), *Viburnum fragrans*, lilac, azaleas, hydrangea
Low-growing herbs – thyme, marjoram
Low-growing spreading plants – *Stachys lanata* 'Silver Carpet' (lamb's ears)
Medium annuals – busy Lizzie (impatiens), petunia, salvia
Medium perennials – *Alchemilla mollis* (lady's mantle), ornamental grass, astrantia (masterwort)
Scented flowers – night scented stock, tobacco plant (nicotiana), dianthus (pinks)
Self-seeders – forget-me-not, poppies, aquilegia, foxgloves, honesty, nasturtiums, marigolds
Tall perennials – echinops (globe thistle), delphinium, lily, lupin, foxgloves, hollyhock
Tall shrubs – *Ribes sanguineum* (flowering currant), *Hamamelis mollis* (Chinese witch hazel)
Wild flowers – cornflowers, geranium (crane's-bill), foxglove

The plan (above) is an example of how you could plant up a flower bed for a cottage garden look. A list of suitable plants is given, left. The ideal depth for this flower bed is 1.2-1.5m/4-5ft.

gardeners tend to plant them not only for fruit, but for the spring blossom and as supports for climbers which scramble up through their branches. Again, really old varieties with evocative names like 'Devonshire Quarrenden', 'D'Arcy Spice' and 'Cornish Aromatic' are still occasionally available from specialist growers. Though not heavy croppers, the flavour of these apples is truly delicious – far better than most fruit you buy from the supermarket.

Vegetables – the mainstay of real old cottage gardens – don't have to make the place look like an allotment. They can be grown in your border, mixed in with the flowers, where they look most attractive. When vegetables are grown to eat, it is the fruit of the plant that is all-important, but they often have interesting foliage and flowers too.

Try scarlet runner beans or climbing pea varieties growing on a wigwam of rustic bean-poles at the back of a flower bed; globe artichokes alongside delphiniums; or an edging of parsley or thyme by a path.

Romantic disorder
The essence of the traditional, romantic cottage garden is its overcrowded look, with plants filling every bit of space and spilling out over paths and grass. In the past, this look took many years to achieve – largely as a result of neglect! Nowadays we tend to create a more orderly version of the same look, with the emphasis on carefully selected cottage garden plants. Invasive plants still have their place – they are best grown together in a bed of their own where they make an ideal low-maintenance cottage border. The most important beds, however, or those where growing conditions are best, should be reserved for the less pushy plants which can then grow quite safely without risk

PERFECT PARTNERS

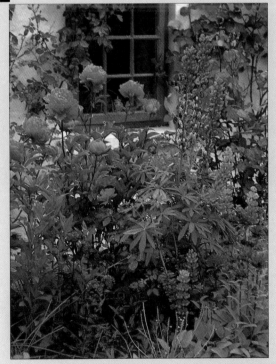

A vibrant and daring mixture of reds (lupins and sweet William), pink (peonies) and purple (campanula) creates an unusually striking effect.

of suffocation. If choice plants happen to self-seed, then you can think yourself lucky and either leave them where they fall or transplant them to another part of the garden.

Attractive combinations

Having decided which kinds of plants you want to grow, the next trick is deciding how to

Same family, different flower: the gladiolis in the main picture (below) are an old-fashioned variety, G. communus ssp. byzantinus, with delicate flowers and a wild look which suits the cottage garden style; whereas a modern hybrid (left) would look out of place with its huge red blooms.

out of hand. The main chores include snipping off dead flowers and cutting back dead or dying stems, pruning, feeding and watering (especially if you have plants in containers) and mulching between plants with garden compost.

The reason for snipping back (deadheading) the dead flowers is to encourage further

put them together, making pleasant contrasts of shape, texture and colour throughout the summer.

A typical small cottage border in a fairly sunny situation might, for instance, contain some old-fashioned roses, lavender, irises, several different kinds of hardy cranesbills (geraniums), a few salvias and perhaps some summer flowering bulbs like allium or lilies.

For late summer and early autumn flowers, there might

also be a clump or two of Japanese anemones and some Michaelmas daisies.

Roses and honeysuckle make an attractive partnership and, next to them, you could plant night-scented stock or nicotiana for truly wonderful perfumed evenings.

Easy maintenance

Cottage gardens need little work to maintain: just some sensible clearing from time to time when things start getting

Bumble-bees (inset), along with other nectar-loving insects, will be keen visitors to a flower-filled garden of 'wild' species.

flowering. A plant's purpose in life is to flower, set seed, then die. If you take off the dead flowers before they can seed, you are, in effect, frustrating this course of events, and forcing the plant to try again with new flowers.

If you grow tall flowers, like delphiniums, they will need tying loosely and unobtrusively to canes or stakes to keep their stems straight, but most cottage flowers look more natural if they flop gently.

HEDGES

Hedges can do more than mark the boundaries of a garden. Use them to create patterns and secret spaces, protect plants – even deter burglars!

It may just be a collection of shrubs or trees growing together to make a living screen, but a hedge can provide a range of creative possibilities for your garden.

Hedges are used to form physical boundaries between properties. In a front garden, they often mark the limits between public and private ground. If a hedge is very high it will provide privacy from neighbouring houses or passers-by; it may lower noise levels from a nearby road or school playground and it can even keep stray animals out. It will also provide shelter and protect your garden plants from strong winds.

Part of the design

As well as these practical functions, however, hedges also play a decorative role and can be an essential part of your garden design. To increase your enjoyment of your garden there are many ways you can get both practical value and

Conifers are a good choice for a formal hedge, but they do need regular clipping to keep them in shape (above). Hedges do not have to be high to be effective (left). These low clipped hedges combine with formal topiary specimens to add interest to a cottage front garden.

169

good looks from a hedge.

Hedges can be grown for either a formal or an informal look. Traditionally, formal hedges are made from plantings of evergreen shrubs including yew, box and privet.

These evergreens look the same all year round, which gives them their unchanging, formal character. All three plants respond well to regular clipping into a trim shape. They are all hardy and long-lived and provide a rich foliage backdrop for the other plants in the garden.

The informal look

If you want a hedge that is more relaxed in form then choose plants that suit an informal look. *Skimmia japonica*, an evergreen shrub with gold-spotted leaves and autumn berries, is a good choice. For a flush of spring flowers in your informal hedge choose *Forsythia × intermedia* 'Spectabilis'. For summer flowers choose *Potentilla arbuscula*. All will make loose hedges but will provide a screen, offer privacy or mark a boundary.

If you want to attract birds to the garden, *Cotoneaster × watereri* 'Cornubia' and *Pyracantha rogersiana* will provide you with evergreen foliage, summer flowers and autumn berries for the birds to enjoy.

In coastal areas two shrubs are invaluable both as ornamental and practical hedge plants: *Escallonia macrantha* with its red to pink summer flowers, and *Griselinia littoralis*, with its fresh green foliage. Both tolerate salty winds.

Mix and match

Instead of using one type of shrub or tree for the hedge, you can create a very informal effect by planting different species. The overall impression will be of a highly textured surface. Hornbeam, holly, beech and laurel can be mixed together to create this type of look but it will take time as they are long-lived but slow-growing plants.

If you wish to make a wildlife garden and attract birds and butterflies, plant a native hedgerow of sloe, hawthorn, holly and hazel. Plant native climbers such as honeysuckle, wild clematis and hop at intervals along the hedge.

Ring the colour changes with an informal hedge. The foliage of beech (above right) is a bright green in spring, which matures to a darker green before assuming rich russet tones in the autumn. Beech also holds its leaves through the winter until new growth starts in spring. Some forms of berberis (right) also produce spectacular autumn colours.

GOOD HEDGING PLANTS

Plant (suggested hedge height)	Planting distance	Cultivation and care
Barberry (*Berberis x stenophylla*) 1.3-1.8m/4-6ft	75cm/30in	Use this evergreen to make an informal hedge. It produces yellow flowers in spring and berries in autumn. Trim after flowering or in autumn.
Beech (*Fagus sylvatica*) 1.3-1.8m/4-6ft hedge	45cm/18in	A deciduous tree for formal hedges, it holds its old leaves through most of the winter, then produces a flush of young leaves in spring. Trim in autumn.
Cotton lavender (*Santolina chamaecyparissus*) 60cm/2ft	30cm/12in	Use this evergreen plant with its bright yellow flowers in summer for a low formal hedge or edging around a herb garden. Trim lightly in spring or after flowering.
Firethorn (*Pyracantha rogersiana*) 1.3-1.8m/4-6ft	75cm/30in	An evergreen, it can be used for informal hedging. Spring flowers are later followed by berries. Trim lightly after flowering, if you want to keep the berries.
Holly (*Ilex aquifolium*) 1.3-2.5m/4-8ft	90cm/36in	An evergreen shrub, it can be trimmed into a formal shape or allowed to create a more informal hedge. Trim in autumn.
Leyland cypress (*× Cupressocyparis leylandii*) 1.8-2.5m/6-8ft	105cm/42in	This evergreen grows very fast, and can be used to create a neat, formal hedge. Trim in late summer.
Mexican orange blossom (*Choisya ternata*) 1.3-1.8m/4-6ft	75cm/30in	This evergreen shrub produces sweet-smelling flowers and makes a largely informal hedge. Trim after flowering.
Privet (*Ligustrum ovalifolium*) 1-1.8m/3-6ft	45cm/18in	A popular and fast-growing evergreen, it can be trimmed into neat, formal shapes. Clip regularly during the growing season.

Pyracantha (above) makes a very attractive hedge, bearing dense clusters of white flowers in early summer followed by orange-yellow or red fruits. Senecio greyi (left) is particularly suited to coastal areas as it tolerates salt breezes. Privet (right) is one of the most popular hedging plants. This variety, Ligustrum ovalifolium 'Aureomarginatum', has golden leaves and prefers a sunny spot.

For a more whimsical effect, privet, yew and box hedges can be clipped into specific shapes, such as bird or animal forms. This is known as topiary. Remember, though, that these plants are slow-growing, so the topiary shapes will take some time to achieve. In a dense hedge dividing a garden across its width you might wish to cut a circular or other geometrically shaped window, through which you can view the rest of your garden.

Safety first

If you want to deter burglars and vandals plant a dense and prickly hedge in a front garden or where there is a vulnerable point of entry to your property. Holly, although slow-growing, will eventually make a painfully impenetrable hedge. Particularly prickly is the hedgehog holly, *Ilex aquifolium* 'Ferox Argentea'.

Roses, lovely to smell and delightful to look at, will also offer a spiky obstacle. *Rosa rugosa* 'Frau Dagmar Hastrup' has very thorny stems, lovely flowers and fat rosehips in autumn. Berberis, with spring flowers, and mahonia, with autumn flowers and purplish berries later, have thorns and spiky leaves.

Create an illusion

As well as providing a screen along the edge of your garden, you can use hedges in other ways. You can make a long, narrow garden feel larger by using hedges to divide it across the width. You can even divide your garden into 'rooms' or compartments that offer changes of mood. Create doorways by arching the hedge plants, or set an iron or wooden trellis archway in place for roses to grow over.

You do not have to use high hedges to gain this effect: a hedge of low-growing plants such as lavender or rosemary can also be used to break up a plot and the aromatic leaves are an added bonus.

Ideas from the past

Low hedges have, in fact, been a traditional garden feature in Britain since Elizabethan times. They are still used to make strongly outlined geometric or floral designs, known as 'knot gardens'. The hedges mark the outline of the design

A FAST HEDGE

One of the quickest-growing hedge plants is the Leyland cypress (× *Cupressocyparis leylandii*). To make a hedge, follow these simple steps:
- First mark out your straight planting line with string.
- Dig holes large enough to receive the roots of plants at 1m/3ft intervals (the plants will eventually grow to fill the space between).
- Scatter compost in the base of each hole and, if the site is exposed, firm in a stake.
- Place each plant in its hole, cover the roots with soil up to the soil level mark on the stem base, and firm in.
- If you have used stakes, fix the plants to them and, if the site is particularly windy, protect the hedging with a netting windbreak.
- Water regularly until the plants are well-established.

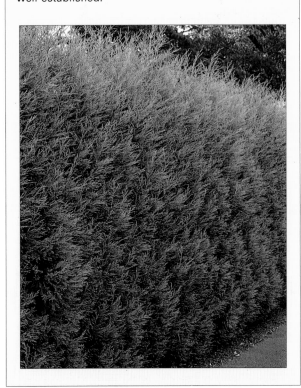

which is best viewed from an upstairs window. Inside the hedge framework, low-growing plants such as violets, marigolds and herbs such as thyme, savory and marjoram are grown to form shapes.

Why not create your own knot garden to frame a selection of summer bedding plants, or to mark out a small herb garden. Use traditional knot garden hedging plants: cotton lavender *(Santolina chamaecyparissus)*, box *(Buxus sempervirens)* or small lavender species.

Protect your plants

A low-growing hedge is particularly useful in a garden where children play regularly. Use it to mark the edge of the lawn – the safest play area for children – and it will protect flowerbeds or vegetable patches from the onslaught of exuberant younger members of the family.

In large, old gardens, hedges were often used in a similar way to keep ornamental areas and productive vegetable areas separate. Few gardens have space for such strict segregation, but if you do want to keep them apart why not grow a specially trained step-over

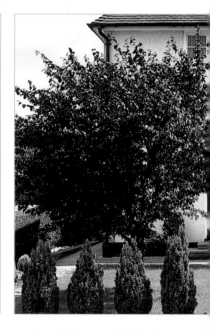

AN EDIBLE MINI-HEDGE

Divide your herb or vegetable garden into a series of decorative sections using short, bushy salad and herb plants grown close together to form bushy edgings. Good plants to try include:
- chives. Plant closely together.
- lettuce. Choose the 'cut and come again' varieties – the hearting types will not grow into each other and picking your dinner would create a hole in your hedge.
- rosemary. Once established, this can be clipped into shape with shears.
- thyme. Choose from among the compact, bushy types rather than the low mat-forming varieties. Plant fairly close together and clip into shape with shears once established.
- pot marigold *(Calendula officinalis)*. Plant close together to add a splash of colour. The bright colour petals are edible and will add decoration to a summer salad.

cordon apple or pear hedge.

On a patio a hedge offers privacy as well as good shelter from prevailing winds. Choose plants that are pretty to look at or have scented, aromatic qualities. Low-growing evergreens such as hebes offer a year-round silvery effect. When you are sitting on the patio the plants may be at eye-level, so choose plants that look attractive from all angles. Mexican orange blossom *(Choisya ternata)* has lovely evergreen leaves with citrus-scented white flowers in

Mixing and matching your plants can result in a very attractive hedge (below). Choose plants that have roughly similar habits and need approximately the same amount of clipping to make your life easier.

spring. Train as a low hedge or use pyramid-shaped formal specimens in tubs lined up to create a neat row.

Make a windbreak

A hedge can also provide the ideal windbreak in a garden. For best wind protection, you need a barrier that allows some wind through. A barrier that blocks the wind completely causes turbulence and gusts that can do as much damage as the wind itself.

A permeable barrier made of hedge plants breaks the

HEDGING TERMS

- **Knot garden:** an ornamental design of interlocking shapes, outlined in low hedging and filled with flowers or herbs.
- **Parterre:** a geometric design of beds and narrow pathways, edged with hedges, usually larger than a knot garden and sited near the house so it can be viewed from above.
- **Topiary:** hedges, trees or shrubs clipped into ornamental shapes, for example cones or spirals, the shapes of animals or birds or even more whimsical, individual designs.

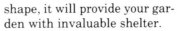

A row of small trees or bushes like these junipers (left) serve many of the same purposes as a hedge while letting in more light.

A forsythia hedge (below) offers a lovely flush of spring colour. Cut it back hard after flowering and then leave alone as the following year's flowers are borne on the current year's growth.

shape, it will provide your garden with invaluable shelter.

Hedges also provide winter shelter and a safe haven for many nesting garden birds.

Routine maintenance

When it comes to pruning your hedge, what you do will depend on the type of hedge you have. The practical reason for pruning hedges is to keep the plant producing shoots from its base. After planting a new hedge cut the plants back by at least half. Leave them to grow unpruned for their first growing season; then in the second year, between spring and summer, clip them every four to six

weeks, especially if they begin to look a little lax in their growth. Keep the upper part of the hedge slightly narrower than the base. This allows plenty of light to get into the growing shoots at the base of the hedge and, if you are in an area with snowy winters, heavy snows will not break the hedge open and damage it.

Informal hedges need very little maintenance. Prune them at least once a year during the growing season. If the hedge bears autumn fruits do not prune it after flowering; wait until the next spring. Trim flowering hedges after their blooming period is over.

strength of the wind, protecting the plants on the other side of it from a battering. The wind will blow through the leaves and branches of your hedge plants, but its effects will not be so damaging by the time it reaches your ornamental garden plants.

Even though they are deciduous, beech hedges provide a successful windbreak all year round. The spring leaves offer a delightful show of foliage and in winter the young plants hold their wispy brown leaves until the new ones show.

For a quick-growing windbreak, Leyland cypress is the best choice. It needs regular clipping or it will grow too fast, but if you manage it well and keep it clipped into a good

Lavender, like this Lavandula angustifolia 'Hidcote' (above right) makes the ideal hedging for a patio or terrace. You can enjoy its fragrance as you sit and relax while it will not grow tall enough to obscure your view.

Rosa rugosa (right) is a vigorous species rose that carries a succession of fragrant single-cupped flowers in summer, followed in autumn by tomato-shaped colourful hips to make a very informal hedge.

KITCHEN HERB GARDEN

Spice up your garden with some summer savory, add a dash of thyme – and before you can say 'oregano' you have a culinary collection of your very own!

Growing herbs is fun and so easy that even those who claim they cannot grow a thing will be sure of success. Herbs need only a little room to grow, so any spare corner of the garden will do.

Try them in window boxes, in hanging baskets or in pots along your window sill. Having them close to hand means you can snip off some chives and add extra 'bite' to your salads, find fresh basil for your authentic bolognese sauce and traditional fresh mint for sauce to enhance roast lamb dinners.

Visual effect

Because herbs have such a variety of uses it is often forgotten that they are also very attractive and versatile additions to any garden.

They can be grown to create many different effects. The unstructured, random grace of a wild flower garden can be captured using herbs. Feathery dill and fennel give a textured effect and chives make soft clumps. In contrast, you may prefer to make a neat and formal 'knot' garden which takes up very little room and yet can be an eye-catching feature.

Many herbs grow well in pots. Chives and lemon balm are suitable for larger containers, while thyme, sage and

This herb garden (right) includes parsley, sage, lemon balm and mint. The brick edging and path are attractive as well as being practical, as they contain the plants and provide access to them.

CULINARY WAYS

Add instant flavour to your cooking with a handful of herbs. Try these ways.
Parsley: sauces, stuffings and garnishes.
Rosemary: spike into lamb before roasting; sprinkle on hot barbecue coals for a tempting aroma and use in marinades.
Tarragon for hollandaise and tartare sauces, herb vinegar and roast chicken.
Basil for all tomato dishes, pizza and sauces.
Chives for soup and salad garnishes or to top a baked potato.
Mint for sauce to serve with roast lamb. Add to cooking water with peas or new potatoes.

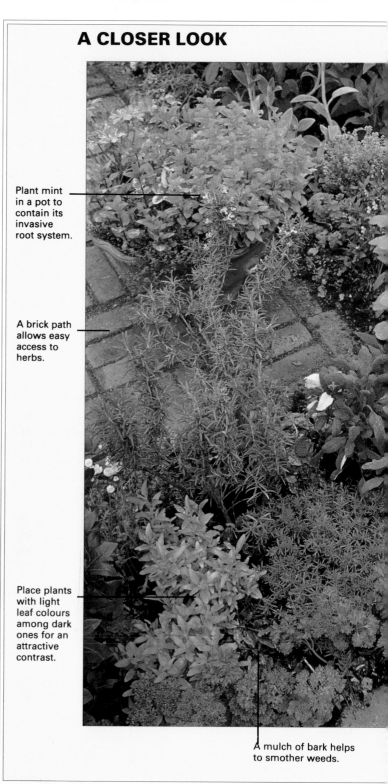

A CLOSER LOOK

Plant mint in a pot to contain its invasive root system.

A brick path allows easy access to herbs.

Place plants with light leaf colours among dark ones for an attractive contrast.

A mulch of bark helps to smother weeds.

marjoram will grow quite happily in smaller pots.

Use herbs to introduce colour as well as interesting shapes. Santolina forms a circular clump with very unusual button-like flowers on long thin stems. Borage is blue, as is sage with its clusters of violet flowers. For yellows and oranges go for marigold, dill and lovage. Bergamot (*Monarda didyma*) has an abundance of beautiful, aromatic flowers in pink and mauve hues. Nasturtiums are not only decorative but can also be grown as vigorous, colourful trailers for boxes and baskets.

Very versatile

Carpeting herbs such as camomile or thyme can be grown so that they spill out of paving cracks and over walls. They can also be grown as lawns

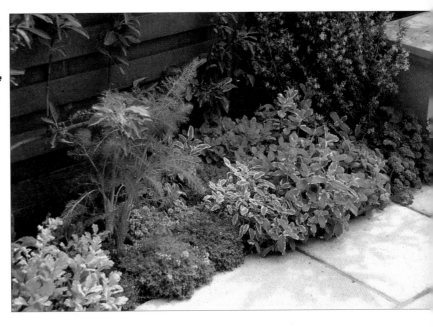

You only need a patch of garden (right) to grow an attractive and useful herb section. A corner of the patio, especially if it is near the kitchen door, is the perfect position for snipping off sprigs to add to your cooking. Regular cutting also encourages neat, healthy growth.

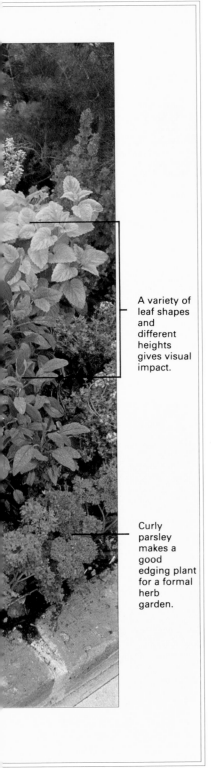

A variety of leaf shapes and different heights gives visual impact.

Curly parsley makes a good edging plant for a formal herb garden.

Herbs can also be trained up poles and around frames. Bay and juniper respond well to clipping and can even be clipped and trained into intricate shapes if you fancy trying your hand at topiary.

Easy growing

Most herbs are not too fussy. They do not require special soil conditions but generally prefer a well-drained situation with some sun.

Many herbs grow quite happily in much warmer climates and can survive a hot dry spell, thriving where other plants would suffer badly from lack of water.

There are three main types of herbs: annuals, biennials and perennials. Annuals last for one year only: they will grow, flower, set seed and die during one season. You will need to re-stock your herb garden with these plants each year, either by growing them from seed each spring or buying plants from garden centres – or some supermarkets even.

A biennial herb develops in two stages: it grows leaves during its first season, then sets seed and dies during its second. The seeds should then be sown to provide more plants ready for the next season.

A perennial herb is there to stay. Some die down in the winter and regrow in spring, forming a bigger clump each year, while others are shrubby and evergreen. You do not have to do much to these plants – just a little tidying now and then.

Clipping an evergreen will encourage it to form a compact

If you don't have room to grow a selection of herbs together, plant them in a border. The chives (below) with their decorative flowers along with tumbling foliage of oregano, soften the edge of a flower bed.

and will not be damaged if you step on them; in fact, this will release their wonderful aroma.

Thyme seeds can be sown between paving stones to produce tough little creeping, mat-forming plants that will soften stark edges of borders and patios. Specimen herbs can be placed in the centre of a flower bed or planted in an attractive container to show them off to the full.

Create a special space for growing herbs (above) by removing a few paving slabs from a patio or pathway.

sheltered, sunny spot in well-drained ground. Regular snipping (for your cooking) will keep your herbs in good, healthy shape.

Here are the most popular herbs, with their culinary uses.

Parsley *(Petroselinum crispum)* is probably the most popular and widely-used herb. The common variety has the familiar curly leaf, but there is also a flat-leafed variety known as French or continental parsley, which has a

stronger, more pungent flavour. Although parsley is a biennial, its leaves are at their best in the first year of growth, so sow parsley seeds annually.

For a successful crop, buy a reputable brand of fresh seed and sow in shallow drills. The best time to sow is in summer (July or August) when the ground is warm and the seed will come up quickly. Dig over the site, enriching the soil with manure or garden compost to ensure the roots get plenty of nourishment. Pick parsley regularly, as this will encourage regrowth, but never remove more than one fifth of the foliage at one time.

Rosemary *(Rosmarinus officinalis)* grows at a slower rate than parsley and forms a medium-sized evergreen bush. Trim your rosemary to keep it in shape, as this herb has a tendency to grow irregularly. Cut the leading shoots to encourage side shoots to develop and form a more attractive shape. Whole plants can be lost in severe cold spells, so if you live in a particularly chilly area site it in a sheltered spot or plant it in a container so

---

WHO'S WHO IN THE HERB GARDEN

Annuals Basil, coriander, dill – all popular herbs for the kitchen, so grow in greater quantities than other herbs, and keep near the kitchen.

Biennials Parsley, caraway and angelica. Parsley is best sown or planted out in late summer for the best results the following summer.

Perennials Mint, fennel, tarragon and chives die down in winter. These plants need little attention – just tidy up the dead foliage in the autumn.

Evergreen Rosemary, thyme, savory, sage, lavender and bay all benefit from regular use and occasional cutting.

---

bush and prevent it becoming too leggy. The best time to trim is just after flowering.

Take your pick

Most herbs are easy to grow. A small selection need not cost too much as many can be grown from seed. Whether planted in a container or in a bed, herbs require little care. The main requirement is for a

Tall, slim **chives** lend a mild onion flavour to dips, baked potatoes and salads.

Chervil (below right) is pale and pretty – it makes a dainty garnish for canapés.

Oregano (below left) is invaluable if you enjoy cooking Italian dishes.

Rosemary (below) is essential when roasting lamb – and great for aromatic barbecues.

There are several types of **mint** (below); use it for salads and mint sauce.

Parsley is available in curly and 'continental' varieties; use either for soups, sauces and, of course, as a garnish.

A SMALL HERB GARDEN

In a sunny position, mark out an area measuring 1m/3ft square and edge this with a double row of bricks or tiles. Dig over the area, adding manure or garden compost to enrich the soil.

Following the planting plan (below left), mark out diagonal divisions and plant a central clump of rosemary, then purple sage (salvia) at each corner. Plant feverfew (not a culinary herb) along the edges, between the clumps of sage, then fill the mid-section with cotton lavender (santolina), leaving gaps in which to stand pots of chives and marigolds (calendula). Keep the santolina trimmed for a formal effect.

You can, of course, vary this plan according to personal taste. Plant curly-leaved parsley in place of the feverfew. Mint is good for growing in pots, as is basil, which can be left outside during the summer months and brought indoors when the weather becomes too cold. Its place can be taken by a herb that is more hardy, such as a tarragon or hyssop. In the central spot, lavender makes a splendid show, while lemon balm sits in the corners.

PLANTING PLAN

For this pretty symmetrical design you will need:
Cotton lavender (8-12 plants)
Rosemary (1 large plant)
Chives (2 plants)
Feverfew 'Golden Ball' (12-15 plants)
Sage (4 large plants)

that it can be brought inside.

Chives *(Allium schoenoprasum)* are another versatile culinary herb. It grows as a clump which dies down each winter and reappears in the spring to form a bigger clump. It thrives in moist, fertile soil and will tolerate shade. If the leaves start to turn brown at the tip they are in need of fertilizer, so apply a liquid feed with a watering can every two weeks and they will soon perk up. When growing strongly a clump can be cut right to the ground if needed and it will quickly regrow with lots of fresh young leaves. In the autumn or early spring, chives can be divided by simply cutting or pulling the clump apart. This creates several smaller plants which can then

Dill (right) has a distinctive flavour; add to fish dishes and pickled cucumbers.

Thyme (below) has a marvellous scent – use in stuffings and meat dishes.

Sage (below left) is the traditional partner for pork – and goes well with duck, veal, liver and sausages.

Savory (below left) has a spicy taste and gives bean dishes delicious flavour.

Marjoram (below right), is a cousin of oregano – use for meat dishes and pizza.

Use **fennel** fronds to flavour fish; add the dried seeds to curries.

be replanted. If potted up they can then be brought indoors and used during winter. Look out for interesting garlic chives, with their flat leaves, pretty white flowers and distinct taste of garlic.

Coriander (*Coriandrum sativum*) is an annual that grows to 45cm/18in. Both the feathery dark green leaves and the small round seeds can be used in cooking. Coriander needs a warm sunny position to thrive. Wait until the seeds have turned from green to grey before picking.

Dill (*Anethum graveolens*) is an annual that grows to 60cm/2ft. This tall decorative herb looks a bit like fennel, with large flower heads and feathery leaves. Sow seeds shallowly in spring, where you want them to grow, as dill does not like being moved.

Fennel (*Foeniculum vulgare*) is a perennial. It grows to 1.5m/5ft and its fine feathery leaves have strong flavour of aniseed. Native to southern Europe, it likes plenty of sun and needs a sheltered position out of the wind.

Lemon balm (*Melissa officinalis*) is a perennial. It grows to 60cm/2ft and will quickly spread once established. Its toothed leaves smell of lemon

Here are two stunning ways of going round in circles: the spokes of a brightly painted cartwheel (above) provide neat divisions for 12 different culinary herbs including parsley, chives, thyme, rosemary, rue, sage, dill and two kinds of mint, making an eye-catching feature for any garden.

For patio gardens, herbs make a convenient culinary centrepiece. Different cartwheel sectors have been created (below) for different heights and varieties of herbs, using old bricks.

and are very attractive to bees. Pinch out the flower buds if you want to use the leaves for cooking. This herb needs a sunny, sheltered spot and, due to its expansive root system, it is a good plant to grow in a pot. The fresh leaves contain an antiseptic, and can be rubbed on insect bites.

Mint (*Mentha*) is a perennial that grows to 45cm/18in. The most common variety grown for using in the kitchen is spearmint. The roots spread rapidly, so it is best grown in a confined area or in a pot. It is very easy to grow from a piece of creeping root. Cut flowering

tops regularly to encourage fresh leaf growth.

Oregano (*Origanum vulgare*) is a perennial. Also known as wild marjoram, it grows to a height of 30cm/12in. If growing from seed, wait until all danger of frost is over and, once established, cut regularly to encourage new, bushy growth.

Sage (*Salvia*) is a perennial evergreen that grows to 45cm/18in. It prefers a warm climate and is best grown from bought plants.

Summer savory (*Satureja hortensis*) is an annual. **Winter savory** (*S.montana*) is a perennial. Both have a peppery, spicy flavour. Sow seed in a sunny, well-drained position in spring. Height is about 30cm/12in.

Tarragon (*Artemisia dracunculus*) is a perennial that grows to 45cm/18in. It cannot be grown from seed, but can easily be propagated from cuttings in spring in well-drained soil. The root system becomes large, so give the plant plenty of room. It must be protected from frost and damp.

Thyme (*Thymus*) is a perennial with a strong scent and taste. Bees are very attracted to the plant, which can be grown from seed or young plants. It needs sun in a well-drained soil and will grow to a height of 25cm/10in.

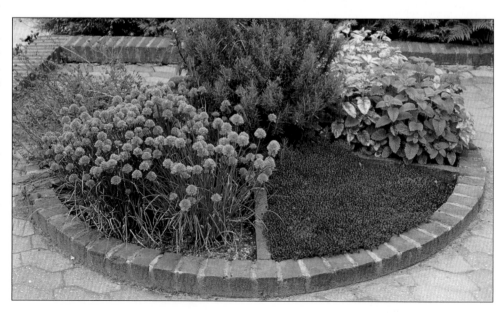

GRAVEL GARDENS

**For creativity, flexibility and covering power,
gravel is the perfect medium. What is more, it requires
the minimum of maintenance and is not as
expensive as you might think.**

There is something rather smart and sweeping about gravel driveways and, surprisingly, they are easy to keep that way. But have you ever considered a gravel lawn or gravel flower bed?

If you have a small area to fill, then gravel is the perfect answer. It is an amazingly versatile material, easy to use and look after, and can be used for so much more than drives or patios, to dramatic effect.

Whereas paving is static, gravel is dynamic, changing

You do not need a large area to obtain the maximum impact from a gravel garden. Beds (above) have been arranged in the gravel and the striking contrast with the background brings out the colour and texture of the plants.

As an alternative to placing beds strategically in the gravel, why not incorporate gravel into your beds? The bold cross (right) divides a flower bed into four symmetrical triangles.

its appearance according to the light and whether it is dry or wet. For instance, some gravels can look glaringly white when dry in bright sunlight, while in damp or dull weather they look mellow and full of different, subtle tones.

No more mowing

Small lawns are the perfect size to convert to gravel. Apart from being more distinctive, it means far less labour. Just imagine, no more weekly mowing during the summer.

179

Flower beds can be retained just as you would have them in a lawn. The added advantage is that you can use spreading or tumbling plants to soften the edges in a way that is often difficult with grass because of the problem of mowing. You may, however, prefer to have the crisp outline of a neat, more formal edging.

A gravel lawn

'Converting' a lawn to gravel is not a lengthy task and you can do it without having to dig up your existing lawn. If it is a shape where you can lay edging stones so that they stand about 5cm/2in higher than the grass, you can kill the grass and simply pour the gravel over this and rake it level.

It is a good idea to destroy the grass with a weedkiller first (but do take special care not to damage plants in the surrounding beds).

If you prefer, simply lay thick polythene over the grass. The weight of the gravel will compact the grass and without light the grass will die.

Mix and match

There is a variety of colours of gravel from which to choose: grey-blue, brown, black, white or tones of yellow. Why not match the gravel to a nearby brick wall or choose a contrasting colour?

You can then add an interesting focal point such as a birdbath or sundial in the centre, or towards one end. Or arrange a group of big boulders in one corner to maintain the

The limited space in the patio area (top left) has been used to the full. A glorious flush of white, pink-tinged star-of-the-Veldt forms a border and the creative use of rocks and potted plants completes the effect.

Brightly coloured potted plants (above left) have been cleverly used in this gravel garden. The lively colour scheme of red, orange and yellow with a touch of hot pink is provided by nasturtiums, pelargoniums, petunias and French marigolds. A path of hexagonal paving slabs has been laid in an area which is frequently used and this enhances the overall effect.

DESIGN FOR A GRAVEL GARDEN

This planting plan can easily be adapted to suit the area you have available – whether it is a large front garden or a small patio. First mark out the gravel area with string. Allow space around the edge for planting. Cover this area with polythene. Mark out the central diamond with string from the centre point of each edge. Mark the central rectangle. Lay the bricks over the polythene. Remove the polythene in the innermost

In a large garden, gravel makes an unusual alternative to grass. It constantly changes its appearance according to the light, the season and the weather. Here (left) a bird bath has been made the central feature, and a border of edging stones further emphasizes the visual effect.

Traditionally a material used in paths, gravel is a much less severe option than paving or concrete. A variety of colours is available so you could even choose your path to match your brickwork. An edging of box gives a more formal look.

...ectangle. Increase the ...soil level in the borders ...o keep bricks in ...osition. Plant up the ...orders leaving room for ... brick path. Plant up the ...entral rectangle ...ositioning a standard ...lant, bird bath or statue ...n the centre as a focal ...oint. Fill in the gravel ...reas in two contrasting ...olours.

GARDEN NOTES

BUYING GRAVEL

Most types of gravel, particularly pea gravel, are available in bags from garden centres. A larger range is available from builders' merchants. To calculate how much you need, multiply the width by the length of the area you want to cover and then by the depth. 1 cubic metre (m^3) will cover an area of 20 square metres (m^2) at a depth of 5cm.

harmony while breaking up the flat surface.

If the gravelled area is one which will be walked across frequently, sink in stepping stones or a staggered path. Not only is this a practical idea, but it will increase the general sense of design.

Gravel can be used to replace other features too, besides lawns. If your garden is so tiny there is simply no space for a lawn and some form of hard surface such as paving seems to be the only practical alternative, gravel might be a better answer. If you pave a very small garden, the stones themselves can be overpowering and may reduce still further the space for growing plants.

Many plants grow happily through gravel, and if you choose dwarf shrubs, the gravel will eventually become like a decorative mulch or background as the shrubs grow. If you want to grow as many different plants as possible in a small space, however, pack in the alpine varieties. These will certainly thrive in the free-draining gravel.

Making beds

Instead of having a gravel area with flower beds set into it, try setting a gravelled area into a lawn as the flower bed. Not only can this type of bed be striking visually, it will provide the perfect conditions for plants which enjoy a dry, well-drained soil. If you have a garden that is too wet for some plants, try making a bed with very good drainage and top this with a layer of gravel.

Rivers of gravel

A gravel bed set into a lawn looks best if it has an irregular and gently curving outline. By the simple addition of a few boulders, you can create the look of a 'dried river bed' if you let it snake through the lawn. The best effect is created by keeping the centre of the river of gravel and stones fairly free of plants, with most of the planting around the edges.

Beds of this kind are best sunk slightly below the surrounding lawn. Because of this there is no trouble containing the gravel, which otherwise may stray over surrounding beds or grass.

Mixing materials

Gravel can be used with other hard surface materials. It

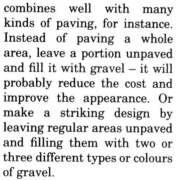

*Irresistible little clumps of **Primula 'Wanda'** (above) have been planted randomly in a gravel garden. The neutral background brings out their vibrant colour.*

*It is a lovely surprise to come across the small evergreen perennial **Armeria juniperifolia** which is almost camouflaged by the large pieces of gravel. A host of colours and textures are captured in the irregular stones.*

combines well with many kinds of paving, for instance. Instead of paving a whole area, leave a portion unpaved and fill it with gravel – it will probably reduce the cost and improve the appearance. Or make a striking design by leaving regular areas unpaved and filling them with two or three different types or colours of gravel.

Do not be tempted to overdo it though, as too many types or colours of gravel or paving will look fussy.

A sunken garden

A sunken garden can bring character and interest to a garden, rather like creating a small garden 'room' to explore, and using gravel gives the advantage of better drainage. Whereas in a paved area surface water can be a problem after heavy rain, gravel allows free drainage. Also, because there are natural boundaries to retain the gravel, it never

---

MAINTENANCE

The beauty of gravel is that it requires so little upkeep. If you lay it on polythene, the weeds that grow near the surface will die off quickly. Light hoeing will take care of most weeds, or use a weedkiller specially formulated for paths. One application should last all season. There are several available and most will not 'creep' through the soil to harm established plants, but do take care not to apply it too close to plants. Be prepared to use a 'spot' weedkiller on weeds that persistently reappear.

---

strays into surrounding beds.

Be prepared, though, because the creation of a sunken garden will no doubt involve a lot of heavy excavation.

Brilliant backdrops

If your interest lies more in plants than in creating eye-catching features, there are several ways in which gravel

---

SIX OF THE BEST

You can grow most of the more vigorous alpines in areas of gravel, but it is best to start with some of the large, bold and bright plants that will not give up and die if you happen to tread on them occasionally, and that will give a good display over a long period, from spring until autumn.

● Thrift (*Armeria maritima*) forms evergreen grass-like tufts, covered in spring and early summer with pink, white or red drumstick flowerheads. Colour depends on variety.
● Maiden pink (*Dianthus deltoides*) is very bright, evergreen, with small red or pink flowers (depends on variety) from early summer through till late summer.
● Euphorbia (*E. myrsinites*) is an evergreen with blue-grey leaves on snaking stems that sprawl over the gravel. Yellowish 'flowers' appear in March and April, but this is really a year-round foliage plant.

● Rock rose (*Helianthemum nummularium*) is another evergreen with greenish or greyish foliage (depends on variety), grown for its prolific flowering. In June and July it is covered with yellow, pink or red flowers 12-25cm (½-1in) across. Dead-heading extends the flowering period.
● Evening primrose (*Oenothera macrocarpa*) is a ground-hugging carpeter that has some of the most brilliant and beautiful flowers of all alpines: big yellow saucers that start to appear in June and will go on blooming until the end of summer.
● Polygonum (*Persicaria affinis*) is a gradually spreading plant that hugs the ground. Choose the variety 'Donald Lowndes' if you have space for only one. It is compact, the old leaves last until the new ones appear in spring, and the small rose-red pokers that appear in early summer remain attractive for months even when they have died.

This stunning iris (left) is one of the many dwarf plants available which are suitable for growing in gravel. Plants with a compact or restrained growth pattern are the best choice.

The sunny, bright yellow Adonis vernalis introduces a splash of vibrant colour into a patio area (below). If your area is small, choose plants that are bold and bright.

The warmth of the dark pink helianthemum and pale pink dianthus is reflected in the colour of these stones (above). The large pieces of gravel deflect the light beautifully.

A succulent, fleshy Euphorbia myrsinites (below) is made more interesting by the stylish arrangement of stones while a border of conifers is given a touch of elegance.

SAFETY FIRST

DON'T FORGET!

- If you have an area of gravel next to a lawn, make sure the gravel does not encroach on to the grass; it could well cause damage to lawnmower blades.
- With smaller children, it is better to choose rounded pea gravel which, unlike gravel chippings, has no sharp edges.

and plants can harmonize. The gravel will form a backdrop for your plants and will help to control weeds.

If the area is large, divide it up into beds with broad gravel paths winding between them. Plant your flowers and shrubs in position and extend a thick layer of gravel from the path over the beds. Provided the gravel is a couple of inches thick over the beds, it will suppress weeds.

As the plants become established and dominate, the gravel links the beds, providing access and an opportunity to explore. You should hoe off the odd weed as it appears or pull it out, or you may prefer to use a suitable weedkiller.

Formal and fancy

Perhaps a sense of design is more important to you than plenty of plants. In this case, gravel is an invaluable material for some types of traditional gardens as well as for more modern, geometric designs.

Elizabethan-style knot gardens, so named for their low hedges which look like knotted ribbons, can look very striking if you introduce areas of various coloured gravels.

Traditionally, dwarf box is used in knot gardens but it is both expensive and slow growing. A cheaper and quick-growing alternative, that can be clipped, is cotton lavender (*Santolina chamaecyparissus*). Improvise with other materials, perhaps picking out a pattern with large beach pebbles instead of plants.

Whatever you choose for the outline shape, use at least two colours of gravel to fill in the areas created by the pattern. You could use one colour for the associated paths and others for the infilling.

If you are feeling bold, try a chequerboard pattern or other geometric design, using bricks to define areas, and fill each 'pocket' with a coloured gravel.

ARCHES AND PERGOLAS

A single arch or a series of inter-connecting structures creates the opportunity to grow climbing and screening plants, forming an attractive architectural feature.

A rustic pergola (left) made of weathered brick and wood adds height and interest to part of a stone terrace. The dappled light which filters through the climbing honeysuckle makes this an ideal place to sit on a hot sunny day.

The obvious place to grow climbing plants is on a wall or fence, but a free-standing structure offers all kinds of possibilities and creates an interesting focus.

Any garden, whether it is large or small, in the town or country, formal or rustic, old-fashioned or ultra-modern, can be enriched by the addition of an arch or pergola. You may choose to site it in the centre of your garden, straddling a path or incorporated into a patio, or you may prefer to attach it to the house or to a garden wall. It can have the additional purpose of hiding an unsightly feature.

Choosing your pergola
Any construction introduced into a garden should blend with the existing design, as well as harmonizing with the house. Cottage-type houses need the old-world charm of rustic arches and cosy arbours, whereas in the garden of a modern house a pergola might be more in keeping.

Some gardens have a neat, symmetrical design: straight paths and flower beds, for example, with perhaps a patio or terrace created from rectangular paving slabs. This style demands a formal pergola and, to create an even more impressive feature, you could paint it to match the colour scheme in your garden. In an architectural-style garden, it could be painted white or even matt black, depending on the effect you wish to create. Alternatively, to produce a

An arch can be used to bring a feeling of depth and perspective to a garden. This one has a rustic style (above). Smothered in red roses and purple clematis with a strip of verdant lawn running through, it perfectly links the two halves of this cottage-style garden.

184

your garden. You may, however, prefer to buy pre-constructed arches and trelliswork from your local garden centre. Sawn-timber pergolas can be bought in sections for later construction. These are mainly free-standing and are intended for straddling paths or for construction on patios or terraces.

A rustic touch

When buying rustic poles to make your own trellis or arch, phone around to ensure the best buy – also check on free delivery. Poles 2.4-2.7m/8-9ft long and 6.5-7.5cm/2½-3in thick are usually sold as uprights, while longer poles are needed for cross-pieces. Because of their extra length – usually 3.6-4.5m/12-15ft or more – these range in thickness from 5-7.5cm/2-3in.

To construct a formal pergola, use sawn timber treated with a wood preservative to stop it rotting in wet weather. Upright posts need to be at least 65mm/2½in square and 2.7m/9ft long, while cross members are 5cm/2in thick and 10cm/5in deep. Their length will depend on the design of the patio, but avoid

widths more than 3m/10ft, especially if constructed adjacent to a house and covered with a roofing material.

Fixing wooden uprights

Rustic poles do not need to be concreted into the ground, though it is advisable. Remove loose bark from the lower 45cm/18in and stand the lower end of each pole in a bucket of plant-friendly wood preservative for 24 hours before use. For a typical pole length of 2.1-2.4m/7-8ft, dig a hole about 60cm/2ft deep and pack about 15cm/6in of broken bricks and rubble into the base. Use more broken bricks, rubble or gravel around the pole. Then add topsoil and firm in well.

Sawn timber (65cm/2½in square) is best bought ready treated with a preservative – preferably where the preservative has been forced into the timber by vacuum or pressure impregnation. There are two main ways to secure sawn timber in the ground.

If the pergola is to be attached to a wall, which will offer rigidity, metal stake supports can be used which means that you do not need to dig holes. These metal, spike-

subdued feature, you can paint your pergola with a natural wood-coloured, plant-friendly wood preservative.

An informal garden, with meandering paths and curved edges to its flower beds, welcomes a less sophisticated approach. It is not only the materials and shape of the construction that enable it to harmonize in informal settings, but also its colour.

Natural colour

A pergola formed of sawn western red cedar may have a hard outline, but it is a wood with a warm and natural-looking colour. This enables it to blend into even the most informal garden.

Your sawn timber or rustic poles can be custom made to fit

A pergola need not only be used to grow plants over; you can also suspend plants from it in hanging baskets (right). Use them to add a splash of instant extra seasonal colour even after the climbers are established or to soften the outlines while the permanent climbing plants make their way over it.

Another area that can often look rather dull is round the base of your climbers. Brighten it up either by planting annuals straight into the bed or by adding a few strategically placed pots.

Honeysuckle (left) makes a delightful covering for an arch. In this case Lonicera × americana has been used; this has the double benefit of a strong, spicy fragrance and colourful flowers, starting as red-purple buds which open to white flowers.

Magnolia stellata (right), though not a climber, makes an unusual plant to decorate a pergola. This is a beautiful, though slow-growing, plant with lovely, star-shaped, fragrant flowers in spring.

This new pergola (far right) has a clematis starting to grow up it. While it grows, there is no need for the pergola to look bare and, in this case, it has been decorated with hanging baskets filled with ivy and geraniums.

A RUSTIC ARCH FOR A COTTAGE GARDEN

A SLIMLINE MODERN ARCH

A DIAMOND TRELLIS ARCH

A tubular steel arch is quickly slotted and linked together and ideal for formal gardens.

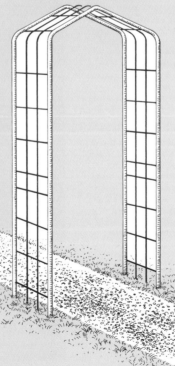

An arch of rustic poles is ideal straddling a path in an informal setting. It can be used to separate one part of the garden from another or create an oasis of scent. Use a series of arches to form a tunnel.

An arch formed of expanded diamond-sha[pe] trellis on a wooden framework is ideal in a[n] informal garden. Use it as a feature on its own, or integrated with hedges to divide different parts of the garden.

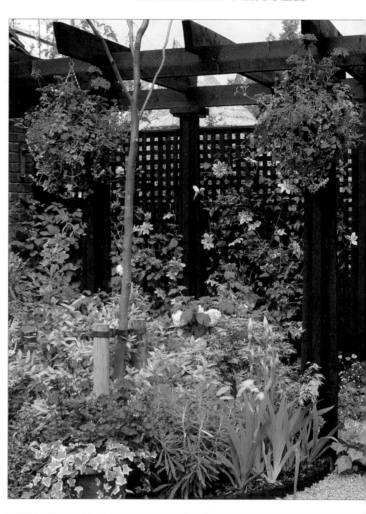

ended supports are driven into the ground and the wooden supports are fitted into them and then secured with screws.

Where the pergola is free standing and exposed to buffeting wind, however, it is preferable to set the posts in concrete. Dig a hole about 60cm/2ft deep, fill the base with rubble, stand and temporarily secure the post in position and pour concrete mix around it. Be prepared to support the posts with temporary bracing for about a week until the concrete has set firmly.

The first year

Many of the climbers you will want to grow over your arch or pergola may take some time to establish themselves. Even while the long-term plants are growing, though, you can quickly create very pretty effects by using fast-growing annuals.

One really stunning annual climber is ipomoea or morning glory. It is a tender plant, so seeds should be planted in the

A STYLISH PERGOLA TO SHADE A PATHWAY

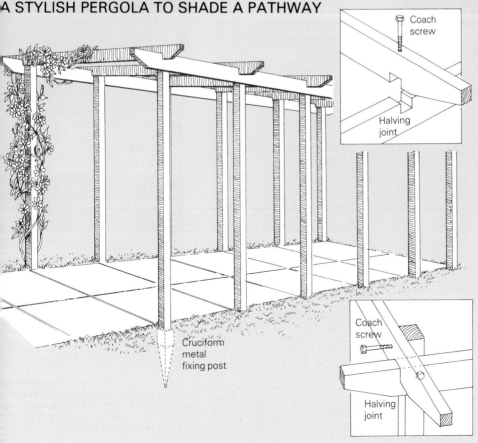

Coach screw

Halving joint

Cruciform metal fixing post

Coach screw

Halving joint

A STYLISH SELECTION

A pergola attached to a house creates an attractive entrance. It can be covered with translucent roofing sheets to form a rain-proof area, or rely on plants to create an overhead canopy of shade during summer. Use a selection of flowering and leafy climbers to create shade and colour.

Bricklaying

Brick pillars, instead of wood, are very attractive but make construction more expensive and time consuming. They can give a formal or informal appearance depending on the types of bricks used. A brick arch connected to the house creates an attractive architectural feature that harmonizes well with a wrought-iron gate. Variegated ivies, such as the Canary Island ivy and the smaller-leaved Hedera helix 'Goldheart', cling tightly to brickwork.

A central focus

A free-standing pergola, straddling a path or paved terrace, creates the opportunity to grow climbers in the centre of a garden. If the pergola is near the house, use climbers such as wisteria and roses, as they will not obscure the view to the bottom of the garden. If the pergola creates a focal point near the bottom of the garden, however, use leafy and rampant climbers such as climbing hydrangea (Hydrangea petiolaris) or the yellow-leaved Humulus lupulus 'Aureus'. Western red cedar creates an attractive shelter with an Oriental feel.

The dark green leaves with gold centres of English ivy, Hedera helix 'Goldheart' (above), have the great advantage of year-round interest.

The soft, yellowish leaves of Humulus lupulus 'Aureus' (above), the hop vine, add a touch of brightness to your garden.

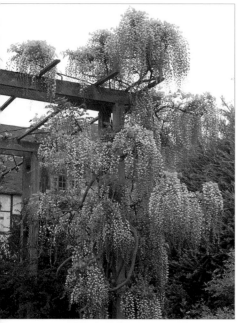

Wisteria (above) has glorious, scented, lilac flowers in early summer and makes a stunning display for a pergola.

PLANTS TO DRESS ARCHES AND PERGOLAS

These climbing plants and wall shrubs will produce beautiful flowers and foliage to soften any hard edges and enhancing the overall effect.

mountain clematis *Clematis montana rubens*	Masses of pink flowers in early and midsummer. Some varieties have slightly scented flowers. Very vigorous climber for large pergolas.
large-flowered clematis hybrids	Wide range of varieties, with eye-catching flowers from early to late summer, depending on the variety. Ideal for clothing the uprights of formal pergolas.
winter jasmine *Jasminum nudiflorum*	A very hardy climbing shrub with bright yellow flowers to brighten winter days from winter to spring. Ideal for training on walls and brick arches.
passion flower *Passiflora caerulea*	Tender evergreen with stunning exotic summer flowers and edible fruits. Suitable for pergolas and arches in warm position.
English ivy *Hedera helix* 'Goldheart'	Green leaves brightly splashed with yellow. Ideal for smothering brick arches.
hop vine (golden hop) *Humulus lupulus* 'Aureus'	Herbaceous climber with large, hop-like, soft-yellow leaves from spring to autumn. Forms a dense screen. Ideal for trellises and arches.
climbing hydrangea *Hydrangea petiolaris*	Vigorous climber with dense foliage and greenish-white flowers during midsummer. Ideal for covering large rustic arches. Also grows on walls so that flowers and foliage trail over arbours.
Japanese wisteria *Wisteria floribunda* 'Macrobotrys'	Large clusters of fragrant, lilac-tinged, blue-purple flowers during early and midsummer. White-flowered varieties are also available. Superb on formal pergolas, it is a large plant and so needs plenty of space to grow.

PROJECT PLANTIN

1 *Dig a hole deep enough to take the entire root ball of the plant comfortably.*

3 *Tie the stems carefully to the arc or pergola but not so tightly or it will cut into the stems.*

The climbing rose 'Madame Grégoire Staechelin' (left) has an abundance of scented, double pink flowers. It grows vigorously and can reach a height of 6m/20ft with a spread of 4m/12ft even in a shady position.

MAKING ROOM FOR ROSES

Rambling roses are ideal for growing over pergolas and arches, as well as trellises. Here are a few beauties from which to make your selection.

'Alberic Barbier' – yellow buds open to creamy white during early summer and often again later in summer. Height: 6m/20ft. Spread 3m/10ft.

'Albertine' – reddish-salmon buds open to coppery-pink from early summer and recurrently throughout summer; strongly scented. Height: 4.5–5.4m/15–18ft.

'Crimson Showers' – bright crimson flowers from early summer until early autumn. Height: 3–3.6m/10–12ft.

'Emily Gray' – rich gold flowers during early summer; scented. Height: 3m/10ft.

'François Juranville' – deep fawn-pink flowers during early summer; sharp apple scent. Height: 4.5–5.4m/15–18ft.

'Veilchenblau' – dark magenta flowers, fading to lilac, during early summer; rich orange scent. Height: 3.6m/12ft.

'Madame Grégoire Staechelin' – pale pink ruffled flowers which darken to carmine appear in large clusters during summer. Height 6m/20ft. Spread 4m/12ft.

IBER

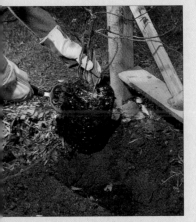

Gently loosen the roots to encourage them to spread the plant in the hole.

Water well especially during dry weather, until the plant is well established.

A ROMANTIC ARBOUR

A few rustic poles can turn a quiet corner into a romantic arbour. Use a selection of old-fashioned, heavily scented flowers to create an intimate atmosphere. Honeysuckle, climbing roses, jasmine and sweet peas are ideal choices.

The hybrid honeysuckle *Lonicera × americana* has a strong fragrance, sweet and spicy, and produces an abundance of pretty white flowers. Jasmines are among the most fragrant of all the climbers.

You can create a romantic arbour as a lean-to against a wall or as a free-standing pergola. You will probably want to put a wooden rustic-looking seat in it so that you can sit there to enjoy the scent on summer evenings.

flowering position in spring, only after any danger of frost has past. It then grows very quickly to a height of about 3m/10ft. It has bright blue trumpet-shaped flowers from late spring through to autumn.

Nasturtiums (*Tropaeolum*) can be grown as climbers and their bright gold, orange and red flowers contrast beautifully with morning glory if you grow the two together. *T. speciosum*, flame nasturtium, has scarlet summer flowers. *T. peregrinum* has small, bright yellow flowers from summer until the first frosts. Both grow to around 2m/6ft and seeds should be sown in flowering position in spring.

Sweet peas (*Lathyrus odoratus*) are not only beautiful to look at, they have the additional advantage of fragrance and this can be a particularly delightful effect for an arch or pergola. Most varieties are climbers growing to 3m/10ft, and dead-heading encourages re-flowering.

Unusual annuals

Cobaea scandens, also known as the cup and saucer plant or cathedral bells, grows remarkably fast, reaching up to 3-6m/10-20ft in a hot summer and in

a sheltered spot. Its greenish-white and purple flowers appear from mid summer to mid autumn. 'Alba' is a variety with pale green flowers.

Eccremocarpus scaber, the Chilean glory flower, is another unusual climber, which in very mild areas of the country is an evergreen, but is usually treated as an annual. It needs plenty of watering in dry weather in order to produce its bright orange, tubular flowers.

Thunbergia alata, better known as black-eyed Susan, has mixed cream, orange and dark brown flowers from summer to early autumn. It reaches a height of 3m/10ft in a good summer and seeds should be sown only when all risk of frost has passed in late spring and early summer.

Edible climbers

Another unusual use for a pergola or arch is to use it for a summer crop of runner beans. Before the beans appear from midsummer to autumn, there are attractive scarlet flowers.

Water the plants often in very dry weather and spray the flowers to encourage them to set. The more beans you pick, the more flowers and beans the plants will produce.

A TOUCH OF FORMALITY

Introduce a touch of formality into your plot, no matter what its size. Whether you choose simply to add a statue or to transform your whole garden, here are some great ideas to get you started.

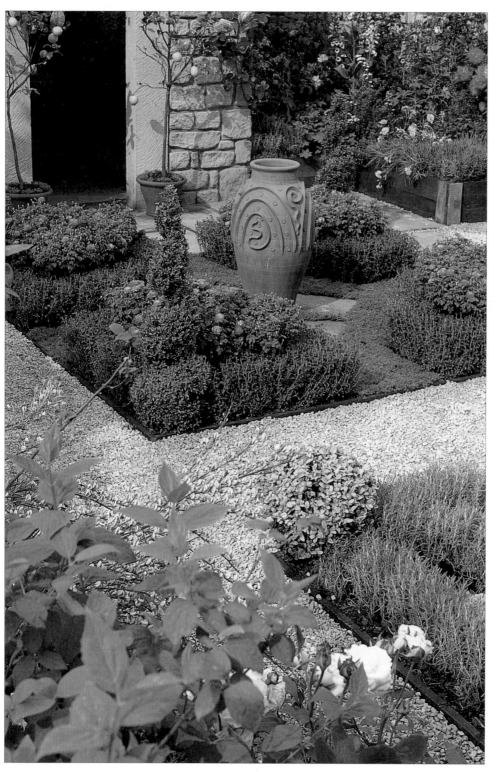

If you wish to create a garden that is well ordered and neat, with straight paths and formal flower beds, a tidy patio and a well-trimmed lawn – perhaps with a statue, bird bath or other decoration – then the classic ornamental garden is the right kind for you.

Whether planning your garden from scratch or making changes to your existing plot, do not make the mistake of considering the garden in isolation. Your design should also take into account the architecture of your home. An intricate design would look out of place next to a simple, modern house, for example.

Perfect symmetry

The overall effect you are looking for in an ornamental garden is one of clean, simple, uncluttered lines. Beds, borders, patios, lawns and other features need to be geometric in shape. They also need to form part of an overall symmetry.

In your quest for a harmonious design, no element should be left 'out on a limb'. Your geometric-shaped flower-beds, for example, should be incorporated into the patio or lawn, or surrounded by neat paths.

Formal beds need formal planting. In spring, a carpet of forget-me-nots, polyanthus or wallflowers punctuated regularly with bedding tulips could be used. The bed could be

An ornamental garden need not be complicated in its design: this garden (left) is all the more pleasing for its simplicity. A pair of lemon trees in pots flank the doorway and a single terracotta urn provides an eye-catching central feature.

If you feel that a statue would be too grand for your garden, why not have a bird bath instead? This one (left) has been placed in the middle of a circular lawn. The round shapes of lawn and bowl are further echoed by the brick-edged bed at the base of the pedestal. As well as being a decorative feature in its own right, a bird bath will also attract birds to your garden.

small number of plants and colours. Go for single colours instead of mixtures when choosing bedding plants and aim to harmonize the beds with the colour of the house, paths, walls and fences.

Low levels

A classic ornamental feature worth considering is a sunken garden. These are usually square or rectangular and the depth should be in proportion

GROWING TIPS

A BEAUTIFUL LAWN

An untidy lawn can ruin the effect of an ornamental garden. If yours is a mess, do not despair. Rather than dig it up and start again, there are ways you can improve it.
- mow regularly and frequently to discourage the growth of coarse rye grasses and encourage finer grasses
- as well as regular cutting, feed frequently with a proprietary fertilizer
- to discourage moss, aerate the lawn in dry conditions and, if soil is acid, add lime
- after aerating, add a top dressing of sharp sand and rake it in
- children and dogs can damage the lawn, so if you really want it to look beautiful, don't allow them to play on the grass or it might end up looking like a football pitch!

edged broadly with a border of double daisies. If you have a group of formal beds, you could stick to the same scheme in each one or different, complementary plantings.

For summer, there are so many bedding plants from which to make your selection that there is an almost infinite variety of combinations.

The right plants

Effective schemes include a carpet of wax begonias or zonal pelargoniums punctuated with silver-leaved *Senecio bicolor*, with a centrepiece of tall cabbage palm (*Cordyline australis*). Remember, however, that these plants are not hardy enough to grow reliably out of doors unless you live in a mild or sheltered area.

Choose plants to suit your own particular climate and soil conditions, following a few simple style guidelines. For an uncluttered effect stick to a

PERFECT PARTNERS

It is best to keep to simple colour schemes in your ornamental garden – a mixture of hues could detract from the orderliness of the design. Here, the white tulip 'Pax' has been combined with 'Crystal Bowl' pansies.

When it comes to deciding on plants to fill your ornamental garden, the choice is huge – but there are some that seem especially 'right' for this style of design. Plants to go for are those that are tidy and echo the orderliness of your design.

Taller plants with straight, upright stems such as tulips can look very effective placed in a sea of neat, low-growing flowers such as pansies. The impressive crown imperial (*Fritillaria imperialis*) can be used in a similar way. When combining different plants, check that their flowering times are the same.

For a traditional touch, why not try a pair of standard roses, placed symmetrically in your design? Surround them with one of the more compact lavenders, such as Dutch lavender (*Lavandula × intermedia* Dutch Group).

Many herbs are ideal plants for the ornamental garden, forming neat clumps and having the added appeal of aromatic foliage and a practical use in the kitchen, too. Combine blue-grey sage, golden balm and parsley.

AN 'ANTIQUE' CONTAINER

A new concrete container can look too bright and clean but by the clever application of a little paint you can easily 'age' it to blend in with its surroundings. Getting the exact shade you want is a matter of trial and error: what you are aiming for is a natural-looking stone colour. Do a test on a piece of scrap paper first.

This method can also be used for 'antiquing' plastic containers – but omit the last stage as sanding is likely to make the paint flake off.

You will need:
raw umber acrylic paint
black acrylic paint
white emulsion paint
2 paintbrushes
medium glass paper

1 *Assemble your materials before you begin. You can paint more than one container at a time.*

2 *Pour some emulsion into a jar and add small amount of raw umber acrylic paint. Paint the container.*

3 *Add more raw umber and dab on paint allowing the lighter base colour to show through.*

4 *Add some black paint to your mixture and paint the hollow parts, softening edges with a dry brush.*

5 *When the paint is dry, rub over the paint surface with glass paper to give a 'distressed' finish.*

BALANCING ACT

Two of the key things to watch out for when planning your ornamental garden are *symmetry* and *balance* – which simply means you should aim to get an equal balance between the different parts on opposite sides of the garden, borders or paths. A tall plant on one side should be matched by a similar plant, or ornament, on the other; a wide border could be balanced by a wide path. Neat, geometric shapes are also the right ones for your beds, paths and ponds.

to the area: the smaller the garden, the shallower it should be. Do not scale down your sunken garden too much, however. It should form a major part of the overall design of your ornamental garden. One possibility is to let it span the width of a narrow plot, creating a split-level effect. Changes of level will add an exciting new dimension to the look of your garden. As a guide, the depth should be about 30-60cm/12-24in.

Decorative details

The low retaining walls of your sunken garden can be built up with bricks. Ideally these should match the house, or be made from decorative concrete walling blocks.

For a really splendid effect, add a central feature such as a statue, sundial, most impressive of all, a small formal pool with a fountain.

Generally this is a wedge shape, broader at the base than at the top, with a rounded or flat top – but you can choose whichever shape you please, of course.

Hedges can also be used within the garden, to divide it into a number of areas. Separate the formal from the informal part of the garden if you have enough space.

Formal hedges should be 1.8m/6ft max. in height and will need regular clipping in the growing season to keep them in shape and prevent them from growing too tall.

Classic features

Low box hedges are an element in another classic formal garden feature, the *parterre*. This consists of geometric beds arranged in a regular pattern and set in a gravel area with space to walk between. The beds are edged with low hedges of dwarf box (*Buxus sempervirens* 'Suffruticosa'), which must be clipped regularly for a neat finish. The beds can be filled with seasonal

bedding or, if you want a more subtle, all-green look, with low-growing culinary and ornamental herbs.

Choosing accessories to dress up your formal garden is probably the most enjoyable part. Make your selection from the array of statues, sundials and ornamental containers you will find on display at most large garden centres.

Finishing touches

Use ornaments in moderation, as it is all too easy to go too far and ruin the simple, elegant effect you are aiming for. If space is limited, a well-chosen piece situated in the corner of the patio, beside a pool or at the far end of the lawn will be more effective than lots of little objects scattered all over the garden.

A statue is a good choice as a focal point, to draw the eye to a particular part of the garden. If you decide to put a statue in your garden, choose one that matches the scale of your plot. Avoid using a life-sized human figure if you have a pocket-

Your sunken garden can be laid out with geometric beds set in gravel or paving and planted with seasonal bedding, or you could create a formal rose garden.

A sunken rose garden can consist of a single bed or a group of geometric beds, perhaps set in a gravel or paved area or in a lawn. Choose formal roses such as large-flowered (hybrid tea) or cluster-flowered (floribunda) varieties. For tiny gardens, scale things down by using miniature roses.

Plant one variety per bed, perhaps with a standard rose, ideally of the same variety, in the centre of each bed, to give additional height.

Hedging bets

The boundaries of a formal ornamental garden are usually planted with formal hedges trained to a regular shape.

Statuary is very much part of the ornamental garden style. A well-placed statue can provide a bold focal point, leading the eye to a particular corner, and can form an essential part of the design. The circular area of gravel (above) cries out for some form of ornament to mark its centre: without the little trumpeter in the middle, it would have seemed very bare. The small figure holds the design together.

In another garden (right), cleverly placed urns and round paving slabs lead the eye naturally across the gravelled area to the statue on the far side. The dark, evergreen hedge behind it provides the perfect foil, accentuating the figure's form.

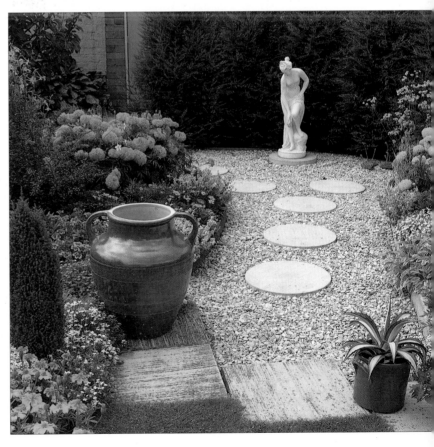

handkerchief-sized garden; a bust might be better, perhaps set on a pedestal or on a wall of a raised bed. Human figures and busts are suited to virtually any garden; those that are naked or carrying a vessel are probably most appropriate near water. If you have a pond, you may also like to consider placing a stone frog, fish or heron by the side of it.

If your statue is light in colour, set it against a dark background such as a hedge or brick wall. Set it next to a formal shrub such as a bay or fatsia, or soften its outlines with a climbing plant.

Modern wood

For an ultra-modern garden, you may prefer to choose a geometric object: a stone obelisk, pyramid, cube or sphere. Use a pair to flank a path or gateway, or place a single object so that it adds drama to a plain lawn or paved area.

A sundial mounted on a pedestal makes a good centrepiece for a sunken bed or the

In the restrained elegance of the ornamental garden, one of the pleasures you can enjoy is variety in colour and texture – and there are plenty of combinations to choose from. Here (left) the deep red of Begonia semperflorens *contrasts with the yellow of* Helichrysum petiolare 'Aureum' *or* 'Limelight'.

centre of a lawn. A container such as a stone urn can perform a similar function, while containers which are set in groups – ideally of similar design but not of the same size – can look extremely elegant.

Containers come in all shapes and sizes. A square wooden Versailles tub looks good in most settings and can be painted to match your

FORMAL HEDGES

These evergreen trees and shrubs are ideal for creating a boundary:
- box (*Buxus sempervirens*) is moderately slow-growing and needs frequent clipping, but forms a good, dense hedge
- Lawson cypress (*Chamaecyparis lawsoniana*) 'Green Hedger' is fast-growing and needs only annual clipping
- holly (*Ilex aquifolium*) is slow-growing, but dense if clipped regularly
- yew (*Taxus baccata*) is moderately slow-growing, but becomes very dense with regular clipping
- western red cedar (*Thuja plicata* 'Atrovirens') is a fast grower with fruity aromatic foliage and needs only annual trimming

cotta which creates a 'warm', rather rustic effect, and may be better suited to more informal parts of the garden. The most stylish – and expensive – garden ornaments are made of stone, but reconstituted stone makes a good substitute. A decorative stone urn can be left unplanted and placed on a matching pedestal to grace a paved area or the centre of a rose garden.

Formal containers are best planted with neat, formal-looking plants – a mass of flowers and greenery tumbling

house. Rounded urns, vases and jars make good focal points, say at the end of a lawn, or as centrepieces for formal rose or sunken gardens. Containers also come in various different materials. At the cheaper end of the range, there is concrete and plastic. These materials may be cheap but in the long run they may be a false economy. Remember

The still surface of this rectangular pond (above left) is uncluttered by plants and calmly reflects the sky. This well-coordinated scheme (above right) has yellow Tagetes 'Lemon Gem' around the edge, with white begonias 'Silver Devil' and a single Artemisia 'Powis Castle' in the middle.

that your garden ornaments may be with you for years, and you may later regret not having splashed out a little more in the beginning to get something that is better quality and continues to be attractive.

Stylish stone

Next in the price range is glass-reinforced cement, a very presentable material, and terra-

loosely over the sides could spoil the tidy effect you have been working to achieve. Good choices would be clipped bay trees or perhaps some topiary in box or yew. You could even try a citrus tree, although if you live in one of the colder areas of the country you would need to bring this indoors into a greenhouse or a conservatory for the winter.

WILD FLOWERS IN THE GARDEN

Do your bit for nature and the environment by making room in your garden for some of our increasingly rare native species.

This carefuly contrived wild garden looks completely natural. Native plants like white and mauve dame's violets, blue cornflowers and bright red poppies are grown in bold patches, while yellow Welsh poppies and spikes of mullein have self-seeded. Heartsease grows in drifts, and daisies dot the grass. Once established, a garden like this thrives on a minimum of attention.

Imagine a summer's day in a garden of wild flowers, where all the colours blend into a pastel haze and the air is filled with the perfume of nectar and the humming of bees. If this is your picture of what a wild flower garden should be, then you will be pleased to know that making your dream come true is easier than you think. If, on the other hand, you imagine an invasion of weeds and a tangle of un-

wanted plants, then it is worth thinking again.

Wild flowers are simply plants that, under natural conditions, would grow in the wild: these plants are our native species and they are all perfectly suited to the weather and soils of this country. Many of our traditional garden plants are descended from these native wild flowers. Cottage gardeners long ago would have grown only wild

flowers because these were the only plants available. It was not until breeders began to select particular colours and shapes they liked, crossing native species with plants imported from abroad, that the cultivated garden plant was born. Over the years, more exotic species were introduced and some of our common wild flowers were forgotten.

Wild flowers are back in fashion. This is partly because

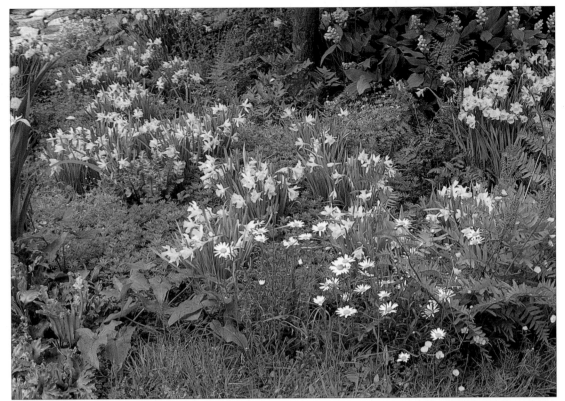

This yellow and white colour scheme (left) has tiny daffodils (Narcissus), as well as the more common larger ones, with ox-eye daisies and tall buttercups growing among green ferns and leaves. The patch of pink campion at the back adds a contrasting note.

The nodding sky-blue harebell (Campanula rotundifolia) (below) must be one of the prettiest small wild flowers, and is perfect for a wild flower garden. Harebells will enjoy a sheltered spot in the rockery, and are ideal for wild meadow areas.

people are aware that too many plants are being threatened with extinction, as their natural habitats are destroyed by agriculture and building developments. Gardens are one of the few safe havens for wild flowers, and by introducing even a few plants to your garden you will be helping to safeguard their future.

Pretty, easy plants

Conservation is not the only reason for growing wild flowers. Cowslips, daisies, columbine and primroses are some of the prettiest flowers to be found anywhere and you do not need any special skills to grow them. On the whole, native flowers are better for wildlife too, attracting a wide range of insects and birds. Last but not least, wild flowers do not need to be fussed over with intensive watering and feeding. They will grow strong and healthy in even the smallest garden, as long you choose the right plants for your soil and situation. You may even find that they grow better in the garden than in the wild places around your home.

The first step towards establishing wild flowers is to take a good look at your garden and see what is growing there. Look closely and you will see flowers that were not planted, but just 'turned up': daisies, clover and dandelions grow in the lawn, thistles and bindweed in the flower beds. Once you get to know and recognize these wild flowers, you can decide which you like and which you do not. It is up to you to decide which are your 'weeds' and which are flowers.

Good management

A wild flower garden, like a conventional one, needs management if you are to grow the plants you want, rather than the ones that just happen to grow. There is a myth that wild flower gardens have to be untidy. The truth is, you can grow wild flowers, just like any other garden flowers, in neat, straight rows if you want to, but to create a more natural feel they are best grouped together in patches, giving a pretty, cottage garden effect. If there is room it is also worth allowing nettles, brambles and

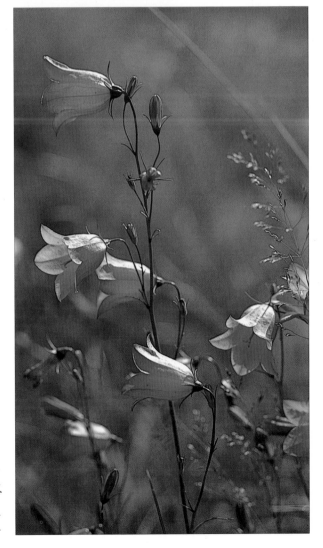

TOP FIVE WILD FLOWERS FOR GARDENS

Bluebell *(Hyacinthoides non-scripta)*
The nodding heads of bluebells used to be common in woods and hedgerows but they are becoming less common now. They prefer a lightly shaded position; under a hedge or decidous tree is ideal.

TYPE: Perennial, bulb
COLOUR: Blue
PLANTING TIME: Autumn
FLOWERING TIME: Spring to early summer
HEIGHT: 30-40cm/12-16in
SOIL: Any

Common poppy *(Papaver rhoeas)*
One of the best-known annual wild flowers, the poppy used to be found in cornfields but is now more likely to be seen on disturbed earth on roadside and motorway verges. It can be grown in a sunny border or as part of a wildflower meadow.

TYPE: Annual, seed
COLOUR: Red
SOWING TIME: Spring
FLOWERING TIME: Early to late summer
HEIGHT: 40-60cm/16-24in
SOIL: Any, particularly on poor, stony soils

Cornflower *(Centaurea cyanus)*
Once a widespread 'weed' in cornfields, it makes a pretty border flower for cutting. It prefers a sunny position, where it will attract bees and several different species of butterfly.

TYPE: Annual, seed
COLOUR: Bright blue
SOWING TIME: Spring
FLOWERING TIME: Summer
HEIGHT: 60-90cm/24-36in
SOIL: Any, except chalk

Foxglove *(Digitalis purpurea)*
A native of woodlands, the foxglove thrives in a damp, partially shaded spot. This stately plant looks good grown under tall trees or to give height at the back of the border.

TYPE: Biennial, seed or young plant
COLOUR: Purple
PLANTING TIME: Autumn for flowers the following year
FLOWERING TIME: Summer
HEIGHT: 120cm/48in
SOIL: Acid, moist

Primrose *(Primula vulgaris)*
The primrose has suffered greatly in the wild from being overpicked, but makes an excellent garden plant. It prefers a moist, partially shaded spot under trees or hedges.

TYPE: Perennial, seed or young plant
COLOUR: Yellow
PLANTING TIME: Early spring
FLOWERING TIME: Spring
HEIGHT: 20cm/8in
SOIL: Moist

other undesirable plants to grow in a tiny patch out of sight. Although they are not particularly attractive to us, butterflies and other wildlife love them. A space behind a shed or garage is ideal.

If you are lucky enough to have taken over a new house with a completely bare plot, you can plan the whole garden for wild flowers. Most people, however, decide to introduce them gradually, perhaps making a single wild flower bed or turning the lawn into a meadow. If you have some trees and shrubs then you might want to create a mini-woodland, with carpets of bluebells and shade-loving plants. Even a small pond can have some wild plants in and around it, or better still you might create a marshy area nearby to grow damp-loving plants like purple loosestrife and marsh marigold. As well as increasing the range of plants you can grow, a marshland makes a great home for frogs and toads.

Making a selection
Whatever size your garden, even if you are gardening on a balcony or patio, there are wild flowers to suit you. The main thing to remember is that you do not have to give the whole garden over to wild flowers straight away (although once you get 'hooked' it's easy to get carried away!). Pick and choose the plants and the habitats that suit your circumstances.

First look at the garden to assess the 'habitats' you already have. A large tree is a good starting point, as you can plant a selection of shade-loving bulbs like snowdrops and bluebells around the base.

Bluebells are a woodland plant and are at home in the dappled shade of trees and larger shrubs (left). If you can give them enough space and the right growing conditions, they will spread themselves happily. Bluebell seeds are available, and are usually sold as Hyacinthoides non-scripta.

To some people, the red dead nettles growing among these primulas in a cool but sunny border (right) are weeds. But a weed is only a plant growing in the wrong place, and if you like a native plant it deserves a place in your flower garden. You may sometimes find you need to thin these plants quite ruthlessly though, as they can be rampant growers if they are made welcome.

You could also put in groups of primroses and sweet violets followed by red campion for the summer. A wet spot or the margins of a pond can be turned into a mini-wetland. This is the place to grow moisture-loving plants like the delicate cuckoo flower, yellow flag iris, meadowsweet and ragged robin. Even the pond itself can have native plants, and planting some curled pondweed or spiked water milfoil which grow under water will help to keep the water clean and clear.

Other wild flowers prefer a

PROJECT   COLLECT YOUR OWN SEEDS

Once you have started growing a few wild flowers in the garden, it is easy and economical to collect your own seed to grow into more plants or to pass on to other gardening friends.

● Wait until the seed pods are ripe. This will vary from plant to plant but is usually when the pods have turned from green to brown.

● Snip off the seed pods with scissors or small secateurs and place them inside a paper bag. Shake the bag until all the seed has been released.

● Lay the contents of the bag on a tray and pick out any bits of stem or plant debris. Leave the seed to dry in the sun or in a warm spot indoors. Store the dry seed in paper envelopes or in clean, sealed jars – spice jars are ideal.

Remember to collect only one type of seed at a time and mark the envelopes and jars clearly to avoid mixing up different species.

No specialist equipment is required for you to begin collecting seeds. Dried seed can be kept in airtight storage jars or an envelope until it is needed. Jars should be clearly labelled (right) as many smaller seeds look very much alike.

sunny spot and a soil that has been turned over and are best grown in a separate flower bed. Poppies, cornflowers, corncockles and corn marigolds are annuals which flower for only one year. Choose a sunny position in the garden and they will provide you with beautiful cut flowers all summer long. It is also easy to add perennial wild flowers to an existing herbaceous border. Plants like meadow cranes-bill, harebell and musk mallow will flower year after year and bring a host of bees and butterflies to your cottage garden border.

height of 5-7cm/2-3in rather than the usual 2.5cm/1in. The only exception is from late spring to mid-summer, the main flowering period, when you need to leave the grass uncut to allow the flowers to produce and spread their seeds.

Wild flowers are perfect for a cottage garden border (above), and they can all be grown from seed. Little pockets of soil in wall crevices will encourage ferns and other plants to make a home there.

IN THE EYES OF THE LAW

DON'T FORGET!

Under the Wildlife and Countryside Act 1981 (UK) it is against the law to dig up or disturb any plant in the wild without the landowner's permission. In addition, there are nearly 100 species which cannot be disturbed *at all* because they are so rare. There is really no need to take plants from the wild as garden centres, nurseries and seedsmen now sell bulbs, plants and packets of seed.

Meadow flowers

You might want to try making a wild flower meadow instead of a smooth lawn. If you have an area of bare earth, you can sow a new flowering lawn with meadow mixture. These seed mixtures, available from some garden centres or by mail order from specialist seedsmen, have the right balance of grasses and low-growing wild flowers and are best sown in the autumn. If you already have an established lawn, let it grow then weed out some of the undesirables such as thistles and dock and put cowslips, ox-eye daisies and lady's bedstraw in their place.

Maintaining a wild flower lawn is quite straightforward; continue to mow it, but to a

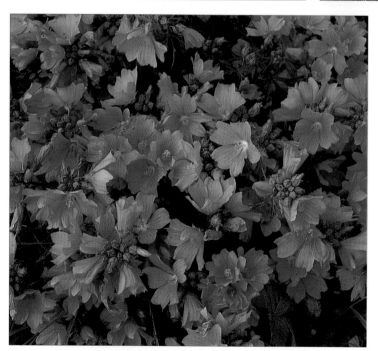

Plants naturally grow best in their favourite type of habitat. A boggy area (above) provides the perfect setting for damp-garden plants. If you have a pond, growing plants in the water will help to keep the water clear, as well as adding to the 'wild' look. There is a wide range of moisture-loving plants available in special garden centres. This sort of garden can be made on a very small scale in a damp, shady corner.

Musk mallow (Malva moschata), (left) is a very colourful wild plant that needs a sunny spot. It can be naturalized in grass.

Growing wild flowers from seed can be time consuming but is not difficult. Annual seeds such as poppies and cornflowers can be sown straight out in the garden in the spring and will flower the same summer.

A wild flower garden is not a neglected garden and will need some regular maintenance, particularly if it is not to become overgrown. Watering is not usually necessary, except for plants grown in containers which dry out quickly in the summer. Likewise, feeding is unnecessary and most wild species prefer no added fertilizer.

The most important task is to deadhead some of the more invasive plants. Simply cut off the heads after they have flowered to stop the seeds being

Whatever you do, do not dig up plants you see in hedgerows or in wild places. Apart from the fact that many of the plants are protected by law, they need all the help they can get to survive. Buy your wild flowers as seeds, bulbs or plants from a reputable nursery, then you can be sure you are helping to increase the species. If you are impatient to see the finished result, the quickest way is to buy small, partly-grown plantlets in spring or summer, which can be planted in a pot or straight into the garden when you get them home. Buy bulbs in the autumn and plant in exactly the same way as daffodils or crocus bulbs.

BRIGHT IDEAS

PRESSING WILD FLOWERS

To prolong the beauty of your wild flowers, you can dry and press them to make pictures or greetings cards. The delicate colours and shapes can be perfectly preserved either as whole flowers or as individual petals. The secret of successful pressing is to cut the flowers on a dry day and to press them immediately, before the colours begin to fade.

You can buy a simple wooden flower press from a craft shop or you can put the flowers between sheets of newspaper or blotting paper weighted down under heavy books. Make sure that the flowers are laid out absolutely flat in one single layer. Leave in a dry room with a minimum temperature of 10°C (50°F) for 3-4 weeks.

Cowslips (below) are a favourite country plant which used to grow wild in huge numbers. Now they are much less common. Like so many wild flowers, the cowslip is a medicinal plant.

spread around. If your aim is to create a cottage garden, this is less important, as a few flowers which have seeded themselves in unexpected places add to the natural, informal effect.

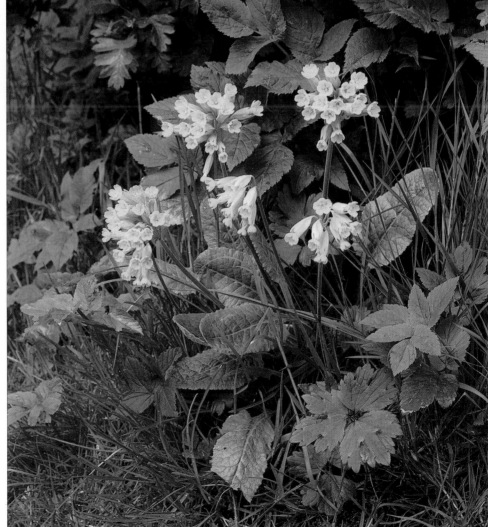

WILDLIFE HAVEN

By creating a haven for wildlife, you can turn your garden into a living landscape full of the incandescent colours of birds and butterflies.

Loss of habitat as a result of intensive farming and land development is becoming a cause for concern to naturalists and amateur nature-lovers alike. By making your garden environmentally friendly, you can help to redress the balance and preserve the beautiful and fascinating natural world around you.

Recently, gardeners have started to take a far greater interest in the natural world on their doorsteps. We have become better informed. A deeper understanding of the importance of habitat has led to a move towards organic gardening methods. Creatures that were once seen as unwanted pests are now viewed with more benevolent eye as vital links in the food chain.

Good news

The good news is that by creating a wildlife haven you can add whole new dimensions to your garden. The gentle hum of insects and the lyrical songs of birds add a soothing counterpoint to the visual aspects of the garden.

Insects such as butterflies will add yet more colour to your flower beds and borders. The darting, fluttering, floating and scuttling of birds and insects gives movement in the air and on the ground.

It is not just a question of throwing a much-needed lifeline to some endangered species but also about encouraging and nurturing those which are not struggling. After all, effective prevention is far better than cure.

By making your garden friendly to wildlife, you will

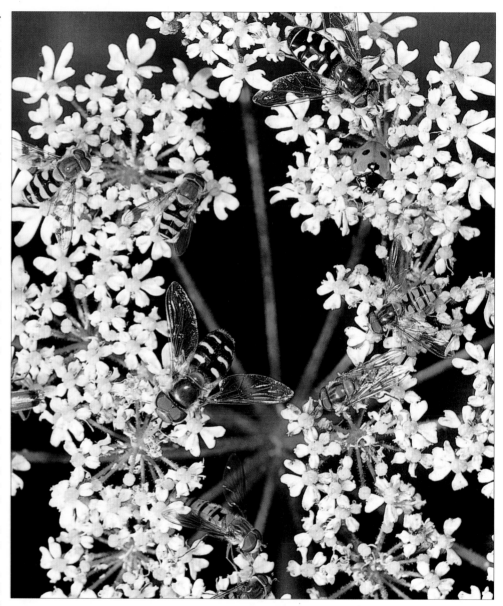

have the deep satisfaction of 'doing good' and the added bonus of creating a sanctuary of breathtaking beauty for you and your family.

If you have children, your garden will become a living classroom. It will teach them to love and respect the natural world and to protect and preserve it in their turn.

Whether you are starting from scratch or intend to adapt an existing garden, you will need to make a plan.

A lot will depend on the size of the area you are working with and the needs of you and your family. Begin by drawing a sketch of your garden showing fixed features, patio area, shed and so on.

Nectar-rich flowers like umbellifers attract hoverflies (above). The darting, hovering flight of these insects makes them attractive, and they also have a practical use. Their young feed on aphids; each larva accounts for around 600 of these garden pests as it matures.

Next, make a list of possible habitats such as a pond, meadowland, woodland, rocky outcrop and hedgerow. Bear in mind that a woodland habitat need not be the size of a small forest and that a serviceable meadow need be no larger than an average lawn. Go back to your plan and see how many habitats you can realistically fit into the space available.

A wildlife garden need not be a wilderness. Many 'wild' habitats are, in fact, managed. Woodlands or hedgerows, for example, both require regular maintenance. A formal setting can be just as inviting to wildlife as an informal one.

You will be astonished at what you already provide for

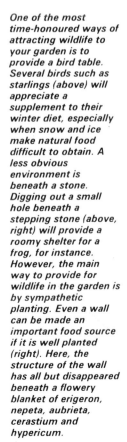

One of the most time-honoured ways of attracting wildlife to your garden is to provide a bird table. Several birds such as starlings (above) will appreciate a supplement to their winter diet, especially when snow and ice make natural food difficult to obtain. A less obvious environment is beneath a stone. Digging out a small hole beneath a stepping stone (above, right) will provide a roomy shelter for a frog, for instance. However, the main way to provide for wildlife in the garden is by sympathetic planting. Even a wall can be made an important food source if it is well planted (right). Here, the structure of the wall has all but disappeared beneath a flowery blanket of erigeron, nepeta, aubrieta, cerastium and hypericum.

CARING FOR BIRDS

Most gardeners like to feed the birds, especially in winter when times are hard. The food you supply should include seeds, nuts, fats (animal or vegetable), fruit and preferably wholemeal bread. Remember to supply water for drinking and bathing. Phase out feeding in spring when natural food supplies are plentiful. Begin again in autumn.

If you want birds to take up residence in your garden then nest sites are essential. A good thick hedge or a selection of trees are ideal. Bird boxes are fine but must be strategically placed. A good bird book will give you the information you need.

You can encourage house-martins to nest by supplying the mud with which they build. Dig a shallow hollow, line it with polythene and place earth on top. Water regularly to keep it moist.

Don't Forget!

wildlife. Seemingly barren areas such as a wall or a patio may already be home to a variety of insects and other creatures. A few simple measures can help to encourage even more to take up residence.

Stepping stones across your lawn could become home to frogs and toads, for example. Dig out a shallow depression about 4cm/1½in deep and supply a small corridor rising up to ground level. Pop your stepping stone over the top, leaving the entrance to the corridor just visible in the grass. Even if you don't have a pond, you may still get visitors, especially if there is a pond in the vicinity.

Bountiful boundaries

Walls and fences provide all sorts of benefits for wildlife. They correspond to rock faces or banks in the wild, and make admirable perches for birds and pupating sites for moths and butterflies without any work from you.

You can enhance their attractiveness as a garden feature and as a wildlife habitat by clothing them with plants. There are many plants that

A birdbath can be incorporated into a design as an ornamental feature (above). Remember, though, that birds are vulnerable when bathing or drinking. It is prudent to site a birdbath away from any features where a predatory cat might lurk waiting to pounce.

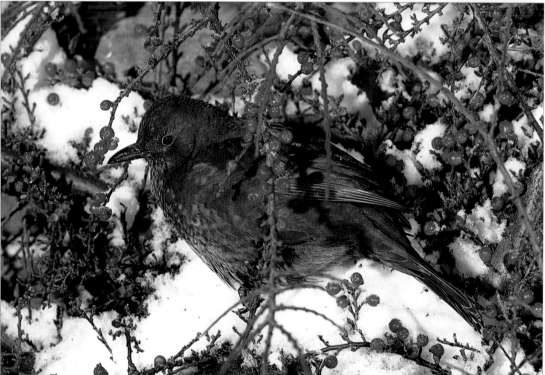

Plants which carry plenty of berries are just as important a winter food source for birds in the garden as the seed and scraps left for them on the bird table. Birds which normally survive on worms or insects, such as blackbirds (left) or other members of the thrush family, will gladly take berries in the depths of winter.

will grow happily in, on or against a wall. *Senecio greyi*, an upright shrub when grown in a border, can be grown against a wall where it provides dense, protective foliage as it drapes itself decorously over the top. Various alpines are only too pleased to settle in crevices, although it is best to plant these as you build.

Honeysuckle is vigorous and full of nectar and pollen during its flowering season. Its fragrance is an added delight.

The common wild ivy (*Hedera helix*) is one of the best all-purpose wildlife garden plants. The nectar-rich flowers which appear in late autumn on mature plants attract a multitude of insects, including the odd butterfly stocking up for hibernation. Birds roost and make nests in it and its protective foliage welcomes

The green flowers which appear on mature ivy plants in autumn are a valuable food source for those insects which have not yet gone into hibernation. Several butterflies, such as the comma, painted lady and red admiral (right) take its nectar.

Tits are basically woodland birds, feeding on insects in the summer and seeds in the autumn and winter. They are also extremely fond of peanuts. Specially-designed feeders, hung from a convenient tree branch, encourage the birds to show off their gymnastic and aerobatic skills (below). Here, two blue tits (on left), a great tit (lower right) and a coal tit (upper right) have flown in for a feast.

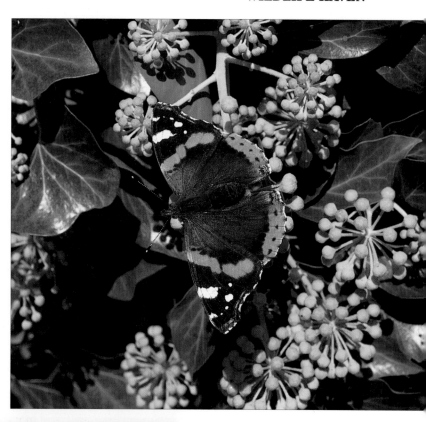

FLOWERY MEADOWS

The traditional, smooth, well-manicured lawn, though good to look at, is not particularly friendly to wildlife.

A miniature flowery meadow makes a wonderful alternative to a traditional lawn. You can turn a lawn into a flowery habitat by the way you maintain it, following a few golden rules.

Do not mow more than once a fortnight; raise the height of your cutter when you do.

Never use chemical aids such as fertilizers or weed killers.

Leave a break in the cutting for about five weeks in the early summer so that the flowers can set seed and self-sow.

In time, slender speedwell, daisies, white clover, spring sedge, bugle and bird's-foot-trefoil will establish themselves to the delight of bees, butterflies and many other insects.

BRIGHT IDEAS

many hibernating creatures, including butterflies.

A warm, sunny, dry stone wall, full of nooks and crannies, is the perfect place for slow worms. These legless lizards are excellent for controlling slugs and other pests. If your wall is brick and mortar, simply chipping out the cement here and there may make it more attractive proposition, not only for slow worms, but for various insects and pupating moths and butterflies as well.

Hedgerows

If you are lucky enough to have a natural hedge made up of native plants such as hawthorn, blackthorn, field maple (*Acer campestre*) and wild privet, count your blessing and hang on to it. If you are planning to plant one, then consider using these species in preference to conifers and other hedging plants.

Such a hedge will attract as many as 20 species of butterfly, a huge variety of birds and some small mammals. Hedges act as a sort of corridor for wildlife, providing them with protection as they wander. They also provide food, nesting sites and a place to hibernate.

You can enhance your hedge by planting native wild flowers such as red campion, wild arum, bluebells and greater stitchwort at the base.

Paths and patios

When planning your patio and paths, leave room between the flag stones to plant pollen and nectar rich plants such as creeping thyme, aubrieta, chamomile, alyssum, apple mint and forget-me-not. Bees and butterflies will be very grateful for such a rich source of pollen and nectar.

There are several other advantages to planting paths and patios. They soften the outlines of otherwise fairly harsh features and stop less desirable plants from filling in the gaps. Creeping or spreading herbs have the added bonus of surrounding you with

FOOD PLANTS

Several decorative plants provide food for birds in the form of fruit and seeds, as well, of course, as attracting insects on which other birds can feed.

The fruit of ornamental apple and cherry trees is unpalatable to us, but welcome to many birds. Varieties of cotoneaster also produce succulent berries, but avoid *C. conspicuus* 'Decorus'.

The hips of the dog rose (*Rosa canina*) are much prized, as are the berries of the elder (*Sambucus nigra*) and holly (*Ilex aquifolium*).

Birds also enjoy hawthorn (*Crataegus monogyna*), honeysuckle, wild privet (*Ligustrum vulgare*), snapdragons (*Antirrhinum* spp.), evening primrose (*Oenothera* spp.) and sunflower (*Helianthus annuus*).

GARDEN NOTES

*The common hawthorn (*Crataegus monogyna*) is a wonderfully decorative plant in late spring and early summer, when it is in full flower (above). It also produces handsome red berries later in the season. The berries and flowers are an important food source and its twisted, thorny branches provide shelter for nesting birds and pupating insects. It can be grown as a specimen tree, but is perhaps more useful to wildlife as part of a hedge.*

No wildlife garden should be without some kind of water feature where birds and animals can drink and bathe. A mature informal pond (left) is the ideal. A mix of native and cultivated plants makes it easy on the eye, as well as providing shelter for drinking animals. Frogs will spawn in a fairly small pond, provided they can get access to it. The common frog (right) is the most likely visitor; it will come to spawn in the spring, and return occasionally in the summer, particularly in hot weather.

HEDGEHOGS

Hedgehogs are the best-loved of our native mammals. They may well be visiting your garden already, as their foraging range is quite large. You can encourage their visits by supplying tasty plates of dog food. Don't be tempted to leave bread and milk for them as it is too rich.

If you wish them to take up residence, you must supply a good place for them to lie up during the day, to hibernate and, with luck, to breed. Underneath the shed is a good place as long as there is plenty of good nesting material such as dry leaves, straw or hay. They also like to nest under a wood pile, with insulation material provided. A weatherproof wooden box, filled with nesting material and placed under a pile of logs and leaves makes a very desirable property for hedgehogs.

Hedgehogs are rarely seen because they do their roaming and hunting at night. They supplement their basic diet of insects, worms, slugs and spiders with fresh carrion, and will gladly take some cat or dog food (above). If, over a period of time, you gradually move the dish nearer the house, they can be encouraged to feed in full view of a window.

fragrance as you sit in the sun or walk your paths.

Water is a vital ingredient in a wildlife garden. A pond is the obvious way of providing it. It needn't be large, as even a tiny pond will support a good selection of life forms.

A good wildlife pond provides a variety of depths. It is best if it slopes gently to a depth of at least 75cm/30in – so it does not freeze solid in winter – with a ledge 30cm/1ft deep at the other end.

If you extend the pond liner beneath the soil you can provide a very desirable wetland area. Remember to provide a hard surface for a viewing point. You don't want to have to wade through bogland to have a close look at the teeming life in your pond.

Some creatures, such as water snails, spend their whole lives in water. Others are tied to it by their breeding habits; these include frogs, toads and dragonflies. Some move from one pond to another – water boatmen and pond-skaters for example. Others just visit for food, for a bath and of course, to drink.

A wildlife pond requires some planning and it is as well to do your research carefully before investing in a pond liner. One thing to consider is the safety of young children.

If you find it is impossible to make the pond out-of-bounds to the very young, put the project on hold until they are old enough not to drown in it. Meanwhile, a few shallow dishes dotted around your garden will provide birds with the much-needed drinking and bathing facilities.

An elegant birdbath can make an excellent focal point while being immensely useful to birds. Do remember to provide fresh water regularly, especially in winter when other supplies are frozen.

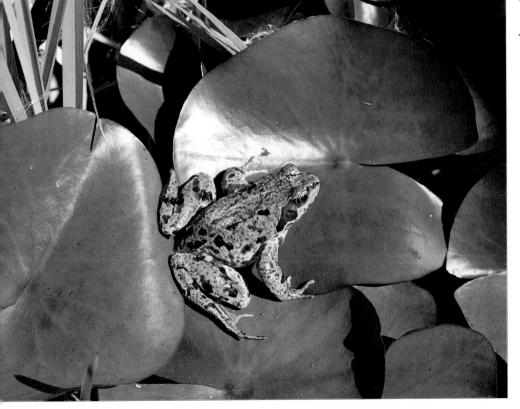

ORNAMENTAL POND

Water brings so many different things to a garden: movement, reflections from the sky, and exciting new plants and wildlife.

A pond is a delightful feature, but is it one that is suitable for every garden? Unfortunately, the answer is no. If a garden is permanently in shade or overshadowed by trees, with little or no open space, then a pond will not be a success. Plants will not thrive and the water will quickly become stagnant.

There are some important aspects to consider before you embark on pond construction. The siting is crucial. It must be open to the sky and not overshadowed by trees. It must also receive sun for a major part of the day.

Water collects at the lowest point of the landscape so bear this in mind: choose the lowest part of the garden, provided it meets with other criteria, especially if you want an informal or 'natural' pond.

Natural landscaping

If you do not have an existing low point try to raise the ground behind the pond so that it appears to be lower than the surrounding ground. For instance, you may be able to create a slope behind it, or construct a rock garden.

Remember also that a pond will create an instant focal point – an object that draws the eye to that part of the garden – so bear this in mind when choosing a site. In

This right-angled pond (above) uses a variety of materials to harmonious effect. The hard edges of bricks and paving slabs are softened by areas of gravel, smooth, round pebbles and plants.

A rockery creates an attractive landscape in an informal garden, echoing the fluid lines of this pond (left). As the dwarf plants already growing on the paving slabs spread further, an even softer effect will be created.

formal surroundings a raised pond makes an especially good focal point, especially if it contains a fountain.

Garden style

Assuming your garden has already been designed and laid out, you will need to choose a pond to suit its style.

Basically gardens can be split into two distinct styles. In a formal garden the layout is geometric, based on regular lines and shapes. An informal

make the plot appear wider than it really is. An L-shaped pond would be suitable for a corner site.

A circular pond might also be suitable in formal surroundings, especially if it has a central fountain. For instance, it could form the centrepiece of a rose garden, or it might be positioned where two paths intersect. This shape would also be suitable for the middle of a lawn.

A half circle would make an excellent focal point at the end of a path or lawn, where it should have a solid background such as a wall or hedge.

A raised pond

If you have a formal garden, you may, of course, prefer a raised pond rather than one on ground level. A raised pond is easily seen so makes an excellent focal point.

A raised pond is certainly highly recommended for two formal areas not so far mentioned: the patio and the courtyard garden. Indeed, a raised pond is the norm in a classic courtyard and often features a fountain. The walls of the pond, which may be square, rectangular or circular, can be

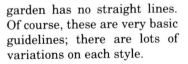

SAFETY FIRST

DON'T FORGET!

A pond can be a great danger to small children. If you start off with a sunken sandpit for toddlers, when they are older it can easily be converted into a pond. Simply line the hole with a rubber or PVC pond liner or instal a preformed pond unit.

A simple, plain, rectangular shape (above) is the perfect choice in this formal paved garden.

Even with only a tiny corner, you can still have a pond. Make sure you have a clear idea of the style, though. This pond (below) would have been a better design with either straight, paved sides or a curved stone edge.

garden has no straight lines. Of course, these are very basic guidelines; there are lots of variations on each style.

Formal gardens

For a garden with beds and borders of regular shapes and straight paths, you should choose a square or rectangular pond. A square pond often makes a good feature in the centre of a formal layout. A rectangular pond positioned across a narrow garden will

This uncluttered patio pool has a cunningly hidden water source feeding into the pond through an overturned urn (above), creating a stylish, modern effect. Another unusual water source (below) is this lion's head. It creates an exciting corner in a walled garden. Note, too, the stunning contrast of scarlet geraniums against whitewashed walls.

capped with coping stones. These give a neat finish and can be used as additional seating.

On a patio, or indeed in any other area of the garden, there is no need to stick to just one raised pond. Why not have several interlocking ponds on different levels? For instance, consider a group of several small square ponds, with a submerged pump to circulate water so that it cascades from one to another.

An informal style

Informal gardens have beds, borders and lawns of irregular shape, with smooth 'flowing' edges and no squared-off corners. The pond should be of similar style.

The shape is up to you, but bear in mind that an informal pond only looks right at ground level or below. One suggestion would be to have a longish pond which is broad at one end, ideal for displaying water lilies, and then gradually tapers to the other end until it becomes quite narrow, making an ideal home for tall aquatic plants.

A natural pond to attract wild creatures would be a good choice for a garden that has areas of long grass and wild flowers. The natural pond should be slightly sunken, with grass right down to the water's edge, to enable any wildlife to reach the water easily.

Practical points

These days ponds are comparatively simple to construct using modern flexible liners or preformed units. These need little or no maintenance if installed correctly.

The pros and cons of ground-level and raised ponds may well influence your choice. The main advantage of a ground-level pond is that you will have lots of soil left over for creating another feature such as a rock garden. It will also work out cheaper. A major disadvantage is that it can be hard work digging out the soil. You may not actually want the soil and will then have the problem of disposing of it.

A raised pond does not have to be excavated and can be built on any site. The building materials are expensive, however. If using bricks or

This unusual formal pond (right) is in an enclosed courtyard. It not only creates an agreeable background to al fresco eating, it gives the unusual impression that the patio is actually floating on the water! Note that care has been taken to site the pond in an area of the garden which is not overshadowed by trees.

This informal pond surrounded by rocks and gravel (left) has a perfect open aspect for its plants to thrive in the sun. The choice of ornaments and plants combine to give the pool a Japanese feel.

This tiny, sunken pond (below) is stocked full of plants and fish and creates a delightfully cooling and informal effect in this very sunny garden.

ornamental concrete walling blocks you have to be quite skilled at bricklaying and, invariably, it will take a little more time to construct.

You will be more restricted as regards size and shape if you opt for a preformed pond unit, although formal and informal designs are available. Make sure you buy a unit that is deep enough, as some preformed ponds are not of the minimum 45cm/18in depth and should be avoided.

The major advantage of a preformed unit is that it enables you to make a pond quickly and easily. Generally it is fitted into a square or rectangular hole with sand in the bottom and packed firmly around with more sand. Always follow the suppliers'

GARDEN NOTES

MATERIALS AVAILABLE

● **Black butyl rubber** is the most expensive type of flexible liner, has the longest life, is less prone to damage and is repairable.

● **PVC liners** are cheaper and of variable quality. A reinforced laminated layer is strongest and will last longest. The best colours are black or stone.

● **Polyester matting** is used to line a pond excavation, as well as sand, if the ground is very stony, prior to installing a flexible liner.

● **Preformed glass fibre** units are strong and have a long life.

● **Preformed plastic** units are cheaper but are still quite strong. They do not last as long as glass fibre. Black is the best colour.

INFORMAL PLANTING

Use these plants for effective planting in informal and natural ponds

- double marsh marigold (*Caltha palustris* var. *palustris* 'Plena') has golden-yellow flowers

- iris (*Iris laevigata*) varieties have sword-shaped leaves

- bog bean *(Menyanthes trifoliata)* has white fringed flowers

- forget-me-not (*Myosotis palustris*) has tiny blue flowers

- greater spearwort (*Ranunculus lingua* 'Grandiflorus') has buttercup-like flowers

- yellow water or pond lily (*Nuphar lutea*) has yellow flowers. It is vigorous and only for large ponds

- soft rush (*Juncus effusus*) has thick green stems

- water mint (*Mentha aquatica)* has aromatic foliage and lilac-pink flowers

- reed mace (*Typha angustifolia*) has brown, sausage-like flower spikes

instructions on installation in case there are any special requirements.

A flexible liner enables you to construct a pond of any shape or size. To calculate the size you need, multiply the overall length of pond required by twice the depth. This will give you the length of liner you need. To find its width, multiply the overall width of pond by twice its depth. For an informal shape, make the calculation by using the greatest width and length. The usual depth for a garden pond is 45-60cm/18-24in.

When you have made the

Once an informal pond is well established, the plants in and around it merge to create a wonderfully romantic effect. This pool (top left) is overhung with peonies and variegated shrubs and filled with water lilies and the sunny, buttercup-like flowers of Ranunculus lingua *'Grandiflorus'.*

The golden-yellow flowers of the double marsh marigold, Caltha palustris *'Plena', (above left), are some of the first to bloom in the water garden. They grow best in shallow water on boggy soil at the side of a natural pond.*

hole for the pond, drape the liner loosely inside it and secure with bricks around the edge, leaving an overlap. Fill with water and gradually ease off the bricks as the liner stretches. Edge the pond with concrete or stone slabs, to hide the overlap.

Pond plants

Water lilies and marginal aquatics (those grown in the shallow water around the edge of a pond) can be planted in most ponds, although the quantity and types used should be determined by the style of your pond.

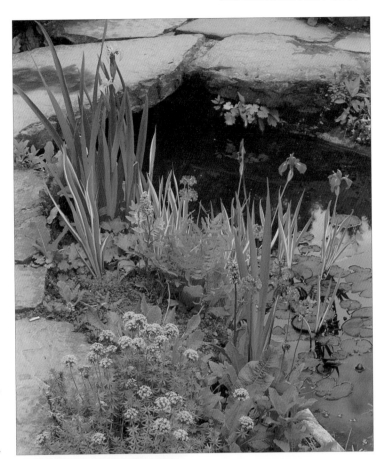

Water marginals, such as flags merge with water lilies in this sunken pond (right) to great effect. Creating a shallow ledge when you build your pond, means you can cultivate a much greater selection of plants and you can also disguise the edge of your pond.

This natural pond (left) merges beautifully into its surroundings. It has an excellent colour balance with its purple iris (I. Laevigata 'Variegata') set against the yellow flag iris (I. pseudacorus).

Water in the garden has many functions. It can, for instance, be used not so much as a feature in its own right but as an integral part of a natural environment (below) which will attract wildlife to your garden.

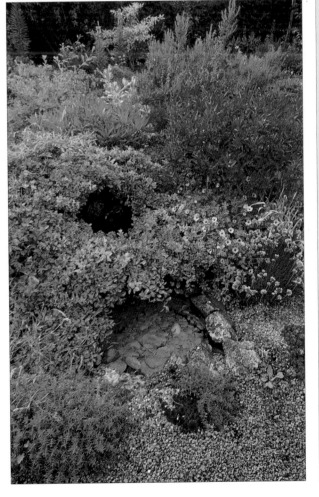

As the water itself is often the main feature of a formal pond, few plants are generally used, but it is up to you to decide what will suit your garden. The surface may be punctuated by a group or two of water lilies, for example, and the edges planted with a few clumps of distinctive bold 'architectural' aquatics. Look at the plant list (far right) for ideas and inspiration.

An informal pond, on the other hand, can be densely planted. Use plenty of water lilies and less formal-looking marginals such as marsh marigolds or flags.

PLANTS FOR FORMAL PONDS

• sweet flag (*Acorus calamus* 'Variegatus') has sword-shaped leaves striped with cream and green

• variegated water grass (*Glyceria aquatica variegata*) has grassy green and cream striped leaves

• variegated yellow flag (*Iris pseudacorus* 'Variegata') has sword-shaped leaves striped with cream and green

• pickerel weed (*Pontederia cordata*) has lance-shaped leaves and blue flowers

• zebra rush (*Schoenoplectus* ssp. *tabernaemontani* 'Zebrinus') has stems barred white and green

• bog arum (*Calla palustris*) has white, sail-like flowers and heart-shaped leaves

• double Japanese arrowhead (*Sagittaria sagittifolia* 'Flore Pleno') has arrow-shaped leaves and white double flowers

• white water lily (*Nymphaea alba*) has white flowers with yellow stamens

SUMMER COLOUR SCHEMES

Your garden is an extension of your home, so why not try a little 'exterior decorating'? Start by selecting and co-ordinating a stunning summer colour scheme.

green'. The resulting garden picture may be 'colourful', but at the same time it is quite monotonous. A muddle of colours which pays no attention to change of tone or mood lacks both harmony and interest.

Make a plan

Start by taking a good look at the colours that are already in your garden, including walls, paving, shrubs, trees and the surrounding landscape. This may give you a good starting point for choosing a harmonious scheme of interrelated colours for your flower beds.

Do not feel you must tackle the whole garden at once. Instead, start with a single flower bed and create a colour

One of the most exciting aspects of garden design is the way in which colour can be used to create certain moods and feelings. Soft blues and mauves are cool and soothing, yellow is warm and cheerful while reds and oranges are hot and exciting.

Using colour in your garden is a little more tricky than it first seems. Mixed shades of bedding plants and seeds are often planted for a colour 'splash', with no consideration given to how those colours will blend with each other or the surrounding plants.

Plants with purple, gold or variegated foliage are quickly snapped up at the garden centres in the belief that anything is better than 'boring old

A swathe of bright yellow blooms (above) will lift your spirits and bring sunshine into your life even on a dull day. A border filled with bright red flowers, on the other hand, creates a bold and dramatic statement. Red provides a powerful contrast to vivid green leaves in this garden (right). The foliage, which is tinged with crimson, echoes the theme.

If you can't decide on the right colour scheme play safe with white. Dazzling, yet calm on a large scale (right), it also works beautifully in a small corner (below). Here, it is used to highlight a range of yellow-green foliage plants. These include water figwort (Scrophularia auriculata), lady's mantle, ferns and hostas. A little stone owl presides over the refreshing combination of colours.

co-ordinated design to make it a beautiful, eye-catching summer focal point.

Colour scheming

Look at the colour wheel on the following pages. By choosing flowers from only one of the colour groups you will be able to create a dramatic display in your flower bed. Select shades of blue, for example, or a range of brilliant reds.

This does not mean you are restricted to using a single colour in your scheme. Take your plan one stage further by 'borrowing' plants from the neighbouring colour group and you can introduce contrast without spoiling the overall theme. A few spots of purple or pink in a blue garden, for instance, will greatly enhance the main colour scheme, creating a much more satisfying picture. If you are still not sure how to mix and blend colours, however, choose white as your contrast, and you cannot go far wrong.

Which plant?

Having chosen a colour theme, you are now ready to choose a selection of plants to match. Those with the longest flowering periods keep your scheme going for longer, and save you lots of work too. Foliage plants can make an excellent basic framework for your scheme, especially if the border already contains shrubs.

Green foliage is always useful, as it enhances other plants and can conceal or divert attention when needed. You do not have to stick to green, however, as plants with silver, gold, purple or variegated foliage can be chosen to harmonize with a surrounding colour scheme of, say, yellows, purples or pinks.

While looking through the plant list of your chosen colour scheme, be sure to select those that suit your site and soil conditions. Choose a key plant, then a second to complement the first one and so on, until you have built up a planting scheme of harmonious colours, textures and shapes. Select each one carefully, considering how it will affect the overall plan. Simplicity and the broad, bold use of colour are the keys to good garden design.

As you arrange and reorganize your plan, you may eliminate some of your original 'key' plants. Keep experimenting until you are happy with the effect. Remember, you are not just selecting plants that will look good side by side, you are creating an overall 'picture'.

Once you are satisfied with your planting scheme, make a

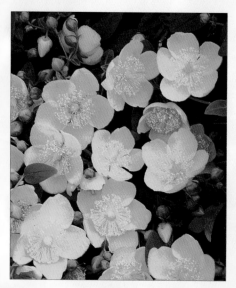

YELLOWS

yarrow (*Achillea* 'Moonshine')
lime-yellow lady's mantle
daylily
St John's wort
creamy honeysuckle (*Lonicera*)
lemon-yellow snapdragons
yellow lilies
golden broom (*Cytisus battandieri*)
evening primrose
mullein (*Verbascum olympicum*)
clematis (*C. tangutica*)
sneezeweed (*Helenium*)
coneflower (*Rudbeckia*)
sunny marigolds
yellow-leaved Japanese maple
   (*A. japonicum* f. *aureum*)
golden bamboo (*Pleioblastus auricomus*
   [formerly *Arundinaria auricoma*])
aucuba (*A. japonica* 'Gold Dust')
yellow ivies
golden creeping Jenny (*Lysimachia*
   nummularia 'Aurea')
golden mock orange (*Philadelphus*
   coronarius 'Aureus')
golden thyme (*Thymus* × *citriodorus*
   'Aureus')

The golden buttercup-like flowers of St John's wort (Hypericum forrestii) provide good bushy ground cover.

Bright yellow flowers and plants with leaves of pale gold create an impact when planted in a large block of 'sunshine' in a mass of green and grey foliage.

The leaves of Acer japonicum f. aureum are a light, soft green.

ORANGES

Plants of vivid orange, orange-reds and golden-yellows are the eye-catchers of the border. They give the extrovert gardener a chance to create excitement.

gold dust (*Aurinius saxatile*)
yarrow (*Achillea filipendulina*)
pot marigold (*Calendula*
   officinalis)
geum (*G. chiloense*)
golden African marigold
yellow-orange coreopsis
   (*C. verticullata*)
bronze Peruvian lily
daylily
busy Lizzie (*Impatiens*)

This bright chrysanthemum (now Dendranthema) is called 'Bronze Gertrude'

red hot poker (*Kniphofia*)
ligularia (*L. dentata*)
lily
honeysuckle (*Lonicera* ×
   brownii 'Fuchsioides')
Iceland and oriental poppies
snapdragon
peony (*Paeonia peregrina*)
candelabra primula
potentilla
chrysanthemum (dendranthema)
montbretia (*Crocosmia* spp.)
flame-coloured rhododendron
apricot and peach roses

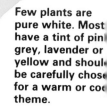

Few plants are pure white. Most have a tint of pin grey, lavender or yellow and shoul be carefully chose for a warm or co theme.

colewort (*Cramb cordifolia*)
thorn (*Crataegus lavallei*)
deutzia
iris
pink-tinged
   flowering crab
   (*Malus species*
sweet cicely
   (*Myrrhis*
   odorata)
rhododendron
wisteria

Reds range from dark, purplish tints to brighter orange, and could overpower if used too freely.

peony
poppy (*Papaver orientale*)
phlox (*Phlox subulata*)
primula (*Primula japonica*)
geraniums
pinks, carnations

Papaver orientalis *(left) is a stunning scarlet poppy – bold and beautiful.*

REDS

rhododendron
red roses
petunia
crimson salvia (*Salvia*
   involucrata)
foxglove (*Digitalis purpure*
cranesbill
daylily (*Hemerocallis* hybri
buddleja
colchicum (*Colchicum*
   speciosum 'Atrorubens')
saffron crocus (*Crocus sativ*
phlox (*Phlox paniculata*)
clematis (*Clematis sp.*)
smoke bush (*Cotinus coggy*
   'Royal Purple')

EENS

milla (*A. conjuncta*)
an wormwood (*Artemesia ntica*)
bore (*Helleborus lividus*)
e variegated dogwood
(*ornus alba* 'Elegantissima')
e variegated euonymus
or variegated plantain lily
(*osta species*)
nettle (*Lamium*)
er-of-thousands (*Saxifraga olonifera*)
egated weigela (*Weigela ida Variegata*')
grass (*Leymus arenarius*)
fescue (*Festuca glauca*)

BLUES

Blues range from deep, inky hues to the palest shades, and have a cool, calming effect.

columbine (*Aquilegia alpina*)
phlox (*Phlox sp.*)
campanula
floss flower (*Ageratum houstonianum*)
Michaelmas daisy
balloon flower (*Platycodon grandiflorum*)
bright blue gentian
blue iris
pale or bright delphiniums
sage (*Salvia azurea*)
monkshood (*Aconitum* x *cammarum*)
blue African lily
California lilac (*Ceanothus*)
lavender (*Lavandula*)
rose of Sharron (*Hibiscus syriacus*)
blue hydrangea (*Hydrangea macrophylla*)

Tall, stately delphiniums are widely available in a vast range of beautiful blues.

Choose a campanula such as C. aucheri (below) for a garden of purples and blues.

nflower
(*Tiarella ordifolia*)
natis
s (*Dianthus Mrs Sinkins*')
y's breath
(*Gypsophila aniculata*)
unia
es
haelmas daisy
e or cream
rysanthemums
rangea
acco plants
fornian poppy
(*Romneya oulteri*)
mone
anium
y Lizzie
(*mpatiens*)

PURPLES

Rich purples give strength to a border, while paler mauves have a delicate, old-fashioned charm.

giant bellflower (*Caryopteris incana*)
bear's breeches (*Acanthus*)
phlox
sedum
sun rose (*Cistus albidus*)
violet-blue *Clematis* 'Lady Betty Balfour'
beauty bush (*Kolkwitzia*

amabilis)
lilac (*Syringa sp.*)
fuchsia

abelia (*Abelia* x *grandiflora*)
mauve hydrangea
Michaelmas daisy
Cupid's dart (*Catananche caerulea*)
cranesbill (*Geranium himalayense*)
drumstick primula (*Primula denticulata*)
monkshood (*Aconitum napellus*)
speedwell (*Veronica longifolia*)
pansies and violas
periwinkle (*Vinca major*)
morning glory (*Ipomoea purpurea*)
purple loosestrife (*Lythrum salicaria*)
crocus
autumn crocus (*Colchicum autumnale*)
purple irises

PINKS

Delicate shades of pink create a feeling of peace and harmony, while brighter shades provide vibrant splashes of warm colour.

hrift (*Armeria maritima*)
ellflower (*Campanula punctata*)
inks, carnations
meadowsweet (*Filipendula palmata*)
ree mallow (*Lavatera maritima*)

Michaelmas daisy (*Aster novi-belgii*)
ornamental onion (*Allium narcissiflorum*)
cranesbill (*Geranium* × *riversleaianum* 'Russell Prichard')
geranium (*Pelargonium species*)
petunia
cyclamen
deep pink *Clematis* 'Walter Pennell'

This shocking pink aster (right) would suit a bold colour scheme.

list of your final plant selection. Decide how many plants you will require to fill the designated area and to create a balanced group. To achieve an unstructured look, plant in uneven numbers. When planting perennials, don't forget to take into account their eventual height and spread. Fill any spaces in between with colour co-ordinated annuals so the bed does not look 'gappy'. Be vigilant about self-sown seedlings – nature certainly won't respect your carefully developed colour scheme!

If you want more than one colour theme in your garden and you have several borders to fill, simply repeat the procedure for each area. The borders can be linked by creating a gradient of colour which spills over from one area into the next. The best way to achieve an effect of total harmony in the garden is to select colours once more from the col-

GARDEN NOTES

CONTRASTS

Strong colours dotted among large areas of softer or weaker shades are very effective, whereas small areas of pale colour among strong, bright tones tend to look washed-out and feeble.

In a misty cloud of pale blue lobelia, for instance, highlight by planting patches of deep blue sage or purple phlox. Or use yellow-orange pot marigolds in small amounts to brighten up a large expanse of paler santolina or alyssum.

A predominantly pink border (above) includes shades of violet and touches of bright red. Generous splashes of white add brightness, while a good balance of fresh green foliage cools down the overall effect. This island bed (right) is very majestic, with its formal planting scheme and predominance of regal purple highlighted by soft pinks. The theme is further enhanced by a background of cool, dark green foliage and further shades of mauve in the surrounding borders.

our wheel. Instead of selecting individual plants from the adjoining colour sections, choose the predominant colours of the beds from neighbouring sections. For example, one bed could be planted with yellow flowers, its neighbour with

COLOUR CONFIDENT

Q I don't feel very confident about choosing colours. Is there a foolproof formula that guards against error?

A Choose plants with grey-green and silvery foliage to mix in with your flowering plants. The grey leaves will act as 'buffers' between incompatible colours, or link different colour themes. Greys and silvers enhance bright colours and emphasize pale ones, so whatever colour flowers you choose, you can't go wrong.

Look out for some of these plants at your garden centre:

- *Tanacetum* × *argenteum*
- *Achillea* 'Moonshine'
- *Artemesia* 'Powis Castle'
- *Euonymus fortunei* 'Silver Queen'
- *Euphorbia myrsinites*
- *Hebe pinguifolia* 'Pagei'
- *Iris pallida* var. *dalmatica*
- *Lavendula* spp.
- *Stachys* spp.
- *Thymus lanuginosus*
- *Tradescantia fluminentis* 'Albovittata'

Create a stunning and very eye-catching effect by choosing plants from opposite sides of the colour wheel. Orange contrasts wonderfully with bright blue, while sunny yellow and rich purple can look simply sensational. Red roses (right) create brilliant splashes in a sea of greeny-yellow fennel.

Dark green and purple (below right) are cool, calm colours. If you select such a deep and dark colour cheme it is a good idea to include some pale fresh colours for light relief. Here, the paler green leaves of Cornus alba *'Spaethii' create a little pool of light.*

shades of orange and flame reds, and a third bed in deep dramatic reds and pinks.

Having carefully chosen and arranged the colours in your garden, the resulting scene will both delight the eye and soothe the soul, and isn't that what a garden is all about? Sit back and await compliments.

WINTER COLOUR

What could be more welcome on a winter's day than a garden aglow with colour? Plan ahead now and you can have plants to please the eye all year round.

When you have spent all spring and summer working away outside to produce a brilliant display that everyone can admire, it is only too easy to forget to plan for the winter months.

A garden that is bare until the first snowdrops appear can be a depressing sight. It is quite possible to have colour in your garden in winter, but this really does need some careful planning. You will have to imagine *now*, before your summer plants have died down, just where a little colour would be most welcome later in the year when the days are shorter and the temperature has plummetted.

Warm indoors

Remember, too, that in winter you will view your garden from the comfort of indoors for most of the time, so you will have to stand at the windows and try to visualize what you will want to see later from inside your home.

Another point to consider is how much space you have. If you have a large garden, it is easy to incorporate areas of winter colour. Smaller spaces can be more difficult to plan: just one patch of late-year colour is not ideal, but you do not want it to be too spread out either, looking as if you are waiting for other plants to emerge in between.

Of course, you do not want anything that requires a lot of attention, or is difficult to find

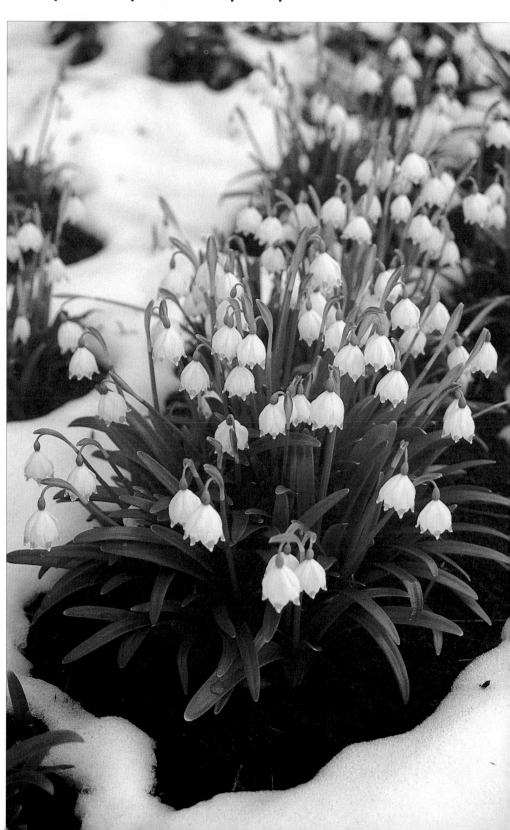

The aptly named snowflake (right) blooms even in the snow. Its petals are gold-tipped and more rounded than those of the snowdrop.

Use the birch (right) as a specimen tree and its incredible bark will help it to earn a place as one of the most unusual features in the winter garden. When the leaves have dropped, the striking colours and texture of the curious bark formation come into view.

This garden (below) is bursting with interest and will take on a magical frosted look when temperatures drop. Silver birch, pink and white heathers, red and yellow dogwoods and conifers in all shades of green prove that winter need not be a sleeping season.

Forget the cold and add a touch of the exotic to a winter garden with Fatsia japonica *(above). The glossy green leaves are palmate in shape, meaning they look like the palm of a hand, but the plant is also interesting for its white pompom-shaped flowers.*

This Viburnum farreri *(left) looks like it should be heralding the spring but in fact it begins to flower in late autumn and continues throughout the winter. The deep pink buds burst into clusters of paler, five-petalled flowers. They have the added advantage of being richly scented so they fill your senses with delight, cheering you up during the long, dark days.*

or expensive to buy. Take advantage of the time you have in the summer months to make your plans, and to visit garden centres to compare prices and choose your plants.

Plant shuffle

Consider the taller plants first and then consider the fronts of borders, any rockeries, containers and window boxes. You may find that you want to move some existing shrubs to fit in with your new plan, and the best time to do this would be in the autumn, when they are dormant.

Winter jasmine (*Jasminum nudiflorum*) produces profuse bright yellow flowers without the slightest trouble, but this wall plant is often misguidedly pushed into corners and against front doors where it can be admired only by visitors or passers-by. How much better it would be to place it

DECORATIVE BARK

Trees with attractive bark can provide a dramatic alternative to colourful flowers and foliage on the winter scene. Here are three to chose from.
- Snake-bark maple (*Acer davidii*) has green bark striped with white, and reaches a height of 6m/18ft.
- Paperbark maple (*Acer griseum*) has papery, reddish bark that peels to a red-brown under-bark. It grows 7.5m/25ft tall.
- Scarlet willow (*Salix alba vitellina* 'Britzensis') has stems that are orange-scarlet in winter.

BRIGHT IDEAS

where you can appreciate it from your own fireside, instead of having to go out in the rain or snow to see it in its only flowering period. Even if you decide to have nothing else in your winter garden at least allow this cheerful plant to persuade you that all is not entirely gloomy until spring.

Another way to provide some interest during winter is to plant trees that have decorative bark. They will provide year round pleasure but many only really take centre stage when the leaves fall away and their bark is fully exposed. It is advisable not to choose a tree with a thick trunk for a small garden, but there are some delicate varieties that are suitable for this purpose.

Beautiful bark

An especially good choice would be the slim and graceful white-barked Himalayan birch (*Betula utilis jacquemontii*). If you buy this tree when it is young and do not remove too many lower side branches, it will grow to about 2.7m/9ft in 10 years. The bark peels to a dazzling white and is shown to best effect if you plant it against a dark background

(but not too near the house, to avoid any structural damage by the roots).

A must for dramatic winter colour in any garden are the dogwoods. The Westonbirt dogwood, *Cornus alba* 'Sibirica' and *C. sanguinea* 'Winter Beauty' can be grown for their bright red winter stems, vivid against snow or wonderful reflected in the surface of a pond.

The *Cornus alba* varieties also produce colourful foliage in autumn. They grow to a height of about 90cm/3ft, but must be pruned back almost to ground level in early spring to encourage plenty of new shoots for the next season.

Another possible addition to the garden in winter would be witch hazel (*Hamamelis mollis*). Defined either as a shrub or a small tree, the 'Pallida' variety produces pure yellow flowers with a wonderful perfume. Witch hazel does not like lime, however, so be sure you have a suitable, fairly acid soil before you buy because the plants are expensive. If your soil meets the requirements, try to get a four-year-old plant with nice, plump buds and no suckers, as younger plants can fail. If your soil is quite heavy

add a large amount of peat or garden compost to the site before planting. The plant will grow to about 1.8m/6ft, and branches brought indoors for flower arrangements will perfume the room beautifully. Take care when cutting, however, as witch hazel dislikes hard pruning.

If you have banks or slopes in your garden, nothing is

Cyclamen coum ssp. coum 'Atkinsii' (right) makes a spectacular sweep of vibrant purple shades when mass-planted in a wide border.

Soft freckled petals of the gently nodding hellebore (above) can soften the effect of a winter garden which often consists only of rugged looking plants like heathers. Their looks are deceptive as the Helleborus orientalis (Lenten rose) is an evergreen in mild areas.

PERFECT PARTNERS

Many people choose just one flowering specimen to add a bright splash of colour to their garden in the winter months. But why choose just one? Once you have an idea of which plants provide winter interest, select a few in colours which complement each other particularly well and plant them together. It doesn't matter whether your garden is small or palatial, you can still achieve an oasis of sunshine shades. Vibrant crocuses in summery tones have been planted here amidst a clump of purple heathers (erica).

For something a little taller in the winter garden, choose the Daphne mezereum (right). The bright blossoms of this bushy shrub appear in late winter/early spring. The dense clusters encase the leafless branches. They are replaced by light green leaves which are grey on their undersides. It gives pleasure all year round as well as making an active contribution to a winter colour scheme.

lovelier than seeing them carpeted in heather (erica). The foliage is evergreen and flowers come in many colours.

Heather carpet

There are over 500 species of flowering heather altogether, many of which bloom in winter so there is no lack of choice. Why not try a pink variety such as *E. × darleyensis*

WINTER FLOWERING SHRUBS

Any one of these shrubs will add shape, interest and colour to your garden all year round—but especially in winter. Make a feature of a single shrub, or plant a selection to create a winter shrub border.

PLANT	HEIGHT	FEATURES
Cornelian cherry (*Cornus mas*)	3m/9ft	This shrub has a rather open, spreading habit and produces a mass of tiny yellow flowers in late winter.
mezereon (*Daphne mezereum*)	90cm/3ft	This popular shrub has fragrant purple blooms in late winter, followed by scarlet berries.
oleaster (*Elaeagnus macropylla*)	3m/9ft	A pretty silvery evergreen, it produces fragrant flowers of a similar silvery colour in autumn.
false castor-oil plant (*Fatsia japonica*)	2.4m/8ft	An evergreen with thick stems and few branches, it has rather exotic white flowers in early winter. This plant does not like being pruned: just cut out any dead wood in spring.
mahonia (*M. japonica*)	2.4m/8ft	This shrub produces long lily-of-the-valley-scented clusters of yellow flowers in mid-winter. For the rest of the year, it provides evergreen background, but it can be invasive if not kept in check.
viburnum (*V. farreri, syn. fragrans*)	2m/6ft	Pale pink buds open to deliciously scented white flowers, that are frost-resistant. Young growth is bronze-coloured.
autumn cherry (*Prunus subhirtella*)	6m/18ft	This is, in fact, a tree, but is compact enough to be grown in a container. 'Autumnalis' has semi-double white blooms and can flower between late autumn and early spring; 'Autumnalis Rosea' has pale pink blooms. It is best grown in mild areas and prefers shelter.

'George Rendall' or the dazzling white 'Molten Silver'?

Heathers require little attention and spread freely, but they, too, dislike lime in the soil. An alternative solution would be to grow them in containers filled with ericaceous lime-free compost. 'George Rendall' and 'Molten Silver' (often sold as 'Silberschmelze') grow to around 45cm/18in tall, while the little *Erica carnea* 'Vivellii', with its carmine flowers and bronze foliage, reaching a height of only 20cm/8in, makes an ideal container plant. Ling (*Calluna vulgaris*) can be used in a similar way to heather, producing a marvellous show of foliage and flowers in reds, oranges, yellows and golds.

Christmas roses

For the front of the border, Christmas rose (*Helleborus niger*) is a good choice, with its nodding white flowers, tinged pink, that appear in the depths of winter. There is also the Lenten rose (*Helleborus orientalis*), that has red, pink, purple, cream or white blooms, and flowers for a long time. Both grow to only about 45cm/

18cm high, and are happy in dappled shade.

Amid all your planning, one garden essential you should not forget about are bulbs such as snowdrops, winter aconites and cyclamen. Snowdrops (galanthus) are best planted and moved 'in the green', which means that, unlike other bulbs, they are best divided after flowering but before the foliage dies back.

Winter bulbs

Winter aconites (*Eranthis hyemalis*) are cheerful but can be too invasive for a small garden. Tuberous *Cyclamen coum* are shy plants but a real delight. Mark them carefully when you plant them because you may forget where you put them. Suddenly, in early winter, one little variegated leaf will appear, a sign that you are about to get masses and masses of tiny, bright flowers right through to early spring.

If you want to bring colour to a balcony or if you only have a patio, there is still much you can do to cheer up the winter months. There are many undemanding little plants for tubs, sink gardens and window

Acers (above) are real all rounders in the garden. Renowned for their remarkably intense autumn colouring they make an excellent choice for a winter garden too. The paper-like outer bark of A. griseum unfurls to reveal the reddish bark beneath.

For a bright, sunny display of pansies (right) you have to plan well ahead. Plant them in early autumn or late summer while the ground is still warm and feed them with a proprietary fertilizer in early autumn to build up their strength for the long winter ahead. They will repay your hard work with a palette of colours.

COLOURFUL CATKINS

GARDEN NOTES

Before many of the spring flowers have appeared, certain trees produce catkins that can add their own sparkle of colour and interest to your garden. Why not try the non-weeping willow, *Salix aegyptiaca* or the Musk willow. Grey catkins that turn to bright yellow adorn its bare branches in late winter and early spring, and are followed by large, oval, dark green leaves. The tree reaches an eventual height of 5m/15ft.

With shiny yellow petals that resemble buttercups, the pretty yellow flowers of the winter aconite, *Eranthis hyemalis* (right), grace the garden in late winter. The long, thin, pale green leaves form a collar around the sunny flower heads.

The winter flowering jasmine (left) is another yellow addition to the winter garden. The bright flowers are produced on leafless stems all through the winter months. This tough climber will survive in practically any position, even against a cold, shady wall. The flowers may be slightly susceptible to damage from very cold winds. Prune flowering stems after flowering to within a few centimetres of the base.

boxes (these would be suitable for rockeries, too). The charming small birch tree, *Betula pendula* 'Golden Cloud', will grow happily in a container, but is rather delicate at first, so surround it with other pots in autumn to keep it sheltered from harsh winds. The plants will then keep each other protected on frosty winter nights, and a grouped display will look attractive when viewed from a window.

The winter flowering dwarf perennial Algerian iris, *Iris unguicularis*, will, if given enough sun, produce lavender blue flowers amid feathery foliage, and reach only about 30cm/1ft in height. It will flower again in summer so it earns its place in the border.

All year colour

Finally, there are Universal pansies and gem-coloured primroses. Use them to fill your winter garden with summer colour by planting them in borders, as edging flowers, in window boxes or in tubs – perhaps surrounding the base of a birch tree. For these, you will have to think well ahead. They are best planted early, while the ground is still warm, then fed well in early autumn to build them up. After this, you can leave them alone, apart from dead-heading the pansies as the blooms fade. You can probably buy them at the same time as your bulbs and, as they may well already be in flower, you will be able to choose from an almost infinite palette of colours.

With careful planning you can create a winter garden for little extra expense.

PROJECT CHRISTMAS WREATHS

Take up the challenge of making your own wreaths. The hard part is already done because florists sell plastic filled with foam and shaped into a circle.

After soaking the shape push the stems of plant material into it. Try brightly-coloured fruits, small fir-cones, painted walnuts, ribbons or other cheerful decorations. For a traditional look use holly with mistletoe and ivy.

To these could be added 'Christmas fern' (*Polystichum acrostichoides*), which is shaped like holly, or variegated ivy. But however plain or elaborate you decide to make your wreath, make sure you put it in a prominent position like a gate, the front door or on an internal door.

This Christmas wreath (right) is made simply of hollies, berries and cones. A bright bow adds colour.

MAKING A ROCKERY

A rockery provides a point of interest in the garden and gives you the chance to be creative with some appealing alpines and garden flowers.

The first garden rockeries were intended to look just like miniature mountains (and some even had models of tweed-clad climbers, complete with ropes), so that the plants in them were completely out of scale. As the idea caught on, rockeries became less fanciful, but were often unimaginative. But nowadays, gardeners have moved away from these unappealing mounds of soil studded with rocks and aubrieta.

Today's rockeries are much more natural-looking, with rocks carefully set into the soil so as to provide the same sort of conditions that rock plants meet in the wild, with horizontal and vertical crevices creating cool, damp places for the plants' roots to run in. The soil has grit added to it, so that it is very well drained, to create a real mountain habitat.

Imitating nature

Alpines make ideal rock plants, but rockeries do not have to be inspired by the Alps. The mountainous areas of Britain, or indeed any high ground with rocky outcrops, can provide a model, as can screes which have become greened over with plants on the lower slopes.

The secret of success is to imitate nature, so that you create a true home for mountain plants, which will then grow and flower happily for many years. Of course, the plants you choose should be in scale with your rock garden. You should try to avoid rampant plants that will take over in a small area. It is also best

PLANTS FOR ROCK GARDENS

CONIFERS AND SHRUBS

Juniper	*Juniperus communis* 'Compressa'
Silver fir	*Abies balsamea* f. *hudsonia*
Spruce	*Picea abies* 'Pumila'
	P. mariana 'Nana'
Cypress	*Chamaecyparis lawsoniana* 'Minima'
	C. obtusa 'Nana Compacta'
Broom	*Cytisus ardoinoi* (alpine broom)
	C. × *beanii*
Daphne	*D. arbuscula*
	D. blagayana
Heather	*Erica carnea* (alpine heather)
	E. mackayana
Rock rose	*Helianthemum alpestre*
	H. nummularium
Rhododendron	*R. campylogynum*
	R. calostrotum keleticum
	Radicans Group *R.* hybrid 'Curlew'

FLOWERING BULBS AND CORMS

Anemone	*A. blanda*
Allium	*A. moly*
Glory of the snow	*Chionodoxa sardensis*
	C. luciliae
Cyclamen	*C. coum*
	C. purpurascens
Snowdrop	*Galanthus nivalis*
Iris	*I. danfordiae*
	I. histrioides
Daffodil	*Narcissus cyclamineus*
	N. assoanus
Scilla	*S. siberica*
Tulip	*Tulipa tarda*

FLOWERING ROCK PLANTS

Thrift	*Armeria maritima*
Aubrieta	*A. deltoides*
Dwarf campanula	*C. arvatica*
	C. carpatica
Gentian	*Gentiana acaulis*
	G. verna
Cranesbill	*Geranium cinereum*
	G. dalmaticum
Phlox	*P. douglasii*
	P. subulata
Auricula	*Primula auricula* (alpine species)
Saxifrages	*Saxifraga* species and varieties
Thyme	*Thymus* species and varieties

GARDEN FLOWERS FOR ROCKERIES
(late spring and summer flowering)

Ageratum	*Ageratum* spp.
Alyssum	*Alyssum* spp.
Californian poppy	*Eschscholzia californica*
Geum	*Geum* spp.
Candytuft	*Iberis umbellata*
Poached egg plant	*Limnanthes douglasii*
Mesembryanthemum	*Mesembryanthemum* spp.
Forget-me-not	*Myosotis* spp.

In a well-established rock garden (left), a colourful carpet of spreading flowers all but obscures the rocks. A stone feature, such as a birdbath, in a similar rock is a happy addition.

The low-growing spruce Picea abies 'Pumila' (above) forms rounded evergreen hummocks.

The alpine primula P. auricula (right) is a colourful addition to any rockery, available in shades of blue, red and yellow.

Few natural colours can match the heavenly blue of the gentians. The trumpet gentian (Gentiana acaulis) (below) is easy enough to grow, but can be temperamental, in some years failing to flower at all.

to choose a variety of mountain plants – it is a waste of a rockery to use it just for heathers.

Rock gardens, despite being mini-mountain habitats, can come in all sorts of styles. There is such a wide variety of plants and shrubs, including evergreens, and flowering plants for all seasons, in all shapes and sizes, that you can make your mini-garden very individual. The style you choose will depend both on the layout of the rest of the garden and on what other features you may want to add.

Special features

You may want the rockery to include a pond, perhaps with a watercourse and even a fountain. Oddly enough, although a fountain is an entirely artificial feature, fountains always seem in keeping with the most naturalistic of rockeries.

One reason for the popularity of the rockery/water feature combination is that you can use the soil dug out for the pond to give the rock garden the height it needs. However, if you do this you should be very careful not to create a dull-looking mound, which can happen all too easily.

If you have a natural bank in your garden you are lucky,

RECOMMENDED ROCKS

Sandstone A sympathetic, soft-edged rock that weathers well and looks attractive. There are many kinds, nearly all of which are good.

Limestone is an ideal rock, and most limestones weather beautifully. If you choose a hard one, you will still be able to grow lime-hating plants. Limestone 'paving' is natural, weathered limestone, formed during the Ice Age, and a vital home for rare wild flowers. It is not environmentally friendly to buy this type of stone for your garden.

Tufa is a very soft limestone into which alpines can be planted directly, and is perhaps the best of all for rock gardens, but is very expensive indeed. To do it credit you need to be an alpine expert.

Local stones such as Yorkshire stone, millstone and gritstone, are attractive, and are often sold in garden centres for crazy paving. Being in such flat pieces they make rockery building easy on the back and produce a fine, natural effect.

Rockeries are usually placed at the side or the back of a garden, against a wall or fence, but this is not a hard and fast rule. A rockery may act as a foreground to the rest of the garden, with a lawn flowing around it (above). Here, a mixed planting of alpines and conifers gives colour and height without having to pile up rocks.

An alternative solution for those who do not want to lift heavy loads is to use hollow artificial rocks (right). Though conveniently and naturalistically shaped, these manufactured rocks do not weather as well as some natural stone.

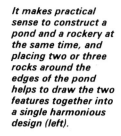

CHOOSING ROCKS

Good rock is nearly always expensive, but you are making a permanent feature and an attractive addition to your garden, so it is well worth spending out on good materials. Do not make the mistake of buying enormous pieces of rock, even if you want to create a dramatic cliff-face. It is always better to use two or three medium rocks rather than one huge one, and plant up the crevices between them. It is best, if possible, to choose a type of rock that is found locally in your area, for a natural effect.

It makes practical sense to construct a pond and a rockery at the same time, and placing two or three rocks around the edges of the pond helps to draw the two features together into a single harmonious design (left).

Limestone (below) is the best rock for a rock garden; it comes in a variety of colours, from pure white through every imaginable shade of cream, buff and grey, and weathers both along and at right angles to the strata.

as this is ideal for a rock garden. Here you can have great fun with rocks without having to move masses of soil. On the other hand, making a rockery in a normal, flat garden need not involve too much digging, as small outcrops can be made on flat ground without too much difficulty.

You dig out a wide, shallow depression and pile the soil behind it, moulded so that it is higher in the middle and tapers to the sides. The rise can then become a rock face, perhaps just 60cm/2ft high and, say, 3.5m/12ft wide. This is a very good way of turning a boringly flat lawn into an undulating, interesting one.

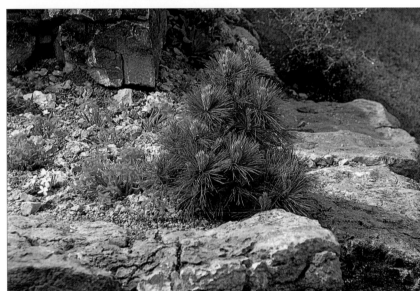

Where to put a rockery

Once you have decided on the shape and size of your rock garden, there are some other important decisions to be made. You may have a general idea where you want it, but there are factors that you must take into consideration. Rockeries should, where possible, be in sun. But you could

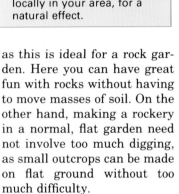

create a rockery as an integral feature of the garden so that where it runs into shade it changes into a mini-woodland garden or even a bog. A rockery does not have to stand on its own as a naked garden feature; indeed the best gardens are those where each element merges with the next.

Although it should be in the sun, a well-built rockery will have its own shady areas,

created by the way the rocks are arranged. Some of these will provide quite deep shade, while others will allow plants to have just a little shade in the middle of the day. The flatter, higher areas will, of course, be in full sun.

Good drainage

Drainage is extremely important for rock garden plants and it is no good trying to make a rockery if the ground under it is waterlogged. Even if you build up over it using imported soil, it never seems to work satisfactorily; so it is much better either to have the ground drained properly or to dig out a bed at least 45cm/18in deep and fill it with plenty of good drainage material to

DIFFICULT ROCKS

Granite is hard, and extremely heavy. It can be used if flattish pieces 30cm/1ft across or less can be found, but it takes skill to create a natural effect with granite. In any case, it is often difficult to obtain.

Gypsum This is the glaringly white 'rockery stone' that comes in difficult, lumpy shapes. It never weathers and is unattractive.

229

provide a base. The soil you use must also have grit added to it to make it drain well.

It is also important not to site your rockery under trees. This stops plants from flourishing, not only because of the shade cast by the trees, but also because it keeps the rain off, with any moisture that does reach the rockery plants falling as heavy drips from the trees.

If you plan to have a pond in your rockery you should decide on the shape of the pond first, and then dig it out. As the soil is thrown up, make sure that

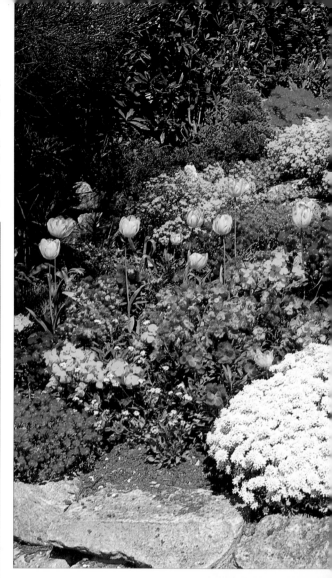

PROJECT — BUILDING A ROCK GARDEN

Some planting can be done as you go along. Put a plant's teased-out root ball on one rock and put another on top, then fill with compost. Otherwise, water the rockery well and allow to settle for a few days before planting. You could put a layer of scree or gravel on the slope to protect the collars of the plants and cut down weeding.

1 Set the first rocks very firmly, ramming an 'alpine' compost – one part sand and gravel to three parts soil – between and behind them.

3 The next layer can curve back into the rockery and out almost to meet the first layer. This creates flat pockets for planting.

2 Curve in the bottom layer so that it creates a natural line rather than a wall. The rocks should slope back so rain runs into, not off, the rockery.

4 Put smaller rocks at the end of each layer. This gives the effect of the rocks disappearing into the soil for a more naturalistic effect.

the subsoil (the compacted soil from below the topsoil) is either discarded or spread out in a layer (never a mound) in the area where the rockery is going to be. This is because plants will not grow in subsoil, and setting rocks in it is not easy. If you do not intend to have a pond, you will either have to sculpt your garden into a hollow and use the hollowed-out earth for your rockery, or buy in topsoil.

The next stage is to use the topsoil to make a shallow mound. When the mound has been completed and shaped to your satisfaction, you can begin to place the rocks in it, starting at the bottom and working up, making sure that each rock is so firmly set that you can stand on it without it rocking. About one-third of each rock should be buried, and the rocks should all tilt slightly backwards.

The brightly coloured zoned flowers Dorotheanthus bellidiformis (above) are an excellent way of introducing summer colour to the rockery.

Many alpines and other rock plants are spring-flowering. Though you should be sure to include other plants that will give colour and interest through the summer, a rockery can be a stunningly colourful sight in the first flushes of spring (left top).

An alternative to the wild riot of a spring-time rockery is to intersperse the flowering alpines with foliage plants (left). The blue-green dwarf cypress Chamaecyparis lawsoniana 'Minima Glauca' and the mid-green spruce Picea abies provide a context for the white flowers of Iberis sempervirens and the yellow blooms of St John's wort, Hypericum cerastioides meuselianum.

Lay the rocks in layers, or strata, just as you see them in nature. Each rock should bear a good relationship to the next and the strata should meet and break here and there, creating flat pockets of soil and interesting shapes. If you use rocks that are fairly flat, you will be able to make a fascinating garden feature without having to build it very high at all. If you have a pond, you can make a cliff at one side of it, and slope the rockery gently down until it merges with the lawn or a border.

Plants to choose

A rock garden plant is any plant that looks 'right' in a rock garden. The plants to grow will depend to an extent on the size of your rockery and the kind of soil you have (for example, some plants prefer limy, alkaline soil and some hate it). Small alpines offer great variety and you can gradually build up a collection of these fascinating plants. On the other hand, there are plenty of other plants that look in keeping and do not grow too high or spread too far.

For the best effect, choose plants in a variety of shapes and heights. If there is a specialist nursery near you, you

ESTIMATING QUANITITES OF ROCK

Do not try to work out how much rock you will need. It is very difficult to do so and depends entirely on how the building goes. It is much better to buy a little at a time, and this means that you are less likely to overspend.

will be able to get useful advice, and the best choice of plants, there. Mound-forming and trailing plants can be mixed with miniature perennials, while dwarf shrubs and conifers add interest in larger rockeries.

Miniature bulbs are at home in rockeries of any size; winter-flowering aconites, scilla and small hyacinths for early spring, followed by miniature daffodils, dwarf tulips and then the smallest irises, and fragile autumn crocuses, will give year-round colour.

One of the most common mistakes people make in selecting plants is to choose only spring-flowering ones. Remember that a rockery which is colourful only in spring is a waste of an opportunity. You can have flowers and interest all year round if you are careful.

Everyone knows which flowers they prefer. Once you know the best conditions for growing your particular favourite, you can fill your garden with them, and give yourself, your friends and family, hours of pleasure as you admire them.

CHAPTER FOUR
Favourite Flowers

HARDY FUCHSIAS

With their elegant, ornamental flowers in a range of eye-catching colours, the sturdy shrub fuchsias are firm summer favourites.

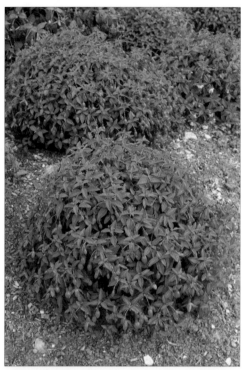

The aptly named 'Tom Thumb' (left) with its plump cherry-red and mauve flowers is the best known of the hardy miniature varieties and looks stunning in a rock garden. Whereas F. magellanica (below) is a prolific and sprawling flowering species from Mexico which grows up to 1.8./6ft in mild areas. This hardy shrub is often used for hedging in favourable areas with a mild climate.

Among the most popular and easy-to-grow garden plants, fuchsias carry masses of nodding, bell-shaped flowers from midsummer until the first autumn frost. Perfect in shrubberies and mixed borders, some varieties can be grown as hedges in mild areas, while dwarf carpeting forms add colour and interest to rockeries and sink gardens.

Spoilt for choice

Most fuchsias form multi-stemmed, upright, dense bushy shrubs, 30-90cm/1-3ft high and wide; though in mild climates, hardy fuchsias can reach 1.8m/6ft or more. Some varieties have gracefully arching branches, while large-flowered forms often start the season upright but become weighed down by their abundant flowers.

Hardy fuchsias can be left outdoors all year round, though in cold winters they tend to die back to ground level and sprout back to life again in spring.

Flushed pink

Hardy fuchsia flowers vary from white and ivory through to shades of pink, crimson,

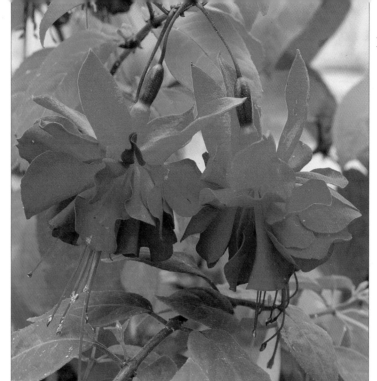

PLANT PROFILE

Suitable site and soil: fuchsias will grow in a variety of soils, including acid and chalky, but preferably well-drained. Organic matter such as peat or garden compost should be added to less fertile soils. Sunshine is needed for a good floral display but full sun is not necessary. They appreciate a sheltered position as wind can damage the flowers.

Planting: all young growth and foliage is prone to frost damage, so do not plant out until fear of frost has passed (late spring or early summer). Set the plants deeper in the soil than they were in the container, to protect the buds.

Cultivation and care: most of the top growth of the plant will be killed back during the winter. Wait until new buds are visible then prune away any dead branches. Water regularly and feed weekly during the growing season.
  In cold areas the stem bases can be protected in winter by covering them with coarse sand or peat.

Propagation: in mid-summer, short tip cuttings root easily in potting compost. Rooting takes between two and four weeks.

Pests and diseases: healthy plants are usually trouble-free, but look out for aphids, capsid bugs (which eat irregular holes in leaves) and froghopper (which suck the sap of plants, causing distortion). Remove pests by spraying off with a jet of soapy water.

THE FUCHSIA FLOWER

This most elegant flower is made up of these delicate parts:

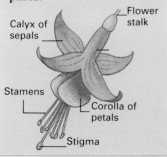

Flower stalk
Calyx of sepals
Stamens
Corolla of petals
Stigma

'Tennessee Waltz' (left), excellent as a standard, has flowers which sweep up their rose-pink 'skirts' to reveal pretty lilac underskirts.

Although small, 'Alice Hoffman' (below left) flowers freely with bright pink sepals over white petals.

'Gay Fandango' (below right) has carmine flowers with delicate rose-pink petals.

'Lena Dalton' (bottom) provides an eye-catching display of pale pink and stunning mauve flowers.

235

PROJECT

PLANTING A FUCHSIA HEDGE

Fuchsia magellanica makes a very decorative informal hedge that will grow quickly and require only occasional pruning – in the autumn or early spring. Follow these simple guidelines and you will be rewarded with an attractive, bushy display like the *F.m.* 'Variegata' pictured here, with its cream-and-pink-edged leaves and vivid red and purple flowers.

● Plant in late spring, spacing individual plants 30cm (1ft) apart. Firm soil well around roots and water frequently until well established.

● Keep the surrounding area free of weeds and other plants to a radius of 30cm (12in), by adding a layer of pulverized wood, bark or mulch.

● To ensure a good, bushy shape, encourage sideways rather than upward growth at first by pinching out the growing tips of young plants.

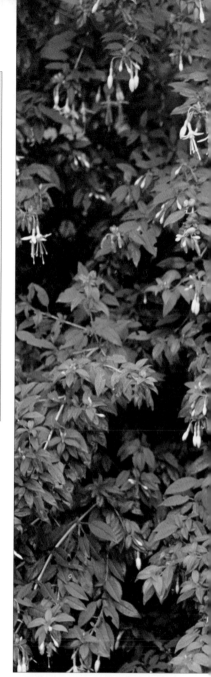

scarlet, lavender and violet blue. They come in pastel shades and really vivid hues – a marvellous range of very attractive colours.

Flowers can be all one colour. Though most, such as the scarlet and purple, single-flowered 'Mrs Popple', are bicoloured. A few varieties are even flushed or veined with a third colour.

Most fuchsia leaves are plain green, but a few are variegated, such as the green, grey and white-leaved *F. magellanica* 'Versicolor'.

Fuchsia fruits

If faded flowers and their stalks are not removed, green seed pods eventually form, swelling and ripening to a rich red colour.

Though decorative, fuchsia fruits hinder further flowering, so it is advisable to snap them off as soon as they begin to form. The ground-covering *Fuchsia procumbens* has huge colourful fruits, 2.5cm/1in long – three times as big as its tiny flowers.

Buyer's guide

Hardy fuchsias are sold in pots all year round, but early summer is the best planting time.

Look for plump, woody growth and a well-balanced leafy branching system with no sign of wilting, yellowing, pests or diseases. You should not be tempted to buy the one with most flowers, since many are liable to drop off during planting, and could disguise a weak or poorly shaped plant.

Planting fuchsias

Fuchsias thrive in any well-drained but moist, fertile soil, in sun or light shade. Those with pale leaves, however, can scorch in full sun, and need a degree of shade. No fuchsia likes prolonged, dry heat.

Once you have selected a suitable location, dig a planting hole 15cm/6in wider than the pot, and 5cm/2in deeper. Remove all weeds.

In hot weather, or if you have a free-draining soil, fill the hole with water and let it drain. Add moist peat or leaf mould to the bottom, and a little bone meal.

Water the fuchsia, then carefully remove it from the pot. Place the plant in the hole, so that it is 4cm/1½in lower in the soil than it was in its pot. Even when the tops are cut back by frost, the spring buds will have protection and

'Alba' (right) the hardiest of all the F. magellanica varieties, contrasts pretty white flowers tinged with mauve and bright green foliage.

In spring, prune back (below) to ground level any leafless, shrivelled stems or branches of hardy types that may have been killed by frost. To encourage bushiness and flowering, lightly cut back the remaining stems by about 20 per cent, to just above a pair of leaves.

then get off to a good start next year. Fill the gap between the root ball and edge of the hole with soil, mixed with more peat or leaf mould. Firm the soil as you go, then water thoroughly.

Room to grow

Space your plants according to variety, allowing 20cm/8in between the dwarf 'Tom Thumb', 60cm/2ft for the ground-covering *procumbens* and 1.8m/6ft or more for the vigorous 'Riccartonii'.

Always keep the area immediately around a young fuchsia free of other plants so it has a chance to settle in.

Pots of blooms

Use a nutrient-rich, loam-based potting compost. Clay pots are more attractive and stable than plastic ones – important if you are growing top-heavy standards!

Plant newly bought fuchsias in pots 2.5cm/1in wider than their garden centre container, or even larger if they are to form part of a mixed group. Place a drainage layer of gravel or crocks in the base of the pot, then fill with potting compost. Water and plant, leaving a 1cm/½in space between the top of the root ball and the rim, then water again.

Leave the pot in a shady spot for a few days, to give the plant a chance to recover and settle in. Re-pot only when the roots fill the existing pot.

Cultivation

Water the plants daily until they are well established, then continue regularly, particularly in hot, dry weather.

Feed your fuchsias weekly in the growing season with a general-purpose fertilizer or a specially prepared fuchsia feed. Follow the instructions on the packet carefully, as overfeeding results in lush foliage but few, if any, flowers.

Pinch out the growing tips of young plants, to stimulate side shoots to form. This encourages bushy growth, making a more attractive plant.

In mid-to-late autumn, before the first frost, surround the bases of hardy fuchsias with a mulch.

Root fuchsias from 7.5-10cm/3-4in tip cuttings, taken in mid summer and make a cut just below a pair of leaves. Lightly dip the base of each stem in rooting powder, and insert to half its length in peat-based potting compost. Cover with a polythene bag to create humidity, and provide a constant temperature of about 16°C/61°F.

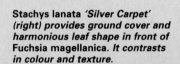
PERFECT PARTNERS

The less hardy fuchsia, 'Amy Lye' (below), is protected by Hydrangea macrophylla.

Stachys lanata *'Silver Carpet'* (right) provides ground cover and harmonious leaf shape in front of Fuchsia magellanica. *It contrasts in colour and texture.*

WATER LILIES

Aquatic aristocrats, water lilies are breathtakingly beautiful. They are often regarded as difficult to grow but they are easy, even if you don't have a pond.

The very name water lily conjures images of beauty and elegance, and even the Latin name has romantic and graceful overtones: *Nymphaea* means water nymph.

The roots of these water plants embed themselves in the mud at the bottom of the pond (or in the soil in their planting containers). From these strong roots grows a thick root stock, topped with leaves and flowers that float gracefully on the surface.

As a family, water lilies are surprisingly varied. Some have blue flowers that stand

Water lillies are easy to grow and quick to multiply. N. 'Marliacea Chromatella' (above), has an exquisite, delicate shape and a beautiful, translucent yellow colour.

above the water; others are so small you can grow them in a tiny sink garden. Their large, flat leaves, which float on the surface of the water, provide shade for fish and help to inhibit the growth of algae.

Variegated and scented varieties are popular today and long ago there were even some which were regarded as an edible delicacy. The ancient Egyptians pounded the seeds and roots to make a bread or would eat the roots both raw and cooked. In Australia they were eaten by aborigines. Different parts of these plants have also been used medicinally and as an aphrodisiac.

Cures for cold

All the hardy water lilies mentioned here will survive cold winters, but take care if you are planting them in very shallow ponds as the roots must be below the ice to survive if the pond freezes over. You are unlikely to lose any water lilies planted in 30cm/ 12in or more of water.

Dwarf and miniature varieties grown in raised containers should be moved to a more sheltered spot or even indoors during severe cold spells. Plants left in a pond will certainly be damaged if the water freezes solid.

Tropical water lilies can be grown outside as long as they are brought indoors for the winter months. Lift the roots and plant them in moist sand in a cool, sheltered place that escapes the frost.

When to plant

The best time to plant the hardy kinds is when the first young leaves appear, but any time from early spring to early summer is suitable. Tropical kinds, however, should not be planted out until later in the summer.

You can plant lilies directly into soil in the bottom of the pond or container, but it is generally more convenient to plant them in special plastic

PLANT PROFILE

NYMPHAEA (WATER LILY)

Suitable site and soil:
In ornamental pools, in a fertile, loamy soil.

Cultivation and care:
They require little attention after planting, though they may need thinning occasionally. This is best done in spring.

Propagation:
Divide roots or remove young offsets. Insert in small pots filled with loam, stand in a bowl, fill with water to 1.5 cm/½in above pot rim and leave in full sun until well rooted, before planting out into permanent position.

Pests and diseases:
Leaves may attract water lily beetle (although this is rare). Leaves and flowers attract aphids. Insects can simply be hosed off. Leaf spot (pale brown circles of fungus) and stem rot (blackened stems) are more serious. Remove affected leaves and/or stems.

Under the surface:
It is just as important to know what is going on under water. Different types of water lily grow to different heights, so it is important to choose a variety suitable for the depth of your pond.

'Mrs. Richmond' (above) has perfectly flat leaves and succulent pink flowers. Lifting its face to the sun on an elegant long neck this fragrant 'Director George T. Moore' flower (left) has a sunny yellow centre. The brilliant red water lily 'Escarboucle' (below) sits in striking contrast on flat, circular, deepest green leaves.

RECOMMENDED VARIETIES

The first process of selection is to find the variety of water lily most suitable for the size of your pond or container. Then decide on the particular colour you would like.

Planting depth is the depth of water above the soil or compost level – not to the bottom of the pond. The depth is only a guide as some of the miniatures will grow in just a few inches of water while others will happily tolerate 30cm/12in deeper than indicated.

Although some of those lilies listed are species (*N. candida* for example) others are hybrids and you often find them listed on plant labels and in catalogues as 'varieties'.

For a dish, sink or tub

Planting depth 10-23cm/4-9in

- *N. candida* (white)
- *N.* 'Pygmaea Alba' (white)
- *N.* 'Pygmaea Helvola' (yellow)

For a small pond

Planting depth 15-30cm/6-12in

- 'Froebeli' (deep red, free-flowering and fragrant)
- 'Laydekeri Purpurata' (masses of flowers over a long season, wine red pointed petals and leaves splashed with maroon)
- 'William Falconer' (dark red)
- 'Odorata Minor' (white, scented, suitable for a tub as well as a small pool)
- 'Paul Hariot' (opens pale yellow, then deepens to copper-red; fragrant)
- 'Rose Arey' (large pink flowers; very fragrant)

For a large pond

Planting depth 23-45cm/9-18in

- 'Albatros' (white)
- 'Director George T. Moore' (light green leaves, purple flowers with yellow centres, tropical type)
- 'Laydekeri Lilacea' (pink and fragrant)
- 'James Brydon' (crimson, peony-shaped flowers and leaves flecked with maroon)
- 'Marliacea Chromatella' (yellow and slightly fragrant)
- 'Mme Wilfon Gonnère' (pink)
- 'Odorata Alba' (white, cup-shaped and fragrant)
- 'René Gerard' (pink, blotched and splashed crimson towards the centre)

N. 'Pygmaea Helvola' (above) has small olive-green leaves and star-shaped flowers. N. 'Froebeli' (left) is a deep-pink lily with mottled leaves.

The reddish tinged leaves and pink flowers are typical of 'Rose Arey' (below). 'James Brydon' (bottom) has fragrant crimson flowers.

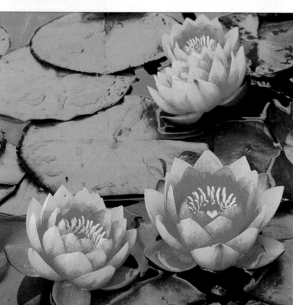

pond baskets available from garden centres. Line these baskets with squares of hessian to prevent the soil falling through. An old plastic washing basket will do the job just as well. The advantage of planting in a container is that it is much easier to lift out the container than to cope with fleshy roots that have penetrated the whole pond.

Nurseries that specialize in aquatic plants sell heavy loam, but ordinary garden soil is perfectly adequate. Avoid soil that has been enriched with powerful chemical fertilizers or manure, however, as this will encourage the invasive growth of algae in the pond. Mix in a handful of bone meal, or add a sachet of special slow-release fertilizer sold for aquatic plants.

Growing tips

To reduce the amount of clouding that occurs when you first immerse the container in water, cover the surface of the

POTENTIAL PESTS

You can grow water lilies for years and never have any problems, but there are a couple of pests of which you should beware.

- *Water lily aphids* are like the common blackfly that you may find in other parts of the garden. Do not spray them with an insecticide – you will harm other wildlife and fish in the pond. Just hose the pests off and let the fish eat them.
- *Water lily beetles* are fortunately rare. The shiny black larvae with yellow undersides and the small dark brown beetles severely damage the leaves, which then start to rot. Pick off and destroy badly affected leaves; otherwise hose the insects off.

GO ORGANIC!

INCREASING YOUR INVESTMENT

Divison is the simplest way of raising water lilies. Lift the roots in late spring and remove some of the 'branches' from the original root. Provided they have a healthy shoot at the end, they should grow. Place in loam-filled pots or simply replant them straight into the pond.

container with a thick layer of gravel. If the water lilies are going in a pond, this will also deter the fish from stirring up the soil in the container. Instead of plunging the container directly into the pond, it is best to lower it over a period of time as the leaf stems elongate. Rest the container on a few bricks initially and remove them in stages, as the plants begin to grow.

The only requirement for good flowering is a sunny position. Provided you choose a variety suitable for your size of pond and depth of water, hardy water lilies will flower well, the number of blooms increasing after the first year or two.

You do not even need a pond

Make a wonderful table centrepiece by growing a miniature water lily in a bowl. The roots are planted in a smaller dish in a complimentary colour. This pink hued lily makes a striking contrast with the black bowl.

Water plants are sometimes sold separately in garden centres and nurseries, from early spring to early summer. They are also available by mail from water plant specialists. Check the mature size before you buy as some varieties spread very quickly.

CUT FLOWERS

One of the drawbacks of water lilies is that they can be rather inaccessible and you may have to get down on your knees to enjoy their scent. Try cutting a few and floating them on water in a dish indoors; many will last for days.

A BUYER'S GUIDE

Popular varieties are available from most good garden centres from early spring to early summer. Outside the main planting season you may be able to obtain them from water garden specialists.

If you do not have a stockist in your area, you can buy them by mail from water plant specialists. New or rare old varieties can be expensive but most are relatively cheap. Beware though of any not listed here that seem very cheap – they may be very vigorous varieties which will quickly invade small ponds.

PROJECT A SUNKEN BARREL POND FOR WATER LILIES

Naturalize the sunken barrel by surrounding it with large pebbles and gravel. This will also serve as a safety measure and will prevent the careless from stumbling into it! If you have small children it will be safer not to sink the barrel, but to leave it free standing.

Sink a watertight half barrel into a hole so that it fits snugly. Use a spirit level to make sure that it is horizontal. Put a 7.5cm/3in layer of loam or good garden soil in the bottom. Part fill the tub with water. Plant the water lilies. N. 'Pygmaea Alba' is a good choice for a small tub as it is hardy and small, yet produces a

stunning display of white flowers. Allow the water to settle before adding a layer of gravel to anchor the plant. Finally top up the water to a total depth of 22-30cm/9-12in. You are likely to lose lilies in bad weather if the water is too shallow. Divide plants in years to come to prevent the tub becoming overcrowded.

to grow the smaller ones. The true miniatures such as *N. × helvola* can be grown in a small dish on a windowsill or in an old sink. The most compact varieties of the larger types, such as 'Froebeli' are perfect for small barrels – try sinking them to the trim in the ground, then plant a lily in each one.

PLANT PROFILE

Suitable site and soil: different species have different requirements. Border varieties love moisture retentive, humus-rich soil in a partially shaded area. Alpine species must have well-drained sandy or gritty soil in a sunny position. Do not allow conditions to become too dry.

Planting: plant in spring or autumn when the ground is moist, but not waterlogged or frozen. It also helps to water the plant in its pot before planting into position. Add peat at planting time. Water well and sprinkle with fertilizer.

Cultivation and care: do not allow primulas to dry out, particularly while in growth. Dead-head faded blooms. In spring, apply mulch. Divide clumps to prevent overcrowding.

Propagation: clump-forming varieties can be lifted and divided every three to four years in spring; primrose (vulgaris) types, every two years. Place in new position in enriched soil.

Take 5cm/2in cuttings from auricula types in summer, plant in a mixture of peat and sand and over-winter in a cold frame or under glass. Plant out in position next spring.

Pests and diseases: in the main, trouble free, although caterpillars are partial to the leaves. Grey mould may appear if conditions are damp during growth. There is no cure and affected plants must be burned to prevent further infection.

Shapes and sizes: there are many varieties of primula. **Auricula** may be alpines or border plants. The flowers are grouped in an umbel on a stem above the foliage. **Candelabra,** as their name suggests, have tiered whorls of flowers on the stem. **Drumstick** types have a pompon of flowers on top of the stem. **Polyanthus** have profuse clusters of yellow-eyed flowers on erect stems.

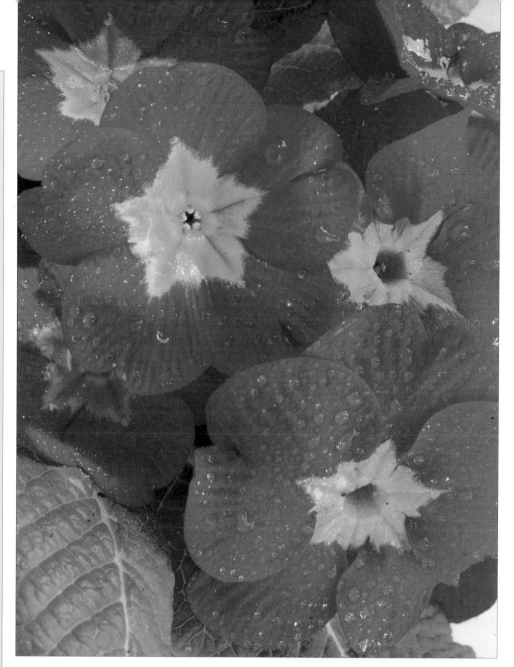

The most distinctive feature of many primulas is their bright central 'eyes' in contrasting colours. Shown here (above) to spectacular effect, this variety 'Insight' has deep red petals which compliment its yellow, winking star-like eyes.

Among a bed of brightly coloured polyanthus, this Primula vulgaris 'Viridiflora' (below) would hold its own with its unusual, exquisite green flowers. Each flower is borne on a single stem, surrounded by oval leaves.

Blooms in blue: this primrose (right) has no contrasting central eye, but boasts beautifully delicate double flowers and petals tinged with white. Falling in the vulgaris group, these primulas grow to a neat mound which reaches a height and width of 15cm/6in.

The traditional soft yellow primrose, Primula vulgaris (above), looks most at home when set with other 'natural woodland' flowers like delicate purple violas. A moist, well-drained bank in partial shade provides the perfect conditions.

TWELVE OF THE BEST PRIMULAS

Name	Type	Height x width	Flower
'Crescendo' F1 hybrids	Polyanthus	20cm/8in x 20cm/8in	various colours, large blooms
'Posy series' F1 hybrids	Polyanthus	7.5cm/3in x 7.5cm/3in	various colours and bi-colours
P. alpicola (moonlight primula)	Sikkimensis	30-60cm/1-2ft x 30cm/1ft	fragrant, creamy white to yellow
P. auricula (dusty miller)	Auricula	15cm/6in x 15cm/6in	various colours and multi-colours
P. beesiana	Candelabra	60cm/2ft x 45cm/1½ft	reddish purple, yellow eye
P. bulleyana	Candelabra	60-75cm/2-2½ft x 45cm/1½ft	golden yellow to orange red
P. denticulata	Drumstick	30cm/1ft x 25cm/10in	pale lilac to deep purple, yellow eye
P. japonica (Japanese primrose)	Candelabra	60-75cm/2-2½ft x 45cm/1½ft	various colours, most with yellow eye
P. florindae (giant cowslip)	Sikkimensis	60-120cm/2-4ft x 60cm/2ft	fragrant, pale-to-deep yellow
P. veris (cowslip)	Vulgaris	15-25cm/6-10in x 15cm/6in	fragrant, bright yellow, orange eye
P. vulgaris (primrose)	Vulgaris	15cm/6in x 15cm/6in	pale yellow
'Wanda'	Vulgaris	10cm/4in x 10cm/4in	wine-purple

Primulas of the auricula group produce fragrant flowers carried in an umbel on a stem. This golden-hued variety (below) can grow up to 15cm/6in. Unlike the crinkly leaves of other primulas, these plants are smooth-leafed, often with a fine powdery surface.

Primula denticulata Alba (right) is a beautiful example of the perfectly formed 'drumstick' variety. Sturdy stems that reach up to 30cm/1ft are topped by dense pompons of petals. The leaves, which fan around the stems in dense clumps, are 'toothed' with softly jagged edges.

autumn, it is better to use slow-release fertilizer such as bone meal to prepare the plant for its major flowering period.

Moisture loving

Water primulas whenever the soil becomes dry. Mulch around plants with damp peat in spring, to smother weeds and retain soil moisture. Remove faded flowers to encourage further blooms. Lift and divide clump-forming types every three to four years, and vulgaris types every two years: this will prevent overcrowding.

You can lift bedding primulas after flowering and replant them in an out-of-the-way spot until the following autumn.

Alpine primulas dislike cold, wet soil, so work a layer of grit around and under the plants in autumn to help keep their crowns dry. Place a horizontal pane of glass (across brick supports) above the plant to help prevent rot, while allowing air to circulate.

Many primulas die back in hot summers, but sprout again once cooler, autumn weather sets in, so don't worry if your plant temporarily disappears!

Plentiful plants

Divide established clumps after flowering. With a hand fork or trowel, lift the clump and gently prise apart the roots into several sections. Replant in a new, ready-prepared spot, or enrich the existing soil with a light sprinkling of all-purpose fertilizer, dug in before replanting.

Auriculas and other dwarf and mat-forming types of primula are propagated by 2.5-5cm/1-2in cuttings or by small rooted shoots. These are taken in summer and placed in trays of loam-based compost, overwintered in a cold frame, then

PERFECT PARTNERS

Polyanthus look lovely alongside tulips, daffodils, hyacinths, and wallflowers because they provide the horizontal ground cover and low-level interest needed around upright-growing bulbs.

In moist borders and bog gardens, primulas associate well with ferns, hostas, arum, marsh marigold, lady's mantle, astilbe and iris. In moist, peaty soil, they complement azaleas or rhododendrons.

In rockeries and sink gardens, grow primulas with saxifrage, aubrieta, fritillaria, anemone, alyssum, in sun or shade, according to type.

Although colourful and eye-catching on their own, primulas can be set off to great effect when set with other plants. Here, the stately candelabra Primula japonica rises above Claytonia sibirica in a woodland setting.

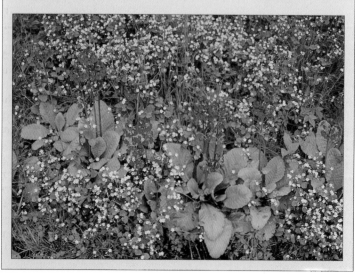

GARDEN NOTES

PRIMULA POSIES

You or your children can bring a breath of spring into your home by picking a pretty posy of primulas from your garden.

Picked with their leaves, they look best in a small container. Cluster them together in a wine glass, milk jug or pretty cup for an informal effect.

Polyanthus are ideal for miniature displays. To keep them fresh, prick gently just below the flower head to release air bubbles, then give them a long drink before arranging the stems.

Auriculas will last longer if at first they are left for several hours in a basin of deep, warm water.

A PRIMULA PLANTER

PROJECT

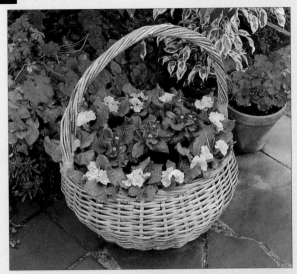

A prettily designed basketful of primulas will brighten any corner. Cut up a black bin liner and use it to line a wicker basket. Pierce a few drainage holes. (To help drainage put some pieces of broken polystyrene at the bottom – this will be much lighter than pieces of broken clay pots.) Fill the basket three-quarters full with moist potting compost. Water primulas then remove from their pots. Arrange them in the basket, add more compost and firm them in. Water the primulas in well.

A wicker basket makes a pretty, portable container for a colourful collection of primulas on a patio or balcony.

Primula 'Wanda' (left) makes a tumbling crimson carpet. One of the primrose types, it prefers to be in a woodland-like setting.

For striking but neat swatches of colour in spring borders, try the hardy **Primula denticulata** *(right) with its bold spheres of bright pink petals.*

Mix an assortment of Primula vulgaris together (below) for a long-lasting cushion of colour. Divide in the autumn.

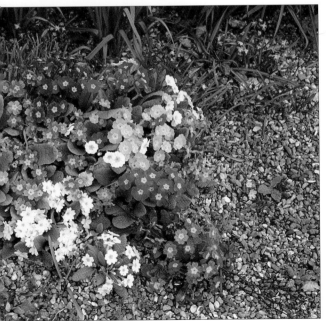

planted out the next spring.

Species can be grown from seed, but named varieties do not breed true to type. Rinse the seed in warm water, to remove the natural germination inhibitor, then simple 'surface sow' – scattering the fine seed on the surface of damp, peat-based compost. Cover with a pane of glass as described above and keep cool, shaded and moist until seedlings appear, then remove the glass. When the seedlings are large enough to handle, pot up into trays or boxes of John Innes No 1 compost. Keep the young plants cool and shaded, and plant them out in early autumn or spring. Do not plant them in waterlogged soil.

Any problems?

Primulas are generally trouble-free. But here is what to do if the following occurs:
- If aphids or greenfly attack flowering shoots, try removing them with soapy water.
- If caterpillars eat the leaves, pick them off individually if there are only a few, or spray or dust with derris.
- If grey mould appears or if the leaves develop orange or brown spots, remove and burn diseased leaves and spray the plant with a suitable fungicide.
- If any viral diseases occur, dig the plant up and burn it to prevent any infection.

HYDRANGEAS

The massive domed flower heads of hortensia hydrangeas are a familiar sight in gardens, but they are far from all that this fascinating genus has to offer.

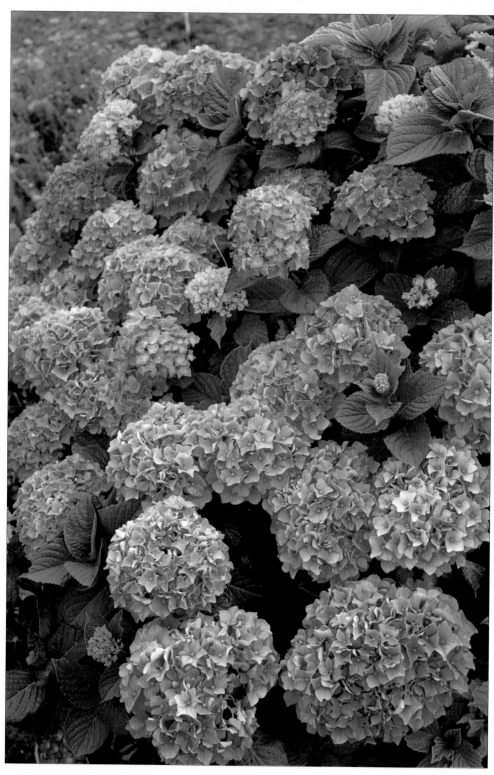

Hydrangeas are shrubs grown for their decorative flowers. These delightful plants may be used in several ways. Larger varieties look well as part of a shubbery or as hedging, as well as making excellent architectual plants at the back of herbaceous and mixed borders. They are often planted beside gates and entrances to extend a cheerful welcome to visitors.

Some smaller ones make good subjects for large pots and tubs – their growth is restricted by the cramped conditions and by cutting back in autumn – while others will flourish as houseplants in a cool, draught-free room or a conservatory.

One species will even provide vertical cover; *Hydrangea petiolaris* is a hardy climber that produces lacy, white flowers in summer. It clings in much the same way as ivy and makes an excellent choice for decorating a large, bare wall. It is one of only a few climbers that do well in shade.

The hydrangeas that are most frequently seen in gardens, however, are all varieties of *H. macrophylla*. They are divided into two groups, hortensias and lacecaps.

Handsome hortensias

The hortensias are the most instantly recognizable members of the hydrangea family; their blooms are large, showy and impossible to overlook. These lovely shrubs have been cherished by generations of gardeners and are equally at home in neat suburban surroundings or in the homely

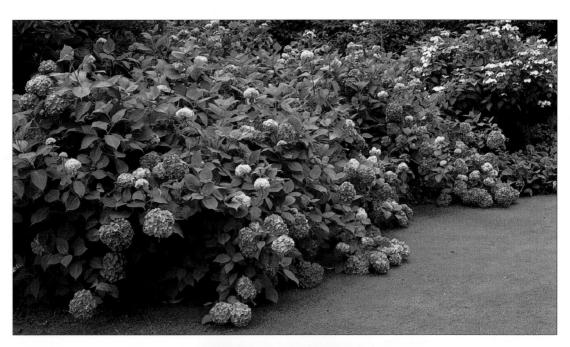

The colour of many hydrangeas is affected by the pH value of the soil, which affects the plants' abilities to take up iron, essential if blue flowers are to be produced. Iron is readily available in acid soils, where varieties such as 'Générale Vicomtesse de Vibraye' display lovely shades of blue and lilac (right). Iron is 'locked up' in very alkaline soils, where no blues are produced. Between these extremes, pink and blue flowers may appear on the same bush (left). The creamy white heads in both pictures are not yet fully open.

PLANT PROFILE

Suitable site and soil Most varieties thrive in sun or partial shade. Best in semi-shade if the site is on the dry side. Will tolerate almost any soil as long as it is both moist and well-drained.

Planting Dig a hole big enough to take the roots in comfort and add rich compost and sand to the planting mixture. Plant in early autumn. Container grown varieties may be planted at any time as long as the soil retains some warmth.

Cultivation and care Many popular varieties are on the tender side of hardy, so root protection is advisable for the first few winters until the shrubs are mature. In areas where hard winters are inevitable, either protect the roots with a liberal covering of straw or grow it in a container and bring it inside during harsh conditions.

Remove dead flower heads. Pruning is not really required but remove any dead or frost-damaged growth, cutting back lightly to good buds in early spring. Pruning for shape may be done in the same way, if necessary.

Hydrangeas must have plenty of moisture during the growing season. Water during dry spells and mulch in early spring to avoid moisture loss at the roots. Do not plant too near to thirsty trees.

Container subjects need feeding and watering regularly in the growing season. All types benefit from a top dressing of well-rotted manure or compost in early spring.

Propagation By softwood cuttings in summer. Choose sturdy, non-flowering shoots about 8cm/3in long. Cut just below a leaf joint or node and strip away the lower leaves. Plant cuttings in a good quality cutting compost and root them in gentle heat, 16°C/61°F.

Pests and diseases The common green capsid bug attacks young leaves and causes distortion. It also attacks young flower buds, resulting in misshapen blooms. Use a proprietary winter wash or an appropriate spray in spring.

Mildew may be a problem if conditions are too dry. Treat at the first sign of trouble or prevent it altogether by spraying with a precautionary systemic fungicide after watering.

Some varieties are a little on the tender side, but, kept well pruned, flourish in containers in a greenhouse or conservatory (left).

The pink 'Altona' (below) is definitely not one for a container; it grows into a substantial bush that is almost completely smothered with flower heads in season.

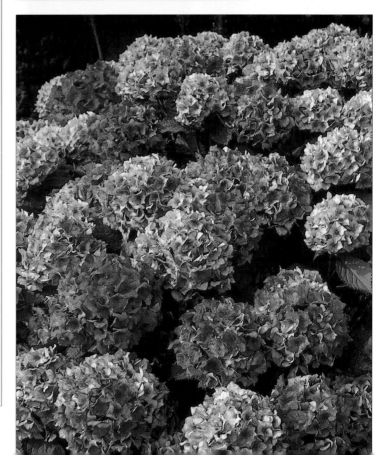

sprawl of a cottage garden.

The large, domed flower heads are made up of dense clusters of mainly sterile flowers. Their colour depends both on the variety you choose and on the nature of the soil.

White varieties are unaffected by soil type, but others may be blue, purple, pink or red depending on the acidity of your soil. Acid soils with plenty of available iron will produce startling blue or purple blooms, while alkaline or neutral soils will bring forth gorgeous pink or red flowers. This is because the iron in low acid soils cannot readily be taken up by the plant's roots.

There are dozens of varieties of hortensia hydrangeas in cultivation, varying from small, compact plants to large

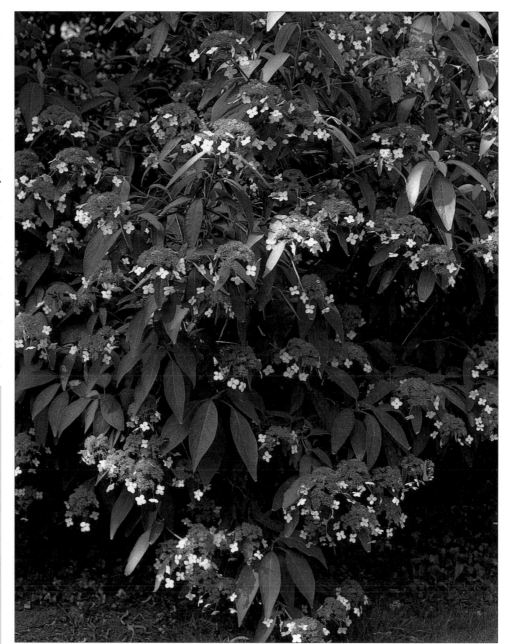

RECOMMENDED VARIETIES

Hortensias
'Altona' Rose pink.
'Ami Pasquier' Crimson or purple-blue.
'Blue Bonnet' Rich blue or pink.
'Générale Vicomtesse de Vibraye' Pale pink or pale blue.
'Goliath' Rich pink or blue-purple.
'Mme E. Mouillère' White; centres flushed with pink.
'Preziosa' Pink maturing to crimson.
Lacecaps
'Blue Wave' Blue or pink.
'Lilacina' Deep lilac centres; white outside.
'Mariesii' Rich blue or pink.
'Veitchii' Lilac centres, white to pink outside.
'White Wave' White.
Species hydrangeas
H. aspera Villosa Group Upright shrub with blue-purple inner flowers, white outers.
C. involucrata 'Hortensis' Late-flowering compact shrub; cream, green and pink.
H. paniculata Shrub with loose, white, conical flower heads; good varieties include 'Brussels Lace', 'Floribunda' and 'Grandiflora'.
H. petiolaris Greenish-white self-clinging climber with toothed leaves.

substantial shrubs.

Among the smaller ones is 'Ami Pasquier', which grows to a height and spread of 1m/3ft. This lovely variety produces deep crimson or blue-purple flowers in midsummer.

'Générale Vicomtesse de Vibraye' has a height and spread of 1.5m/5ft when fully mature. It flowers between mid and late summer and the blooms are either pale pink or pale blue.

'Blue Bonnet' is very bushy and reaches a height of about 1.5m/5ft. Blooms appear in mid and late summer and are a rich blue or pink.

One of the better white varieties is 'Mme E. Mouillère', whose gorgeous flowers turn a pale pink. This one prefers partial shade. *H.* 'Preziosa' bears pink flowers that turn a glorious deep crimson colour as they mature.

Lovely lacecaps

Lacecap hydrangeas have very different blooms to other *H. macrophylla* varieties. They have flat, open heads with tiny, fertile flowers at the centre and larger, sterile flowers on the outside. These flower heads give these beautiful shrubs a more delicate air

Hydrangea aspera Villosa Group (above) is a fully hardy species with lacecap flower heads. It will make a tall, upright bush.

'Lilacina' (above right) is one of the loveliest of the H. macrophylla *lacecap varieties, with late summer flower heads in shades of blue and lilac.*

The pink flowers of H. *'Preziosa' turn a deep crimson as they mature, and are attractively complemented by the bronzed early autumn foliage (right).*

than the hortensias.

Like hortensias, lacecaps are deciduous, and the pH balance and iron content of the soil will have an effect on the colour of all but the white varieties. Given plenty of iron, 'Blue Wave' has rich blue flowers in the latter half of the summer; without it, they are pink or lilac. It is a substantial shrub, growing to 1.5m/5ft tall and up to 2.4m/8ft across.

Of a similar size is the handsome 'Veitchii', which has lilac-blue central flowers surrounded by white outer bracts which turn a pretty pink as they mature. 'Veitchii' enjoys partial shade, as does 'Lilacina', whose lovely late summer blooms are deep lilac at the centre of the head and a paler colour outside.

Hardiness

Opinions differ about the hardiness of *H. macrophylla* in either of its forms. Some garden authorities say it will only

TRUE BLUE

Good blues are relatively difficult to find in the plant world. This problem has led to real blues being much sought after by plantsmen and gardeners.

It is possible for enthusiasts with alkaline or neutral soils to tinker with *H. macrophylla* so that they produce blue flowers more or less at will. All that is required is a blueing agent, readily available at garden centres, which is usually watered in at regular intervals. Failure to keep it up will lead to the flowers reverting to pink.

Cottage gardeners used to bury old iron nails beneath their hydrangeas to make blue flowers. Some managed to get both pink and blue flowers on the same shrub.

GROWING TIPS

PERFECT PARTNERS

The strong colours and bushy habits of hydrangeas make many unsuitable companion plants, but the white of 'Madame Emile Mouillère' perfectly sets off crimson regal pelargoniums.

survive mild winters in sheltered parts of the country, but others make no such stipulation. The truth is that it hovers on the borderline of tenderness.

A well-sheltered spot in a northern garden may happily support a hydrangea for years. An exposed frost pocket in a southern garden may kill it off in its first winter.

The only way to find out whether a hydrangea will survive in your garden is to try it and see. You can take elementary precautions by protecting its roots with straw during the winter months for the first two or three years, until it is fully established.

In areas with cold, harsh winters, you could grow a small hydrangea in a container and bring it indoors over the winter months.

Keeping stock

Another possibility is to grow your plant in a pot for the first year or two and to take several cuttings in summer. When you are sure that your cuttings have rooted, you can risk planting your shrub in a bed or border. If the frosts do damage it, you have several back-up plants with which to experiment in other sites around your garden. Always keep at least one container grown specimen to act as a stock plant in case of disaster.

Not only, but also

Although the *H. macrophylla* varieties are the commonest, other species in the genus make good garden plants.

Hydrangea aspera Villosa Group is an upright, deciduous shrub which reaches a height of 3m/10ft. Narrow at its base, it swells out to a spread of almost 3m/10ft at its widest point.

Flowers appear between late summer and mid autumn. They have small blue or purple central flowers and large white outer ones that are sometimes flushed a pinkish purple. This pretty shrub likes moist soil with good drainage and a partially shaded site. It suits harsh climates as it is fully hardy.

Another hardy subject is *H. paniculata*. 'Brussels Lace', as its name suggests, has delicate, white, frothy blooms. *H. p.* 'Floribunda' is another lovely white variety but is not as hardy as 'Brussels Lace', so check the labels carefully.

H. p. 'Grandiflora' is fully hardy and has large conical panicles of white flowers that turn pink or red as they mature. This variety requires hard pruning in spring if you want an impressive display.

If space is limited, you could grow the compact *H. involucrata* 'Hortensis', which is not to be confused with any of the Hortensia varieties of *H. macrophylla*. This one has beautiful clusters of pink, green and cream flowers in late summer and autumn. It is on the tender side and would make a good container subject.

Hydrangea paniculata *is distinguished from other hydrangeas by its flowers, which form loose, conical panicles rather than flat or domed heads. 'Floribunda' (above left) is more tender than 'Brussels Lace', the other widely-grown variety.*

'Ami Pasquier' (above) is a small form of **H. macrophylla,** *but its domed flower heads (above) are no less imposing than its larger relatives.*

The lacecap 'Blue Wave' (above right) normally makes a mounded shrub some 2.1m/7ft tall, but it can be grown to good effect against a wall, as here, where it is tumbling attractively over into a neighbouring garden.

The confusingly-named **H. involucrata** *'Hortensis' (right) has delicately-coloured flowers that resemble a lacecap rather than a hortensia.*

COLD COMFORT

If you have tried and failed to grow *H. macrophylla* hortensia varieties because your winters are just too harsh or your garden is too exposed, do not lose heart. These lovely plants can be grown indoors.

Choose an attractive container and make sure you provide good drainage. Use good quality, rich compost. Water and feed regularly in the growing season. Cut hard back at the very end of the growing season and water sparingly during this rest period.

Apply a good top dressing of rich humus in early spring and begin to water and feed regularly again. Pot on as necessary.

Keep the plant in good light, but not direct sunlight. It prefers cool conditions.

PEONIES

With their larger-than-life blooms, peonies are among the most popular herbaceous perennials. Luckily, they are as easy to grow and as long lived as they are gorgeous.

The much-loved peony vies with the rose for the title 'Queen of the Garden' in late spring and early summer. With their huge yet delicate-looking blooms in dazzling white, spun-sugar pastels and rich, deep hues, they have an old-fashioned, romantic appeal. Traditional mainstays in informal, country-cottage gardens and formal herbaceous borders, peonies are just as happy in the mixed beds and patio tubs of today's smaller gardens.

Peonies grow 45-90cm/1½-3ft high, with single, semi-double or double bowl-shaped flowers, up to 15cm/6in across and often fragrant. Colours range from white through cream, yellow, pink, lilac, scarlet and crimson to deep wine red. Some are two-toned, and many single varieties have showy yellow centres, or stamens.

The young spring shoots are delicately tinged with red and, unlike many other herbaceous perennials, whose leaves get tatty after flowering, the peony's glossy, deeply cut leaves remain attractive all summer long, providing a backdrop for other flowers. The leaves often take on rich, ruddy tones in autumn. Peonies also have exotic-looking, scarlet seed pods filled with shiny, midnight blue seeds to add interest in the garden or dried flower displays.

Peonies' fleshy, tuberous roots can take a year or two to settle down and start flowering after planting, but once they do, they virtually look after themselves, gradually forming sizeable clumps and producing generous crops of their beautiful satiny flowers for up to 50 years! Peonies are tolerant of intense heat and cold, too, and take severe winters and even the hottest summers in their stride.

Buying and planting

Buy container-grown plants, in early to mid-autumn or spring. Peonies like a deep

WHAT'S IN A NAME?

Peony was named after Paeon, physician to the Gods in Greek mythology, and has long been valued for its medicinal properties. Its seeds were worn to repel evil spirits; steeped in wine, to cure nightmares; and taken to ease childbirth pains. Peony roots, dried and ground and taken orally, were used to treat nervous disorders, including epilepsy. Don't however, attempt to treat yourself with peonies – see a doctor first!

root run, so dig a hole generously wider and deeper than the container. Remove all weeds, fork over the bottom and work in well-rotted garden compost, manure or bagged organic compost from garden centres.

Remove the plant from its pot. Plant with the crown 2.5cm/1in below ground level, replace the soil, mixed with more organic matter, and firm. Sprinkle a handful of bone meal over the soil, and water if the soil is dry. If planting more than one, space them 60-90cm/2-3ft apart, according to type.

Using peonies

Depending on height, peonies can go in the front, middle or back of a bed or border. Their clumpy foliage is ideal for hiding bare or awkward-looking stems, such as those of hybrid tea or floribunda roses. They are also most attractive when planted as an infill between

The combination of glossy, lance-shaped leaves and nodding crimson double flowers makes a dramatic splash in a mixed spring border (above), where it is set off by the golden-green bracts of euphorbia.

There are hundreds of varieties of Chinese peony (P. lactiflora). 'Sarah Bernhardt' (left) is a particularly attractive double, with large, scented flowers.

Often classified as semi-doubles, anemone-form peonies have a double row of outer petals and a centre that fills as the flower matures with modified stamens. In 'Bowl of Beauty' (right), these petaloids make a delicious, creamy contrast to the pink petals.

PLANT PROFILE

Suitable site and soil: Choose a sheltered spot in sun or light shade, and rich, well-drained but moisture-retentive soil. In very hot climates, the flowers last longer in light shade. Peonies dislike being moved, so choose your spot with care!

Cultivation and care: Peonies survive neglect, but flower better if you water them in dry weather, remove the faded blooms and mulch every spring with well-rotted garden compost, manure or organic matter. Support tall-growing types, especially in windy gardens, with twiggy sticks or metal plant supports. When cutting flowers, take only a few stems from each plant. In late autumn, cut plants back to ground level.

Propagation: You can raise peonies from seed, but it takes four years or more for them to flower, and they vary in colour and quality.

Sow seeds in early autumn in a cold frame and prick out into a nursery bed in late spring of the following year. Grow on for three or four years, then plant out from early autumn to early spring.

It is quicker and easier to lift, divide and replant mature crowns in early autumn. Using a sharp knife, cut the crown into three or four pieces, each with roots and at least one bud. Coat the cut surfaces with a fungicide and replant in prepared soil. They will take a season or two to recover before flowering.

Pests and diseases: Brown patches on the leaves and soft, mushy stems near the ground, covered with grey fuzz, indicate peony wilt. Cut off infected stems, treat the crown with fungicide, then spray the leaves regularly with a fungicide.

A virus causes yellow patches or rings on the leaves. Dig up and destroy infected plants, and plant new peonies elsewhere.

Swift moth caterpillars eat holes in the roots and crowns, causing unexplained wilting. Treat the soil with gamma-HCH dust.

WATCH POINTS

- When hoeing the ground near peonies, be careful not to pierce or nick the fleshy crowns; they are liable to rot. It is also best not to fork the ground very near peonies.
- If couch grass, bindweed or ground elder gets into peony crowns, it is a real nightmare, so check regularly and remove any weeds while they are still small.
- When applying a mulch, spread it around, not over, the peony crown, or it may fail to flower properly.

The single-flowered species P. mascula *ssp. arietina (above) is very similar to* P. mascula. *The main distinguishing feature is that the underside of the former's leaves are covered in fine hairs.*

shrubs in a mixed border.

A long, narrow border of one peony variety edging a path or wall is stunning in flower.

For a wild garden, single varieties look most natural, and for an authentic cottage garden look, use one of the old-fashioned favourites such as double crimson *P. officinalis* 'Rubra Plena'.

For container growing, choose a compact type, such as the fern-leafed peony, 45cm/ 18in high and wide.

Tree peonies

In spite of their name, tree peonies grow no more than 1.2-1.8m/4-6ft high and wide, and form picturesque, multi-stemmed, wide-spreading shrubs. These unusual and striking plants are a little more challenging to grow, but a tree peony in full flower is a sight you won't forget!

Like herbaceous peonies, tree peonies are long lived,

P. lactiflora 'Nancy Lindsay' (right) can be hard to find. It is well worth tracking down, however, for its pale apricot flowers containing a nest of golden yellow stamens.

CLOSED BUDS

Q Why do my peonies look healthy, but the buds stay hard and small, and never open?

A It could be a number of things; dry soil, lack of food, being planted too deeply, disturbed roots or frost damage. By process of elimination, you should be able to sort this out, and correct it.

The leaves of P. tenuifolia *(top) are deeply divided into long, thin segments, making a finely-textured backdrop for a single crimson flowers with their contrasting yellow anthers.*

PERFECT PARTNERS

- Peonies, lupins, bearded iris, delphiniums and campanulas are the backbone of a traditional early summer border.
- For a handsome trio, combine double pink peonies with rich blue delphiniums behind and lady's mantle (alchemilla) in front.
- For an all-pink theme with old-fashioned charm, plant pink roses, hardy geraniums, sweet Williams and peonies.
- Orange wallflowers, yellow species roses, yellow tulips and the yellow 'Molly the Witch' peony *(P. mlokosewitschii)* make a bright, sunny late spring display.

- Plant hyacinths among Chinese peonies, whose shoots are rosy red when the hyacinths flower. When the hyacinths finish, the peonies come into their own.
- The tall pink and mauve flower spikes of foxgloves *(Digitalis purpurea)* make a pleasing backdrop for pink double peonies (right).
- Plant a late-flowering clematis to ramble through a clump of peonies, adding interest after the peonies finish. *C. flammula,* with scented white flowers, or the orange peel clematis, *C. orientalis,* with thick-petalled, yellowy orange bell flowers, are just two possibilities.

The single flowered P. mlokosewitschii, *'Molly the Witch' (above) is an old garden favourite, and is much valued for its large lemon-yellow flowers and soft, faintly bluish foliage.*

with deeply divided, deciduous leaves and large, showy flowers in late spring and early summer. The flowers come in single, semi-double and double forms, and whites, pinks, yellows and reds, some with contrasting blotches.

Tree peonies make lovely focal points in mixed borders and woodland gardens, but are also impressive enough to be used as specimen plants on a lawn. For an exquisite garden 'painting', underplant a tree peony with violets.

Growing tree peonies

Tree peonies are very hardy, but young growth is easily damaged by spring frost, especially after a mild winter. Fertile, moist but well drained soil in sun or light shade is best; shelter from the wind and late frosts is essential .

Container-grown tree peonies should be planted in early to mid-spring. Plant them deeply, with any graft, or join, between the named variety and rootstock 10cm/4in below

Some peony varieties have flowers so large that they flop over unless each bloom is individually supported. This need not be a disaster (above); the delicate pink of the double lactiflora shows well against the grey of the gravel path.

PICK A PEONY

Among the most popular cut flowers and superb focal points for flower arrangements, peonies are long lasting if you pick them in bud, but with colour showing. Lay them down flat on a cool floor overnight, then re-cut the stem ends and place in a deep container of warm water for several hours before arranging. Only take one or two flowers per plant.

Pick the seed pods while still green, and hang them upside down to dry. You can preserve the leaves of tree peonies by picking them when mature but still green, and placing them in a tall container of half glycerine, half warm water. Leave them until they turn leathery and grey green, topping up the liquid if necessary.

BRIGHT IDEAS

P. 'Smouthii' (right) is an old lactiflora variety that came to Britain from France in 1845. Now rarely seen, it was once highly valued for its lacy leaves and crimson, single flowers, which appear earlier than most peony varieties.

RECOMMENDED VARIETIES

TREE PEONIES

- *Paeonia delavayi* is a suckering species with deep-red, cup-shaped flowers, up to 10cm/4in wide, with golden stamens.
- *P. × lemoinei* hybrids have yellow flowers 15-20cm/6-8in wide, and include the double, lemon yellow 'Alice Harding'.
- *P. delavayi ludlowii* has cup-shaped, single yellow flowers with a lily-like scent.
- *P. suffruticosa* varieties have large, bowl-shaped flowers 15-30cm/6-12in wide.

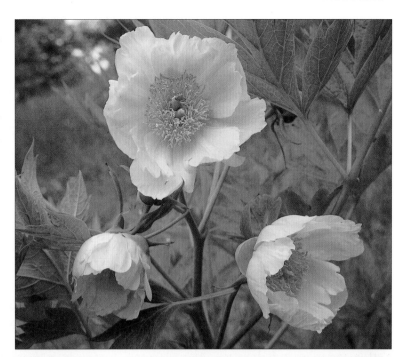

P. delavayi ludlowii (right) is a tree peony which grows to a height and spread of 2.4m/8ft. Attractive though its fragrant, cup-shaped single yellow flowers are, it is more often planted for its show of vivid green, deeply divided leaves.

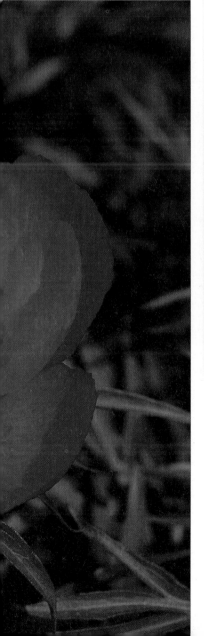

The flowers of the tree peony P. suffruticosa have a splash of colour at the base of each petal. 'Rock's Variety', also known as 'Joseph Rock' (above), has white petals and a maroon blotch. Other varieties are pink, with chocolate-brown splashes.

the soil surface. Scatter bone meal on top.

You can grow species tree peonies from seed, but they take several years to flower. Varieties are usually propagated by grafting, a technique best left to experts, but if you have a variety growing on its own roots, you can divide it in early autumn.

Once established, tree peonies need to be mulched, fed and dead-headed in the same way as herbaceous varieties. Otherwise the only maintenance necessary is to cut back any damaged or dead wood in the spring.

Peony wilt also affects tree peonies, especially those planted in damp or crowded conditions. Their roots may be susceptible to honey fungus; there is no cure, and affected plants should be destroyed.

DAHLIAS

Dahlias offer you dazzling colour all summer and into autumn, along with plenty of cut flowers – all with the minimum of care.

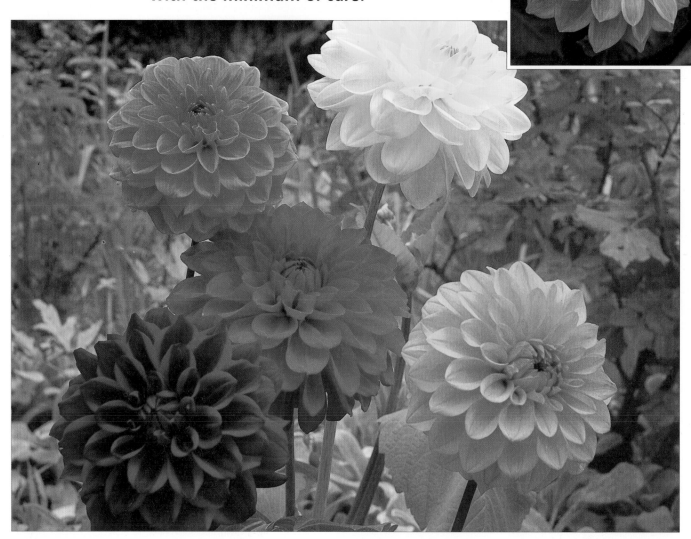

You could not choose more worthwhile plants than dahlias and, what is more, you do not even need a garden to grow them – dwarf varieties are ideally suited to tubs or window boxes on a balcony.

Dahlias are perennials, capable of living for a number of years, but they are tender, so cannot be left outdoors over winter. The first frosts of autumn will blacken and kill the leaves and stems. The plants form large fleshy tubers, which allow them to have a long rest over winter as they store food and water.

Dahlias are split into two groups: the dwarf kinds which can be used for mass planting or formal summer bedding, as well as for tubs and window boxes, and the tall border varieties. The dwarf varieties grow 30-60cm/1-2ft high and border dahlias reach an average height of 90-120cm/3-4ft.

The flowers, especially those of the taller dahlias, vary greatly in shape. Dwarf bedding types have either single blooms, with a ring of petals, or double, with many petals forming a ball shape.

Tall dahlias
The most popular groups among the tall dahlias include decorative flowered, which have double flowers formed of broad flat petals; cactus-flowered, with double spiky flowers; and semi-cactus-flowered, midway between the

Decorative dahlias, whose broad, flat petals tend to curve in slightly at the edges, are available in a dazzling range of colours (above), though there is no blue. Many of the double flowers are multi-coloured, such as 'Master Robert' (above, inset).

PLANT PROFILE

Suitable site and soil: full sun and any well-drained yet moisture-retentive soil.

Planting: dormant tubers are planted in mid-spring, at least 10cm/4in deep. Young pot-grown plants are set out in late spring or early summer, when danger of frost is over. Space bedding dahlias 30-60cm/1-2ft apart each way and tall kinds 45-90cm/18-36in apart each way, according to height (the taller they are, the more space required).

Cultivation and care: before planting, dig in plenty of peat, coconut fibre or garden compost. Give the plants plenty of water in dry spells to prevent the soil drying out. Check containers daily. Feed border dahlias fortnightly, using a liquid flower-garden fertilizer. Cut off dead flowers regularly.

To keep plants from year to year, cut down stems when they have become blackened by frost, lift tubers and dry them off thoroughly, then store them in a cool but frost-proof, dry, airy place over the winter.

Propagation: large clumps of dormant tubers can be split into smaller portions just before planting. Each division must consist of at least one stem base and tuber.

Pests and diseases: the main ones are slugs and snails which chew soft stems and leaves. Sprinkle slug pellets around new shoots or young plants.

two. Flower size in each group ranges from miniature to giant.

Other popular forms include water-lily-flowered, where the blooms look like water-lilies; collerette, single flowers which have a central collar of contrasting petals; ball dahlias with blooms the size of tennis balls; and pompon dahlias, with golf-ball-sized flowers.

Dahlias come in almost every colour you can imagine. There are all shades of red, pink, orange, yellow, purple and white. Some varieties are bi-coloured, consisting of two contrasting colours; others have several colours blending into each other. In many dahlias the colours are brilliant and dazzling, but others come in quieter pastel shades.

Dahlias are divided into groups according to the size and type of their flower heads and, in fact, the shapes of dahlia flowers are almost as varied as their colours. Cactus-flowered varieties (above) have a shock of long, thin petals. Semi-cactus varieties have flowers of similar shape although the petals are slightly wider.

Collerette dahlias, such as 'La Cierva' (left), are single-flowered with an inner ring, often of another colour (as in this example). They typically display dramatic – some may say – melodramatic – colour contrasts. Collerette dahlias usually have strong stems, so they are particularly good for flower arrangements.

Compact ball dahlias such as 'Wootton Cupid' (right) have densely packed, almost tubular petals. This popular variety reaches a height of about 90-120cm/3-4ft with flowers 8-10cm/3-4in across and is a favourite exhibition dahlia. Pompon dahlias bear a close resemblance to ball varieties but are much smaller, being only about 5cm/2in across.

There are various ways of buying dahlias. Undoubtedly the easiest is to purchase dormant tubers in winter or spring from a garden centre, supermarket or mail order dahlia specialist. Young plants can be bought in spring from garden centres or specialists, but these may be inconvenient for some people as they cannot be planted out until all danger of frost is over; in the meantime they must be kept in a light, frost-proof place such as a heated greenhouse. You could also raise your own bedding dahlias from seeds.

Dahlias are fussy about growing conditions, but if

Dahlia enthusiasts tend to grow taller varieties in special beds; they can, however, look very well at the back of a mixed border (left), where their dense foliage provides a backdrop for smaller plants and their blooms add a crowning splash of colour. Tall dahlias do, however, need to be staked, as here, to support the stems as they grow.

these are right they are very easy plants to grow. Full sun is absolutely essential for strong growth and prolific flowering. In partial or full shade growth will be weak and spindly and few flowers will be produced.

Soil types

Most soil types are suitable for dahlias provided they are well drained – if they stay extremely wet, or pools of water lie on the surface after rain, the plants are liable to rot. The soil needs to be able to hold on to moisture during dry periods though, as dahlias are thirsty plants. In very dry soil conditions, growth will be stunted and flowering reduced.

The best way to prepare the ground for dahlias is to dig in plenty of peat, peat substitute such as coconut fibre, or garden compost before planting.

Containers such as tubs and window boxes should be filled with a soil-less potting compost, either peat-based or one of the new coconut-fibre composts. Dahlias are also greedy feeders, so before planting apply a flower garden fertilizer according to the instructions on the pack.

If all you want is masses of

The single-flowered 'Coltness Hybrids' (below) are dwarf varieties with lobed leaves and daisy-like flowers. Though perennial like all dahlias, they are often grown as annuals.

colour in the garden without much work, there is no doubt that dwarf dahlias are your best bet. They are also the first choice for containers.

Tall dahlias are best for cutting but they need more time spent on cultivation as they must be provided with supports to which the stems are tied as they grow. The best

A FLOWER ARRANGER'S DREAM

Dahlias are ideal for cutting, producing a succession of flowers in summer and autumn that last a long time in water (right).

Cutting blooms regularly will also ensure plenty more follow. The tall varieties are generaly considered best for cutting as those produce longer stems than the dwarf kinds.

BEST OF THE BUNCH

These readily available varieties are among the very best and the most easily grown, all of them flowering profusely with the minimum of attention.

Dwarf
These are seed-raised types offered by major seed companies.
'Coltness Hybrids' (single, mixed colours)
'Gypsy Dance' (semi-double, mixed colours)
'Redskin' (double, mixed colours, bronze foliage)
'Sunny Yellow' (double, lemon yellow)

Tall
Red
'Doris Day' (small cactus)
'Pontiac' (small cactus)
'Rotterdam' (medium semi-cactus)
Pink
'Gerrie Hoek' (water-lily flowered)

'Vicky Crutchfield' (water-lily flowered)
'Wootton Cupid' (miniature ball)
Orange
'Jescot Jess' (small decorative)
'Kym Willo' (pompon)
'Symbol' (medium semi-cactus)
Yellow
'Clair de Lune' (collerette)
'Glorie van Heemstede' (water-lily flowered)
'Klankstad Kerkrade' (small cactus)
Purple
'Edinburgh' (white, purple tips, small decorative)
'Moor Place' (pompon)
'Winston Churchill' (miniature decorative)
White
'Hamari Bride' (medium semi-cactus)
'Matterhorn' (small decorative)
'White Moonlight' (medium semi-cactus)

supports for dahlias are the 2.5cm/1in square wooden dahlia stakes that are available from garden centres. Alternatively, you could use very thick bamboo canes. Before buying stakes, it is best to find out the final height of the particular variety of dahlia. You can then choose a stake that is a little bit shorter than the plant after being inserted 30cm/12in into the ground, so that is does not tower above it in an unsightly way. The stakes, one for each plant, should be inserted before planting the tubers or young plants.

As the stems grow, loosely tie in each one to the stake with soft green garden string, making a figure-of-eight loop around stake and stem.

Plant combinations

In the garden dahlias can be effectively combined with various other plants. It is important to grow them only with plants that need the same conditions.

These days many people grow all their plants in mixed borders of shrubs, perennials, bulbs and annuals. Dahlias can be included, too, with tall varieties in the centre or back, and dwarf forms at the front.

Dahlias look superb mixed with shrubs noted for autumn leaf colour or berries, such as cotinus, rhus, cotoneaster, euonymus and berberis. The

basically rounded or ball-shaped blooms of dahlias also contrast strikingly with hardy perennials that have spikes of flowers, such as delphiniums.

Dwarf bedding dahlias can be combined with other summer bedding plants. There are many combinations but an idea that works well is to have foliage plants like the silver-leaved *Senecio cineraria* (usually sold as *Cineraria maritimus*) or artemisia dotted among massed dahlias.

Dahlias can be used as a focus in the creation of a subtropical bedding scheme. For example, the main planting

can consist of dwarf bedding dahlias. Among these plant varieties of canna (Indian shot) and tender fuchsias, whose delicate colours and pendulous flower forms provide a delightful contrast.

'Doris Day' (below), a tall cactus-flowered dahlia with relatively small blooms, is one of the most richly-coloured red varieties available.

RHODODENDRONS

Everyone can grow these beautiful, dazzling shrubs – the aristocrats of the plant world – either in the garden or in tubs and window boxes.

From the dense forests of the Himalayas, across Burma and Tibet into south-west China, intrepid plant hunters of the past have searched the mountains to discover many of the beautiful rhododendron species that people enjoy today. One can also find the rhododendron family growing naturally across Alaska, through Canada and down the East and West coasts of North America.

In the wild there are over 500 different species of all sizes from tall 20m/65ft trees to ground-hugging alpines.

From the wide range of these beautiful shrubs found in nature, plant breeders have hybridized a vast choice of the most attractive flowering shrubs that can brighten your garden. There is a dazzling

GARDEN NOTES

RHODODENDRON OR AZALEA?

The plants that we call azaleas are really rhododendrons – you will find them listed under rhododendrons in some books and catalogues. They differ from rhododrendrons in that they are often deciduous (and those described as evergreen are not true evergreens because the leaves formed on the lower parts of the shoots fall in autumn). In this feature we have included only the true rhododendrons and not azaleas. The popular tender azalea sold as a pot plant in the winter is really *Rhododendron simsii*.

display of colours from pinks to white, creamy yellows, orange, scarlet, crimson and lavender. A number of rhododendrons also have an exquisite scent and others have highly aromatic foliage. Flowering seasons of the different types occur at various times of the year from winter through to summer.

In terms of size, the vast range of rhododendrons available from garden centres and nurseries ensures that everyone has an opportunity to enjoy these beautiful flowering shrubs. The smallest will adorn a window box, there are many suitable for tubs, and the largest will need a woodland site to spread themselves.

Wherever rhododendrons are planted, in a small garden (above) or an area of natural woodland, they will produce a splash of dramatic colour in spring or summer. Several planted together will produce a bank of one colour or a variety of complementary hues.

Nearly all rhododendrons are evergreen and belong to the ericaceous family, which includes azaleas and heathers. This whole family has one particular requirement – the soil must be acid. This means that no quantity of lime should be present. Planted into the wrong soil your rhododendron's leaves will look yellow and sad. But do not despair if you have alkaline soil. It is quite easy to grow rhododendrons in pots and tubs using

Growing a rhododendron in a large flowerpot (above) is a way of introducing colour to an otherwise drab corner of a patio. The variety above is 'Baden-Baden'.

The pure white flowers of the dwarf variety 'Ptarmigan' (below) contrast well with more colourful plants such as primulas.

PLANT PROFILE

Site and soil:
Rhododendrons require well drained soil, moist, acid and rich in humus. Avoid badly drained soil that stays wet in winter. Also, don't subject them to dry conditions. They need plenty of water during drought. Use rainwater if possible; mains water is often quite alkaline (chalky).

Alkaline soil is also no good for them. But if your garden soil is chalky, you can give your rhododendron its own special soil within a tub or other container, using ericaceous compost.

All rhododendrons are happy in light shade which guards them from late spring frosts and keeps the ground cool and moist. Few enjoy heavy shade but some dwarf alpines tolerate a sunny site or even a rockery.

Cultivation and care: Care at the planting stage almost guarantees success. First make sure the site and soil are right. Then make the hole suitably wide and shallow for the rootball, so that the final soil level comes to the base of the stem, not above!

Inside the hole, provide plenty of moss peat or, better, leaf mould or coconut fibre. Water in well, using rainwater if you can. Keep rhododendrons well watered during dry spells, or whenever their leaves hang.

The best soil conditioning is to add mulch each spring: at least 2.5cm/1in of humus (leaf mould etc.). Fertilizer is seldom necessary at all.

To ensure strong growth, remove old flowerheads a month or so after flowering. This makes sure that all the energy goes into growing and not into forming seeds.

Little pruning is necessary except where suckers on a hybrid grow from below a graft and these should be cut away. You will notice the different leaf form (usually it is *Rhododendron ponticum*) which characterizes the sucker growth.

Problems, pest and diseases:
Rhododendrons have few problems. If the leaves look pale, a spring application of sulphate of ammonia may help and will increase the soil acidity a little, but it may be necessary to use Sequestrene (see box).

Browning of the leaf tips indicates too much or too little water, and the growing conditions need to be adjusted accordingly.

Bark split can occur after a very cold spring. Shoots appear to die back beyond where bark has split away, and need to be pruned back to healthy wood.

Greenfly can attack the fresh shoots of young plants – this can be controlled with a pyrethrum-based spray.

Weevils cut tell-tale notches in the leaves. Although disfiguring, these will not kill the plants.

Propagation:
Rhododendrons are quite easy to propagate from cuttings or by layering. Grafting is sometimes used commercially but is difficult for an amateur, as you will need a suitable rootstock as well as a fair amount of skill.

They can be raised from seed, but this is a slow method and only suitable for the species – the large hybrids will not produce plants like the parent.

Take cuttings from semi-ripe shoots, choosing a healthy plant, preferably in late summer. The length of the cutting depends on the species: 5-8cm/2-3in for the tender *R. simsii*, about 15-23cm/6-9in for most hardy species.

Rooting is usually accelerated by dipping the end in a rooting hormone. Lightly wounding the base first may help. Insert the cuttings in pots in a mixture of equal parts moss peat and sharp sand (or perlite). They should root if kept in a cold frame, but they will probably root best if you can place them in a propagator.

Once they have rooted, pot each one in an ericaceous compost, and grow on until large enough to plant out. It may take up to five years before they flower.

Layering is a good way to propagate rhododendrons. See pages 78-81 for instructions on how and when to layer.

RECOMMENDED VARIETIES

For very small gardens and rockeries

Blue Diamond	(blue)
Baden-Baden	(red)
Carmen	(deep scarlet)
Cilpinense	(pink)
Curlew	(yellow)
Dora Amateis	(white)
R. impeditum	(lavender)
Scarlet Wonder	(scarlet)
Ptarmigan	(white)
Patty Bee	(yellow)
Ginny Gee	(white and pink flush)

For pots and tubs

Percy Wiseman	(pink and cream)
Pink Cherub	(soft pink)
Golden Torch	(pale yellow)
Surrey Heath	(rose pink)
Titian Beauty	(geranium red)
Elizabeth	(scarlet)
Praecox	(lavender)

For hedges and screens

Britannia	(scarlet)
Cunningham's White	(white)
R. ponticum	(lavender)

For large woodland gardens

Autumn Gold	(apricot/ salmon)
Christmas Cheer	(pink; winter flowering)
Doncaster	(scarlet)
Elizabeth de Rothschild	(cream)
Gomer Waterer	(white flushed lavender)
Kluis Sensation	(scarlet)
Lord Roberts	(red)
Nova Zembla	(bright red)
Pink Pearl	(pink)
Purple Splendour	(deep purple)
Unique	pink fading to cream

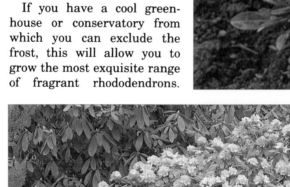

an acid compost and watering with soft rainwater.

Since many rhododendrons originate from the high, often snow-covered hills of the Himalayas, they are fairly used to occasional cold winters and can generally be described as quite hardy. However, there are a few very early spring varieties and the beautiful flowers of these are sometimes damaged by the frost. Try to find a well sheltered site for such plants, perhaps tucked under the shade of a suitable tree or shrub to give protection from frost and cold dry winds.

If you have a cool greenhouse or conservatory from which you can exclude the frost, this will allow you to grow the most exquisite range of fragrant rhododendrons.

GROWING TIPS

CURING A SICKLY PLANT

Rhododendrons growing on soil that is not sufficiently acid for their liking often grow poorly and the leaves may look pale and yellow. You can often help the plant survive by feeding it with Sequestrene, which contains iron and other elements in a form that the plant can absorb even though it is not growing in an acid soil.

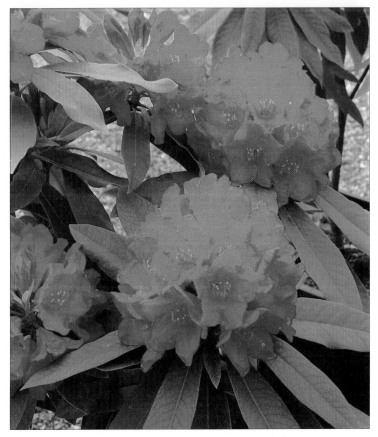

RHODODENDRONS

These give you wonderful colour and scent during the first days of early spring. Like all your rhododendrons, the greenhouse ones require exactly the same acid, lime-free compost. After flowering they can be plunged, with their pots, into the garden, provided you are sure the soil is not alkaline. However, remember to bring them back indoors before the first frost of autumn.

A wide choice

Across many regions of Britain the large *Rhododendron ponticum* has become naturalized in woods and on open moorlands, producing a mass of deep purple in late spring and early summer. This lovely plant was introduced into the country from Turkey about 200 years ago. Unfortunately, it has been almost too successful in spreading from seed, and foresters are liable to look upon it as quite a serious weed. However, in the garden it remains useful because it offers you a quick-growing plant that will form an excellent, hardy evergreen hedge or high screen that will flower profusely in late spring. Equally effective as hedges and screens are 'Cunningham's White' and the brilliant scarlet 'Britannia'.

Many smaller rhododendron species naturally occur at quite high altitudes on open mountain sides, some as high as 3,600m/12,000ft. These and their hybrids can be quite truthfully described as al-

Rhododendron 'Blue Diamond' (above) is one that likes full sun. It grows to a height of 1.5m/5ft and flowers from mid- to late spring.

Gardeners with space will want to contrast several varieties (above right). They can be underplanted with flowering and foliage plants. Here foxgloves, ferns, lady's mantle and epimedium have been used.

The correct choice of varieties planted next to each other can give a succession of flowers over a sustained period. 'Christmas Cheer' (left) is in flower in late winter, ahead of other species.

The large but compact cherry-red flowers of 'Britannia' (right) appear in late spring and early summer.

CUT FLOWERS

GARDEN NOTES

If you can bear to cut your rhododendrons they will make marvellous cut flower arrangements for the house. Cut just as the buds are showing colour. They will quickly burst into flower indoors in the warm atmosphere and give many days of enjoyment.

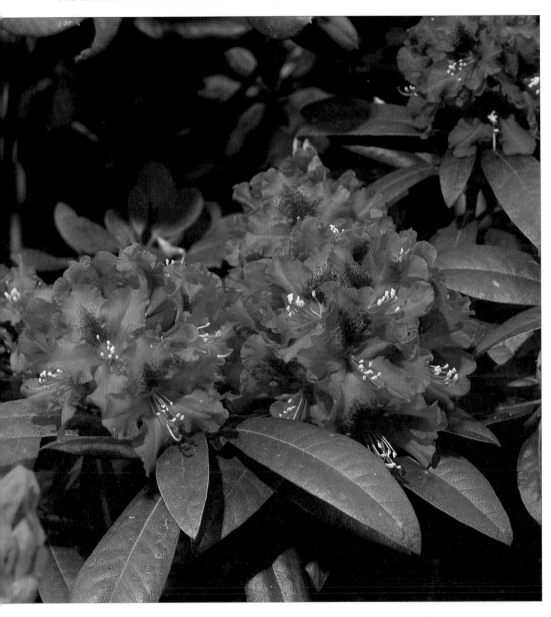

'Purple Splendour' is one of the larger varieties, growing to 3m/10ft. The rich purple blooms have black speckles in the throat and creamy stamens.

pines. They offer us a wide selection of low-growing plants that will tolerate full sun and thrive in cool, moist conditions. All these dwarf plants can be put to great use in a small garden and can be equally effective in a rock garden or raised bed provided the soil is suitable.

Maximum interest and colour throughout the year is what everyone would like to achieve in the garden. However, because rhododendrons have a limited flowering season, careful thought must be given to suitable companion planting for them.

Suitable companions

Attractive trees which give rhododendrons the necessary frost protection and the light dappled shade which keeps the roots cool and moist, can add some colour of their own.

Flowering cherries contribute lovely pastel shades and the showy mespilus (*Amelanchier canadensis*), a most effective white. Many varieties of mountain ash (*Sorbus aucuparia*) look well among rhododendrons, and the lovely autumn tints of Japanese maples add a touch of brightness at the end of the year.

On the ground below the usual hybrid rhododendrons it is good to plant groups of heather or perhaps hostas, whose bold leaves may be striped green and white or pale yellow. One obvious sort of companion is the lovely azalea. This is a close relation of the rhododendron and requires the same conditions.

It says something about rhododendrons that over the past 100 years the rich and famous have fallen deeply in love with their exotic charm. Here we have what must surely be the aristocrats of the plant world, yet they provide a magnificent range of flowering evergreens that are now available for all to enjoy. With some care, it is possible for everyone to share their beauty.

PERFECT PARTNERS

Trees that grow well with rhododendrons are small acers (Japanese maple); birch; flowering cherries (spring varieties); *Prunus autumnalis* (autumn flowering cherry); liquidambar; rowan (mountain ash); and malus (flowering crab apple).

Shrubs that associate well with rhododendrons include azaleas, heathers, pernettyas, daphnes, viburnums, skimmias, dwarf berberis and pieris.

PANSIES

**Pansies' velvety textures and friendly little faces
make them one of the best-loved garden flowers,
providing colour all year round.**

Perhaps the pansy's place in our affections comes from its long association with lovers. The word pansy comes from the French *pensées*, meaning 'thoughts'. The charming flowers both of pansies and of their close relatives, violas, were said to turn a person's thoughts to their loved one. Their old English name, heartsease, symbolized the peace and rest that came to the hearts of lovers who died of love.

Yet, in stark contrast to this romantically melancholy image of tormented sweethearts, the pansy itself is essentially a cheerful plant. Not only does it present a bright and breezy countenance to the world, but it is amenable and obliging by nature too.

Pansies are simple to grow from seed and will put up with almost any soil. They are also very easy to obtain as bedding plants. Garden centres always carry a thorough selection and carry a thorough selection and most little local stores such as greengrocers, florists and even pet shops often offer trays of pansies for sale.

There are a host of varieties available, in almost every colour. Most varieties have at least two contrasting shades. In some cases this is a fringe around the petals; others have 'faces' of another colour at their centres.

If you browse through catalogues or the seed racks at your local garden centre, you

The rich and varied colours of pansies (above) allow you to create an air of profusion in a small space and for little cost or effort. Some of the tones are unique and magical and, with care and a little luck, you can produce fine blooms throughout the year.

will discover varieties of pansies for every season and, with care and a mild winter, you could have a colourful display all year round.

Winter pansies

Winter can be a very dull time in your garden. This is especially true if your space is limited to a small patch, a balcony or a window box or two. There is simply no room for the shrubs, trees and heathers that provide most of the winter interest in larger gardens.

The ever-obliging pansy can brighten up the winter gloom. 'Winter Smiles' and 'Forerunner Mixed' are two colourful varieties which will flower from autumn through to early spring in mild winters.

The 'Universal' F1 hybrid varieties are also winter flowering and come in selections of

You can really let your creativity show when you put pansies in hanging baskets. This ball-like effect (right) has a simple colour scheme. Just think what you can do with a richer mix! Pansies are hardy plants so your hanging basket can endure harsh days.

'King of the Blacks' (below) are among the most mysterious of all garden pansies. They are robust plants with flowers nestling deep in the foliage. They reach a breadth of 10cm/4in or more.

PLANT PROFILE

Suitable site and soil: will tolerate most soils but benefit from some prior preparation. Dig well and add well-rotted manure and a dusting of bone meal to the top 23cm/9in.

Planting: in spring or autumn, about 20-30cm/8-12in apart in full sun or partial shade.

Propagation: from seed or cuttings. Sow seeds according to the instructions on the packet. May be sown indoors or out. Cuttings should be taken from fresh new growth in spring or autumn. Stop the parent plant from flowering in July by removing buds, encouraging the vigorous new growth you will need in autumn. Choose sturdy stems and cut just below a joint. Trim away lower leaves. Add horticultural sand and perlite to the compost and fill trays to 10cm/4in. Make holes and add a little sand to the bottom of each. Firm in 6-8cm/2½-3in

cuttings and water well. Place in a shady spot. Plant out spring cuttings in autumn but over-winter autumn cuttings in a sunny, unheated cold frame.

Pests and diseases: rarely troubled by common pests such as slugs, snails and aphids. Red spider mite can sometimes be controlled by directing a jet of water at the creatures and their webs until all trace is washed away. The rare, soil-borne *pansy sickness* can kill off healthy plants almost overnight. Discard infected plants and start again in another site, or replace the topsoil in the infected area. Sinking pansies in pots into the bed is another solution.

Recommended varieties: Any 'Universal' will give winter flowers. Try 'Padparadja' and 'Clear Crystals' for self-colour and, for fun, 'Jolly Joker', the dwarf 'Baby Lucia' or 'Rippling Waters'.

Looking like a butterfly, the 'Joker Light Blue' pansy (left) has sharp colours and commands attention anywhere. The Joker varieties are among the ever-growing number of novelty plants whose patterns can be blended endlessly.

'Padparadja' (below) is named after a real jewel of the Orient. This plant takes on even more luxurious tones when planted among other pansies. A summer pansy, it offers a garden a broad swathe of colour or a rich splash in a drab corner.

DEAD-HEADING

Remove the dead flowers from your pansies regularly so that they do not go to seed. Diligent dead-heading ensures that your plants continue to produce masses of flowers over a long period.

and summer varieties, plant some earlies. 'Eclipse' is one such variety, beginning its flowering very early in the season and finishing at the end of the summer. Another possible choice is 'Supremo', which offers yellow, bronze, red, rose, purple and white in its colour combinations. It has very large flowers.

'Ruffled Earlies', as their name suggests, have ruffled edges and flower in early spring. To add to their charms, they may sometimes have contrasting borders, veins, stripes or blotches.

Summer blooms

Most pansies flower in summer and early autumn and there are many varieties to choose from in this category. Some of these can produce very large flowers, bi-coloured, tri-coloured or multi-coloured. 'Majestic Giant', 'Swiss Giant' and 'Monarch Giant' are all mixtures and will provide rich colours. Some of the blooms in these mixtures will have strongly marked faces.

For self-coloured pansies with a wide selection of colours, it is hard to beat the 'Clear Crystal Mixed' variety.

Fancies

Among the summer lovers there is a wide choice of what Victorian gardeners referred to as 'fancies'. These are strikingly-coloured novelty plants whose numbers are added to every year. 'Jolly Joker', for instance, is an orange and purple bi-colour with a fairly small flower. 'Rippling Waters'

colours and types. The multi-coloured 'Delft', for example, has flowers that are lemon, cream, purple, white and midnight black, while 'Beaconsfield' is a beautiful royal purple shading to lilac, with light blue upper petals.

The unromantic sounding 'White Blotch' is a neat, compact plant, pure white with a deep violet blue face or 'blotch'. There is also a 'Blue Blotch', whose petals are a deep, rich blue tinged with purple. It has a distinctive velvet blue face.

If you prefer flowers in all one colour, without a face, the self-coloured varieties are for you. Amongst the winter flowerers there is 'True Blue', which is a clear mid-blue and has rather fetching whiskers. Other single-coloured varieties include a pure white and a wonderful apricot.

For smaller winter flowering plants choose 'Floral Dance', which will give you a lovely mixture of blooms. To ensure that there is no gap in flowering between the winter

BRIGHT IDEAS

CREATING VARIETIES

Pansies are very obliging and you can have a lot of fun developing your own new varieties. Simply set aside a small area devoted to a few favourites and allow nature to take its course. Allow the plants to set seed and see what happens next. Some plants produced this way will be truly gorgeous; others, unfortunately, may turn out to be more useful in the compost bin.

is a splendid dark purple bloom enhanced with rippled white edges.

'Joker' is pale blue with a dark blue face and a little white for contrast. 'Love Duet' is cream suffused with pale pink and has a rich rose face.

For intensity of colour and a stunning display you could not do better than to choose 'Pad-paradja', which is a really deep, rich orange variety. It glows like the Sri Lankan jewel after which it is named. If you enjoy a really dramatic effect, plant it with the equally exotic 'Midnight Black' or another variety of the same colour, 'Black Star'.

Choosing

Pansies offer such a wealth of possibilities in terms of colour, design and flowering season, that it is easy to get confused.

The first thing to decide is when you want them to flower. With care you can select varieties which will flower one after another so that every month of the year is graced by their presence in your garden.

The next consideration is where you want to plant them. Pansies are equally happy as border plants or container dwellers. They also make very effective edging plants.

Like most bedding plants, pansies enjoy full sun, but they will tolerate some shade.

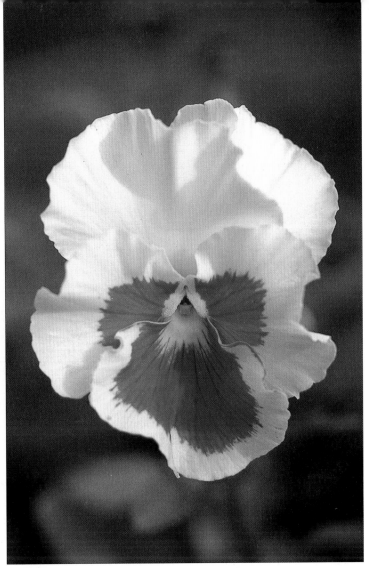

This array of 'Monarch' pansies (left) have been orchestrated to resemble a painting. 'True Blue' pansies (below left) are a reminder that they can be subtly shaded as well as vibrantly coloured.

The aptly named 'Jolly Joker' (above) is among the most reliable pansies for summer blooms.

The exquisite 'Love Duet' (right) is one of the most striking of all pansy varieties.

PERFECT PARTNERS

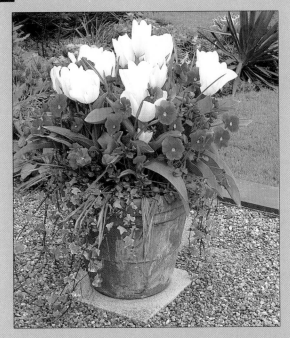

Potted pansies look good when combined with slightly taller flowers. These blue violas and white tulips (above) make a dramatic effect.

Unlike their close relatives, violets and some violas, they are not suited to brightening a very shady corner.

Mix and match

Design is the next consideration. Many devotees of the pansy feel that they are at their resplendent best when masses of the same variety are planted together in a border or container. This is particularly true of self-coloured varieties.

However, pansies also make good companion plants. The more old-fashioned varieties, for example, make a handsome addition to a knot garden. Their old-world charm blends beautifully with the historical theme of this type of planting scheme. Box hedges and the foliage of selected herbs make a wonderful background for their jaunty, colourful blooms. Choose fairly tidy herbs such as chives, thyme, parsley and basil. Pansies cannot compete with unruly types such as mint.

Pansies look well with small bulbs such as snowdrops, *Iris reticulata,* cyclamen and muscari. Their bold colours and markings complement the more delicate features of miniature bulbs. The shapes go well together too.

GROWING TIPS

PROLONGING LIFE

Many people discard pansies after a year of two because of their tendency to get straggly, but can prolong their useful life by cutting back at the end of flowering.

A top dressing of manure in autumn and regular foliar feeding during the flowering season will also ensure good, healthy plants for next year.

273

BUSY LIZZIES

If you are looking for an easy, reliable annual to add colour to your garden throughout the summer, then the aptly-named busy Lizzie is the plant for you.

Everything about busy Lizzies suggests bright, cheerful bustle. This bushy, succulent-stemmed and almost perpetual-flowering plant was given its common name because of its fast growth and the persistence with which it flowers. Seedlings begin to produce blooms when they are only an inch or so tall, and carry on doing so all through the summer months.

Even its generic name, *Impatiens*, suggests swift movement, though in this case it is named not for its growth habits but rather for the speed with which it discharges its seeds when ripe.

Busy Lizzies are enormously versatile plants. Several different varieties planted together in a bed make a colourful ground cover (right), while a single variety will grace a tub or window-box (below). If they are left in their pots, other options arise. Wedging the pots in the gaps in a honeycomb wall, for example, enables the plants to make lovely vertical cover (opposite above).

A striking alternative to conventional busy Lizzies is provided by the new, larger-flowered New Guinea hybrids, some with variegated foliage (opposite below).

STRIPED STARS

The candy-stripe varieties, in eye-catching shades of red, pink, orange or purple, striped with white, are striking when used alone.

Try planting up a container with several plants of a single variety spaced just 8-10cm/3-4ins apart for a truly dazzling effect.

The ancestral strains of *Impatiens* originated in the tropical and sub-tropical areas of Africa and the Far East.

From these tall, rangy ancestors have been developed a vast range of hybrids that have all of the good habits and none of the drawbacks of the parent plant. Most busy Lizzie hybrids are notable for their compact, low-growing habit and for their profuse blooming. The flowers are generally single, though there are some spectacular doubles, and have a pronounced spur at the back.

None of the new compact strains is likely to grow beyond a height of 30-40cm/12-15in, which makes them ideal candidates for hanging baskets, small tubs and window boxes, though they are equally good performers when planted out as summer bedding. They are extremely versatile and can safely be used in difficult, shady parts of the garden or in full sunshine: not many half-hardy annuals tolerate both conditions. There will, naturally, be more flowers if the plant is grown in full sun.

Among the many hybrid strains of *Impatiens* are plants with flowers of all shades of

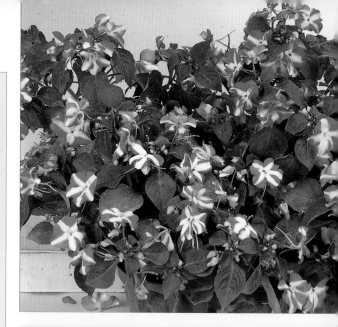

PLANT PROFILE

Suitable site and soil Does well in full sun or partial shade. Will tolerate most soil conditions if kept moist, but not waterlogged.

Planting Plant out young specimens when all danger of frost has passed. Prepare the border by working in a little well-rotted garden compost and sprinkle in a handful of bone meal to enrich the area around the roots of each plant; they should be placed 15-23cm/6-9in apart. Water in.

Cultivation and care Require little attention apart from regular watering when the rain does not oblige.

Propagation If growing from seed, this should be sown indoors or under glass in spring. Use peat-based compost and cover the seeds lightly. Seedlings must be kept at a temperature of at least 18°C/65°.

When they are about 4cm/1½in high, transplant them into individual pots of loam-based compost. Alternatively, tip cuttings 5-8cm/2-3in long can be taken in summer or early autumn and rooted in water before being potted up.

Pests and diseases Slugs can be a problem to younger, weaker plants and aphids may occasionally take a fancy to the odd specimen.

Recommended varieties So many varieties have been developed that it is difficult to make a choice. Here are some to look out for.

● The fast-growing 'Imp' and 'Super Elfin' strains grown to around 23cm/9in high and produce large flowers in a full range of colours.

● 'Novette' mixture, with plants only 10cm/4in high, and 'Florette' (15cm/6in) are good for edging and for the front of mixed borders.

● 'Futura', which has a trailing habit, is ideal for window boxes and hanging baskets.

● 'Camellia flowered Mixed' (45cm/18in) and 'Tom Thumb Mixed' (20cm/10in) are best for the balsam-type double flowers.

● 'Confection Mixed' is the choice for conventional doubles.

● 'Zig-Zag', which has striped blooms, is extremely eye-catching, while 'Grand Prix' bears the largest flowers.

pink, red, orange, mauve and white. There are also bi-coloured varieties – for instance, red or pink striped with white.

The leaves may be elliptic or heart-shaped and can be coloured in almost every imaginable shade of green; some have a bronze or purple sheen and reddish or brown speckles on the undersides.

Named varieties

Although they are raised from named types, in garden centres you may be faced with rows of plants marked simply '*Impatiens* F1 Hybrid', giving the colour and brief information on the height, spread and general care of the plant.

However, if you wish to look further into the various varieties, a specialist grower should be able to identify and supply a much wider range of named

Impatiens hybrids.

The best way to get a named variety, though, is to raise plants from seed. As a basic bedding plant for borders and large containers, it is difficult to beat the fast-growing 'Imp' and 'Super Elfin' varieties. Both grow to around 23cm/9in tall and produce large flowers in a full range of colours.

If you have smaller containers, try the dwarf 'Novette' mixture. This free-flowering variety grows to just 10cm/4in tall, making it a good choice for edging a border. The same is true of the slightly taller (15cm/6in) 'Florette' series.

The compact colour they provide make busy Lizzies a good choice for window boxes; the semi-pendulous habit of the 'Futura' variety makes it ideal for boxes and for hanging baskets, where it makes a good companion for trailing

Named varieties are not always available as bedding plants, but they can be raised from seed without much difficulty, and are well worth the effort. The striped blooms of 'Zig Zag' (left) make a striking display for a container or hanging basket, while the small blooms of the dwarf form, 'Novette Mixed' (below left) make excellent bedding plants for the front of a border. 'Super Elfin Mixed' (right) is a taller variety, with correspondingly larger flowers. Large flowers are also characteristic of the New Guinea hybrids; the pink and white blooms of 'Fanfare' (below right) are set off by handsomely variegated leaves. Impatiens F1 hybrids include several double-flowered varieties. Although some are named, others are simply sold as 'Double Mixed' (below). Sometimes the double flowers resemble roses; others are more open.

GARDEN NOTES

HARDENING OFF

It is essential that you wait until the possibility of frost is past and the soil is beginning to warm up before planting out. This means the beginning of summer at the earliest.

Accustom the plants to outside conditions by introducing the pots to the garden for lengthening periods, making sure that you bring them in at night. Do not allow them to dry out during this hardening-off period – this can happen very quickly to plants in small pots – but be very careful not to over-water either, as the plants will rot in water-logged soil.

pelargoniums, fuchsias, petunias and lobelia.

Complex double varieties, no less free-flowering, are available for those who want to put on a little more show in their borders.

The camellia-flowered busy Lizzies (which are usually called balsam, the name under which you will find them in some catalogues) are varieties of *I. balsamina*, and come in shades of rose, blush pink, scarlet and white. 'Camellia Flowered Mixed', one of the largest busy Lizzie varieties, grows to 45cm/18in. The same type of showy flower can be had in smaller plants; try 'Tom Thumb Mixed' (25cm/10in).

There are double-flowered forms of the more conventional busy Lizzie, too, such as 'Confection Mixed' (20-30cm/8-12in tall, with fine, double and semi-double flowers).

Growing busy Lizzies

Strictly speaking, *Impatiens* is a perennial. Growers of houseplants will be well aware of the busy Lizzie's sterling service indoors – a well cared for specimen can be kept at peak performance for years.

However, when grown as a garden plant in temperate conditions it must be regarded as a tender half-hardy annual. Most modern *Impatiens* hybrids are started off in spring under glass and discarded in the autumn before the first frosts puts paid to them. Young plants can be purchased through mail-order catalogues and begin to appear in garden centres in late spring.

They may, of course, be propagated from seed at home, though this will have to be done indoors, as seedlings must be kept at a minimum temperature of 18°C/65°F.

Seed should be sown on a growing medium based on peat or a peat substitute in spring and lightly covered. When the seedlings are large enough to handle (about 4cm/1½in tall), transplant them into individual pots of loam-based compost. Pinch out the growing tips of young plants regularly to ensure bushiness.

Alternatively, you can take tip cuttings 5-8cm/2-3in long from existing plants in the summer and root them in water. Transfer them to a soil-based compost when roots 1½cm/½in long have formed, and over-winter them indoors.

Whole plants can also be lifted from the garden and

NEW BLOOMS

Striking new hybrids with larger flowers have recently been developed as a result of a plant-gathering expedition to New Guinea. Some strains reputedly produce flowers over 8cm/3in across. Many of the most colourful have strongly variegated foliage.

These New Guinea hybrids are now becoming available through garden centres and mail-order catalogues.

The camellia flowered busy Lizzies (above) are varieties of I. balsamina and are often sold as balsam. Unlike other Impatiens hybrids, they are true annuals. Most varieties have an upright growth habit, and do not branch. While the species has small, single flowers, hybrids are fully double; the flower stems are very short and the blooms appear to burst out from between the lance-shaped leaves.

GROWING TIPS

INDOOR PESTS

When you are raising plants indoors, they can be susceptible to pests which also enjoy the warm conditions. This is especially true if you have a large collection of houseplants.

Red spider mite can be a real menace if conditions become very dry, causing mottling and bronzing of leaves, which may begin to drop.

Whitefly is another nuisance. It disfigures and weakens the plants. In each case, treat with a suitable systemic insecticide such as dimethoate.

then over-wintered indoors. Usually, though, they have become so leggy by the end of the summer that they are not worth hanging on to.

Planting out

Whichever method of propagation you choose, or whether you simply decide to start again with new plantlets each year, do take care not to plant them out too early. Always harden them off gradually, accustoming them to lower temperatures and more airy conditions for a week or two before planting them out in their final positions.

Once the danger of their main enemy, frost, is past, busy Lizzies could not be ea-

sier to grow. There are, however, always the usual garden pests around, ready to prey on vulnerable individuals.

Slugs and snails may attack seedlings and young plants, especially in periods of wet weather. A sprinkling of slug pellets from time to time should keep them at bay.

Also, keep an eye out for infestations of aphids on leaves or stems, which will weaken the plants, make them sticky and encourage mould.

Once summer is under way, all you really need to do is keep your plants well-watered, and they will reward you with a heartening display of colour throughout the season and well into the autumn.

SPRING BULBS

Spring bulbs act as the heralds of summer, providing the first flushes of colour in the garden, lifting the spirits and setting the tone for the coming season.

Few sights in the garden are more stirring than green spikes forcing their way through bare ground or frosted lawns. In a matter of weeks, these unfurl to display an array of brightly coloured, often fragrant, flowers.

Most of this early season show is provided by spring bulbs, a name given to a group of widely different plants – including daffodils, narcissi, crocuses, snowdrops, tulips, hya-cinths, grape hyacinths and bluebells – linked by their ha-bits of growth.

Bulb or corm?

Although they are all known as spring bulbs, some of these plants grow from corms or tu-bers. A corm is a swollen stem base where reserve nutrients are stored overwinter, and a tuber is a thickened fleshy root, while a bulb is a modified shoot with fleshy scales that take the place of leaves. New flower buds develop quickly from the centre of this tightly packed bundle.

All new plantings of spring bulbs have to be completed in autumn to ensure spring flowers. Some, such as snow-drops, do best if planted 'in the green', just after flowering has finished and their leaves are still showing.

In the garden, bulbs will fit just about any growing plan,

One of the greatest joys of spring bulbs is the colourful profusion they bring to gardens which, just a month or so before, were bleak wastes. Here, tulips, daffodils, narcissi, dwarf irises and snowdrops have thrust their way up through a bed covered in a handsome, weed-suppressing mulch of bark chippings.

NATURALIZING BULBS IN LAWN

Lift a piece of turf and dig a planting hole deep enough and wide enough to hold ten bulbs of your choice. Daffodils need a depth of 10cm/4in.

Apply a slow-release fertilizer, replace the soil and then cover the hole with the lifted turf.

Firm the turf in and water well for a few weeks. In a dry spring, keep it well-watered.

After flowering, remove faded flowers and leave the area unmown for at least six weeks so the leaves can build up reserves for vigorous growth next year.

provided they have sun and well-drained soil. They are often used as temporary bedding plants that delight for several weeks in spring before being lifted to make room for summer bedding plants.

Small, dwarf-growing bulbs can have permanent positions in rockeries, while plants such as grape hyacinth can be used as edging for beds and borders.

Bulbs suit mixed borders, too, though you have to mark the spot where they are planted before the leaves die back, or you may accidentally spike them with a fork or slice them with a spade when you are working on the border.

The natural look

The most attractive way to grow bulbs in the garden is by allowing them to look as natural as possible. This means either growing them in the lawn or in the dappled shade cast by deciduous trees.

Daffodils and crocuses make the best subjects for naturalizing in the lawn. Although the intended effect is one of informality, the bulbs are best grouped together according to colour, rewarding you with a drift of harmonizing tones. Each year, as the bulbs increase naturally, the drifts will intensify.

To keep the planting as informal as possible, use older,

short-stemmed and strong-growing varieties; modern, perfect daffodils bred for show purposes are wasted in this setting. 'February Gold' and 'Carlton' are good choices. Both are plain yellow; 'Carlton', a short-stemmed variety, is a paler shade. For a drift of white use 'Poeticus', with its red-rimmed cup, or 'Mount Hood', a plain white trumpet.

To make a good display of crocuses, you will need a dense mass of corms. Large-flowered Dutch hybrids grow well in grass, but they are not as natural-looking there as the small-flowered species crocuses. Keep mauves, whites and purples separate from yel-

KEEP OFF

Mice, cats and birds are potential pests that will affect bulb performance. To keep mice off, place a few prickly holly leaves in the ground around the bulbs.

Cats and mice may be deterred by pepper dust scattered on the surface. This will have to be renewed in wet weather.

Keep birds away from crocus flowers with lengths of black cotton tied between short pieces of cane.

GO ORGANIC!

low varieties for the most harmonious effects.

A good choice is *Crocus* 'Vanguard', whose light mauve cups with yellow stamens appear early in spring.

A woodland setting

Even in a small garden, it is possible to create a miniature woodland scene under fruit trees or hazels, the perfect place for snowdrops, bluebells or crocuses to naturalize.

Snowdrops need sunny, open, well-drained sites to increase in any great quantity, but can be grown in light or dappled shade, where you will need to plant them in a good mass to create a strong effect.

The early-flowering *Crocus tommasinianus*, with mauve flowers, and the deep golden *C. flavus flavus* give the best display in a sunny position, while bluebells grow well if you can offer them cool, moist and partially shaded sites.

Border bridges

For a natural effect, avoid putting the bulbs in circles or rows. Plant them as they fall, if you spread them by hand. Allow some space for their nat-

ural increase by separating off several clumps as you plant.

In a mixed herbaceous border, spring bulbs bridge the colour gap between seasons. You can use a wide range of bulbs including daffodils, tulips and anemones as well as the tall-growing crown imperial fritillary (*Fritillaria imperialis*). Plant crown imperials at the back of the border and leave them undisturbed to ensure dramatic displays of hanging, rich yellow or orange, ball-shaped flowers. Be particularly careful to mark these bulbs; they do not show above ground in the summer, and have an unpleasant, foxy smell if cut into or damaged.

When planting bulbs in a mixed border, group them according to colour, several to a

Daffodils naturalize in drifts on banks, in lawns, and under deciduous trees (above left), where they provide colour and interest before the tree is in leaf.

Forget-me-nots and pansies are often planted with taller bulbs such as tulips (left) to provide colour on more than one level.

The crown imperial fritillary, with its pendulous flowers crowned with a rosette of bracts, is a handsome ornament to any bed; here (above) it is combined with harmonizing hyacinths and tulips.

The mottled-leaved dog's-tooth violet (Erythronium dens-canis, right) grows from a tuber.

BULB VARIETIES

Naturalizing in lawns
Narcissus 'February Gold' and 'Carlton' are yellow, with shortish, sturdy stems. 'Poeticus' has white flowers with a red-rimmed cup. 'Mount Hood' is white.
Crocus vernus 'Vanguard' has early mauve flowers.
For woodland setting
Snowdrops, bluebells and *Crocus tommasinianus* grow in sun or dappled shade.
For the border
Crown imperial (*Fritillaria imperialis*) grows to 90cm/3ft and flowers in mid-spring.
Anemone blanda has daisy-like flowers in white, blues and pastel pinks and flowers in early spring. It suits the front of the border.
Grape hyacinth (*Muscari armeniacum*) makes a good edging plant and multiplies freely.
Iris reticulata grows to 10-15cm/4-6in and suits the front of a border or the rockery.
Rockery bulbs
Dog's-tooth violet (*Erythronium dens-canis*) grows well in dappled shade or sun.
Spring starflower (*Ipheion uniflorum*) needs protection from winds.

KEEP ON BLOOMING

By planting several different bulbs at varying planting depths you can ensure a continuity of spring bulb flowers from early to late spring.

Snowdrops, crocus, *Anemone blanda* and grape hyacinths flower early in spring and need a depth of 5cm/2in. Species tulips such as *Tulipa turkestanica*, Forsteriana tulips, hyacinths, daffodils, Darwin hybrid tulips and crown imperials grow best if they are planted to a depth of 10cm/4in. They all flower in mid-spring. Late-flowering tulips, Dutch iris and the ornamental onion, *Allium giganteum*, provide colour in late spring and early summer.

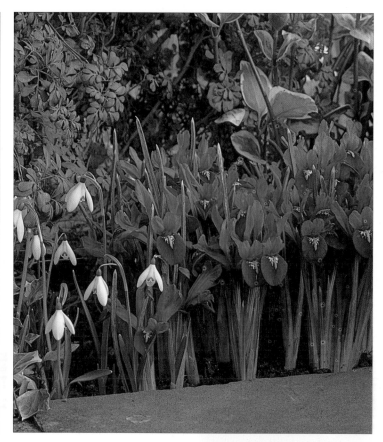

The miniature iris (I. reticulata) is small enough for a rockery, and also combines well with snowdrops at the edge of a mixed bed (above left); they flower at the same time, are more or less the same size, and offer an attractive contrast of shapes and colours.

Snowdrops and crocuses are traditional partners. They look their best in an informal, semi-wild setting, such as here (right), where they are scattered in colourful clumps along a stepping-stone path.

The smaller tulip varieties also grow well in rock gardens alongside dwarf narcissi (below).

clump for the best effect, and position them in the border according to height.

If they can be left in place after flowering, allow their foliage to die down naturally so that they can build up their food reserves and flowering vigour for the following year.

Plant the corms of *Anemone blanda* at the front of a spring border, where their shades of white and blue make a pretty edge. Grape hyacinths (*Muscari* spp.) make a strong blue edging for a raised bed. However, they increase and spread invasively, so you will need to lift, divide and move grape hyacinth clumps in autumn.

Room with a view

If you have room, it is always a good idea to plan a special bulb bed near the house so that you can see and enjoy a succession of flowers from indoors at a time when you will not necessarily wish to linger outside. First to flower is the miniature iris (*Iris reticulata*) interspersed with snowdrops. Hyacinths and grape hyacinths follow, with tulips in late spring.

The key to success lies in the depth to which the bulbs are planted. Snowdrops have to be planted to a depth of 5cm/2in. Hyacinth, grape hyacinth and iris go deeper, to 10cm/4in, while hybrid tulips need a depth of 20cm/8in.

If you are less concerned with a natural look than with

WILD ABOUT BULBS

To protect the naturally occuring wild populations of bulbs try to ensure that the bulbs you buy for your garden come from stock that has been specially cultivated.

Soon, labelling will be compulsory to show whether bulbs have been collected in the wild or specially propagated.

At present a voluntary agreement exists and most suppliers try to distinguish between wild-collected and specially grown bulbs.

creating geometric blocks of colour, bulbs can lend themselves to formal planting. A circular bed in the lawn, formal squares or rectangular beds suit a display of this kind. Choose one type of bulb, such as tulips, all in one colour.

Formal bulbs beds

When you plant the bulbs, combine them with suitable spring bedding that will provide a contrasting or complementary colour. The foliage of the bedding plants will soften the look of bare soil at the feet of the bulb plants.

Blue flowered forget-me-nots are the traditional accompaniment for pink tulips such as 'Clara Butt'. Dwarf wallflowers and primroses also mix well with tulips. Winter-flowering Universal pansies, freely available in solid shades of purple and apricot, are a popular choice under white or yellow daffodils.

Rockery bulbs

Dwarf bulbs, including grape hyacinths, *Crocus tommasinianus* and *C. aureus,* look attractive in clumps on the rockery. They will grow through

the fresh green foliage of rockery perennials.

An unusual bulb, dog's-tooth violet (*Erythronium denscanis*), grows well in dappled shade on a well-drained rockery. It also looks attractive in a woodland setting around the base of trees.

Spring starflower (*Ipheion uniflorum*) makes a welcome display in blue, white or yellow on a sunny rockery but needs protection from wind. 'Wisley Blue' is a good variety.

Striped squill (*Puschkinia scilloides*), with its delicately striped, star-like pale blue flowers, is another suitable plant for a spring rockery.

Bulb care

Plant new bulbs early in the autumn when the ground is moist and pliable. Mulch and apply a slow-release fertilizer.

In spring, remove faded flowers before they set seed, but once flowering is over, allow the leaves to die down naturally. Before they disappear they will have obtained nutrients for next years' flowers.

If you can leave the bulbs or corms in position from year to year, they will continue to increase and flower. Well-established clumps should be lifted, divided and replanted in the autumn.

If you have to use the bulb bed for a succession of summer planting, remove the bulbs before their foliage has died down and replant them in a special shallow trench where they can continue undisturbed. In autumn, return them to their flowering sites.

PERFECT PARTNERS

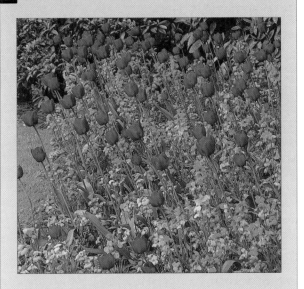

Though they grow from seed rather than bulbs, spring-flowering wallflowers (*Erysimum cheiri*) make a fragrant, colourful setting for tall tulips.

ROSES

The rose is one of the most versatile of plants, with literally hundreds of varieties offering soft-petalled, fragrant blooms and stunning ornamental effects.

A rose bed need not be a rigid, regimental affair; informal plantings of mixed varieties (above) can produce a dazzling kaleidoscope of colour throughout the season.

The rose has attracted an army of specialist growers over the last few centuries. Their enthusiasm has created an almost limitless variety of plants with a wealth of flower shapes, colours and scents.

Within the broad categories of modern garden roses, old garden roses and wild roses, there are rampant climbers, bushy shrubs and ground-cover varieties. Some have delicate single flowers with 5-8 petals, some semi-double blooms with 10-25, while others produce full double roses with more than 40.

Many modern varieties carry one flower to a stem, while others, the floribundas, produce clusters or trusses of smaller blooms; there are also several miniature varieties.

Roses can provide floral display in a mixed bed or stand alone as a specimen plant in a patio tub. Climbers and ramblers can screen the garden shed or cloak an archway in colour and fragrance. Ground cover varieties may be the answer on a difficult bank, while its thorns make the rose particularly effective in a barrier hedge. Miniature varieties can do well in a window box.

This abundance means that the key to using roses as part of a creative plan in the garden is first to decide what effect you require and then to choose the varieties whose colours and growing habits best suit what you have in mind.

A special rose bed

Rose enthusiasts usually prefer to keep them apart from other plants, so they can lavish attention on them, and a separate rose bed is the best place to display many of the modern varieties, grown as shrubs or standards.

Hybrid tea roses are best suited to a formal rose bed. They produce well shaped double flowers, typically one bloom on each flowering stem. Their elegance makes them the perfect choice if you aim to fill the rooms of your house with bowls of cut flowers.

If you prefer a less formal look, you can soften the appearance of a rose bed by underplanting standards with border plants such as forget-me-nots and lady's mantle (*Alchemilla mollis.*) The soft, delicate foliage and host of small flowers that characterize these plants soften the edges of a bed and provide interest when the roses are not in bloom.

A standard rose, either with a round, bushy head or trained into a weeping shape, can be used as a central focus in a formal herb garden. These

specimen plants are very useful as centrepieces in any circular bed, offering height and shape all year round and a cascade of scent and colour when in full seasonal bloom.

Good bedfellows

In contrast to the hybrid tea varieties, **old garden roses** grow in a very informal way,

blending harmoniously into all kinds of mixed shrub and herbaceous borders.

Many of these varieties have been grown for centuries, but can still offer a modern garden much to treasure. Gentler in style than the modern roses, their buds and flowers have a delicate beauty.

Rosa × *odorata* 'Mutabilis', also known as 'Tipo Ideale', for instance, produces papery flowers for much of the summer and bronze foliage in spring. Another eye-catching old rose is *R. gallica* 'Versicolor', a variety that is at least 300 years old, whose petals are streaked with shades of pink.

Old roses tend to be available only from specialist growers, but they are well worth seeking out to soften and add interest to mixed bor-

ders. Their foliage often makes a more dramatic contribution to a border than their flowers.

R. glauca, for instance, produces short-lived and unspectacular blooms, but its almost thornless stems and leaves of pinky-grey earn it a place in many gardens. Grown next to a plant with silver

Several varieties of rose give good ground cover. Rosa 'Pheasant' (below) produces masses of small pink semi-double flowers. Other 'game bird' roses give different colours; R. 'Grouse' is pale pink, and R. 'Partridge' white.

A collection of miniature roses makes an excellent, free-flowering subject for a container or a raised bed (above).

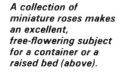

ROSES FOR EVERY PURPOSE

- For a formal rose garden choose the large-flowered hybrid tea rose *'Peace'* with its pink-tipped yellow petals.
- For an informal shrub border choose *'Iceberg'* or the red-flowered *'Fragrant Delight'*. Both are cluster-flowered roses.
- Choice climbing roses for a wall or screen include *'Zéphirine Drouhin'*, a thornless pink-flowered rose that flowers continously through the summer and has a deep fragrance. For a sunny effect choose *'Golden Showers'*.
- Rambling roses that can be trained over arches, fallen trees and across the front of a house include *'American Pillar'* with its deep red roses; the fragrant pink *'Albertine'* and the rampant *'Kiftsgate'*.
- If you prefer to try old garden roses in a mixed shrubbery, *Rosa glauca* offers pretty foliage and attractive hips.
- For hedges use *'Frau Dagmar Hastrup'*.
- Good ground cover roses include the Japanese rose, *'Nozomi'*, and *'Pheasant'* with masses of small flowers.

leaves, it makes a strong decorative focus. Both the filigree foliage of artemisia and the huge indented leaves of an ornamental artichoke, for example, provide a striking contrast to the delicate leaves of this old garden rose.

Containers

You do not need a bed of any kind to enjoy roses, which will happily grow in containers on a patio or balcony; some will grow in a window box. Wooden tubs make the best containers for all types of rose, from miniature to standard.

Make sure that any rose you choose for container cultivation is disease-resistant, as it will be more vulnerable in its tub than in the ground. For all-year interest, plant the container with trailing ivy, and in late spring add annual plants such as lobelia to make a froth of colour at the base.

Miniature roses, such as 'Baby Masquerade', which grows to 38cm/15in high, look well as the focal point of a tub. Small-flowered annual bedding plants chosen to complement the colour of the rose will soften the edge of the container. Dwarf varieties can also be used in a window box, as a short-term house plant, as edging at the front of a border, or as a splash of colour on a small rockery.

Not all roses grow upwards. Some make spreading horizontal growth and are ideal ground cover. They provide a ready solution to a 'difficult' slope or bank, transforming it into a colourful, flower-strewn bed requiring the minimum of maintenance.

Floral carpets

The variety 'Nozomi', with its profusion of single pearly-pink blooms, is particularly suited to this purpose, as are 'Partridge' and 'Red Blanket', which are both smothered with flowers and boast disease-resistant leaves.

Weed the site carefully before planting, since the roses will not actually suppress weeds, and it is difficult to remove them from between the roses once established.

Roses can be used to mark out short internal hedges between parts of the garden. For

Many shrub roses, although classified as modern garden varieties, have the timeless appeal of old garden roses. The creamy-pink scented flowers, dense foliage and arching habit of R. 'Nevada' (above) make it an inspired choice for framing a garden gate.

PERFECT PARTNERS

In a garden where space is short, the stems of a tall-growing shrub rose can act as a support for annual sweet peas, whose blooms will intertwine with those of the rose to make a living bouquet.

MAINTENANCE

All roses should be kept well-watered until they are established. As their roots go deep, it should not be necessary to water them again except in long, dry spells. Water them direct from the spout of the can, held close to the ground. They should be fed in spring and the area round the stem mulched with compost or manure (do not let it come into direct contact with the stem).

Apart from this, old garden roses need very little attention, apart from dead-heading and removing diseased or damaged wood in spring. They do not need to be pruned like modern varieties, simply clipped back.

DON'T FORGET!

anything on a larger scale, a rose hedge tends to be rather too expensive.

Hedges and screens

The best choices for hedging are the *R. rugosa* varieties, which have a compact shape and flower repeatedly. Their bright, fat hips extend interest into the autumn and winter. Miniature roses make an interesting and attractive alternative to edging a formal herb garden or shrub border.

Rambling and climbing roses make the best screens, masking rubbish bins, unsightly downpipes or simply a dull wall. Both will grow quickly along a support. This can be a lattice of wires or trellis fixed to the wall, or a free standing screen over which the plants can be trained.

Roses are often the first choice for covering arches and pergolas. Rambling varieties, though they tend to have a short flowering season, pro-

vide good foliage cover; 'Albertine', with its heavy scent and attractive, full-blown flowers, is a favourite choice.

For more dramatic effect, climbers can be planted to sweep along rope swags trained from wooden pillars or formal tripods. On the pillars, they will thicken up and make a dense show of flowers; along the ropes they become a ribbon of linking colour.

Such effects take time to produce and require varieties

The Bourbon rose, R. 'Zéphirine Drouhin', has no thorns, which reduces its effectiveness as a barrier. However, it makes a fine, fragrant hedge for dividing up the garden (top).

A miniature rose can stand alone as a specimen plant in a pot or tub (above); where its perfectly-shaped flowers and foliage can be easily appreciated.

287

Roses can make fine border plants as here (right) where the floribunda 'August Seebauer' is combined with santolina to stunning effect.

Many roses have attractive hips, but those of R. rugosa (below) are especially fine, full and plump and set off to perfection by the variety's glossy, crinkled leaves.

with a fairly rampant growth habit such as 'Schoolgirl', 'New Dawn' or 'Pink Perpetué'.

Fringe benefits

Roses offer so much in terms of colour and abundant flower that it is easy for gardeners to overlook the plant's less obvious delights.

The seed-heads, known as hips, of many varieties are an attraction in their own right. Plump, sleek and scarlet, they stay on the plant throughout the winter. 'Frau Dagmar Hastrup', a rugosa rose that is good for hedging and for planting in a mixed shrub border, has round, fat hips, while *R.*

'Geranium' has long rich red ones.

The pretty hips of the grey-leaved *R. glauca* make a welcome decorative addition to both the garden and the house in the depths of winter.

Moss roses originated as a chance sport from cabbage roses. Their mossy stems and buds are almost as stunning as the full blooms that follow. This effect is best seen in the beautifully-scented *R. × centifolia* 'Muscosa'.

Scent

Fragrance can play a large part in choosing and siting a rose. Part of the traditional appeal of growing roses around a doorway is the heavenly scent which greets you when you open the door on a summer's evening.

Many of the old garden roses, such as the free-flowering 'Rose d'Amour' and 'Gloire de Dijon', otherwise known as 'Old Glory', also have delicious, evocative perfumes, while 'Zéphirine Drouhin' offers a sea of fragrant pink flowers.

For some rose-lovers, though, it is the large red thorns that are the attraction. *R. sericea omeiensis* f. *pteracantha* is a spiny rose with filigree foliage. In the sunlight, its thorns give a very different kind of ornamental effect.

ROJECT

TRAINING A CLIMBER

The image of a rose clambering over a cottage wall and framing the door is deeply embedded in English country life, but in fact this may not be the perfect place to grow a rose. Beds right up against a wall often prove too dry for roses. The growth of their roots can be restricted, which makes them vulnerable to disease.

Climbing roses should be planted some 45cm/18in from

the wall. Lay the roots so that they slope away from the wall. Tie the lower parts of the stem into the

supports, laying the branches horizontally across the wall to encourage new shoots to grow upwards.

IRISES

Versatile and easy to grow, irises make an elegant addition to the flower garden. Plant them around the pond, in borders or in rockeries for year round colour.

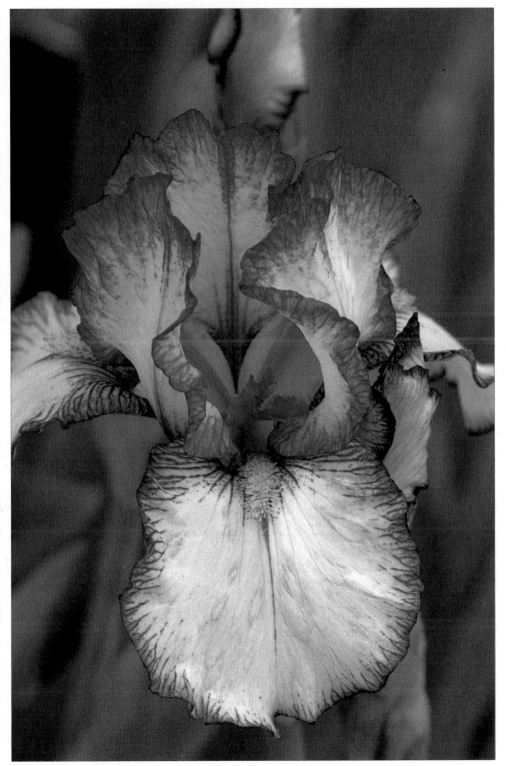

Irises form a very large genus of flowering perennials with more than 300 members, most of them ideally suited to gardens. There is, quite literally, an iris for every situation, from a pond, through moist boggy areas to a dry sun-parched border.

By choosing the right varieties you can have irises blooming in every season, their flowers ranging from the purest white, through sunny yellows to the deepest, velvety purple. With some varieties there is the added bonus of a delicious scent, and nearly all types make good cut flowers.

A typical iris is easily recognized by its erect, sword-shaped leaves and distinctive flowers, made up of three inner petals (standards) which usually stand upright, and three larger, outer ones (falls) which fall downwards.

Iris groups

For convenience, commonly-grown garden irises can be split into three main groups, each serving a different purpose in the garden. Bulbous irises include the various border kinds, popular as florists' cut flowers, as well as dwarf, winter and spring alpine species. Water irises grow best in moist soil or shallow water and are ideal for ponds and pools. Bearded irises – so-called because of a line of fleshy hairs on the falls which looks like a beard – are traditionally grown in the herbaceous border and include the

The aptly-named bearded iris, I. 'Bold Print', is remarkable for its striking colour contrasts.

PLANT PROFILE

Suitable site and soil *Iris reticulata* prefers light, well-drained, limy soil; English irises, light moist soil; Dutch irises, light fertile soil, and Spanish irises, light, well-drained soil. Water irises need damp, marshy soil or shallow water, and bearded irises fertile, neutral or slightly alkaline soil. All prefer full sun.

Planting Plant bulbs in early autumn; *I. reticulata* should be 8cm/3in deep, larger bulbs 10-15cm/4-6in deep. Water irises should be planted in early spring or late summer. *I. pseudacorus* should be up to 45cm/18in below water level and *I. laevigata* 15cm/6in deep. Put *I. ensata* into damp soil.

Cultivation and care After flowering, *I. reticulata* can be fed once a month for three months with a general liquid fertilizer to ensure good flowers the following year. Do not allow it to get waterlogged. Keep the rhizomes of bearded irises well-watered for the first three weeks and dead-head the flowers in summer.

Propagation Divide bulbs after flowering if required. Divide clumps of rhizomous irises and grow new plants from the offsets. This should be done every three to four years even if you do not want new plants, to ensure continued vigour.

Pests and diseases Generally trouble free, though may suffer aphid attack.

In late winter, I. reticulata (right) can bring vibrant colour to a rockery or window box.

The delightful water iris, I. laevigata 'Alba' (above right), flowers in midsummer.

I. laevigata (far right), flanked by Euphorbia griffithii 'Fireglow', can make a striking display.

The tiny I. danfordiae (below), with glowing yellow flowers, is perfect for a rockery.

popular 'flag' irises.

The most popular hybrids found in garden centres and bulb catalogues are known as English, Dutch and Spanish irises. English irises derive from *I. latifolia*, Spanish from *I. xiphium*, while the Dutch are hybrids. They have similar, wide ranges of colour.

Given a sunny position in the garden, they are as trouble-free as any of the common spring bulbs, and should be planted in the autumn for a succession of flowers throughout the summer months.

Continuous flowers

The Dutch are the first to flower, in early summer, followed in a few weeks by the Spanish and then by the English. By planting a few bulbs of each type, it is possible to have a continuous supply of white, yellow, blue, mauve and purple flowers for cutting, or simply for enjoying in the garden border. The plants will grow to a height of 30-60cm/12-24in.

The Dutch and Spanish irises may not be hardy in some colder areas, and will need

protecting in winter with a cloche. The English irises are the easiest of all to grow, needing no winter protection.

Equally pretty are the dwarf irises, which flower in early spring. They prefer a well-drained soil and make ideal specimens for rockeries and alpine beds, or for growing in pots on the patio; they also make a brave show in a winter window box, where their bright colours are especially welcome in late winter.

I. reticulata grows to just 15cm/6in in height, and produces a delicate, sweetly-scented, blue or purple flower, while *I. danfordiae* is strongly scented and even smaller, just 5-10cm/2-4in tall. The yellow flowers have green spots on the fall petals, while the standards are under-developed; the flowers are rarely as much as 5cm/2in across.

Water lovers

Water irises grow from rhizomes, or fleshy roots, and are best suited to waterside planting. Two particular species, *Iris ensata* and *Iris laevigata*, have beautiful, big flowers, 12-15cm/5-6in across. *I. ensata* is happiest in moist soil on

DIVIDE AND RULE

You can increase your stock of irises by dividing up clumps which have become overgrown.

Lift bulbous irises when the foliage has died down (usually in late summer). The bulbs will spilt naturally by hand and once replanted will often flower the following year.

Rhizomes can be divided in the same way. Lift them after flowering, then, using a sharp knife, cut off new pieces from the outside and discard the old centre. Each piece should have one or two strong offshoots. Replant immediately.

GARDEN NOTES

The water iris, I. ensata (left), is best planted at the edge of a pond, where its glorious flowers are seen to maximum effect.

The beautiful yellow flag iris, I. pseudacorus (right) is another water lover but tends to be invasive in a pond. It grows wild in Britain.

The delicate colours of I. 'Shepherd's Delight' (below right) make it a popular border plant and ideal for cut-flower displays.

A favourite border plant, I. 'Jane Phillips' (far right) bears delightful pinkish-mauve flowers in early summer.

the edge of the pool, while *I. laevigata* is a true water plant, and ideally likes 15cm/6in of water above the rhizome. Both varieties flower in early to midsummer.

Many water irises originate in Japan – indeed the group is sometimes known as Japanese irises – but *I. sibirica* comes from Siberia. It prefers boggy soil, and grows to 1.2m/4ft, with blue or purple flowers in early summer. Its hybrids, in blue, violet and white, are good garden choices.

The yellow flag iris (*Iris pseudacorus*), with its butter-coloured flowers, grows wild in Britain and is very adaptable, accustoming itself to any water depth up to 46cm/18in. It can reach 1.8m/6ft tall.

Water irises are completely hardy and need no special care. If they start to outgrow the pond, the rhizomes can easily be divided and replanted every three years or so.

Border favourites

The bearded irises also grow from rhizomes, but they are distinguised by a 'beard' of hairs on the downward petals. This group, mainly derived from *I. pallida* and *I. germanica*, contains most of the com-

---

RECOMMENDED VARIETIES

Dwarf bulbs
I. reticulata 'Harmony'; velvet blue with yellow blaze. 'Violet Beauty'; purple with orange streak. *I. danfordiae*; yellow.

Other bulbs
'White Excelsior'; white Dutch. 'Imperator'; deep blue. 'Golden Emperor'; gold.

Water irises
I. ensata; purple, pink, lavender or white marginal or bog plant.
Yellow flag (*I. pseudacorus*); yellow water plant.
I. laevigata; blue or purple marginal. 'Snowdrift' is a pure white double, 'Regal' is red. 'Variegata' has blue flowers and leaves striped with white.

Bearded irises
Purple flag (*I. germanica*); medium-sized rich purple with white beard.
I. pallida 'Bold Print'; medium, white and purple. 'Early Light'; tall, cream and yellow. 'Marhaba'; dwarf blue. 'Mary Frances'; tall, pink to lavender. 'Sable'; tall, with purple petals verging on black. 'Shepherd's Delight'; tall, pale pink.

for the front of the border, where they will form colourful clumps through into the beginning of summer.

The tall ones flower slightly later, and are best grown at the back of the border, where other plants will give them some support. As well as the usual blue, purple and yellow, the colour range includes the pale pink of 'Shepherd's Delight', the lavender of 'Mary Frances' and the unusual golden brown, russet and white shades of 'Flamenco'.

Plant choice

The sheer number of iris varieties can make choosing the right plants for your garden a confusing task. It is really a case of deciding exactly where in the garden you want to grow them and then checking that the conditions are right for each group – moist soil or water for the Japanese irises, a sunny border for bearded and bulbous irises and a rock garden for *Iris reticulata* and the dwarf forms. Having got that right, it is simply a matter of choosing your favourite colours and getting going on the planting.

Iris reticulata bulbs should be planted 8cm/3in deep in a well-drained soil during late summer and early autumn. English, Spanish and Dutch iris bulbs should also be

planted at this time, at a depth of 10-15cm/4-6in.

Water irises can be planted in either spring or autumn on the margins of the pond, while the rhizomes of bearded irises can be planted at the beginning or end of the summer.

The top of the rhizome should be just visible above the surface of the soil and it is important to keep them moist for the first few weeks after planting has been done.

Once established, all irises are easy to care for. They do not need attention or special watering or feeding. However, the taller varieties will benefit from staking with a bamboo cane during their first year of growth. If, after three or four years, the clumps have outgrown their allotted space, or if the flowers are poor, it is a simple task to divide them up to create new plants.

mon garden hybrids. They are excellent plants for the late spring and early summer herbaceous border, as long as they have plenty of sun. Heights vary from the tiniest dwarf varieties, measuring only 10cm/4in, to the majestic tall forms which reach heights of up to 1.5m/5ft.

The spring-flowering dwarf irises, including the deep blue 'Marhaba', are best suited to rockeries where the drainage is good, while the medium-sized ones, such as 'Bold Print', whose white petals are edged with purple, are ideal

LILIES

Despite their exotic appearance, many lilies are perfectly hardy plants that will reward a little care with a long-lasting, spectacular display of flowers.

Lilies are among the most aristocratic of all garden plants, bearing their large, strikingly shaped flowers aloft on a single tall and stately stem. The flowers are often graced with exotic spots and stripes, and there are varieties in every colour bar blue.

Because lilies are so remarkably beautiful, they are considered difficult to grow, and they do generally need a little more care than more commonplace plants. But the lily family is a vast one, and far from all of its members are overly demanding. Over the last 50 years lily breeders have produced many new hybrids which are hardier and more disease-resistant than the parents, and possessed of even more magnificent flowers.

Magnificent obsession

Growing lilies is so fascinating that many gardeners become addicted, studying catalogues avidly each spring and autumn and gradually amassing large collections, featuring every lily that will flourish in their particular garden.

Although some lilies can grow very tall – the leopard lily (*Lilium pardalinum*) can exceed 2.4m/8ft – the single erect stems do not take up a lot of elbow room, so they are well suited to small gardens where they can be studied at close quarters in all their splendour. Many varieties also look well in a patio tub.

Many people are put off buying lilies because the bulbs are relatively expensive – several pounds for a single bulb in some cases. But for a small

PLANT PROFILE

Suitable site and soil
Sheltered but well-ventilated spot, usually sunny, though some prefer shade. Roots must always be in shade. Rich well-drained soil – most lilies prefer acid or neutral soil, but a few tolerate or even prefer lime.

Planting Plant in spring or autumn, as soon as possible after purchase to reduce risk of drying out. If bulbs look shrivelled, keep in moist peat for 10 days first. Work coarse grit or sand into the soil to improve drainage, if necessary. Set bulb so that tip is 2½ times its height below soil level – about 7.5cm/3in for small bulbs, 10-20cm/4-8in for larger ones. Set stem-rooting lilies more deeply, and *L. candidum* and *L. × testacum*

with the tips almost showing. Plant about 23cm/9in apart, depending on ultimate height. Mark planting spot with a stick.

Cultivation and care Mulch after planting and replace regularly. Protect newly planted lilies from frost with a covering of peat. Water in dry weather, avoiding leaves. Tall plants may need staking. Cut off the flower spike when the blooms have withered.

Propagation Divide mature plants in autumn every 3-4 years, or plant bulblets or bulbils if produced.

Pests and diseases Prone to attack by a large number of pests, fungi and viruses, but spraying at the first sign of trouble will control most of them. Use wildlife-safe pellets to deter slugs.

There is plenty of choice in lily species. L. hansonii (left) has pendent orange blooms. The white petals of L. auratum (above) are up to 18cm/7in long, while the turk's caps of L. martagon (below) are smaller. The white Madonna lily (L. candidum), yellow L. 'Citronella' and orange lily make a vibrant group (right).

DON'T FORGET!

VIRUS DISEASES

Lilies are unfortunately prone to virus disease such as lily mosaic. If possible, buy guaranteed virus-free bulbs. In the growing season, keep a sharp look out for aphids, as they spread the disease. Spray at the very first sign of them.

garden, where quality should take precedence over quantity, the expense is more than justified by the results. Besides, once they are established, most lilies will spread, and after a few years they can very easily be divided up to produce several new plants.

A historic plant

Lilies have been cultivated for literally thousands of years. One of the best known, the pure white Madonna lily (*Lilium candidum*), was almost certainly brought to Britain by the Romans, and by medieval times had become a symbol of Christianity and the special flower of the Virgin Mary. Even today it is widely used to decorate churches.

In more recent times, the lily-lover's focus has switched from Europe to Asia, and particularly to China. The famous plant hunter, Ernest Henry Wilson, found *Lilium regale* growing in an inaccessible val-

RECOMMENDED VARIETIES FOR BEGINNERS

L. hansonii (orange-yellow turk's cap)
L. henryi (yellow turk's cap)
L. martagon (rose-purple, spotted turk's cap)
L. pyrenaicum (greenish-yellow turk's cap)
L. regale (white funnels flushed pink)
L. lancifolium, previously *L. tigrinum* (orange-red turk's cap)
'Black Dragon' (trumpets, white inside, dark red outside)
'Bright Star' (white cups with orange stripe)
'Casablanca' (large white cups)
'Citronella' (lemon to golden yellow)
'Connecticut King' (bright yellow cups)
'Enchantment' (orange-red cups with black spots)
'Green Dragon' (white cups streaked brown and green outside)
'Harlequin' strain (all colours)
'Pink Perfection' (pink trumpets)
'Star Gazer' (crimson-red with white border)

ley in tens of thousands – its heady fragrance must have been overpowering.

The nodding, scarlet turk's cap blooms of L. pumilum, previously known as L. tenuifolium (right) are among the smallest of all true lily flowers.

Fascinating flowers

There is a tremendous variation in lily flowers. Although always recognizable as lilies, they appear in no less than six different shapes.

Those that have bell-shaped flowers, such as *L. nanum*, have petals that are either straight or curve inwards towards the tips. In bowl-shaped flowers (*L. auratum*, for exam-

INCREASING YOUR INVESTMENT

After a few years, if all goes well, your lilies should have spread into a large clump. To increase your stock, dig the clump up in autumn, and break it apart into groups of bulbs. Replant immediately, so that the bulbs will have time to grow new roots before winter comes.

If your lily produces bulbils in the leaf axils, or bulblets on the underground stem, detach these in autumn and replant immediately in a nursery bed. Keep them there for two years before moving to permanent quarters.

GROWING TIPS

Many years of work by dedicated lily lovers have produced some truly spectacular varieties and hybrids. The tiger lily (L. lancifolium *syn.* L. tigrinum), *with its large, spotted turk's cap flowers, has long been a favourite; the variety* L. l. splendens *(above) has even bigger flowers in a brighter shade of orange.*

The golden yellow cups of the hybrid 'Connecticut King' (left) are held aloft on stems some 1m/3ft high with their faces to the sun.

PERFECT PARTNERS

The pale, shapely blooms of the Madonna lily are an excellent foil for colourful border plants. Here they set off the pale pinks and yellows of *Alstroemeria* Ligtu hybrid.

ple), the petals are more widely spaced and slightly recurved or reflexed (that is, rolled back) at the tips.

Cup- or star-shaped flowers, as in the hybrid 'Bright Star', are similar but more compact, and may or may not roll back at the tips. *L. regale* has funnel-shaped flowers. These are more tubular, flaring out towards the mouth. Trumpet-shaped flowers, like those of the popular Easter lily (*L. longiflorum*) are the same but longer and narrower.

Perhaps the best-known flower form is the turk's cap or martagon type, with strongly recurved petals – sometimes so much so that the flower becomes actually ball shaped and the long, graceful stamens are fully exposed.

This is not the end of the lily flowers' variety. While some are pendent, nodding their heads to the ground, others point outwards, or upwards to face the sun.

Many lilies add to their attractiveness with a rich fragrance, although some, such as *L. pyrenaicum*, actually smell rather unpleasant.

Most lilies flower in midsummer, but some flower earlier or later, so it is perfectly possible to have a succession of lilies blooming in your garden for almost half the year.

The flowers are produced at the top of a single upright stem, grouped in pairs or bunches. The number of flowers can be up to 50 or more, and they appear over a period of several weeks. They vary in size from the modest 2.5cm/1in blooms of *L. pumilum* to those produced by the golden-rayed lily (*L. auratum*), which can reach 30cm/12in across. Lily leaves are stalkless and relatively insignificant, growing in whorls or scattered evenly up the stem.

True and false lilies
All true lilies – members of the genus *Lilium* – grow from bulbs. This distinguishes them

LILIES IN CONTAINERS

Growing lilies in containers means that you can put them somewhere inconspicuous while they are developing, and move them into the limelight when in flower. Do not forget, though, that very large containers become too heavy to move once filled with compost.

Container growing also means that you have full control over the type of soil, and the position, to suit the lily's needs.

Add interest by planting a small companion plant around the lily – this will help keep the bulbs cool by shading the soil. Choose small annuals in a colour that complements the lily. Use white flowers, or grey-leaved plants such as senecio, to cool down a very brightly coloured lily.

GROWING TIPS

from plants like arum lily (*Zantedeschia*) and day lily (*Hemerocallis*). The bulbs are different from ordinary ones like those of the daffodil, having no papery covering, and consisting of a large number of fleshy scales.

Like the flowers, the bulb shapes vary – some are round and some shaped like the rhizome of an iris, while others produce chains of round bulbs linked by stolons.

Many lilies produce bulblets on the underground part of the stem, just above the bulb. A few produce bulbils where the leaves join the stem. Both can be used for propagation.

Where to plant

Lilies can be grown in many parts of the garden. Those that like full sun thrive in herbaceous or mixed borders, or in tubs. Those that prefer dappled shade are excellent for planting under trees, or can be used among shrubs to provide

The funnel-shaped flowers of L. regale *are pink in bud, but open to a dazzling white (far left).*

'Enchantment' (left) has become a popular cut flower in recent years. Very like the tiger lily in colour, it is distinguished by its upturned, cup-shaped flower form.

The flowers of L. pyrenaicum *are lovely to look at (below left), but many find their scent unpleasant.*

Cardiocrinum giganteum (below), sold as a giant lily, produces a tall, flamboyant flower spike, then the bulb dies, producing offsets that will flower again in five years.

LILY CLASSIFICATIONS

Botanists divide the vast family of lilies into nine groups. The largest contains all the original species lilies found growing wild in different parts of the world, many of which are hardy and easily grown. The other eight contain the huge number (over 3,500 registered!) of hybrids – some hardy, some tender – which have developed by crossing and recrossing the species plants. The six main groups readily available to gardeners are listed below.

● **Asiatic hybrids** are generally compact, no more than 1.2m/4ft high. Many are unfussy as to soil and aspect. The Mid-century hybrids contained within this group are especially easy.

● **Martagon and *L. hansonii* hybrids** all have small, pendent, turk's cap flowers and do best in partial shade.

● **Candidum and *L. chalcedonicum* hybrids** have long, pendent, trumpet-shaped flowers.

● **Bellingham hybrids** do best on acid soil in semi-shade.

● **Trumpet and Aurelian hybrids** mostly have large, trumpet-shaped flowers. They prefer rich, lime-free soil and semi-shade.

● **Oriental hybrids** have striking white, crimson or pink flowers, but may not be quite so hardy as others; they are good subjects for tubs in the sun.

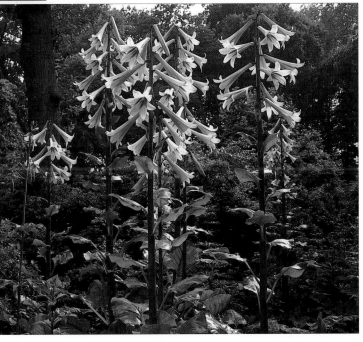

colour when these have finished flowering.

Plant lilies singly or in groups of three, in a spot where they can be admired at close quarters – though of course the really tall ones will need to go in the back of a border. If you grow several varieties, for the best effect keep them apart from one another.

Secrets of success

It is best to buy lily bulbs from specialist nurseries by mail order. They are normally des-

patched between autumn and spring – if the ground is frozen, plunge the bulbs into moist peat and wait. It is best not to choose a lily just for its looks – you **must** be able to give it the right conditions.

Most lilies offered by nurseries thrive in free-draining but not dry soil – work coarse sand or grit into heavier soils before planting lilies – and in sun or partial shade. Make sure that those preferring alkaline or acid soils get what they want – plant them in tubs if necess-

ary. Good air circulation is needed, to avoid fungal infection – but strong winds can badly damage the plants.

Observe the recommended planting depth exactly, and mark the spot with a stick so that you remember where they are. (Also do this when the stems die down in autumn, so there is no risk of digging up or damaging the precious bulbs while they are dormant.)

In winter, avoid frost damage to lilies in borders by mulching thickly with peat; bring containers into a frost-free shed. Protect bulbs from snails and slugs, and keep watch for aphids, which can spread virus diseases.

SUPERLILY

Some lily nurseries also offer *Cardiocrinum giganteum*, a species of giant lily. The bulbs are among the most expensive, but a giant lily in full flower is a real talking point. The stem grows to 2.4m/8ft high or more, and each one can carry 25 flowers. These are 15-20cm/6-8in long, pure white trumpets, striped reddish purple inside, and give way to decorative seed heads.

GARDEN NOTES

HYACINTHS

Sweet-smelling hyacinths bring spring colour to the garden and can banish the drabness of winter from normally flowerless rooms.

Of all the spring bulbs, hyacinths are perhaps the most widely used for indoor cultivation, providing bold colour and a sweet, pervasive fragrance from Christmas to Easter when grown indoors in bowls or pots. But these versatile performers can also give fine displays in outdoor beds or in window-boxes and tubs through the spring. Indeed, they may start their lives as indoor plants, perhaps as Christmas gifts, and go on to give many years of pleasure in the garden.

For most people, the image of the hyacinth that will most immediately spring to mind is that of the tubular-flowered hybrids commonly known as Dutch hyacinths, varieties of *Hyacinthus orientalis*. This large bulb produces a single, heavily-scented flower spike 10-15cm/4-6in long. This spike is tightly packed with small, bell-shaped flowers.

Varieties of Dutch hyacinth can be purchased in a wide range of clear colours: its blooms may be white, cream, yellow, pink, red or blue. New varieties and shades appear every year.

Left to their own devices in the garden, Dutch hyacinths will flower from mid to late spring, although they can be persuaded to flower earlier indoors by a technique known as 'forcing'. Special, treated bulbs which can be forced into flower by Christmas are also widely

Hyacinths are famed for their sweet scent and vivid colour, especially shades of blue. H. 'Ostara' (right) verges on indigo.

PLANT PROFILE

Suitable site and soil Both Dutch hyacinths and grape hyacinths will grow in full sun or light shade, in well-drained soil.

Planting Plant Dutch hyacinths 15cm/6in deep in early to mid autumn. Grape hyacinths should be planted at the same time, but at half the depth.

Cultivation and care They need little care during the growing season except for water in dry spells. After flowering, remove dead blooms but leave the stalk intact. Leaves and flower stems should be left to wither and die naturally.

Propagation Prepare Dutch hyacinths by slitting the base of the bulb two or three times with a sharp knife in the autumn before planting. This encourages the growth of small offsets which may later be separated and planted out. Prepared bulbs cannot be propagated.

Grape hyacinths seed themselves rapidly: alternatively, lift and divide them every three years when the foliage has yellowed.

Pests and diseases Stem and bulb eelworm causes pale stripes on leaves, followed by twisted growth and deformed flowers and leaves. Infested bulbs are soft and may have a white woolly substance on the base. Healthy bulbs from reputable sources are usually grown in sterilized soil. Infested bulbs must be dug up and destroyed. Soft rot bacteria can occasionally attack pot-grown hyacinths. Flowers fail to develop and topple over at soil level while still in bud. This is precipitated by moist, humid conditions. Beware of over-watering.

Hyacinths are usually sold and planted in single colours. If you want a multi-coloured display in flower at the same time, buy a collection such as 'Multiflora Mixed' (above).

The Roman hyacinth (H. orientalis albulus) is smaller than the species but produces two or three headily fragrant, loosely packed, flower spikes. 'Rosalie' (right) is a good pink variety; others are blue or white. Dutch hyacinths such as the rich pink 'Jan Bos' (below) have a single, more compact spike.

available in garden centres.

A smaller subspecies, the Roman hyacinth (*H. orientalis albulus*) produces two or three flower spikes 15cm/6in high. These are thinner than those of the species, with fewer, more widely-spaced and stronger-scented white, pink or blue flowers. Like all hyacinths, it is frost hardy, but it does best when grown indoors and is the easiest of the varieties to force.

Outdoors, it will flower slightly earlier than the Dutch hyacinth; indoors, any time

CHRISTMAS BLOOMS

If you want your bulbs to be in flower for Christmas it is essential to buy specially prepared bulbs. These are widely available in garden centres from late summer and the same instructions apply as for untreated bulbs, but the pots should be brought in when shoots are 2.5cm/1in high, not later than the beginning of winter.

GARDEN NOTES

301

RECOMMENDED VARIETIES

Dutch Hyacinth All share the same characteristics of size and shape and differ mainly by their colour. There are several in differing shades of pink, ranging from the pale pink 'Lady Derby', and the slightly darker 'Pink Pearl' to the crimson 'Jan Bos'. 'L'Innocence' is a creamy white and 'City of Haarlem' a pale yellow. At the other end of the spectrum come the delicate pale blues of 'Bismark' and 'Delft Blue', and the striking indigo 'Ostara'.

Grape Hyacinths Most commonly available are *Muscari azureum* (also known as *Hyacinthus azureus*), which has clear blue flowers, darker towards the base of the spike, and *Muscari armenaicum*, which has pale blue flowers tipped with white. It can often also be found in the white form 'Album'. Both grow to a height of about 20cm/8in.

Muscari latifolium is sometimes seen. This is slightly larger (25cm/10in), and its long, two-tone flower is a deep blackish-violet, topped by a smaller layer of bright blue petals. The rather odd-looking tassel or feather hyacinth (*Muscari comosum*), as its name suggests, looks something like a feather duster. It is most often available in a form known as 'Plumosum' or 'Monstrosum', which has light, pinkish-blue flowers and grows to around 30cm/12in.

from midwinter to early spring.

The very large-bulbed Multiflora hyacinth produces nine to twelve 15cm/6in flower stalks per bulb, with blooms in shades of white, pink or blue. Like the Roman hyacinth, it does best indoors, where it has the same flowering season.

Grape hyacinths

The smaller plants known as grape hyacinths belong to a different, but closely related genus of bulb, *Muscari*. However, with their tightly-packed flower spikes, they are suffi-ciently reminiscent of their larger cousin to merit their common name. In most species the petals of the individual flowers curve in, rather than out, giving them narrow mouths. Colours range from white through various shades of blue to a deep bluish purple which is almost black; only some species are fragrant.

Fast growers

Grape hyacinths are easy to grow and look their best in groups at the front of borders or as edging to mixed beds. They are also ideal rock garden plants and do well in tubs and window-boxes. The many different varieties can be seen in flower any time from early spring to midsummer.

Their only drawback is the speed with which they proliferate, especially *Muscari neglectum* syn. *Muscari race-mosum*, which is really only suitable for wilder parts of the

Planting mixed colour schemes (right) can be problematical because different varieties can flower a few days, even weeks apart. Here, 'Delft Blue' is fully mature, while the white spikes of 'L'Innocence' have yet to emerge completely from the green.

As with most other Dutch hyacinths, the leaves of 'Pink Pearl' (left) do not develop fully until after the plant has flowered.

'City of Haarlem' (left) has a distinct, pale yellow tint.

Varieties of the grape hyacinth Muscari armenaicum such as 'Blue Spike' (right) have a distinctive white fringe around the flower openings.

garden. With other species, divide and replant bulbs every three years after the leaves have turned yellow at the end of the growing season.

Rocky origins

The species form of *Hyacinthus orientalis*, which resembles the modern Roman hyacinth, is a native of western Asia, where it can be found growing amongst the rocks. The numerous wild varieties of grape hyacinths are also found in scrubby, rocky areas of western Asia and the eas-

RECYCLING HOUSE PLANTS

After a forced hyacinth has flowered, remove the dead heads by running a hand up the stem from the base of the flower spike. Do not cut off the stalk. Continue watering until the leaves have withered and died down, then allow the compost to dry out, remove the bulbs and, having picked off any dried compost, dead roots or foliage, store in a cool, dry place until the autumn, when they may be planted out in the garden, with a little slow-acting fertilizer, such as bone meal, worked into the soil.

Bulbs grown in compost will often flower outdoors during their first spring, but those grown in bulb fibre will need more time to recover. Neither can be brought in and used again as houseplants.

GROWING TIPS

FORCING

Hyacinths can be made to flower indoors from midwinter. Bulbs for forcing should be potted up at the end of the summer. They can be planted singly in 10-12cm/4-5in pots but look best when planted together in larger pots or bowls. Whatever you choose, make sure the bulb has room to develop roots. It is not a good idea to mix colours in containers as it is difficult to bring all of the colours into flower together.

In pots without drainage holes, a special bulb fibre should be used. For those with drainage holes, use a good potting compost – John Innes No. 1 or No. 2 would be fine.

Place a layer of moist compost or very moist (but not sodden) bulb fibre at the bottom of the container and set the bulbs on it, close together but not touching. Press them down very gently so that their bases are in firm contact with the compost. Making sure that they remain steadily upright, continue adding compost until the tops of the bulbs are just showing.

They now need about six to ten weeks of complete darkness in a temperature of not more than 5°C/40°F. Commercial growers bury them under peat until they are rooted and it is quite possible to do this at home, but it is just as effective to place the container in a black polythene bag and stand it in a cool corner of the garden. Check the bulbs occasionally to ensure the compost is still moist, but take care not to over-water.

When the shoot tips are around 2.5-5cm/1-2in high, bring the bowl indoors into a cool place (not more than 10°C/50°F), gradually increasing the amount of light and raising the temperature as more shoots appear.

As the leaves develop and flower buds appear, move the container to a bright, draught-free site around 15-20°C/60-70°F. Keep the compost moist at all times and turn the bowl occasionally to make sure you get even growth.

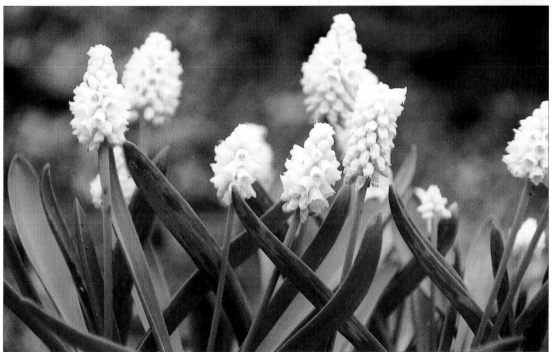

Far and away the most unusual plant in the hyacinth group is the tassel grape hyacinth (Muscari comosum 'Plumosum' syn. 'Monstrosum'), whose sterile flowers are superseded by a mass of purple threads (above). More conventionally shaped, but a startlingly clear white, is M. azureum 'Album' (left). The most vigorous member of the genus, though, is the deep blue M. neglectum syn. M. racemosum (right), which self-seeds rapidly and will soon take over a formal planting; it is best used in a semi-wild setting.

PERFECT PARTNERS

Hyacinths do not always suit companion planting. However, H. 'L'Innocence' is at home among the pink blooms of the low-growing double daisy Bellis perennis *'Rose Carpet'.*

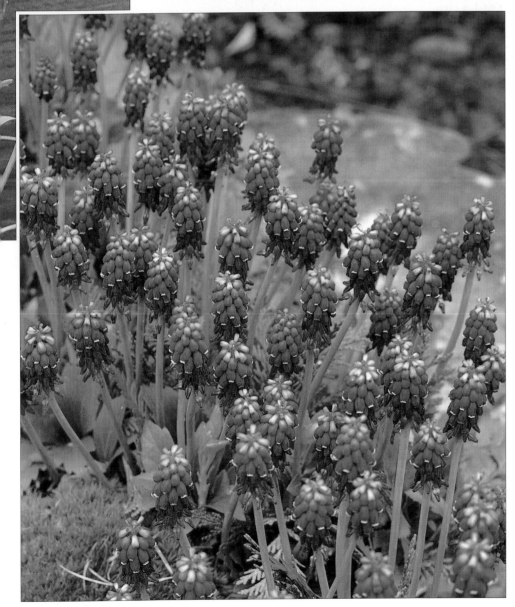

tern Mediterranean.

Given their origins, it is not surprising that both will flourish best in open, sunny situations with well-drained soil, although both will also tolerate partial shade, which will in fact extend their flowering period for a month or so.

Buying hyacinths

Dutch hyacinth bulbs are usually sold by size. For outdoor planting it is advisable to buy the smaller sized bulbs (16-17cm in circumference). The flower heads may not be as big, but they will be better able to withstand the squally weather of early spring.

For outside flowering, both hyacinth and grape hyacinth bulbs should be planted in early or mid autumn. Both look their best planted in small clumps rather than standing in rows like well-drilled soldiers, and both blend very well with daffodils.

Hyacinths should be planted to a depth of 15cm/6in and spaced 15-20cm/6-8in apart, and grape hyacinths to a depth of 8cm/3in, 10cm/4in apart. Some well-rotted compost or peat dug into the site a few days before planting will get your bulbs off to a good start.

HYACINTH JARS

Single hyacinths are often grown in glass bulb jars, which are sold in most gardening shops. The jar should be filled with water to a point just below the base of the bulb (*not* touching it). A small piece of charcoal in the bottom of the jar will help to keep the water fresh.

The jar should be kept in a cool, dark place until the roots are about 10cm/4in long and the leaves have begun to show, when it should be moved into a warmer and lighter spot.

Make sure the jar is kept topped up with water to the required level. Water-grown bulbs should be discarded at the end of their growing season as they will not flower again.

CLEMATIS

The clematis genus contains many of the very best climbing plants, producing attractive flowers in an enormous variety of shapes and colours.

If ever a plant deserved the title 'Queen of Climbers', clematis does. This handsome genus of plants offers literally hundreds of gorgeous varieties. The choice of flower colour ranges from subtle, pastel shades of pink, blue and mauve, to the more regal hues of crimson, magenta and purple. Rich creams are available, as are stunning whites and vibrant yellows.

Some varieties produce an abundance of small, delicate, single or double blooms, while others have fewer, but more imposing flowers. Some have seed heads so beautiful that they are much sought after for flower arrangements.

Clever clematis

The clematis family can supply a glorious climber suitable for virtually any site. Exposed, chilly, north-facing walls are absolutely no problem to *C. alpina* or *C. macropetala* varieties, for example, while an ugly shed, wall or outbuilding can soon be camouflaged by any member of the vigorous *C. montana* branch of the family.

Clematis will clothe and soften the outlines of arches and pergolas with enchanting displays of flowers. By selecting your varieties carefully, you can have blooms from spring to autumn.

Trees and shrubs whose interest is limited to early spring need not be an embarrassment for the rest of the season. You can grow a clematis through them. The varieties

The early summer blooms of 'Nelly Moser' are best in semi-shade; the carmine stripe fades in full sun.

PLANT PROFILE

Suitable site and soil Likes a deep, moist, cool root run. Will thrive in almost any good quality garden soil. Sandy or chalky soils must have plenty of organic matter added to help retain moisture. Do not plant too near to thirsty hedges (especially privet) or trees as these will rob the clematis of moisture. Clematis appreciates a bit of lime, but it is not essential.

Planting Container grown clematis may be planted at any time as long as the soil retains some warmth. Early autumn or late spring are best.

Cultivation and care When, where and how to prune depends on the variety; read the instructions carefully when you buy.

Clematis must be fed regularly with a liquid fertilizer in the growing season. In autumn, mulch with farmyard manure or work in bone meal around the stem.

Propagation Cuttings are best left to the professional. Layering in summer is an easier method. Fill a 10-15cm/4-6in flowerpot with cutting compost and sink into the ground a little away from the parent so you do not damage roots. Bend a young shoot until it touches the soil in the pot. Make a slit upwards from below a leaf node, and dust it with hormone rooting powder. Cover with soil and clip into place with a bent piece of wire. Cover with a stone or slate to keep pot moist and cool. Keep pot damp. Sever the young plant from the parent the following spring and plant in the usual way.

Pests and diseases Clematis wilt tends to attack young plants. Remove and destroy infected stems immediately. With luck new stems will form. Spraying the leaves and soaking the immediate root area with a benomyl fungicide will help to protect new growth. If you lose your plant, replace the surface soil at the site and grow a different variety. If the trouble persists, plant a species clematis in new soil, as they are less susceptible than cultivated varieties.

Mildew may be a problem, especially to some hybrids. Spray with a proprietary fungicide.

C. jackmanii and *C. viticella* are useful for this. *C. montana* is a particularly handy choice if you wish to cover a large tree or to disguise a dead one.

Clematis can be used as ground cover. Once again *C. montana* may be called into service. Other suitable subjects are varieties of *C. alpina*, *C. macropetala*, *C. orientalis* and *C. tangutica*. Any of these plants also look lovely if allowed to tumble down a bank. There are even a few herba-

ceous species suitable for the mixed border, including *C. integrifolia* and *C. recta*.

Flowering types

There are so many species and varieties of clematis that it is useful to split them into three groups, depending on the season when they flower, their growing habit and their pruning requirements.

The first group includes the *Clematis montana* varieties, along with *C. macropetala* and

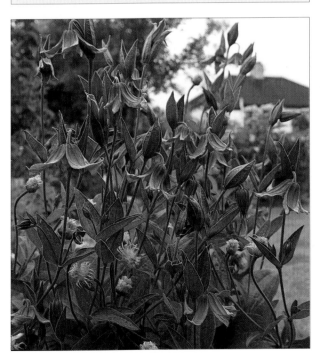

There is great variety in the shapes, as well as the colours, of clematis flowers. The late flowering, pendulous, golden yellow blooms of C. tangutica (above) have a lantern shape, while the summer flowers of the herbaceous, late-flowering C. integrifolia (left) are deep blue bells. These are succeeded later in the year by very attractive, light-brown seed heads. The most readily recognizable of all clematis flower forms, though, are the abundant, flat, single blooms of C. montana (right) which appear in late spring.

C. alpina. All are vigorous, fully hardy, and produce masses of blooms in late spring. Pruning should be restricted to merely tidying up the plant. Dead flower heads and stems should be removed immediately after flowering so the new growth ripens before winter.

C. montana 'Elizabeth' can reach a height of 10-12m/30-40ft and bears soft pink, scented flowers, while *C. m.* 'Tetrarose' is a stronger, satin pink variety that reaches a height of 7-8m/23-26ft.

Macropetala and alpina varieties are good looking and very hardy. *C. macropetala* 'Markham's Pink' has delicate, bell-shaped flowers in a glorious dusky pink. It grows to a height of 3m/10ft and blooms appear in late spring and summer. It is a suitable clematis for a small garden.

C. alpina 'Frances Rivis' is a lovely bell-shaped variety in a mid-blue colour. 'Ruby' has purplish-pink blooms. They are free flowering in spring with an occasional second flush in summer. The delicate, fluffy, silver seed heads are produced in the summer months. These varieties also suit small gardens, reaching a height of 2-3m/6-10ft.

Early flowers

The second group includes early flowering, frost hardy subjects. These should be pruned back to the lowest pair of strong buds in their first season, so that growth is more vigorous. In subsequent seasons, pruning should be restricted to removing dead growth only, because the flowers are only produced on the previous year's stems.

'Nelly Moser' is an old favourite in this group. It produces large, single, flat rose coloured flowers that have a carmine stripe on each petal. Blooms appear in early summer on plants that reach a height of 3.5m/11ft. The flower colours fade in strong sunlight so it is best to plant these in a shaded east, west or north facing site.

'Proteus' has wide, double mauve-pink flowers. This handsome variety produces blooms in early summer and a second flush of single flowers later in the season. It reaches

---

RECOMMENDED VARIETIES

'Crimson King'. Height 2.4-3m/8-10ft. Has large, striking, clear crimson flowers in summer and autumn.

C. alpina 'Willy'. Height 2-3m/6-10ft. Has delicate white, lantern-shaped flowers in abundance in spring. Flowers have an attractive pinkish flush at the base. Suits north facing and exposed sites.

'Elsa Späth'. Height 2-3m/6-10ft. Has masses of deep mauve-blue, single flowers throughout summer.

C. montana 'Elizabeth' reaches a height of 10-12m/30-40ft and bears soft pink, scented flowers.

C. macropetala 'Markham's Pink' has delicate, bell-shaped dusky pink flowers and grows to a height of 3m/10ft.

'Nelly Moser' has large, single, flat, rose coloured flowers with a carmine stripe on each petal. It reaches a height of 3.5m/11ft.

C. orientalis has deep yellow, bell-shaped flowers between late summer and autumn. Grows to 3-6m/10-20ft and requires hard pruning early in the year.

'Vyvyan Pennell' is one of the best doubles. Has lavender or violet flowers with magnificent, golden yellow anthers. Height 2.4-3m/8-10ft.

The alpine clematis (C. alpina) is the best choice for very exposed sites. The blooms of 'Frances Rivis' (above left) are enhanced by a cluster of white stamens – looking very much like petals – in the centre.

'Vyvyan Pennell' produces large, double flowers (above) in early summer, followed by a later flush of single, slightly darker blooms.

The semi-double blooms of C. macropetala are small, just 5cm/2in across, but make up in numbers what they lack in size (above right).

The yellow flowers of C. orientalis (right) appear in late summer.

a height of 2.4-3m/8-10ft.

'Rouge Cardinale' flowers on new wood only, so it needs hard pruning every year. This lovely variety produces masses of velvety, crimson, single flowers in summer and makes an excellent subject for small gardens, growing to a height of 2.4-3m/8-10ft.

'Henryi' is a vigorous plant that boasts lovely, white, single flowers with handsome, chocolate coloured anthers that contrast well with the petals. Flowers appear in summer on a plant that reaches a height of 3m/10ft.

Spring pruning

The third group produces large, flattish flowers in late summer and early autumn. All

'Proteus' is another variety which has a first flush of double flowers with a greenish tint to the outer petals (left), followed by a second of single blooms.

One of the more unusual forms of clematis is C. florida 'Sieboldii' (right), whose flat, star-shaped blooms resemble those of the passion flower. The petals, usually described as creamy-white, can have a green flush, as here, and the central mound is made up of stamens which mature from green to purple.

The crimson petals of 'Rouge Cardinal' (below) have a lovely, soft, velvety texture.

are frost hardy. This group is dominated by 'Jackmanii' varieties. It is very important to prune these annually because the flowers are borne on new growth. For best results, cut them back to the lowest two or three strong buds on each stem in early spring.

C. viticella 'Purpurea Plena Elegans' is a gorgeous variety with double, rose-purple flowers that form tight rosettes. Sometimes the outer petals are green. It reaches a height of 3-4m/10-12ft.

'Jackmanii Superba' grows to about the same height. A vigorous plant, it has large, single, deep purple blooms.

C. florida 'Sieboldii' is really only suitable for a very shel-tered site as it is a bit weak and tender. What it lacks in vigour it makes up for in beauty, however. The flowers are creamy white, with rich, purple stamens. It reaches a height of 2-3m/6-10ft.

Caring for clematis

Clematis like a deep, rich, moist and cool root run. Although they will thrive in almost any good quality, well-cultivated garden soil, good preparation is essential if you want your plant to flower profusely and live long.

Dig a hole 45cm/18in square and deep. Fork over the subsoil at the base and add two or three handfuls of bone meal. Next, add a fairly generous layer of well-rooted manure. Then fill the hole with a mixture of rich garden compost or John Innes No 3, some peat or peat substitute and sand.

Place the crown 5-8cm/2-3in below soil level, burying the first pair of leaves or nodes. Top off with tiles, stones or a thick mulch to keep roots cool and to retain moisture.

Feeding time

Clematis are hungry plants and it pays to feed them regularly as they will soon exhaust the nutrients provided at

HOT HEADS

Many clematis like their feet in the shade and their heads in the sun. All of them like cool roots; place tiles, stones or slates around the stems to keep the ground cool.

Although it is not essential for their well-being, clematis like lime. Covering the roots with a piece of limestone allows some of the mineral to leech into the ground.

GROWING TIPS

planting. Mulch with farmyard manure in autumn or work in some bone meal around the stem. Provide sulphate of potash in spring and feed with a liquid fertilizer every two weeks during the growing season.

Make sure that your plant never goes thirsty by watering during dry spells and by providing a good, thick layer of mulch to prevent the evaporation of precious water from the soil when the sun shines.

Support your clematis

Clematis require support. They do not attach themselves to walls the way ivy does, but twine, so they need something to twine around, either another, preferably woody, plant or an artificial support.

When you wish to clothe a wall or fence, use a trellis or a framework of 23cm/9in squares made with plastic covered wire. Make sure that there is a gap of 1cm/½in between the support and the wall. When planting, allow a gap of at least 30cm/1ft between the clematis and the wall.

If you want a clematis to scramble through a tree, plant it outside the overhang of the branches on the north side.

Bridge the gap between your clematis and the wall or tree with a cane, placed at an angle, so that the plant may twine its way along it to its permanent support.

PERFECT PARTNERS

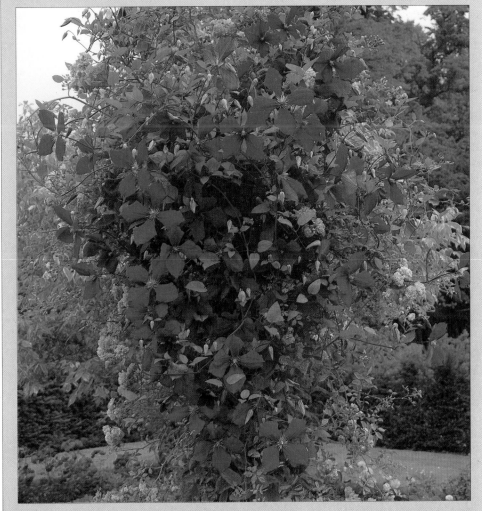

The twining habit of clematis makes them adept at climbing through other plants. Here, *C.* 'Jackmanii Superba' is supported by a double shrub rose.

CHRYSANTHEMUMS

From tiny alpines to cottagey daisies and the handsome blooms of the show tents, chrysanthemums give us an outstanding range of flower forms and colours.

As summer beds begin to fade, the chrysanthemums come into their own. From late summer right through to the onset of winter, these magnificent plants provide a spectrum of brilliant colour that echoes the flaming hues of autumn.

Their enormous popularity is well earned. The diversity of flower shape and size from the huge, flawless globes nurtured for exhibition to the small, smiling daisy-like faces at the edge of a border, is exceptional, while their long flowering season and lasting blooms ensure a continuing array of almost every imaginable colour and hue. Chrysanthemums will grace borders, tubs and window boxes, as well as making good indoor pot plants.

Eastern origins

Chrysanthemums have been cultivated and admired in the Orient since 500 B.C., but it was not until late in the 18th century that they first came to Europe, brought from China by a French navigator.

In 1843, the Royal Horticultural Society sent the famous plant collector, Robert Fortune, to the Far East in search of new species, and some of his discoveries became the forebears of many of today's modern chrysanthemums.

The cultivation of modern varieties for exhibition is an exciting and all-consuming passion for a large number of enthusiasts, professional and amateur alike. These plants, though, are only part of a very large and diverse group.

The genus has been broken

up in recent years, with species allocated to new genera, particularly dendranthema, but, since these are not yet in common usage, we shall still love them as chrysanthemums. All have their individual virtues and delights, and all merit a place in our gardens.

The modern garden varieties give us the greatest range of flower shapes and vibrant, jewel-like colours. They are classified according to the time at which they flower: early-flowering varieties bloom from late summer; late-flowering from the middle of autumn.

Late-flowering varieties are grown in pots, standing outside during the summer then being brought in to flower in the greenhouse. In temperate climates, only the early flowers will bloom successfully in the garden.

Flower forms

Modern chrysanthemums are also classified by the form and size of the flower and whether they are borne singly or in sprays (see box page 316).

Large blooms are achieved

PLANT PROFILE

Suitable site and soil Fertile, well-drained soil, in sun and with some shelter from winds for the taller varieties. Alpines prefer a gritty soil.
Planting Plant early-flowering varieties at the end of spring, adding plenty of humus to the site. Plant hardy perennials and alpines between September and April. Always give the root balls a good soaking before transplanting.
Cultivation and care Taller chrysanthemums need support in the form of canes or peasticks. Mulch early-flowering varieties in summer to help retain moisture, and water once a week unless rainy weather does this for you. Pinch out the growing tips of early-flowering and perennial varieties when about 15-20cm/6-8in tall to encourage lateral growths.

After flowering, cut hardy perennials back to ground level in early winter. Cut early-flowering varieties down to about 20cm/8in from the ground in autumn, right after flowering. The remaining stem and roots (known as the 'stool') must be lifted for storage in damp compost over the winter. Encourage new growth of stools after Christmas by providing a little warmth and moisture.
Propagation For early-flowering varieties, take basal cuttings from the stools towards the end of winter, and encourage rooting in a propagator. Established hardy perennials should be divided in autumn after flowering or in early spring. Take cuttings of alpines in early to mid-summer, root in a cold frame, then pot up in autumn. Seeds of annuals are sown on-site in spring and thinned out as required. *C. frutescens* is increased by cuttings of non-flowering side-shoots taken in early autumn or February and planted out after frost.
Pests and diseases These unfortunately seem to like chrysanthemums just as much as we do. Problems include aphids, leaf miners, slugs, snails and caterpillars, frog hoppers, earwigs, chrysanthemum viruses, mildew, leafy gall, leaf spot, verticillium wilt and rust. A system of regular spraying should go a long way towards guarding against such unwelcome guests.

The public face of the chrysanthemum is represented by the extravagant blooms of the modern varieties (left), seen on the show bench or in florists.

'Pennine Gambol' (above) is anemone-centred, with several layers of ray florets surrounding a large, raised centre.

Korean chrysanthemums, like many others, are now classified as members of the genus Dendranthema. However, despite their obvious charms, few varieties are offered for sale under any name. 'Raquel' (right) is a rare exception.

through disbudding: all but four or five flower buds are nipped out, so all the plant's energy is channelled into producing sizeable blooms on stems reaching 1-1.5m/3-5ft in height. Though mostly grown for cutting or exhibiting, the reflexed form is excellent in the garden, shedding the rain from its downward-curving petals or florets. 'Brietner' is a lovely pink variety; 'Bruera' a superb white.

Spray and pompon chrysanthemums bring an invaluable abundance of smaller flowers to borders, and provide some of the best cut flowers for the home. They are generally shorter and bushier plants (though sprays can grow to

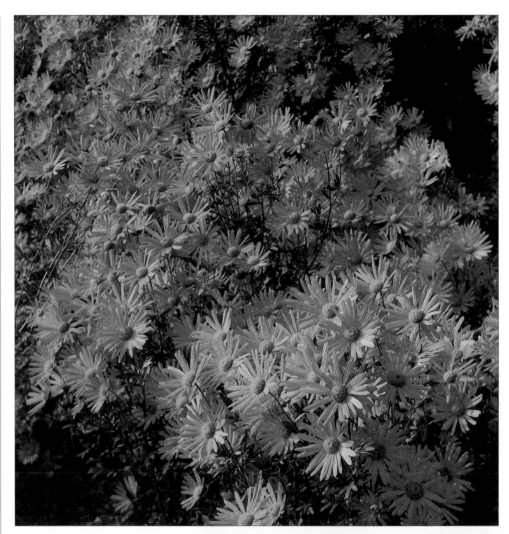

RECOMMENDED VARIETIES

Nurseries have to make their selections from a vast number of varieties cultivated today. Consequently, you will have to make your own choices from those available to you locally or by post. Here are some you may find without too much difficulty.

Early-flowering Reflexed: 'Brietner' (pink); 'Bruera' (white); 'Alice Jones' (light bronze); 'Yvonne Arnaud' (cerise).

Intermediate: 'Bill Wade' (white); 'Ginger Nut' (light red-bronze). Sprays: 'Margaret' (pink double); 'Lemon Margaret' (pale yellow double); 'Pennine Gambol' (pink anemone); 'Pennine Tango' (bronze single). Pompons: 'Bronze Fairie' (bronze); 'Cameo' (white); 'Jante Wells' (yellow). Also, do try the very rewarding Korean hybrids.

Hardy perennials *Chrysanthemum rubellum* (syn. *D. Zawadskii*): 'Clara Curtis' (clear pink); 'Mary Stoker' (soft yellow); 'Duchess of Edinburgh' (bright crimson). Shasta daisy (*C. maximum*, syn. *Leucanthemum* × *superbum*): 'Wirral Supreme' and 'Esther Read' (double white); 'Phyllis Smith' (fringed white petals with almost shredded effect); 'Snowcap' (small variety, to about 45cm/1½ft).

Annuals Marguerite (*C. frutescens*, syn. *Argyranthemum frutescens*): 'Jamaica Primrose' (soft yellow); 'Mary Wootton' (pink). Feverfew (*C. parthenium*, syn. *Tanacetum parthenium*): 'Aureum' (white flowers and gold-tinted foliage).

1.2m/4ft) and are not disbudded since their beauty lies in the sheer number of flowers.

The sprays have various flower forms, while pompoms bear small, globe- or button-shaped blooms. Together they offer a kaleidoscopic range of colours, from the single bronze flowers of the spray variety, 'Pennine Tango', to the pink,

anemone-centred sprays of 'Pennine Gambol' and the yellow pompons of 'Jante Wells'.

Korean chrysanthemums are, sadly, not easily found nowadays but are well worth looking for, since they continue to provide colour when the early-flowering varieties are starting to look a little battered. They are bushy plants, growing to about 60cm/2ft and clothed in sprays of small flowers in gorgeous hues.

All these varieties need to be lifted and stored away from damaging frosts. There are species, however, which are fully hardy and happy to remain in the garden throughout the year.

Daisy flowers

Chrysanthemum C. rubellum (now *D. zawadskii*) is compact and bushy, about 45-75cm/1½-2½ft in height, and

The clear pink single blooms of C. rubellum (or Dendranthema) 'Clara Curtis' (left) are so abundant, the dense, bushy foliage almost disappears.

The feverfew (C. parthenium) is a perennial usually treated as an annual. Here (below) it is growing through a clump of irises.

At the other end of the floral spectrum from the showy modern varieties is the tiny alpine C. hosmariense (right above).

The pyrethrums may be found as C. coccineum, Pyrethrum roseum or Tanacetum coccineum. The species is not encountered, but the colourful hybrids (right) are a staple of summer flower beds.

The marguerite (C. frutescens syn. Argyranthemum frutescens) is a tender perennial, in demand for containers as well as beds and borders. 'Jamaica Primrose' (right below) is an excellent variety.

GARDEN NOTES

CUT FLOWERS

Their long-lasting blooms and outstanding variety of colours and forms make chrysanthemums among the best cut flowers.

Cut them in the morning and immediately slit the stems from the base upwards for about 5cm/2in. Cut the slit stem diagonally and place in deep water for 24 hours in a cool place before using. If you change the water every few days, re-cutting the stems each time, they should continue to provide gorgeous splashes of colour for as much as three weeks.

covered from late summer through autumn with clusters of single flowers in a cheerful array of colours. One of the oldest varieties, and still deservedly popular, is the delightful 'Clara Curtis' which has lovely, clear pink, golden-centred blooms.

The Shasta daisy (*Chrysanthemum maximum*, syn. *Leucanthemum × superbum*), a relative of our wild ox-eye daisies, has long been cherished for its large white flowers borne singly through summer. 'Wirral Supreme' and 'Esther Read' are much-loved varieties with double flowers. About 1m/3ft tall, Shasta daisies look splendid with golden-flowered neighbours.

Chrysanthemum coccineum is more commonly known as pyrethrum (*Tanacetum coccineum*). It is lovely in borders, with single or double flowers on long stems (60-90cm/2-3ft tall), and an array of colours from white through pink to red, accentuated by attractively feathery foliage.

There are even alpine species for rock gardens, such as *Chrysanthemum hosmariense* (*Rhodanthemum hosmariense*), just 20cm/8in

FLOWER FORMS

Chrysanthemum flowers are actually heads of numerous small florets. A central circle of disc florets is surrounded by longer ray florets like petals. Modern chrysanthemums are classified according to the shape of the florets and the character of the resulting bloom.

Incurved These have a very compact, globe-like head, the ray florets tightly curved upwards and inwards. They are not suitable for the garden, since rain tends to be caught in the centre of the bloom.

Reflexed The florets curve out and down, forming more of a mushroom shape.

Intermediate The ray florets curve upwards, but more loosely than those of incurves, and do not close over the top. The lower florets may be reflexed.

Single Simple, daisy-like flowers with up to five rows of ray florets around the central disk.

Anemone-centred Single daisy-like flowers, again with up to five rows of ray florets, but the central disc is very enlarged and dome-shaped.

Spidery Long, quill-like ray florets.

Spoon Similar to the single types, but the ray florets are tubular and flattened at the tips.

Spray Several flowers borne on each stem.

Pompon Several small, spherical or button-shaped flowers borne on each stem.

Charms and cascades with their profusion of small flowers are generally grown as late-flowering decorative pot plants. Charms are low, very compact bushes, while cascades are trained down canes for a flowing effect.

tall, with white flowers set against finely-cut silvery green leaves, or the even smaller, pink-flowered *C. weyrichii* (*D. weyrichii*) (4-6in/10-15cm).

Annuals

Annuals, of course, are invaluable for adding shots of colour quickly and easily. *C. carinatum* (syn. *C. tricolor*) provides stunning, rainbow hues and attractive, feathery foliage. The flat, daisy-like summer flowers, borne singly on erect stems 60cm/2ft tall have dark purplish centres surrounded by ray petals decorated with concentric rings of contrasting colours. 'Court Jesters' gives large flowers with a magnificent colour range.

Though a perennial, feverfew (*C. parthenium* syn. *Tanacetum parthenium*) is short-lived, and commonly grown as an annual. 'Aureum' is a lovely variety with fragrant, golden tinted foliage and small, daisy-like white flowers in summer and early autumn. A

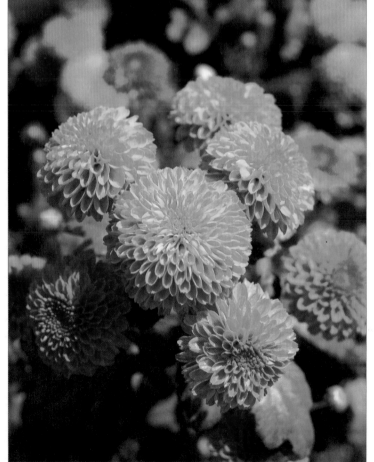

'Phyllis Smith' (above) is a variety of C. maximum with particularly ragged ray florets and a handsome, golden, central dome.

'Bronze Fairie' (left) is an early-flowering modern variety which boasts perfectly formed pompon blooms that are just 4cm/1¹/₂in across.

'Yvonne Arnaud' (right) is another modern early flowering variety. This time the flowers are reflexed, and much larger than those of 'Bronze Fairie', reaching 12cm/5in in diameter.

Jolly 'Court Jesters', with their multi-coloured flowers, do not fit into formal schemes and are best used in a riotous mixed bed with other annuals like nicotiana and mignonette.

bushy plant, 20-45cm/8-18in high, it makes a neat edging for borders and a splendidly decorative addition to containers.

The marguerite (*C. frutescens*, syn. *Argyranthemum frutescens*) has recently seen a revival in popularity, and is another excellent choice for tubs and containers, bearing a profusion of white, yellow or pink daisies through summer and into autumn.

Chrysanthemum care

While those who grow chrysanthemeums for exhibition have their own recipes for success, it is quite easy to grow them in the garden. They like sun and fertile, well-drained soil, and dislike very acid and waterlogged sites. Some shelter from winds is helpful for the taller varieties which also benefit from support with canes or peasticks. Chrysanthemums are prone to a number of pests and diseases, but regular spraying should take care of these. After flowering, cut all the hardy perennial chrysanthemums back to ground level.

Early-flowering modern varieties need a little more attention. Plant them out once the danger of severe frosts has passed, then, just under two weeks later, pinch out the growing tip to channel the plant's energy into its side shoots. These will produce healthy 'breaks' which will eventually bear the blooms.

The size of the flower will depend to a large extent on the number of breaks that are allowed to develop. About four to six breaks produce the best results, so you should remove any others as they appear. For disbuds, remove any sideshoots which emerge on the lengthening breaks.

In mid summer, the flower buds appear on the top of each break, surrounded by a cluster of smaller buds. Take off these smaller buds, leaving just the central one, if you want large blooms. After flowering, cut them back to about 20cm/8in, then lift for storage over winter away from frosts.

COVER UP

SAFETY FIRST

Chrysanthemum leaves can cause allergic reactions such as soreness or itching of the skin. If you think you may be affected, avoid skin contact by wearing gloves and keeping your arms and legs covered when working with them.

*Index compiled by Indexing
Specialists, Hove*

PICTURE CREDITS